SURGEON T. H. PARKE, A.M.D.   CAPTAIN NELSON.   H. M. STANLEY.   A. J. MOUNTENEY JEPHSON.

LIEUT. W. G. STAIRS, R.E.

IN DARKEST AFRICA

OR, THE QUEST, RESCUE, AND RETREAT OF EMIN PASHA, GOVERNOR OF EQUATORIA

VOLUME I

By Henry M. Stanley

THE NARRATIVE PRESS
TRUE FIRST PERSON ACCOUNTS OF HIGH ADVENTURE

The Narrative Press
P.O. Box 2487, Santa Barbara, California 93120 U.S.A.
Telephone: (805) 884-0160 Web: www.narrativepress.com

ISBN 1-58976-044-1 (Paperback)
ISBN 1-58976-045-X (eBook)

Produced in the United States of America

TABLE OF CONTENTS

PREFATORY LETTER

To Sir William Mackinnon, Bart.,
of Balinakill and Loup,
in the County of Argyleshire,
The Chairman of the Emin Pasha Relief Committee.
&c. &c. &c.

My Dear Sir William,
I have great pleasure in dedicating this book to you. It professes
to be the Official Report to yourself and the Emin Relief Committee of what we have experienced and endured during our mission of
Relief, which circumstances altered into that of Rescue. You may
accept it as a truthful record of the journeyings of the Expedition
which you and the Emin Relief Committee entrusted to my guidance.

I regret that I was not able to accomplish all that I burned to do
when I set out from England in January, 1887, but the total collapse
of the Government of Equatoria thrust upon us the duty of conveying in hammocks so many aged and sick people, and protecting so
many helpless and feeble folk, that we became transformed from a
small fighting column of tried men into a mere Hospital Corps to
whom active adventure was denied. The Governor was half-blind
and possessed much luggage, Casati was weakly and had to be carried, and 90 per cent. of their followers were, soon after starting,
scarcely able to travel from age, disease, weakness or infancy.
Without sacrificing our sacred charge, to assist which was the
object of the Expedition, we could neither deviate to the right or to
the left, from the most direct road to the sea.

You who throughout your long and varied life have steadfastly
believed in the Christian's God, and before men have professed
your devout thankfulness for many mercies vouchsafed to you, will
better understand than many others the feelings which animate me

when I find myself back again in civilization, uninjured in life or health, after passing through so many stormy and distressful periods. Constrained at the darkest hour to humbly confess that without God's help I was helpless, I vowed a vow in the forest solitudes that I would confess His aid before men. A silence as of death was round about me; it was midnight; I was weakened by illness, prostrated with fatigue and worn with anxiety for my white and black companions, whose fate was a mystery. In this physical and mental distress I besought God to give me back my people. Nine hours later we were exulting with a rapturous joy. In full view of all was the crimson flag with the crescent, and beneath its waving folds was the long-lost rear column.

Again, we had emerged into the open country out of the forest, after such experiences as in the collective annals of African travels there is no parallel. We were approaching the region wherein our ideal Governor was reported to be beleaguered. All that we heard from such natives as our scouts caught prepared us for desperate encounters with multitudes, of whose numbers or qualities none could inform us intelligently, and when the population of Undusuma swarmed in myriads on the hills, and the valleys seemed alive with warriors, it really seemed to us in our dense ignorance of their character and power, that these were of those who hemmed in the Pasha to the west. If he with his 4000 soldiers appealed for help, what could we effect with 173? The night before I had been reading the exhortation of Moses to Joshua, and whether it was the effect of those brave words, or whether it was a voice, I know not, but it appeared to me as though I heard: "Be strong, and of a good courage, fear not, nor be afraid of them, for the Lord thy God, He it is that doth go with thee, He will not fail thee nor forsake thee." When on the next day Mazamboni commanded his people to attack and exterminate us, there was not a coward in our camp, whereas the evening before we exclaimed in bitterness on seeing four of our men fly before one native, "And these are the wretches with whom we must reach the Pasha!"

And yet again. Between the confluence of the Ihuru and the Dui rivers in December 1888, 150 of the best and strongest of our men had been despatched to forage for food. They had been absent for many days more than they ought to have been, and in the meantime 130 men besides boys and women were starving. They were supported each day with a cup of warm thin broth, made of butter, milk and water, to keep death away as long as possible. When the provisions were so reduced that there were only sufficient for thirteen men for ten days, even of the thin broth with four tiny biscuits each per day, it became necessary for me to hunt up the missing men. They might, being without a leader, have been reckless, and been besieged by an overwhelming force of vicious dwarfs. My following consisted of sixty-six men, a few women and children, who, more active than the others, had assisted the thin fluid with the berries of the phrynium and the amomum, and such fungi as could be discovered in damp places, and therefore were possessed of some little strength, though the poor fellows were terribly emaciated. Fifty-one men, besides boys and women, were so prostrate with debility and disease that they would be hopelessly gone if within a few hours food did not arrive. My white comrade and thirteen men were assured of sufficient for ten days to protract the struggle against a painful death. We who were bound for the search possessed nothing. We could feed on berries until we could arrive at a plantation. As we travelled that afternoon we passed several dead bodies in various stages of decay, and the sight of doomed, dying and dead produced on my nerves such a feeling of weakness that I was well-nigh overcome. Every Soul in that camp was paralysed with sadness and suffering. Despair had made them all dumb. Not a sound was heard to disturb the deathly brooding. It was a mercy to me that I heard no murmur of reproach, no sign of rebuke. I felt the horror of the silence of the forest and the night intensely. Sleep was impossible. My thoughts dwelt on these recurring disobediences which caused so much misery and anxiety. "Stiff-necked, rebellious, incorrigible human nature, ever showing its animalism and brutishness, let the wretches be for ever accursed! Their utter thought-less and oblivious natures and continual breach of promises kill more men, and cause more anxiety, than the poison of the darts or barbs and points of the arrows. If I meet them I will —." But before the resolve was uttered flashed to my memory the dead men on the road, the doomed in the camp, and the starving with me, and the thought that those 150 men were lost in the remorseless woods beyond recovery, or surrounded by savages without hope of escape, then do you wonder that the natural hardness of the heart was softened, and that I again consigned my case to Him who could alone assist us. The next morning within half-an-hour of the start we met the foragers, safe, sound, robust, loaded, bearing four tons of plaintains. You can imagine what cries of joy these wild children of nature uttered, you can imagine how they flung themselves upon the fruit, and kindled the fires to roast and boil and bake, and how, after they were all filled, we strode back to the camp to rejoice those unfortunates with Mr. Bonny.

As I mentally review the many grim episodes and reflect on the marvelously narrow escapes from utter destruction to which we have been subjected during our various journeys to and fro through that immense and gloomy extent of primeval woods, I feel utterly unable to attribute our salvation to any other cause than to a gracious Providence who for some purpose of His own preserved us. All the armies and armaments of Europe could not have lent us any aid in the dire extremity in which we found ourselves in that camp between the Dui and Ihuru; an army of explorers could not have traced our course to the scene of the last struggle had we fallen, for deep, deep as utter oblivion had we been surely buried under the humus of the trackless wilds.

It is in this humble and grateful spirit that I commence this record of the progress of the Expedition from its inception by you to the date when at our feet the Indian Ocean burst into view, pure and blue as Heaven when we might justly exclaim "It is ended!"

What the public ought to know, that have I written; but there are many things that the snarling, cynical, unbelieving, vulgar ought not to know. I write to you and to your friends, and for those who desire more light on Darkest Africa, and for those who can feel an interest in what concerns humanity.

My creed has been, is, and will remain so, I hope, to act for the best, think the right thought, and speak the right word, as well as a good motive will permit. When a mission is entrusted to me and my conscience approves it as noble and right, and I give my promise to exert my best powers to fulfil this according to the letter and spirit, I carry with me a Law, that I am compelled to obey. If any associated with me prove to me by their manner and action that this Law is equally incumbent on them, then I recognize my brothers. Therefore it is with unqualified delight that I acknowledge the priceless services of my friends Stairs, Jephson, Nelson and Parke, four men whose devotion to their several duties were as perfect as human nature is capable of. As a man's epitaph can only be justly written when he lies in his sepulchre, so I rarely attempted to tell them during the journey, how much I valued the ready and prompt obedience of Stairs, that earnestness for work that distinguished Jephson, the brave soldierly qualities of Nelson, and the gentle, tender devotion paid by our Doctor to his ailing patients; but now that the long wanderings are over, and they have bided and laboured ungrudgingly throughout the long period, I feel that my words are poor indeed when I need them to express in full my lasting obligations to each of them.

Concerning those who have fallen, or who were turned back by illness or accident, I will admit, with pleasure, that while in my company every one seemed most capable of fulfilling the highest expectations formed of them. I never had a doubt of any one of them until Mr. Bonny poured into my ears the dismal story of the rear column. While I possess positive proofs that both the Major and Mr. Jameson were inspired by loyalty, and burning with desire throughout those long months at Yambuya, I have endeavoured to ascertain why they did not proceed as instructed by letter, or why Messrs. Ward, Troup and Bonny did not suggest that to move little by little was preferable to rotting at Yambuya, which they were clearly in danger of doing, like the 100 dead followers. To this simple question there is no answer. The eight visits to Stanley Falls and Kasongo amount in the aggregate to 1,200 miles; their journals, log books, letters teem with proofs that every element of success was in and with them. I cannot understand why the five officers, having means for moving, confessedly burning with the desire to move, and animated with the highest feelings, did not move on along our tract as directed; or, why, believing I was alive, the officers sent my personal baggage down river and reduced their chief to a state of destitution; or, why they should send European tinned provisions and two dozen bottles of Madeira down river, when there were thirty-three men sick and hungry in camp; or, why Mr. Bonny should allow his own rations to be sent down while he was present; or, why Mr. Ward should be sent down river with a despatch, and an order be sent after him to prevent his return to the Expedition. These are a few of the problems which puzzle me, and to which I have been unable to obtain satisfactory solutions. Had any other person informed me that such things had taken place I should have doubted them, but I take my information solely from Major Barttelot's official despatch (See Appendix). The telegram which Mr. Ward conveyed to the sea requests instructions from the London Committee, but the gentlemen in London reply, "We refer you to Mr. Stanley's letter of instructions." It becomes clear to every one that there is a mystery here for which I cannot conceive a rational solution, and therefore each reader of this narrative must think his own thoughts but construe the whole charitably.

After the discovery of Mr. Bonny at Banalya, I had frequent occasions to remark to him that his goodwill and devotion were equal to that shown by the others, and as for bravery, I think he has as much as the bravest. With his performance of any appointed work I never had cause for dissatisfaction, and as he so admirably conducted himself with such perfect and respectful obedience while with us from Banalya to the Indian Sea, the more the mystery of Yambuya life is deepened, for with 2,000 such soldiers as Bonny under a competent leader, the entire Soudan could be subjugated, pacified and governed.

It must thoroughly be understood, however, while reflecting upon the misfortunes of the rear-column, that it is my firm belief that had it been the lot of Barttelot and Jameson to have been in the place of, say Stairs and Jephson, and to have accompanied us in the advance, they would equally have distinguished themselves; for such a group of young gentlemen as Barttelot, Jameson, Stairs, Nelson, Jephson, and Parke, at all times, night or day, so eager for and rather loving work, is rare. If I were to try and form another African State, such tireless, brave natures would be simply invaluable. The misfortunes of the rear-column were due to the resolutions of August 17th to stay and wait for me, and to the meeting with the Arabs the next day.

What is herein related about Emin Pasha need not, I hope, be taken as derogating in the slightest from the high conception of our ideal. If the reality differs somewhat from it no fault can be attributed to him. While his people were faithful he was equal to the ideal; when his soldiers revolted, his usefulness as a Governor ceased, just as the cabinet-maker with tools may turn out finished wood-work, but without them can do nothing. If the Pasha was not of such gigantic stature as we supposed him to be, he certainly cannot be held responsible for that, any more than he can be held accountable for his unmilitary appearance. If the Pasha was able to maintain his province for five years, he cannot in justice be held answerable for the wave of insanity and the epidemic of turbulence which converted his hitherto loyal soldiers into rebels. You will find two special periods in this narrative wherein the Pasha is described with strictest impartiality in each, but his misfortunes never cause us to lose our respect for him, though we may not agree with that excess of sentiment which distinguished him, for objects so unworthy as sworn rebels. As an administrator he displayed the finest qualities; he was just, tender, loyal and merciful, and affectionate to the natives who placed themselves under his protection, and no higher and better proof of the esteem with which he was regarded by his soldiery can be desired than that he owed his life to the reputation for justice and mildness which he had won. In short, every hour saved from sleep was devoted before his final deposition to some useful purpose conducive to increase of knowledge, improvement of humanity, and gain to civilization. You must remember all these things, and by no means lose sight of them, even while you read our impressions of him.

I am compelled to believe that Mr. Mounteney Jephson wrote the kindliest report of the events that transpired during the arrest and imprisonment of the Pasha and himself, out of pure affection, sympathy, and fellow-feeling for his friend. Indeed the kindness and sympathy he entertains for the Pasha are so evident that I playfully accuse him of being either a Mahdist, Arabist, or Eminist, as one would naturally feel indignant at the prospect of leading a slave's life at Khartoum. The letters of Mr. Jephson, after being shown, were endorsed, as will be seen by Emin Pasha. Later observations proved the truth of those made by Mr. Jephson when he said, "Sentiment is the Pasha's worst enemy; nothing keeps Emin here but Emin himself." What I most admire in him is the evident struggle between his duty to me, as my agent, and the friendship he entertains for the Pasha.

While we may naturally regret that Emin Pasha did not possess that influence over his troops which would have commanded their perfect obedience, confidence and trust, and made them pliable to the laws and customs of civilization, and compelled them to respect natives as fellow-subjects, to be guardians of peace and protectors of property, without which there can be no civilization, many will think that, as the Governor was unable to do this, that it is as well that events took the turn they did. The natives of Africa cannot be taught that there are blessings in civilization if they are permitted to be oppressed and to be treated as unworthy of the treatment due to human beings, to be despoiled and enslaved at will by a licentious soldiery. The habit of regarding the aborigines as nothing better than pagan *abid* or slaves, dates from Ibrahim Pasha, and must be utterly suppressed before any semblance of civilization can be seen outside the military settlements. When every grain of corn, and every fowl, goat, sheep and cow which is necessary for the troops is paid for in sterling money or its equivalent in necessary goods, then civilization will become irresistible in its influence, and the Gospel even may be introduced; but without impartial justice both are impossible, certainly never when preceded and accompanied by spoliation, which I fear was too general a custom in the Soudan.

Those who have some regard for righteous justice may find some comfort in the reflection that until civilization in its true and real form be introduced into Equatoria, the aborigines shall now have some peace and rest, and that whatever aspects its semblance bare, excepting a few orange and lime trees, can be replaced within a month, under higher, better, and more enduring auspices.

If during this Expedition I have not sufficiently manifested the reality of my friendship and devotion to you, and to my friends of the Emin Relief Committee, pray attribute it to want of opportunities and force of circumstances and not to lukewarmness and insincerity; but if, on the other hand, you and my friends have been satisfied that so far as lay in my power I have faithfully and loyally accomplished the missions you entrusted to me in the same spirit and to the same purpose that you yourself would have performed them had it been physically and morally possible for you to have been with us, then indeed am I satisfied, and the highest praise would not be equal in my opinion to the simple acknowledgment of it, such as "Well done." My dear Sir William, to love a noble, generous and loyal heart like your own, is natural. Accept the profession of mine, which has been pledged long ago to you wholly and entirely.

Henry M. Stanley

Chapter 1

INTRODUCTORY CHAPTER

Only a Carlyle in his maturest period, as when he drew in lurid colours the agonies of the terrible French Revolution, can do justice to the long catalogue of disasters which has followed the connection of England with Egypt. It is a theme so dreadful throughout, that Englishmen shrink from touching it. Those who have written upon any matters relating to these horrors confine themselves to bare historical record. No one can read through these without shuddering at the dangers England and Englishmen have incurred during this pitiful period of mismanagement. After the Egyptian campaign there is only one bright gleam of sunshine throughout months of oppressive darkness, and that shone over the immortals of Abu-Klea and Gubat, when that small body of heroic Englishmen struggled shoulder to shoulder on the sands of the fatal desert, and won a glory equal to that which the Light Brigade were urged to gain at Balaclava. Those were fights indeed, and atone in a great measure for a series of blunders, that a century of history would fail to parallel. If only a portion of that earnestness of purpose exhibited at Abu-Klea had been manifested by those responsible for ordering events, the Mahdi would soon have become only a picturesque figure to adorn a page or to point a metaphor, and not the terrible portent of these latter days, whose presence blasted every vestige of civilization in the Soudan to ashes.

In order that I may make a fitting but brief introduction to the subject matter of this book, I must necessarily glance at the events which led to the cry of the last surviving Lieutenant of Gordon for help in his close beleaguerment near the Equator.

To the daring project of Ismail the Khedive do we owe the original cause of all that has befallen Egypt and the Soudan. With

5,000,000 of subjects, and a rapidly depleting treasury, he undertook the expansion of the Egyptian Khediviate into an enormous Egyptian Empire, the entire area embracing a superficial extent of nearly 1,000,000 square miles – that is, from the Pharos of Alexandria to the south end of Lake Albert, from Massowah to the western boundary of Darfur. Adventurers from Europe and from America resorted to his capital to suggest the maddest schemes, and volunteered themselves leaders of the wildest enterprises. The staid period when Egyptian sovereignty ceased at Gondokoro, and the Nile was the natural drain of such traffic as found its way by the gentle pressure of slow development, was ended when Captains Speke and Grant, and Sir Samuel Baker brought their rapturous reports of magnificent lakes, and regions unmatched for fertility and productiveness. The termination of the American Civil War threw numbers of military officers out of employment, and many thronged to Egypt to lend their genius to the modern Pharaoh, and to realize his splendid dreams of empire. Englishmen, Germans, and Italians, appeared also to share in the honours that were showered upon the bold and the brave.

While reading carefully and dispassionately the annals of this period, admiring the breadth of the Khedive's views, the enthusiasm which possesses him, the princely liberality of his rewards, the military exploits, the sudden extensions of his power, and the steady expansions of his sovereignty to the south, west, and east, I am struck by the fact that his success as a conqueror in Africa may well be compared to the successes of Alexander in Asia, the only difference being that Alexander led his armies in person, while Ismail the Khedive preferred the luxuries of his palaces in Cairo, and to commit his wars to the charge of his Pashas and Beys.

To the Khedive, the career of conquest on which he has launched appears noble; the European Press applaud him; so many things of grand importance to civilization transpire that they chant paeans of praise in his honour; the two seas are brought together, and the mercantile navies ride in stately columns along the maritime canal; railways are pushed towards the south, and it is prophesied that a line will reach as far as Berber. But throughout all this brilliant period the people of this new empire do not seem to have been worthy of a thought, except as subjects of taxation and as instruments of supplying the Treasury; taxes are heavier than ever; the Pashas are more mercenary; the laws are more exacting, the ivory trade is monopolised, and finally, to add to the discontent already growing, the slave trade is prohibited throughout all the territory where Egyptian authority is constituted. Within five years Sir Samuel Baker has conquered the Equatorial Province, Munzinger has mastered Senaar, Darfur has been annexed, and Bahr-el-Ghazal has been subjugated after a most frightful waste of life. The audacity manifested in all these projects of empire is perfectly marvelous – almost as wonderful as the total absence of common sense. Along a line of territory 800 miles in length there are only three military stations in a country that can only rely upon camels as means of communication except when the Nile is high.

In 1879, Ismail the Khedive having drawn too freely upon the banks of Europe, and increased the debt of Egypt to £128,000,000, and unable to agree to the restraints imposed by the Powers, the money of whose subjects he had so liberally squandered, was deposed, and the present Khedive, Tewfik, his son, was elevated to his place, under the tutelage of the Powers. But shortly after, a military revolt occurred, and at Kassassin, Tel-el-Kebir, Cairo, and Kafr Dewar, it was crushed by an English Army, 13,000 strong, under Lord Wolseley.

During the brief sovereignty of Arabi Pasha, who headed the military revolt, much mischief was caused by the withdrawal of the available troops from the Soudan. While the English General was defeating the rebel soldiers at Tel-el-Kebir, the Mahdi Mohamet-Achmet was proceeding to the investment of El Obeid. On the 23rd of August he was attacked at Duem with a loss of 4500. On the 14th he was repulsed by the garrison of Obeid, with a loss, it is said, of 10,000 men. These immense losses of life, which have been continuous from the 11th of August, 1881, when the Mahdi first essayed the task of teaching the populations of the Soudan the weakness of Egyptian power, were from the tribes who were indifferent to the religion professed by the Mahdi, but who had been robbed by the Egyptian officials, taxed beyond endurance by the Government, and who had been prevented from obtaining means by the sale of slaves to pay the taxes, and also from the hundreds of slave-trading caravans, whose occupation was taken from them by their energetic suppression by Gordon, and his Lieutenant, Gessi Pasha. From the 11th of August, 1881, to the 4th of March, 1883, when Hicks Pasha, a retired Indian officer, landed at Khartoum as Chief of the Staff of the Soudan army, the disasters to the Government troops had been almost one unbroken series; and, in the meanwhile, the factious and mutinous army of Egypt had revolted, been suppressed and disbanded, and another army had been reconstituted under Sir Evelyn Wood, which was not to exceed 6000 men. Yet aware of the tremendous power of the Mahdi, and the combined fanaticism and hate, amounting to frenzy, which possessed his legions, and of the instability, the indiscipline, and cowardice of his troops – while pleading to the Egyptian Government for a reinforcement of 5000 men, or for four battalions of General Wood's new army – Hicks Pasha resolves upon the conquest of Kordofan, and marches to meet the victorious Prophet, while he and his hordes are flushed with the victory lately gained over Obeid and Bara. His staff, and the very civilians accompanying him, predict disaster; yet Hicks starts forth on his last journey with a body of 12,000 men, 10 mountain guns, 6 Nordenfelts, 5500 camels, and 500 horses. They know that the elements of weakness are in the force; that many of the soldiers are peasants taken from the fields in Egypt, chained in gangs; that others are Mahdists; that there is dissension between the officers, and that everything is out of joint. But they march towards Obeid, meet the Mahdi's legions, and are annihilated.

England at this time directs the affairs of Egypt with the consent of the young Khedive, whom she has been instrumental in placing upon the almost royal throne of Egypt, and whom she is interested in protecting. Her soldiers are in Egypt; the new Egyptian army is under an English General; her military police is under the command of an English ex-Colonel of cavalry; her Diplomatic Agent directs the foreign policy; almost all the principal offices of the State are in the hands of Englishmen.

The Soudan has been the scene of the most fearful sanguinary encounters between the ill-directed troops of the Egyptian Government and the victorious tribes gathered under the sacred banner of the Mahdi; and unless firm resistance is offered soon to the advance of the Prophet, it becomes clear to many in England that this vast region and fertile basin of the Upper Nile will be lost to Egypt, unless troops and money be furnished to meet the emergency. To the view of good sense it is clear that, as England has undertaken to direct the government and manage the affairs of Egypt, she cannot avoid declaring her policy as regards the Soudan. To a question addressed to the English Prime Minister in Parliament, as to whether the Soudan was regarded as forming a part of Egypt, and if so, whether the British Government would take steps to restore order there, Mr. Gladstone replied, that the Soudan had not been included in the sphere of English operations, and that the Government was not disposed to include it within the sphere of English responsibility. As a declaration of policy no fault can be found with it; it is Mr. Gladstone's policy, and there is nothing to be said against it as such; it is his principle, the principle of his associates in the Government, and of his party, and as a principle it deserves respect.

The Political Agent in Egypt, Sir Evelyn Baring, while the fate of Hicks Pasha and his army was still unknown, but suspected, sends repeated signals of warning to the English Government, and suggests remedies and means of averting a final catastrophe. "If Hicks Pasha is defeated, Khartoum is in danger; by the fall of Khartoum, Egypt will be menaced."

Lord Granville replies at various times in the months of November and December, 1883, that the Government advises the abandonment of the Soudan within certain limits; that the Egyptian Government must take the sole responsibility of operations beyond Egypt Proper; that the Government has no intention of employing British or Indian troops in the Soudan; that ineffectual efforts on the part of the Egyptian Government to secure the Soudan would only increase the danger.

Sir Evelyn Baring notified Lord Granville that no persuasion or argument availed to induce the Egyptian Minister to accept the policy of abandonment. Cherif Pasha, the Prime Minister, also informed Lord Granville that, according to Valentine Baker Pasha, the means at the disposal were utterly inadequate for coping with the insurrection in the Soudan.

Then Lord Granville replied, through Sir Evelyn Baring, that it was indispensable that, so long as English soldiers provisionally occupied Egypt, the advice of Her Majesty's Ministers should be followed, and that he insisted on its adoption. The Egyptian Ministers were changed, and Nubar Pasha became Prime Minister on the 10th January, 1884.

On the 17th December, Valentine Baker departed from Egypt for Suakim, to commence military operations for the maintenance of communication between Suakim and Berber, and the pacification of the tribes in that region. While it was absolutely certain in England that Baker's force would suffer a crushing defeat, and suspected in Egypt, the General does not seem to be aware of any danger, or if there be, he courts it. The Khedive, fearful that to his troops an engagement will be most disastrous, writes privately to Baker Pasha: "I rely on your prudence and ability not to engage the enemy except under the most favourable conditions." Baker possessed ability and courage in abundance; but the event proved that prudence and judgment were as absent in his case as in that of the unfortunate Hicks. His force consisted of 3746 men. On the 6th of February he left Trinkitat on the sea shore, towards Tokar. After a march of six miles the van of the rebels was encountered, and shortly after the armies were engaged. It is said "that the rebels displayed the utmost contempt for the Egyptians; that they seized them by the neck and cut their throats; and that the Government troops, paralysed by fear, turned their backs, submitting to be killed rather than attempt to defend their lives; that hundreds threw away their rifles, knelt down, raised their clasped hands, and prayed for mercy."

The total number killed was 2373 out of 3746. Mr. Royle, the excellent historian of the Egyptian campaigns, says: "Baker knew, or ought to have known, the composition of the troops he commanded, and to take such men into action was simply to court disaster." What ought we to say of Hicks?

We now come to General Gordon, who from 1874 to 1876 had been working in the Upper Soudan on the lines commenced by Sir Samuel Baker, conciliating natives, crushing slave caravans, destroying slave stations, and extending Egyptian authority by lines of fortified forts up to the Albert Nyanza. After four months' retirement he was appointed Governor-General of the Soudan, of Darfur, and the Equatorial Provinces. Among others whom Gordon employed as Governors of these various provinces under his Vice-regal Government was one Edward Schnitzler, a German born in Oppeln, Prussia, 28th March, 1840, of Jewish parents, who had seen service in Turkey, Armenia, Syria, and Arabia, in the suite of Ismail Hakki Pasha, once Governor-General of Scutari, and a Mushir of the Empire. On the death of his patron he had departed to Niesse, where his mother, sister, and cousins lived, and where he stayed for several months, and thence left for Egypt. He, in 1875, thence travelled to Khartoum, and being a medical doctor, was employed by Gordon Pasha in that capacity. He assumed the name and tide of Emin Effendi Hakim – the faithful physician. He was sent to Lado as storekeeper and doctor, was afterwards despatched to King Mtesa on a political mission, recalled to Khartoum, again despatched on a similar mission to King Kabba-Rega of Unyoro, and finally, in 1878, was promoted to Bey, and appointed Governor of the Equatorial Province of *Ha-tal-astiva,* which, rendered into English, means Equatoria, at a salary of £50 per month. A mate of one of the Peninsular and Oriental steamers, called Lupton, was promoted to the rank of Governor of the Province of Bahr-el-Ghazal, which adjoined Equatoria.

On hearing of the deposition of Ismail in 1879, Gordon surren-dered his high office in the hands of Tewfik, the new Khedive, informing him that he did not intend to resume it.

In 1880 he accepted the post of Secretary under the Marquis of Ripon, but resigned it within a month.

In 1881 he is in Mauritius as Commandant of the Royal Engi-neers. In about two months he abandons that post to proceed to the assistance of the Cape authorities in their difficulty with the Basu-tos, but, after a little experience, finds himself unable to agree with the views of the Cape Government, and resigns.

Meantime, I have been labouring on the Congo River. Our suc-cesses in that immense territory of Western Africa have expanded into responsibilities so serious that they threaten to become unman-ageable. When I visit the Lower Congo, affairs become deranged on the Upper Congo; if I confine myself to the Upper Congo there is friction in the Lower Congo. Wherefore, feeling an intense inter-est in the growth of the territory which was rapidly developing into a State, I suggested to His Majesty King Leopold, as early as September 1882, and again in the spring of 1883, that I required as an associate a person of merit, rank, and devotion to work, such as General Gordon, who would undertake either the management of the Lower or Upper Congo, while I would work in the other section, as a vast amount of valuable time was consumed in travelling up and down from one to the other, and young officers of stations were so apt to take advantage of my absence. His Majesty promised to request the aid of General Gordon, but for a long time the replies were unfavourable. Finally, in the spring of 1884, I received a letter in General Gordon's well-known handwriting, which informed me I was to expect him by the next mail.

It appears, however, that he had no sooner mailed his letter to me and parted from His Majesty than he was besieged by applications from his countrymen to assist the Egyptian Government in extricating the beleaguered garrison of Khartoum from their impending fate. Personally, I know nothing of what actually happened when he was ushered by Lord Wolseley into the presence of Lord Granville, but I have been informed that General Gordon was confident he could perform the mission entrusted to him. There is a serious discrepancy in the definition of this mission. The Egyptian authorities were anxious for the evacuation of Khartoum only, and it is possible that Lord Granville only needed Gordon's services for this humane mission, all the other garrisons to be left to their fate because of the supposed impossibility of rescuing them. The Blue Books which contain the official despatches seem to confirm the probability of this. But it is certain that Lord Granville instructed General Gordon to proceed to Egypt to report on the situation of the Soudan, and on the best measures that should be taken for the security of the Egyptian garrisons (in the plural), and for the safety of the European population in Khartoum. He was to perform such other duties as the Egyptian Government might wish to entrust to him. He was to be accompanied by Colonel Stewart.

Sir Evelyn Baring, after a prolonged conversation with Gordon, gives him his final instructions on behalf of the British Government.

A precis of these is as follows: –

1. "Ensure retreat of the European population from 10,000 to 15,000 people, and of the garrison of Kartoum."[1]
2. "You know best the when and how to effect this."
3. "You will bear in mind that the main end (of your Mission) is the evacuation of the Soudan."
4. "As you are of opinion it could be done, endeavour to make a confederation of the native tribes to take the place of Egyptian authority."
5. "A credit of £100,000 is opened for you at the Finance Department."

Gordon has succeeded in infusing confidence in the minds of the Egyptian Ministry, who were previously panic-stricken and cried out for the evacuation of Khartoum only. They breathe freer after seeing and hearing him, and according to his own request they invest him with the Governor-Generalship. The firman, given him, empowers him to evacuate the respective territories (of the Soudan) and to withdraw the troops, civil officials, and such of the inhabitants as wish to leave for Egypt, and if possible, after completing the evacuation (and this was an absolute impossibility) he was to establish an organized Government. With these instructions Lord Granville concurs.

I am told that it was understood, however, that he was to do what he could – do everything necessary, in fact, if possible; if not all the Soudan, then he was to proceed to evacuating Khartoum only, without loss of time. But this is not on official record until March 23rd, 1884, and it is not known whether he ever received this particular telegram.[2]

General Gordon proceeded to Khartoum on January 26th, 1884, and arrived in that city on the 18th of the following month. During his journey he sent frequent despatches by telegraph

---

1. No. 2 clashes with No. 3 somewhat. Khartoum and the Soudan are not synonymous terms. To withdraw the garrison of Khartoum is an easy task, to evacuate the Soudan is an impossibility for a single person.

2. This is the only clearly worded despatch that I have been able to find in the Blue Book of the period.

abounding in confidence. Mr. Power, the acting consul and *Times* correspondent, wired the following despatch – "The people (of Khartoum) are devoted to General Gordon, whose design is to save the garrison, and for ever leave the Soudan – as perforce it must be left – to the Soudanese".

The English press, which had been so wise respecting the chances of Valentine Baker Pasha, were very much in the condition of the people of Khartoum, that is, devoted to General Gordon and sanguine of his success. He had performed such wonders in China – he had laboured so effectually in crushing the slave-trade in the Soudan. he had won the affection of the sullen Soudanese, that the press did not deem it at all improbable that Gordon with his white wand and six servants could rescue the doomed garrisons of Senaar, Bahr-el-Ghazal, and Equatoria – a total of 29,000 men, besides the civil employees and their wives and families; and after performing that more than herculean – nay utterly impossible task – establish an organized Government.

On February 29th Gordon telegraphs, "There is not much chance of improving, and every chance is getting worse," and on the 2nd of the month "I have no option about staying at Khartoum, it has passed out of my hands." On the 16th March he predicts that before long "we shall be blocked." At the latter end of March he telegraphs, "We have provisions for five months, and are hemmed in."

It is clear that a serious misunderstanding had occurred in the drawing up of the instructions by Sir Evelyn Baring and their comprehension of them by General Gordon, for the latter expresses himself to the former thus: –

"You ask me to state cause and reason of my intention for my staying at Khartoum. I stay at Khartoum because Arabs have shut us up, and will not let us out."

Meantime public opinion urged on the British Government the necessity of despatching an Expedition to withdraw General Gordon from Khartoum. But as it was understood between General Gordon and Lord Granville that the former's mission was for the purpose of dispensing with the services of British troops in the Soudan, and as it was its declared policy not to employ English or Indian troops in that region, the Government were naturally reluctant to yield to the demand of the public. At last, however, as the clamour increased and Parliament and public joined in affirming that it was a duty on the country to save the brave man who had so willingly volunteered to perform such an important service for his country, Mr. Gladstone rose in the House of Commons on the 5th August to move a vote of credit to undertake operations for the relief of Gordon.

Two routes were suggested by which the Relief Expedition could approach Khartoum – the short cut across the desert from Suakim to Berber, and the other by the Nile. Gordon expressed his preference for that up the Nile, and it was this latter route that the Commanding General of the Relief Expedition adopted.

On the 18th September, the steamer "Abbas," with Colonel Stewart (Gordon's companion), Mr. Power, the *Times* correspondent, Mr. Herbin, the French Consul, and a number of Greeks and Egyptians on board – forty-four men all told – on trying to pass by the cataract of Abu Harold was wrecked in the cataract. The Arabs on the shore invited them to land in peace, but unarmed. Stewart complied, and he and the two Consuls (Power and Herbin) and Hassan Effendi went ashore and entered a house, in which they were immediately murdered.

On the 17th November, Gordon reports to Lord Wolseley, who was then at Wady Halfa, that he can hold out for forty days yet, that the Mahdists are to the south, south-west, and east, but not to the north of Khartoum.

By Christmas Day, 1884, a great part of the Expeditionary Force was assembled at Korti. So far, the advance of the Expedition had been as rapid as the energy and skill of the General commanding could command. Probably there never was a force so numerous, animated with such noble ardour and passion, as this under Lord Wolseley for the rescue of that noble and solitary Englishman at Khartoum.

On December 30th, a part of General Herbert Stewart's force moves from Korti towards Gakdul Wells, with 2099 camels. In 46 hours and 50 minutes it has reached Gakdul Wells; 11 hours later Sir Herbert Stewart with all the camels starts on his return journey to Korti, which place was reached January 5th. On the 12th Sir Herbert Stewart was back at Gakdul Wells, and at 2 p.m. of the 13th the march towards Abu Klea was resumed. On the 17th, the famous battle of Abu Klea was fought, resulting in a hard-won victory to the English troops, with a loss of 9 officers and 65 men killed and 85 wounded, out of a total of 1800, while 1100 of the enemy lay dead before the square. It appears probable that if the 3000 English sent up the Nile Valley had been with this gallant little force, it would have been a mere walk over for the English army. After another battle on the 19th near Metammeh, where 20 men were killed and 60 wounded of the English, and 250 of the enemy, a village on a gravel terrace near the Nile was occupied. On the 21st, four steamers belonging to General Gordon appeared. The officer in command stated that they had been lying for some weeks near an island awaiting the arrival of the British column. The 22nd and 23rd were expended by Sir Chas. Wilson in making a reconnaissance, building two forts, changing the crews of the steamers, and preparing fuel. On the 24th, two of the steamers started for Khartoum, carrying only 20 English soldiers. On the 26th two men came aboard and reported that there had been fighting at Khartoum; on the 27th a man cried out from the bank that the town had fallen, and that Gordon had been killed. The next day the last news was confirmed by another man. Sir Charles Wilson steamed on until his steamers became the target of cannon from Omdurman and from Khartoum, besides rifles from a distance of from 75 to 200 yards, and turned back only when convinced that the sad news was only too true. Steaming down river then at full speed he reached Tamanieb when he halted for the night. From here he sent out two messengers to collect news. One returned saying that he had met an Arab who informed him that Khartoum had been entered on the night of the 26th January through the treachery of Farag Pasha, and that Gordon was killed; that the Mahdi had on the next day entered the city and had gone into a mosque to return thanks and had then retired, and had given the city up to three days' pillage.

In Major Kitchener's report we find a summary of the results of the taking of Khartoum. "The massacre in the town lasted some six hours, and about 4000 persons at least were killed. The Bashi Bazouks and white regulars numbering 3327, and the Shaigia irregulars numbering 2330, were mostly all killed in cold blood after they had surrendered and been disarmed." The surviving inhabitants of the town were ordered out, and as they passed through the gate were searched, and then taken to Omdurman where the women were distributed among the Mahdist chiefs, and the men were stripped and turned adrift to pick a living as they could. A Greek merchant, who escaped from Khartoum, reported that the town was betrayed by the merchants there, who desired to make terms with the enemy, and not by Farag Pasha.

Darfur, Kordofan, Senaar, Bahr-el-Ghazal, Khartoum, had been possessed by the enemy; Kassala soon followed, and throughout the length and breadth of the Soudan there now remained only the Equatorial Province, whose Governor was Emin Bey Hakim – the Faithful Physician.

Naturally, if English people felt that they were in duty bound to rescue their brave countryman, and a gallant General of such genius and reputation as Gordon, they would feel a lively interest in the fate of the last of Gordon's Governors, who, by a prudent Fabian policy, it was supposed, had evaded the fate which had befallen the armies and garrisons of the Soudan. It follows also that, if the English were solicitous for the salvation of the garrison of Khartoum, they would feel a proportionate solicitude for the fate of a brave officer and his little army in the far South, and that, if assistance could be rendered at a reasonable cost, there would be no difficulty in raising a fund to effect that desirable object.

On November 16, 1884, Emin Bey informs Mr. A. M. Mackay, the missionary in Uganda, by letter written at Lado, that "the Soudan has become the theatre of an insurrection; that for nineteen months he is without news from Khartoum, and that thence he is led to believe that the town has been taken by the insurgents, or that the Nile is blocked"; but he says: –

"Whatever it proves to be, please inform your correspondents and through them the Egyptian Government, that to this day we are well, and that we propose to hold out until help may reach us or until we perish."

A second note from Emin Bey to the same missionary, on the same date as the preceding, contains the following: –

"The Bahr-Ghazal Province being lost and Lupton Bey, the governor, carried away to Kordofan, we are unable to inform our Government of what happens here. For nineteen months we have had no communication from Khartoum, so I suppose the river is blocked up."

"Please therefore inform the Egyptian Government by some means that we are well to this day, but greatly in need of help. We shall hold out until we obtain such help or until we perish."

To Mr. Charles H. Allen, Secretary of the Anti-Slavery Society, Emin Bey writes from Wadelai, December 31, 1885, as follows: –

"Ever since the month of May, 1883, we have been cut off from all communication with the world. Forgotten, and abandoned by the Government, we have been compelled to make a virtue of necessity. Since the occupation of the Bathr-Ghazal we have been vigorously attacked, and I do not know how to describe to you the admirable devotion of my black troops throughout a long war, which for them at least, has no advantage. Deprived of the most necessary things for a long time without any pay, my men fought valiantly, and when at last hunger weakened them, when, after nineteen days of incredible privation and sufferings, their strength was exhausted, and when the last torn leather of the last boot had been eaten, then they cut away through the midst of their enemies and succeeded in saving themselves. All this hardship was undergone without the least arriére-pensée, without even the hope of any appreciable reward, prompted only by their duty and the desire of showing a proper valour before their enemies."

This is a noble record of valour and military virtue. I remember the appearance of this letter in the *Times,* and the impression it made on myself and friends. It was only a few days after the appearance of this letter that we began to discuss ways and means of relief for the writer.

The following letter also impressed me very strongly. It is written to Dr. R. W. Felkin on the same date, December 31, 1885.

"You will probably know through the daily papers that poor Lupton, after having bravely held the Bahr-Ghazal Province was compelled, through the treachery of his own people, to surrender to the emissaries of the late Madhi, and was carried by them to Kordofan."

"My province and also myself I only saved from a like fate by a stratagem, but at last I was attacked, and many losses in both men and ammunition were the result, until I delivered such a heavy blow to the rebels at Rimo, in Makraka, that compelled them to leave me alone. Before this took place they informed us that Khartoum fell, in January, 1885, and that Gordon was killed."

"Naturally on account of these occurrences I have been compelled to evacuate our more distant stations, and withdraw our soldiers and their families, still hoping that our Government will send us help. It seems, however, that I have deceived myself, for since April, 1883, I have received no news of any kind from the north."

"The Government in Khartoum did not behave well to us. Before they evacuated Fashoda, they ought to have remembered that Government officials were living here (Equatorial Provinces) who had performed their duty, and had not deserved to be left to their fate without more ado. Even if it were the intention of the Government to deliver us over to our fate, the least they could have done was to have released us from our duties; we should then have known that we were considered to have become valueless.

... *"Anyway it was necessary for us to seek some way of escape, and in the first place it was urgent to send news of our existence in Egypt. With this object in view I went south, after having made the necessary arrangements at Lade, and came to Wadelai.*

... "As to my future plans, I intend to hold this country as long as possible. I hope that when our letters arrive in Egypt, in seven or eight months, a reply will be sent to me viâ Khartoum or Zanzibar. If the Egyptian Government still exists in the Soudan we naturally expect them to send us help. If, however, the Soudan has been evacuated, I shall take the whole of the people towards the south. I shall then send the whole of the Egyptian and Khartoum officials viâ Uganda or Karagwé to Zanzibar, but shall remain myself with my black troops at Kabba-Rege's until the Government inform me as to their wishes."

This is very clear that Emin Pasha at this time proposed to relieve himself of the Egyptian officials, and that he himself only intended to remain until the Egyptian Government could communicate to him its wishes. Those "wishes" were that he should abandon his province, as they were unable to maintain it, and take advantage of the escort to leave Africa. In a letter written to Mr. Mackay dated July 6th, 1886, Emin says: –

"In the first place believe me that I am in no hurry to break away from here, or to leave those countries in which I have now laboured for ten years.

... "All my people, but especially the negro troops, entertain a strong objection against a march to the south and thence to Egypt, and mean to remain here until they can be taken north. Meantime, if no danger overtakes us, and our ammunition holds out for some time longer, I mean to follow your advice and remain here until help comes to us from some quarter. At all events, you may rest assured that we will occasion no disturbance to you in Uganda."

"I shall determine on a march to the coast only in a case of dire necessity. There are, moreover, two other routes before me. One from Kabba-Rega's direct to Karagwé; the other viâ Usongora to the stations at Tanganika. I hope, however, that I shall have no need to make use of either."

... *"My people have become impatient through long delay, and are anxiously looking for help at last. It would also be most desirable that some Commissioner came here from Europe, either direct by the Masai route, or from Karagwé viâ Kabba Rega's country, in order that my people may actually see that there is some interest taken in them. I would defray with ivory all expenses of such a Commission."*

"As I once more repeat, I am ready to stay and to hold these countries as long as I can until help comes, and I beseech you to do what you can to hasten the arrival of such assistance. Assure Mwanga that he has nothing to fear from me or my people, and that as an old friend of Mtesa's I have no intention to trouble him."

In the above letters we have Emin Bey's views, wherein we gather that his people are loyal – that is, they are obedient to his commands, but that none of them, judging from the tenour of the letters, express any inclination to return to Egypt, excepting the Egyptians. He is at the same time pondering upon the routes by which it is possible to retreat – elsewhere he suggests the Monbuttu route to the sea; in these letters he hints at Masai Land, or through Unyoro, and west of Uganda to Usongora, and thence to Tanganika! If none of the black troops intended to follow him, he certainly could not have done so with only the Egyptian officials and their families.

From the following letters from the Consul-General, F. Holmwood, to Sir Evelyn Baring, dated September 25th and September 27th, we gather Mr. Holmwood's views, who, from his position and local knowledge, was very competent to furnish information as to what could be done in the way of the proposed relief.

"In Emin's letters to me he only reports his situation up to 27th February, 1886, when he proposed evacuating his province by detachments, the first of which he proposed to despatch at the close of the rains toward the end of July; but both Dr. Junker and Mr. Mackay inform me that they have since heard from Emin that the majority of the 4000 loyal Egyptian subjects who have remained faithful to Egypt throughout, and have supported him in the face of the constant attacks from the Mahdi's adherents, aggravated by an imminent danger of starvation refuse to leave their country, and he had therefore determined, if he could possibly do so, to remain at his post, and continue to protect Egyptian interests till relief arrived.

... "Were Uganda freed from this tyrant (Mwanga), the Equatorial Province, even should the present elementary system of communication remain unmodified, would be within eight weeks' post of Zanzibar, and a safe depôt on the Albert Nyanza would provide a base for any further operations that might be decided upon.

"Dr. Junker states that the country to the east of the Ripen Falls[3] has proved impracticable, and that Emin has lost many troops in endeavouring to open communication through it. If such be the case the alternative line by which Dr. Fischer tried to relieve Junker, and which I believe he still recommends, could not be relied on for turning Uganda and its eastern dependency, and the well-known route viâ Uganda would be the only one available for an Expedition of moderate size.

... "As far as I am able to judge, without making any special calculation, I consider that 1200 porters would be the smallest number that would suffice, and a well-armed guard of at least 500 natives would be necessary.

---

3.   This route would be through Masai Land.

... "General Matthews, whom I had consulted as to the force necessary for the safety of the Expedition, is of opinion that I have formed far too low an estimate, but after weighing the testimony of many experienced persons acquainted with Uganda, I must adhere to my opinion that 500 native troops armed with modern rifles and under experienced persons, would, if supplemented by the irregular force, fully suffice."

An American officer of the Khedivial Government writes to Mr. Portal, and suggests that communication with Emin might be opened by the Zanzibar Arabs, but that to send stores and ammunition to him was impossible; that the Arabs might manage for his passage, though his safest line of retreat was westward to reach the Congo.

Mr. Fred Holmwood, in his despatch to the Foreign Office of September 23rd, 1886, writes that, "had it not been for the dangerous attitude of the King of Uganda, the question of relieving Emin would have been merely one of expenditure to be settled at Cairo; but under present circumstances, many other serious considerations are involved in it which will have to be referred to Her Majesty's Government.

"I would call attention to the account contained in Mr. Mackay's letter regarding the alternative route to Wadelai which Dr. Fischer endeavoured to take and, I believe, still recommends. If this statement be correct, any attempt to turn Uganda or its Eastern dependency by this unexplored line would probably fail."

Mr. A. M. Mackay writes from Uganda, May 14th, 1886: –

"From Dr. Junker's letter you will have seen that Emin Bey has had the good fortune to have secured the loyalty of the people he governs. Emin seems to have learned Gordon's secret of securing the affection of his subjects, and has bravely stuck to them. There can be no doubt at all but that had he been anxious to leave he would with a few hundred of his soldiers have easily made a dash for the coast either

through the Masai Land or this way, asking no permission from Mwanga (King of Uganda) or anyone else. He knows that there is no power here able to stop him. In fact years ago he wrote me that it would be nothing to him to storm this wretched village and drive off the cattle."

"But what would be the fate of thousands of people who have remained loyal on the Upper Nile? Dr. Junker speaks of thousands. They do not want to be taken out of their own fertile country, and taken to the deserts of Upper Egypt."

"Dr. Emin is on all hands allowed to be a wise and able Governor. But he cannot remain for ever where he is, nor can he succeed himself, even should the Mahdi's troops leave him undisturbed in the future. His peculiar position should be taken advantage of by our country, which undertook to rescue the garrisons of the Soudan.

... *"Mwanga's action with respect to, the letters forwarded him for Dr. Emin, was as disrespectful as possible to the British Government which had received with such kindness his father's envoys. We asked him merely to forward the letters in the first place until he should receive word from Emin as to whether or not he was prepared to come this way, but he detained your packet altogether."*

In Mr. Mackay's letter to Sir John Kirk, June 28th, 1886, he says: –

"Dr. Fischer's difficulties would also only really begin after Kavirondo, as he then had the country of the dreaded Bakedi to cross, and Dr. Junker tells me that whole parties of Dr. Emin's soldiers have been repeatedly murdered by them."

Dr. Fischer, it will be remembered, was engaged to proceed to Equatoria in search of Dr. Junker by that traveller's brother, and chose the road *viâ* East coast of the Victoria Lake. Arriving at the N.E. corner of the Lake he returned to the coast.

Mr. Mackay proceeds: –

"Dr. Junker is living here with us. He brought me a letter from Emin Bey dated the 27th January (1886). He then proposed sending his people at once this way – some 4000 – in small detachments. This policy would be fatal. He also asked me to go to meet him with a view to bringing here two steamers which otherwise he would have to abandon. One of them he meant for the King, and the other for the mission."

"Since then, however, he finds that his people, officers and men, refuse to leave the Soudan, hence he is prepared to remain some years with them provided only he can get supplies of cloth, etc."

Mr. Mackay always writes sensibly. I obtained a great deal of solid information from these letters.

Naturally he writes in the full belief that Emin's troops are loyal. We all shared in this belief. We now see that we were grossly misled, and that at no time could Emin have cut his way to the coast through Uganda or any other country with men of such fibre as his ignorant and stolid Soudanese.

Mr. Joseph Thomson, in a letter to the *Times,* suggested a route through the Masai Land, and proposed to be responsible for the safe conduct of a Relief Expedition through that country.

Mr. J. T. Wills suggested that the Mobangi-Welle would prove an excellent way to Emin.

Mr. Harrison Smith expressed himself assured that a way by Abyssinia would be found feasible.

Another gentleman interested in the African Lakes Company proposed that the Expedition should adopt the Zambezi-Shire-Nyassa route, and thence *viâ* Tanganika north to Muta Nzige and Lake Albert, and a missionary from the Tanganika warmly endorsed it, as not presenting more difficulties than any other.

Dr. Felkin, in the 'Scottish Geographical Magazine,' after examining several routes carefully, came to the conclusion that a road west of Lake Victoria and Karagwé, through Usongora to Lake Albert, possessed some advantages over any other.

Early in October, 1886, Sir William Mackinnon and Mr. J. F. Hutton, ex-President of the Manchester Chamber of Commerce, had spoken with me respecting the possibilities of conveying relief to Emin, with a view to enable him to hold his own. To them it seemed that he only required ammunition, and I shared their opinion, and they were very earnest in their intention to collect funds for the support he required. But many of their friends were absent from town, and they could not decide alone what should be done without consultation. We discussed estimates and routes, and Mr. Hutton informs me that the rough estimate I furnished him then exceeds by £500 the actual cost of the Expedition.

As for routes, I intimated to them that there were four almost equally feasible.

The first, *viâ* Masai Land, was decidedly objectionable while carrying a vast store of ammunition which absolutely must reach Emin. Mr. Thomson had tried it, and his account of the extremities to which he was driven on returning from the Lake Victoria, for want of water and grain, were extremely unfavourable. In proceeding to the lake his people were dispirited, and deserted in such numbers that he was obliged to return a short distance, to Kilima Njaro, leave his camp there, and proceed with a few men back to the coast to recruit more men. In ease of a pressing necessity like this it would be extremely unwise to return a mile after commencing the march. The tendency of the Zanzibaris to desert also was another disadvantage, and desertion of late from East Coast Expeditions had assumed alarming proportions owing to the impunity with which they could decamp with rifles and loads, and the number of opportunities presented to them. Many of the Zanzibaris had become professional advance-jumpers, and the greater the expedition the greater would be the loss in money, rifles, and stores.

The second, *viâ* Victoria Nyanza and Uganda, which was naturally the best, was rendered impossible for a small expedition because of the hostility of Uganda. Even this hostility could be avoided if there were any vessels on Lake Victoria capable of transporting across the lake such an expedition as was needed. The danger of desertion was just as imminent on this as on the first.

The third was *viâ* Msalala, Karagwé and Ankori, and Unyoro and Lake Albert. Immense loss of men and goods would assuredly follow any attempt from the East Coast. Fifty per cent. loss was unavoidable, and no precautions would avail to prevent desertion. Besides, Karagwé was garrisoned by the Waganda, and no expedition could pass through that country without persistent hostility from the Waganda. If fortunate enough to force our way through Karagwé, we should have to reckon with the Wanyankori, who number 200,000 spears, and if introduced to them by fighting the Karagwé natives the outlook would be dismal in the extreme. As for going through any country west of Karagwé to avoid the Waganda that would be impossible, except at a cost that I did not suppose the subscribers would contemplate paying.

"The whole question resolves itself into that of money. With money enough every route is possible; but as I understand it, you propose to subscribe a moderate amount, and therefore there is only one route which is safely open for the money, and that is the Congo. This river has the disadvantage of not having enough transport vessels in its upper portion. I would propose then to supplement the Upper Congo flotilla with fifteen whale-boats, which will take an Expedition to within 200 miles, at least, of the Albert Nyanza. A heavy labour will be carrying the whale-boats from the Lower Congo to the Upper, but we can easily manage it by sending agents at once there to prepare carriers. There is one thing, however, that must be done – which is to obtain the sanction of King Leopold.

"But it may be we are rather premature in discussing the matter at all. You know I am aware of many projects mooted, and much 'talk' has been expended on each and this may end in smoke – collect your funds, and then call upon me if you want me. If you do not require me after this exposition of my views, let Thomson take his Expedition through the Masai Land, and put me down for £500 subscription for it."

As the middle of November drew near, Sir William Mackinnon requested me to write him a letter upon the subject that he might show it to his friends, who would soon be returning to town.

A few days after the despatch of the letter, I sailed for America, and on arrival at New York, the lecture "Tour," as it is called, commenced. But on the 11th December, the fifteenth day after arrival, I received the following: –

London.

Your plan and offer accepted. Authorities approve. Funds provided. Business urgent. Come promptly. Reply.

Mackinnon.

A reply was sent from St. Johnsbury, Vermont, for thus far the lecture tour had reached, as follows: –

Just received Monday's cablegram. Many thanks. Everything all right. Will sail per Eider 8 a.m. Wednesday morning. If good weather and barring accidents arrive 22nd December, Southampton. It is only one month's delay after all. Tell the authorities to prepare Holmwood (Consul General) Zanzibar, and Seyyid Barghash (Prince of Zanzibar). Best compliments to you.

Stanley.

My agent was in despair – the audiences were so kind – the receptions were ovations, but arguments and entreaties were of no avail.

I arrived in England the day preceding Christmas, and within a few hours Sir William Mackinnon and myself were discussing the Expedition.

Of course, and without the least shade of doubt, I was firmly convinced that the Congo River route was infinitely the best and safest, provided that I should get my flotilla of whale-boats, and the permission of King Leopold to pass through his territory with an armed force. I knew a route from the East Coast, and was equally acquainted with that from the West Coast. From the furthest point reached by me in 1876, along the East Coast road, the distance was but 100 miles to Lake Albert – from Yambuya Rapids the distance was 322 geographical miles in an air line to the lake. Yet to the best of my judgment the Congo route was preferable. We should have abundance of water – which was so scanty and bad along the Eastern route; food there must be – it was natural to expect it from my knowledge that unsurpassed fertility such as the Upper Congo regions possesses would have been long ago discovered by the aborigines, whereas we knew from Thomson, Fischer, and Hannington's experiences that food and water was scanty in Masai Land; then again, that wholesale desertion so frequent on the East Coast would be avoided on the West Coast.

Yet notwithstanding they admitted that I might be right, it was the opinion of the Committee that it would be best to adopt the Eastern route.

Very good, it is perfectly immaterial to me. Let us decide on the East Coast route, viâ Msalala, Karagwé, Ankori, and Unyoro. If you hear of some hard-fighting, I look to you that you will defend the absent. If I could drop this ammunition in Emin's camp from a balloon I certainly would do so, and avoid coming in contact with those warlike natives, but it is decided that the means of defence must be put into Emin's hands, and you have entrusted me with the escort of it. So be it.

A Relief Fund was raised, the subscriptions to which were as follows: –

Sir William Mackinnon, Bart	2,000
Peter Mackinnon, Esq.	1,000
John Mackinnon, Esq.	300
Baroness Burdett-Coutts	100
W. Burdett-Coutts, Esq.	400
James S. Jameson, Esq.	1,000
Countess de Noailles	1,000
Peter Denny, Esq., of Dumbarton	1,000
Henry Johnson Younger, Esq., of the Scottish Geographical Society	500
Alexander L. Bruce, Esq., of the Scottish Geographical Society	500
Messrs. Gray, Dawes & Co., of London	1,000
Duncan Mac Neil, Esq.	700
James F. Hutton, Esq., of Manchester	250

Sir Thos. Fowell Buxton............................... 250
James Hall, Esq., of Argyleshire 250
N. McMichael, Esq., of Glasgow 250
Royal Geographical Society, London......... 1,000
Egyptian Government............................. 10,000
Total ....£21,500[4]

In order to increase the funds and create a provision against contingencies, I volunteered to write letters from Africa, which the Committee might dispose of to the press as they saw fit, and accept whatever moneys that might receive as my contribution to it.

The estimate of time required to reach Emin Pasha, after a careful calculation, was formed on the basis that whereas I travelled in 1874-5 a distance of 720 miles in 103 days, therefore: −

1st route. - By Masai Land, march to Wadelai and return to coast 14 months. Reserve for delays 4 months = 18 months.

2nd route. - By Msalala, Karagwe, Ankori, and Usongora to Lake Albert. Land march to and return 16 months, delays 4 months = 20 months.

3rd route. - *viâ* Congo.
Zanzibar to Congo, 1 mth. = 1st April
Overland routh to Stanley Pool, 1 mth. = 1st May
By steam up the Congo, 1 1/2 mths. = 15th June
Halt = 25th June
Albert Nyanza to Zanzibar, land march, 8 mths. = 8th Sept.
Delays, 3 1/2 mths. = 18 months.

The actual time, however, occupied by the Expedition is as follows: −

Arrive at Congo, 18th Mar., 1887
Arrive at Stanley Pool, 21st April
Arrive at Yambuya, 15th June
Halt at Yambuya, 28th June
Albert Nyanza, 13th Dec.
Return to Fort Bodo, 8th Jan., 1888

---

4.   See Appendix for full statement of Receipts and Expenditure.

Halt while collecting convalescents, 2nd Apr.
The Albert Nyanza, 2nd time, 18th Apr.
Halt until 25th May
Fort Bodo again, 8th June
Banalya 90 miles from Yambuya, 7th Aug.
Fort Bodo again, 20th Dec.
Albert Nyanza, 3rd time, 26th Jan. 1889
Halt near Albert Nyanza until 8th May
March to Zanzibar, 1400 miles, 6 months, 6th Dec.

So, that we actually occupied a little over 10 1/2 months from Zanzibar to the Albert Nyanza, and from the Nyanza to the Indian Ocean, 6 months, plus a halt at the Albert = 18 months.

I was formally informed by letter on the 31st of December, 1886, that I might commence my preparations. The first order I gave in connection with the Expedition for the relief of Emin Bey was by cable to Zanzibar to my agent, Mr. Edmund Mackenzie, of Messrs. Smith, Mackenzie & Co., to engage 200 Wanyamwezi porters at Bagamoyo to convey as many loads of rice (= 6 tons) to the missionary station at Mpwapwa, which was about 200 miles east of Zanzibar, the cost of which was 2,700 rupees.

The second order, after receiving the consent of His Highness the Seyyid of Zanzibar, was to enlist 600 Zanzibari porters, and also the purchase of the 27, 262 yards of goods, to be used for barter for native provisions, such as grain, potatoes, rice, Indian corn, bananas, plantains, etc. Also 3,600 lbs. of beads and 1 ton of wire, brass, copper, iron.

The third order was for the purchase of forty pack donkeys and ten riding asses, which necessitated an order for saddles to match, at an expense of £400.

Messrs. Forrest & Son received a design and order for the construction of a steel boat 28 ft. long, 6 ft. beam, and 2 ft. 6 in. deep. It was to be built of Siemens steel galvanized, and divided into twelve sections, each weighing about 75 lbs. The fore and aft sections were to be decked and watertight, to give buoyancy in case of accident.

From Egypt were despatched to Zanzibar 510 Remington rifles, 2 tons of gunpowder, 350,000 percussion caps, and 100,000 rounds Remington ammunition. In England the War Office furnished me with 30,000 Gatling cartridges, and from Messrs. Kynoch & Co., Birmingham, I received 35,000 special Remington cartridges. Messrs. Watson & Co., of 4 Pall Mall, packed up 50 Winchester repeaters and 50,000 Winchester cartridges. Hiram Maxim, the inventor of the Maxim Automatic Gun, donated as a gift one of his wonderful weapons, with shield attached mounted on a light but effective stand.

We despatched to Zanzibar 100 shovels, 100 hoes, for forming breastworks, 100 axes for palisading the camp, 100 bill-hooks for building zeribas.

Messrs. Burroughs & Welcome, of Snowhill Buildings, London, the well-known chemists, furnished gratis nine beautiful chests replete with every medicament necessary to combat the endemic diseases peculiar to Africa. Every drug was in tablets mixed with quick solvents, every compartment was well stocked with essentials for the doctor and surgeon. Nothing was omitted, and we all owe a deep debt of gratitude to these gentlemen, not only for the intrinsic value of these chests and excellent medicines, but also for the personal selection of the best that London could furnish, and the supervision of the packing, by which means we were enabled to transport them to Yambuya without damage.

Messrs. John Edgington & Co., of Duke Street, London, took charge of our tents, and made them out of canvas dipped in a preservative of sulphate of copper, which preserved them for three years. Notwithstanding their exposure to three hundred days of rain, for the first time in my experience in Africa I possessed a tent which, after arrival at Zanzibar in 1889, was well able to endure two hundred days more of rain.

Messrs. Fortnum & Mason, of Piccadilly, packed up forty carrier loads of choicest provisions. Every article was superb, the tea retained its flavour to the last, the coffee was of the purest Mocha, the Liebig Company's Extract was of the choicest, and the packing of all was excellent.

I need not enumerate what else was purchased. Four expeditions into Africa, with my old lists of miscellanea before me, enabled me to choose the various articles, and in Sir Francis de Winton and Captain Grant Elliott I had valuable assistants who would know what magazines to patronize, and who could check the deliveries.

Colonel Sir Francis de Winton was my successor on the Congo, and he gave me gratuitously and out of pure friendship the benefit of his great experience, and his masterly knowledge of business to assist me in the despatch of the various businesses connected with the expedition, especially in answering letters, and selecting out of the hundreds of eager applicants for membership a few officers to form a staff.

The first selected was Lieutenant W. Grant Stairs, of the Royal Engineers, who had applied by letter. The concise style and directness of the application appealed strongly in his favour. We sent for him, and after a short interview enlisted him on condition that he could obtain leave of absence. Lord Wolseley kindly granted leave.

The next was Mr. William Bonny, who, having failed in his epistolary ventures on former expeditions, thought the best way was to present himself in person for service in any capacity. The gentleman would not take a mild negative. His breast was covered with medals. They spoke eloquently, though dumb, for his merits. The end of it was Mr. Bonny was engaged as medical assistant, he having just left service of a hospital of the A.M.D.

The third was Mr. John Rose Troup, who had performed good service on the Congo. He was intimate with Swahili, the vernacular of Zanzibar. He was not dainty at work, was exact and methodical in preserving accounts. Mr. Troup was engaged.

The fourth volunteer who presented himself was Major Edmund Musgrave Barttelot, of the 7th Fusiliers. He was accompanied by an acquaintance of mine who spoke highly of him. What passed at the interview will be heard later on. After a few remarks he was also engaged.

The fifth was Captain R. H. Nelson, of Methuen's Horse, fairly distinguished in Zulu campaigns. There was merit in his very face. Captain Nelson agreed to sign the articles of enlistment.

Our next volunteer was Mr. A. J. Mounteney Jephson, inexperienced as yet in foreign travel, and quite unaccustomed to "roughing" in wilds. On some members of the Committee, Mr. Jephson made the impression that he was unfitted for an expedition of this kind, being in their opinion of too "high class." But the Countess de

Noailles made a subscription in his favour to the Relief Fund of £1,000, an argument that the Committee could not resist, and Mr. Jephson signed the articles of agreement with unshaken nerves. Poor young Jephson! he emerged out of Africa after various severe trials which are herein related.

One of the latest to apply, and when the list was about to be closed, was Mr. James S. Jameson. He had travelled in Mashona and Matabele lands in South Africa to collect trophies of the wild chase, to study birds, and to make sketches. He did not appear remarkably strong. We urged that, but he as quickly defended his slight appearance, and argued that as he had already spent a long time in Africa his experience disproved our fears. Besides, he was willing to subscribe £1,000 for the privilege of membership, and do faithful and loyal service, as though it was indispensable for the Expedition to employ him. Mr. Jameson was firm, and subscribed to the articles.

We were in the full swing of preparations to meet the necessities of the overland march from Zanzibar, east to the Victoria Nyanza, when, as will be shown by the tenor of the following letter, it became necessary to reconsider our route.

Palais de Bruxelles,
7th January, 1887.

Dear Mr. Stanley,

The Congo State has nothing to gain by the Expedition for the relief of Emin Pasha passing through its territory. The King has suggested this road merely so as to lend your services to the Expedition, which it would be impossible for him to do were the Expedition to proceed by the Eastern coast. According to your own estimate, the Expedition proceeding by the Eastern coast would occupy about eighteen months. His Majesty considers that he would be failing in his duty towards the State were he to deprive it of your services, especially as the latter will be certainly needed before the expiration of this lapse of time.

If the Expedition proceeds by the Congo the State will promise to show it all good will. The State likewise gratuitously places at the disposal of the Expedition the whole of its naval stock, inasmuch as will allow the working arrangements of its own administration, which it is, above all, desirous of ensuring, as you know. The Stanley is the largest steamer on the Upper Congo. We are forwarding a second one by the mail of the 15th inst, and we will hasten as much as possible the launching of this steamer at Stanley Pool; she will be a valuable and much-needed adjunct to our flotilla. In the meanwhile the mission steamer Peace would no doubt gratuitously effect certain transports.

Should the Expedition desire it, we would facilitate the recruiting of Bangala; we are very pleased with the latter, as they are excellent soldiers, and do not fear the Arabs like the Zanzibaris.

You will have remarked that the official documents, published this week in Berlin, limit the territory of Zanzibar to a narrow strip of land along the seashore. Beyond this strip the entire territory is German. If the Germans allow the Expedition to cross their territory, the Zanzibaris would be precisely as on the Congo, on foreign soil.

With kind regards, I am, dear Mr. Stanley,

Yours very truly,

Comte de Borchgrave.

That this was not a light matter to be hastily decided will be evident by the following note which was sent me by Sir William Mackinnon: –

Western Club, Glasgow,
January 4th, 1887.

My Dear Mr. Stanley,

I had a pleasant short letter from the King showing how anxious he is the Congo route should be taken, and how unwilling to allow a break in the continuity of your connection with the Congo State, as he considers you a pillar of the State, he asks me to banish (?) any divergent sentiments, and get all parties to agree to the Congo route. I have explained fully all that has been done and is doing, and the difficulties in the way of canceling existing engagements, and get the authorities, home and Egyptian and the Sultan of Zanzibar, to acquiesce in making such a change. I also mentioned the great additional charge involved by sending 600 men, even if the Sultan should consent to their going from Zanzibar to the Congo and bringing them back.

I promised, however, to ascertain whether all interested in the present arrangements would agree in taking the Congo route.

In my diary of January 5th I find written briefly the heads of businesses despatched this day.

As suggested by Mackinnon, who has been written to by King Leopold upon the subject of the Congo route, I saw Sir Percy Anderson, and revealed the King's desire that the Expedition should proceed *via* Congo. I was requested to state what advantages the Congo route gave, and replied: –

1st. Certainty of reaching Emin.

2nd. Transport up the Congo River by state steamers to a point 320 geographical miles from Lake Albert.

3rd. Allaying suspicion of Germans that underlying our acts were political motives.

4th. Allaying alleged fears of French Government that our Expedition would endanger the lives of French Missionaries.

5th. If French Missionaries were endangered, then English Missionaries would certainly share their fate.

6th. Greater immunity from the desertion of the Zanzibaris who were fickle in the neighbourhood of Arab settlements.

Lord Iddesleigh writes me that the French ambassador has been instructed to inform him that if the Emin Pasha Relief Expedition proceeds by a route east of the Victoria Nyanza it will certainly endanger the lives of their Missionaries in Uganda. He suggests that I consider this question.

Visited Admiralty, inquired of Admiral Sullivan respecting the possibility of Admiralty supplying vessel to carry Expedition to Congo. He said if Government ordered it would be easy, if not, impossible.

Wrote to the King urging him to acquaint me how far his assistance would extend in transport on the Upper Congo.

January 8th. – Received letters from the King. He lays claim to my services. Offers to lend whole of his naval stock for transport except such as may be necessary for uses of administration. Wired to Mackinnon that I felt uneasy at the clause; that it was scarcely compatible with the urgency required. Colonel de Winton wrote to the same effect.

Effects of Expedition are arriving by many cwts.

De Winton worked with me until late in the night.

January 9th, 1887. – Colonel J. A. Grant, Colonel Sir F. de Winton, and myself sat down to consider His Majesty's letter, and finally wrote a reply requesting he would graciously respond with greater definiteness respecting quantity of transport and time for which transport vessels will be granted as so many matters depend upon quick reply, such as hire of Soudanese, detention of mail steamer for shipment of ammunition, etc. We therefore send special messenger.

January 10th, 1887 – De Winton visited Foreign Office and was promised as soon as possible to attend to the detention of mail steamer and Government transport round the Cape of Good Hope.

Messrs. Gray, Dawes & Co write Postmaster-General willing to detain Zanzibar mail steamer at Aden to wait *Navarino,* which sails from London on the 20th with the ammunition and officers. I overtake *Navarino* at Suez after settling matters of Expedition in Egypt.

January 12th. – Answer arrived last night. Meeting was called by Honourable Guy Dawnay, Colonel Sir Lewis Pelly, Colonel Sir F. de Winton and self. The answer as regards Congo route being satisfactory was decided upon, and this has now been adopted unanimously.

Was notified at 2 p.m. by the Earl of Iddesleigh that he would see me at 6 p.m. But at 3.13 p.m. the Earl died suddenly from disease of the heart.

January 13th. – Foreign office note received from Sir J. Pauncefote transmitting telegram from Sir E. Baring, also letters concerning Admiralty transport. No help from Admiralty.

Goods arriving fast. Will presently fill my house. Went down with Baroness Burdett-Coutts to Guildhall, arriving there 12.45 p.m. I received Freedom of City of London, and am called youngest citizen. Afterwards lunched at Mansion House, a distinguished party present, and affair most satisfactory.

Telegraphed to Brussels to know if Friday convenient to King. Reply, "Yes at 9.30 a.m."

January 14th. – Crossed over Channel last night towards Brussels *viâ* Ostend to see King Leopold. Saw King and gave my farewell. He was very kind. Left for London in evening at 8 p.m.

Telegram arrived from Sandringham requesting visit.

January 15th. – Sir Percy Anderson requested interview.

Mr. Joseph Thomson at this late hour has been writing to Geographical Society wanting to go with Expedition.

Arranged with Ingham to collect Congo carriers. He goes out shortly.

Telegraphed Zanzibar to recall rice carriers from Mpwapwa. This will cost 2,500 rupees more.

Wrote some days ago to the donor of the *Peace* Mission Steamer on the Congo requesting loan of her for the relief of Emin Pasha. Received the following quaint reply: –

"Leeds, *January* 15th, 1887.

"Dear Mr. Stanley,

"I have much regard for you personally, although I cannot, dare not, sanction all your acts.

"I am very sorry if I cannot give assent to your request; but I fully believe you will be no sufferer by the circumstance of not having the s.s. Peace. Yesterday I was able to come to a decision.

"Mr. Baynes, of the Baptist Missionary Society, Holborn, will, he hopes, make to you any communication he judges proper. If you have any reverential regard for 'the Man of Sorrows,' the 'King of Peace' may He mercifully preserve and save your party.

"I have no doubt of the safety of Emin – till his work is done. I believe he will be brought through this trial in perfect safety. God seems to have given you a noble soul (covers for the moment, if on your sad sin and mistakes), and I should like you should 'repent and believe the Gospel' – with real sense, and live hereafter in happiness, light, and joy – for ever. Here delay in you is more dangerous than delay for Emin.

"Your faithful friend,

"(Signed) Robert Arthington."

January 16th. – Colonel J. A. Grant offered to arrange with Mr. J. S. Keltie, Editor of *Nature,* to discuss Mr. Thomson's offer.

Letters accumulate by scores. All hands employed answering.

January 17th. – Wrote Sir Percy Anderson would call Wednesday 2 p.m. Correspondence increases.

Mr. Joseph Thomson's offer discussed. Mr. J. S. Keltie is to write to him privately – decision of committee.

Arranged with G. S. Mackenzie about Zanzibar matters. He despatched two telegrams. General Brackenbury wrote about coal being furnished requiring Treasury sanction.

January 18th. – Worked off morning's business. Travelled to Sandringham with Colonel de Winton to see His Royal Highness. With African map before us gave short lecture to their Royal Highnesses respecting route proposed to reach Emin Pasha. Had a very attentive audience.

January 19th. – Sir William Mackinnon mustered his friends at the Burlington Hotel at a farewell banquet to me.

Have said "good-bye" to a host of friends to-day. *January* 20th. – The s.s. *Navarino* sailed this afternoon carrying goods of Expedition and officers. Lieutenant Stairs, Captain Nelson, and Mr. Mounteney Jephson. Mr. William Bonny started from my rooms with black boy Baruti to Fenchurch Station at 8 a.m. Arriving there he leaves Baruti after a while and proceeds to Tower of London! He says that returning to station at 2 p.m. he found boat had gone. He then went to Gray, Dawes & Co., shipping agents, and is discouraged to find that the matter cannot be mended. Baruti found deserted in Fenchurch Station, very hungry and cold. Colonel J. A. Grant finds him and brings him to me.

January 21st. – Despatch Mr. Bonny by rail to Plymouth to overtake a steamer bound for India and instruct him to debark at Suez with boy and await me.

Left London at 8.50 p.m. for Egypt. Quite a crowd collected to take a final shake of the hands and to bid me a kindly "God speed."

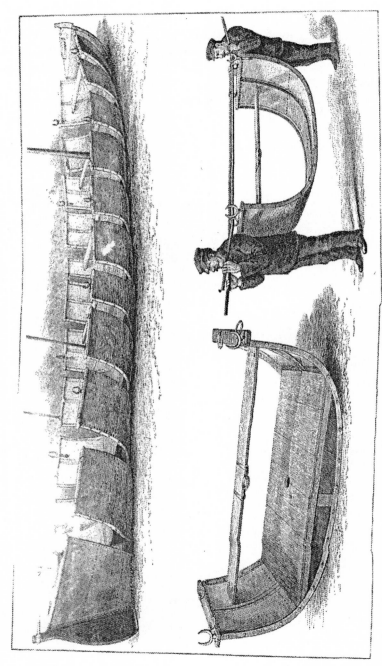

THE STEEL BOAT 'ADVANCE.' (From a Photograph.)

Chapter 2

EGYPT AND ZANZIBAR

January 27th, 1887. – Arrived at Alexandria 6 A.M. Surgeon
T. H. Parke of the A.M.D. came to my hotel and applied for the
position of surgeon to the Expedition. It was the one vacancy not
yet filled to my satisfaction. I considered it a Godsend, though I
appeared distant, as I had had two most unpleasant experiences
with medical men, both of whom were crotchety, and inconsistent
in England. An extremely handsome young gentleman – diffident
somewhat – but very prepossessing. To try if he were in earnest I
said, "If you care to follow me to Cairo, I will talk further with you.
I have not the time to argue with you here."

Left Alexandria at 10 A.M. for Cairo. At the station I met Sir
Evelyn Baring, whom I had read of in Gordon's journals. We drove
to Sir Evelyn's house and was told in his straightforward and clear-
est manner that there was a hitch somewhere. The Khedive and
Nubar Pasha, the Prime Minister, were doubtful as to the wisdom
of the Congo route. Professor Schweinfurth and Dr. Junker had
both been struck with consternation, and by their manner had
expressed that the idea was absurd.

"Well, Sir Evelyn," I said, "do you not think that there are as
clever men in England as Messrs. Schweinfurth and Junker? On the
Relief Committee we have Colonel James Augustus Grant – com-
panion of Speke, Colonel Sir Francis de Winton, late Administrator
General of the Congo, Colonel Sir Lewis Pelly – late Political
Agent at Zanzibar, the Honourable Guy Dawnay of the War Office,
Sir John Kirk – late Consul-General at Zanzibar, the Rev. Horace
Waller and several other distinguished and level-headed men.
Nothing has been settled without the concurrence and assent of the
Foreign Office. We have considered everything, and I have come

thus far resolved to carry the project out as the committee and myself have agreed."

And then I gave Sir Evelyn the pros and cons of the routes, which satisfied him. We then drove to the Prime Minister, Nubar Pasha, and the same explanations had to be entered into with him. Nubar, with a kindly benevolent smile, deferred to Sir Evelyn's superior judgment. Nubar assented to the wisdom and discretion of the change, and as a reward I was invited to breakfast for the morrow.

January 28th, Cairo. – I breakfasted with Nubar Pasha. He introduced me to Mason Bey – the circumnavigator of Lake Albert in 1877, Madame Nubar and three daughters, Tigrane Pasha, his son-in-law, Mr. Fane, formerly Secretary of Legation at Brussels. During breakfast Nubar Pasha conversed upon many things, principally Egypt, Soudan, Africa, and Gordon. Of Gordon he is clearly no admirer. He accredits the loss of the Soudan to him. His views of Baker were that he was a fighter – an eager pioneer – a man of great power.

Showed map to Nubar after breakfast. He examined the various routes carefully, and was convinced the Congo route was the best. He proposes to write instructions to Emin to return to Egypt on the ground that Egypt cannot afford to retain the Soudan under present circumstances. He permits us the use of the Egyptian Flag as the banner of the Expedition. He says he would like to see Emin return with as much ivory as possible and bringing his Makrakas with him. Should any ivory be brought out he will lay claim to some of the money on behalf of the Egyptian Government – because of the £10,000 furnished by it. Uniforms are being ordered for Emin Pasha and principal officers, for which the Relief Fund will have to pay. Rank and pay due to each officer assured.

I saw Schweinfurth and Junker, who have been considered experts here, and I have had a long and interesting conversation, the pith of which I here embody.

Schweinfurth and Junker, it seems, had formed the curious idea that because the Expedition was to be armed with several hundred Remingtons and a machine gun of the latest invention, it was to be an offensive force conducted after strict military rules.

If they had reflected at all the very title of the Expedition ought to have warned them that they were astray; the character of the people who subscribed the major portion of the fund ought to have still more assured them that their conception of the Expedition was wide of the mark. It is the relief of Emin Pasha that is the object of the Expedition, the said relief consisting of ammunition in sufficient quantity to enable him to withdraw from his dangerous position in Central Africa in safety, or to hold his own if he decides to do so for such length of time as he may see fit. Considering the quality of the escort, being mainly Zanzibaris or freed slaves, it would be rash to expect too much from them. It is already known in Zanzibar that Uganda is hostile, that Mwanga massacred some sixty of the followers of Bishop Hannington, that the Masai route has its dangers, that Karagwé is tributary to Mwanga, that the Wahha are numerous and aggressive, that Ruanda has never yet been penetrated, that beyond a certain line whether on the Masai route or the Karagwé route there is certain danger; and no matter with what cheerfulness they would assert at Zanzibar their readiness to defy all and every belligerent, African travellers, remember how weak they are proved to be when in actual presence of danger. Assuming, however, that this band of 600 Zanzibaris were faithful, consider their inexperience of these new rifles, their wild, aimless, harmless firing, their want of discipline and tone, their disposition to be horrified at sight of the effects of fighting – remember that in reality they are only porters and do not pretend to be warriors – and you will see how very unequal such men are to the duties of defending munitions of war in the face of an enemy. It was only by stratagem that I secured their services for the desperate work of discovering the issue of the great river along which we had travelled with Tippu-Tib, when that now famous Arab deserted me in mid-Africa. It was only that there were no other means of escape that enabled me with their help to obtain a quiet retreat from savage Ituru. In many other instances they proved that when menaced with instant death they could be utilized to assist in the preservation of their own lives; but to expect them to march faithfully forward to court the dangers of fighting with the seductions of Unyamwezi and Zanzibar in their rear would be too much. In this Expedition we cannot turn aside as formerly in presence of a pronounced hostility and seek more peaceful countries; but our objective point must be reached, and risk must be run, and the ammunition must be deposited at the feet of Emin Pasha. Therefore to arm these people with Remingtons or machine guns is not enough – you must cut off their means of retreat, allow no avenue of escape – then they will stand together like men, and we may expect the object of the Expedition to be attained, even if we have now and again to meet bows and spears or guns.

Regarding Emin Pasha my information is various.

From Dr. Junker I learn that Emin Pasha is tall,[5] thin and exceedingly short-sighted; that he is a great linguist, Turkish, Arabic, German, French, Italian, and English being familiar to him; to these languages may be added a few of the African dialects. He does not seem to have impressed Junker with his fighting qualities, though as an administrator, he is sagacious, tactful and prudent. His long isolation seems to have discouraged him. He says, "Egypt does not care for us and has forgotten us; Europe takes no interest in what we do." He is German by birth, and is about forty-seven years old.

His force is distributed among eight stations, from 200 to 300 men in each, say about 1,800 in all. The garrisons of the four northernmost stations were discontented and mutinous at last accounts. They answered Emin's advice to consolidate with reproaches; his suggestions that they should all withdraw from the equatorial province *viâ* Zanzibar, were responded to by accusations that he intended only to sell them to Zanzibar as slaves.

Junker cannot give an exact figure of the force itself, or of the Egyptians or clerks or Dongolese with Emin, but being questioned closely as to details replied that the approximate number of those likely to return with the Expedition would be as follows: –

White Egyptian Officers, 10; non-commissioned (black), 15; white clerks (Copts), 20; blacks from Dongola, Wady Halfa, etc., 300, = men 345, Whitewomen, 22; blackwomen, 137; = women 159, children of officers, 40; soldiers' children, 60 = children 100. = Total 604.

---

5.   We consequently bade the tailor make long pantaloons, and they were quite six inches too long.

Besides these, the native troops on perceiving a general withdrawal, may also desire to return with their friends and comrades to Egypt. It is impossible to state what may be the effect on their minds of the appearance of the Relief Expedition. The decision of Emin Pasha, to remain or withdraw, will probably influence the majority.

I expect my men from Wady Halfa to be here this afternoon. They will be armed, equipped, and rationed at the Citadel, and on Thursday will accompany me to Suez. The *Navarino* is supposed to arrive at Suez the day following, when we will embark and be off.

Received telegrams from London. Reports from a well-known person at Cairo has reached newspapers that Emin Pasha had fought his way through Uganda after some desperate struggles, and that the Egyptian Government had placed difficulty in way of Expedition. Replied that such facts were unknown in Cairo.

February 1st. – Saw Sir Evelyn Baring at 10.45 A.M. Accompanied him to Khedive Tewfik. His Highness is most amiable and good-looking. Fine palace within, abundance of room, a host of attendants, &c. Am invited to breakfast with Khedive at noon to-morrow.

Taken later by Sir Evelyn to General Grenfell's office respecting suggestion made to me last night, at General Stephenson's by Valentine Baker Pasha, that I must assure myself that the Remington ammunition furnished by Egyptian Government was sound, as his experience of it was that 50 per cent. was bad. "You must think then," said he, "if the ammunition is so poor already what it will be about a year hence when you meet Emin, after humidity of tropics."

General Grenfell said he had already tested the ammunition, and would make another trial, since Valentine Baker Pasha entertained such an opinion of it.

February 2nd. – Breakfast with Khedive Tewfik. He protests his patriotism, and loves his country. He is certainly most unaffected and genial.

Before leaving Khedive, the following Firman or High Order, was given to me open with the English translation.

Translation.

Copy of a High Arabic Order to Emin Pasha, dated 8th, Gamad Awal 1304, (1st February, 1887. No. 3).

"We have already thanked you and your officers for the plucky and successful defence of the Egyptian Equatorial provinces entrusted to your charge, and for the firmness you have shown with your fellow-officers under your command.

And we therefore have rewarded you in raising your rank to that of Lewa Pasha (Brigadier-General). We have also approved the ranks you thought necessary to give to the officers under your charge. As I have already written to you on the 29 November, 1886, No. 31, and it must have reached you with other documents sent by His Excellency Nubar Pasha, President of the Council of Ministers.

And, since it is our sincerest desire to relieve you with your officers and soldiers from the difficult position you are in, our Government have made up their mind in the manner by which you may be relieved with officers and soldiers from your troubles.

And as a mission for the relief has been formed under the command of Mr. Stanley, the famous and experienced African Explorer, whose reputation is well known throughout the world; and as he intends to set out on his Expedition with all the necessary provisions for you so that he may bring you here with officers and men to Cairo, by the route which Mr. Stanley may think proper to take. Consequently we have issued this High Order to you, and it is sent to you by the hand of Mr. Stanley to let you know what has been done, and as soon as it will reach you, I charge you to convey my best wishes to the officers and men – and you are at full liberty with regard to your leaving for Cairo or your stay there with officers and men.

Our Government has given a decision for paying your salaries with that of the officers and men.

Those who wish to stay there from the officers and men they may do it on their own responsibility, and they may not expect any assistance from the Government.

Try to understand the contents well, and make it well-known to all the officers and men, that they may be aware of what they are going to do.

(Signed) Mehemet Tewfik."

In the evening Tigrane Pasha brought to me Nubar Pasha's – the Prime Minister – letter of recall to Emin. It was read to me and then sealed.

We stand thus, then; Junker does not think Emin will abandon the Province; the English subscribers to the fund hope he will not, but express nothing; they leave it to Emin to decide; the English Government would prefer that he would retire, as his Province under present circumstances is almost inaccessible, and certainly he, so far removed, is a cause of anxiety. The Khedive sends the above order for Emin to accept of our escort, but says, "You may do as you please, if you decline our proffered aid you are not to expect further assistance from the Government." Nubar Pasha's letter conveys the wishes of the Egyptian Government which are in accordance with those of the English Government, as expressed by Sir Evelyn Baring.

February 3rd. – Left Cairo for Suez. At the station to wish me success were Sir Evelyn and Lady Baring, Generals Stephenson, Grenfell, Valentine Baker, Abbaté Pasha, Professor Schweinfurth, and Dr. Junker. The latter and sixty-one soldiers (Soudanese) from Wady Halfa accompanied me. At Zagazig, Surgeon T. H. Parke, now an enrolled member of the Expedition, joined me. At Ismailia our party were increased by Giegler Pasha. At Suez met Mr. James S. Jameson, the naturalist of the Expedition. Mr. Bonny of the Hospital Staff Corps, and Baruti, will arrive to-morrow per *Garonne* of the Orient line.

February 6th. – Breakfasted with Captain Beyts, Agent of the British India Steam Navigation Company. At 2 P.M. Capt. Beyts embarked with us on board *Rob Roy,* a new steamer just built for him, and we steamed out to the Suez harbour where the *Navarino* from London is at anchor. At 5 P.M., after friendly wishes from Captain Beyts and my good friend Dr. Junker, to whom I had become greatly attached for the real worth in him, the *Navarino* sailed for Aden.

February 8th. – Weather grows warm. Ther. Fah. 74° at 8 A.M. in Captain's cabin. My European servant asked me if this was the Red Sea through which we were sailing. "Yes," I replied. "Well, sir, it looks more like a black sea than a red one," was his profound remark.

February 12th. – Reached Aden at 2 A.M. We now change steamers. *Navarino* proceeds to Bombay. The B.I.S.N. steamer *Oriental* takes us to Zanzibar. On board the latter steamer we met Major Barttelot. Cabled to Zanzibar following: –

Mackenzie, Zanzibar.

Your telegram very gratifying. Please engage twenty young lads as officers' servants at lower rate than men. We leave to-day with eight Europeans, sixty-one Soudanese, two Syrians, thirteen Somalis. Provision transport steamer accordingly.

The first-class passengers include self, Barttelot, Stairs, Jephson, Nelson, Parke, Bonny, Count Pfeil, and two German companions bound for Rufiji River.

February 19th. – Arrived off Lamu at 3 P.M. Soon after s.s. *Baghdad* came in with Dr. Lenz, the Austrian traveller, who had started to proceed to Emin Bey, but failing, came across to Zanzibar instead. He is on his way home. Having failed in his purpose, he will blame Africa and abuse the Congo especially. It is natural with all classes to shift the blame on others, and I feel assured Lenz will be no exception.

February 20th. – Arrived at Mombasa. Was told that a great battle had been fought lately between the Gallas and Somalis. The former are for the Germans, the latter are declared enemies to them. We also hear that Portugal has declared war against Zanzibar, or something like it.

Best place for commercial depôt is on right hand of northern entrance, first point within harbour; it is bluffy, dips sheer down into deep water, with timber floated along base of bluff, and long-armed derricks on edge of bluff, steamers might be unloaded and loaded with ease. Cocoa-nut palms abundant. Good view of sea from it. If Mombasa becomes an English port – as I hope it will shortly – the best position of new town would be along face of bluff fronting seaward on island just where old Portuguese port is; a light railway and some draught mules would land on train all goods from harbour.

February 22nd. – Arrived at Zanzibar. Acting Consul-General Holmwood warmly proffered hospitality.

Instructed officers to proceed on board our transport, B.I.S.N. Co. *Madura,* and to take charge of Somalis and Soudanese, and Mackenzie to disembark forty donkeys and saddles from *Madura* – route being changed there was no need for so many animals.

Received compliments from the Sultan of Zanzibar; visits from the famous Tippu-Tib, Jaffar, son of Tarya Topan, his agent, and Kanji the Vakeel of Tarya.

Zanzibar is somewhat changed during my eight years' absence. There is a telegraphic cable, a tall clock-tower, a new Sultan's palace, very lofty and conspicuous, with wide verandahs. The Custom House has been enlarged. General Lloyd Mathews has new barracks for his Military Police; the promenade to Fiddler's grave has been expanded into a broad carriage-way, which extends to Sultan's house beyond Mbwenni. There are horses and carriages, and steam-rollers, and lamp-posts, at convenient distances, serve to bear oil-lamps to light the road when His Highness returns to city from a country jaunt.

There are six German war-vessels in port, under Admiral Knorr, H.B.M.S. *Turquoise* and *Reindeer,* ten merchant steamers, and a few score of Arab dhows, Baggalas, Kanjehs, and boats.

February 23rd. – Paid what is called a State visit to His Highness. As a special mark of honour the troops, under stout General Lloyd Mathews, were drawn up in two lines, about 300 yards in length. A tolerable military band saluted us with martial strains, while several hundreds of the population were banked behind the soldiers. The most frequent words I heard as I passed through with

Consul Holmwood were: "Ndio huyu" – "Yes, it is he!" by which I gathered that scattered among the crowds must have been a large number of my old followers, pointing me out to their friends.

State visits are nearly always alike. The "Present arms!" by General Mathews, the martial strains, the large groups of the superior Arabs at the hall porch, the ascent up the lofty flights of stairs – the Sultan at the head of the stairs – the grave bow, the warm clasp, the salutation word, the courteous wave of the hand to enter, the slow march towards the throne – another ceremonious inclination all round – the Prince taking his seat, which intimates we may follow suit, the refreshments of sherbet after coffee, and a few remarks about Europe, and our mutual healths. Then the ceremonious departure, again the strains of music, – Mathews' sonorous voice at "Present arms!" and we retire from the scene to doff our London dress-suits, and pack them up with camphor to preserve them from moths, until we return from years of travel "Through the Dark Continent" and from "Darkest Africa."

In the afternoon, paid the business visit, first presenting the following letter: –

To His Highness Seyyid Barghash Bin Said,
Sultan of Zanzibar.
Burlington Hotel,
Old Burlington Street, London, W.
28th January, 1887.

Your Highness,

I cannot allow another mail to pass without writing to express to you my grateful appreciation of the kindly response you made to my telegram in regard to assisting the Expedition, which proceeds under the leadership of Mr. H. M. Stanley to relieve Emin Pasha. The cordiality with which you instructed your officers to assist in selecting the best men available is indeed a most important service to the Expedition, and I have reason to know that it has given great satisfaction in England. Mr. Stanley will reach Zanzibar in about four weeks. He is full of enthusiasm as the leader of his interesting Expedition, and his chief reasons for selecting the Congo route are that he may be able to convey the men your Highness has so kindly assisted him in procuring without fatigue or risk by sea to the Congo, and up the river in boats in comparative comfort, and they will arrive within 850 miles of their destination fresh and vigorous instead of being worn out and jaded by the fatigue of a long march inland. His services will be entirely devoted to the Expedition during its progress, and he cannot deviate from its course to perform service for the Congo State.

It is probable also he will return by the east coast land route, and as I know him to be deeply interested in your Highness's prosperity and welfare, I am sure if he can render any service to Your Highness during his progress back to the coast, he will do so most heartily. I have had many conversations with him, and have always found him most friendly to Your Highness's interests, and I believe also the confidence of our mutual good friend. I pray you in these circumstances to communicate freely with Mr. Stanley on all points – as freely as if I had the honour of being there to receive the communications myself.

With the repeated assurance of my hearty sympathy in all the affairs that concern Your Highness's interests.

I remain,

Your very obedient servant and friend,

W. Mackinnon.

We then entered heartily into our business; how absolutely necessary it was that he should promptly enter into an agreement with the English within the limits assigned by Anglo-German treaty. It would take too long to describe the details of the conversation, but I obtained from him the answer needed.

Please God we shall agree. When you have got the papers ready we shall read and sign without further delay and the matter will be over.

At night, wrote the following letter to Emin Pasha, for transmission to-morrow by couriers overland, who will travel through Uganda into Unyoro secretly.

To His Excellency Emin Pasha,
Governor of the Equatorial Provinces.
H. B. Majesty's Consulate. Zanzibar.

February 23rd, 1887.

Dear Sir,

I have the honour to inform you that the Government of His Highness the Khedive of Egypt, upon the receipt of your urgent letters soliciting aid and instructions, have seen fit to depute me to equip an Expedition to proceed to Wadelai to convey such aid as they think you require, and to assist you in other ways agreeably with the written instructions which have been delivered to me for you.

Having been pretty accurately informed of the nature of your necessities from the perusal of your letters to the Egyptian Government, the Expedition has been equipped in such a manner as may be supposed to meet all your wants. As you will gather from the letters of His Highness and the Prime Minister of Egypt to you, and which I bring with me, all that could possibly be done to satisfy your needs has been done most heartily. From the translation of the letters delivered to me, I perceive that they will give you immense satisfaction. Over sixty soldiers from Wady Halfa have been detailed to accompany me in order that they may be able to encourage the soldiers under your command, and confirm the letters. We also march under the Egyptian standard.

The Expedition includes 600 Zanzibari natives, and probably as many Arab followers from Central Africa.

We sail to-morrow from Zanzibar to the Congo, and by the 18th June next we hope to be at the head of navigation on the Upper Congo. From the point where we debark to the southern end of Lake Albert is a distance of 320 miles in a straight line, say 500 miles by road, which will probably occupy us fifty days to march to the south-western or southern end, in the neighbourhood of Kavalli.

If your steamers are in that neighbourhood, you will be able to leave word perhaps at Kavalli, or in its neighbourhood, informing me of your whereabouts.

The reasons which have obliged me to adopt this route for the conveyance of your stores are various, but principally political. I am also impressed with the greater security of that route and the greater certainty of success attending the venture with less trouble to the Expedition and less annoyance to the natives. Mwanga is a formidable opponent to the south and south-east. The Wakedi and other warlike natives to the eastward of Fatiko oppose a serious obstacle, the natives of Kisbakka and Ruanda have never permitted strangers to enter their country. En route I do not anticipate much trouble, because there are no powerful chiefs in the Congo basin capable of interrupting our march.

Besides abundance of ammunition for your needs, official loiters from the Egyptian Government, a heavy mail from your numerous friends and admirers, I bring with me personal equipments for yourself and officers suitable to the rank of each.

Trusting that I shall have the satisfaction of finding you well trod safe, and that nothing will induce you to rashly venture your life and liberty in the neighbourhood of Uganda, with-

out the ample means of causing yourself and men to be respected which I am bringing to you.

I beg you to believe me,
Yours very faithfully,

(Signed) Henry Stanley.

February 24th and 25th – On arriving at Zanzibar, I found our Agent, Mr. Edmund Mackenzie, had managed everything so well that the Expedition was almost ready for embarkation. The steamer *Madura*, of the British India Steam Navigation Company, was in harbour, provisioned and watered for the voyage. The goods for barter, and transport animals, were on board. There were a few things to be done, however – such as arranging with the famous Tippu-Tib about our line of conduct towards one another. Tippu-Tib is a much greater man to-day than he was in the year 1877, when he escorted my caravan, preliminary to our descent down the Congo. He has invested his hard-earned fortune in guns and powder. Adventurous Arabs have flocked to his standard, until he is now an uncrowned king of the region between Stanley Falls and Tanganika Lake, commanding many thousands of men inured to fighting and wild Equatorial life. If I discovered hostile intentions, my idea was to give him a wide berth; for the ammunition I had to convey to Emin Pasha, if captured and employed by him, would endanger the existence of the infant State of the Congo, and imperil all our hopes. Between Tippu-Tip and Mwanga, King of Uganda, there was only a choice of the frying-pan and the fire. Tippu-Tib was the Zubehr of the Congo Basin – just as formidable if made an enemy, as the latter would have been at the head of his slaves. Between myself and Gordon there had to be a difference in dealing with our respective Zubehrs; mine had no animus against me personally; my hands were free, and my movements unfettered. Therefore, with due caution, I sounded Tippu-Tib on the first day, and found him fully prepared for any eventuality – to fight me, or be employed by me. I chose the latter, and we proceeded to business. His aid was not required to enable me to reach Emin Pasha, or to show the road. There are four good roads to Wadelai from the Congo; one of them was in Tippu-Tib's power, the remaining three are clear of him and his myriads. But Dr. Junker informed me that Emin Pasha possessed about 75 tons of ivory. So much ivory would amount to £60,000, at 8s. per lb. The subscription of Egypt to the Emin Pasha Fund is large for her depressed finance. In this quantity of ivory we had a possible means of recouping her Treasury – with a large sum left towards defraying expenses, and perhaps leaving a handsome present for the Zanzibari survivors.

Why not attempt the carriage of this ivory to the Congo? Accordingly, I wished to engage Tippu-Tib and his people to assist me in conveying the ammunition to Emin Pasha, and on return to carry this ivory. After a good deal of bargaining I entered into a contract with him, by which he agreed to supply 600 carriers at £6 per loaded head – each round trip from Stanley Falls to Lake Albert and back. Thus, if each carrier carries 70 lbs. weight of ivory, one round trip will bring to the Fund £13,200 nett at Stanley Falls.

On the Conclusion of this contract, which was entered into in presence of the British Consul-General, I broached another subject in the name of His Majesty King Leopold with Tippu-Tib. Stanley Falls station was established by me in December 1883. Various Europeans have since commanded this station, and Mr. Binnie and Lieut. Wester of the Swedish Army had succeeded in making it a well-ordered and presentable station. Captain Deane, his successor, quarreled with the Arabs, and at his forced departure from the scene set fire to the station. The object for which the station was established was the prevention of the Arabs from pursuing their devastating career below the Falls, not so much by force as by tact, or rather the happy combination of both. By the retreat of the officers of the State from Stanley Falls, the floodgates were opened and the Arabs pressed down river. Tippu-Tib being of course the guiding spirit of the Arabs west of Tanganika Lake, it was advisable to see how far his aid might be secured to cheek this stream of Arabs from destroying the country. After the interchange of messages by cable with Brussels – on the second day of my stay at Zanzibar – I signed an engagement with Tippu-Tib by which he was appointed Governor of Stanley Falls at a regular salary, paid monthly at Zanzibar, into the British Consul-General's hands. His duties will be principally to defend Stanley Falls in the name of the State against all Arabs and natives. The flag of the station will be that of the State.

At all hazards he is to defeat and capture all persons raiding territory for slaves, and to disperse all bodies of men who may be justly suspected of violent designs, he is to abstain from all slave traffic below the Falls himself, and to prevent all in his command trading in slaves. In order to ensure a faithful performance of his engagement with the State, an European officer is to be appointed Resident at the Falls. On the breach of any article in the contract being reported, the salary is to cease.

Meantime, while I was engaged with these negotiations, Mr. Mackenzie had paid four months' advance pay – $12,415 – to 620 men and boys enlisted in the Relief Expedition, and as fast as each batch of fifty men was satisfactorily paid, a barge was hauled alongside and the men were duly embarked, and a steam launch towed the barge to the transport. By 5 P.M. all hands were aboard, and the steamer moved off to a more distant anchorage. By midnight Tippu-Tib and his people and every person connected with the Expedition was on board, and at daybreak next day, the 25th February, the anchor was lifted, and we steamed away towards the Cape of Good Hope.

So far there had not been a hitch in any arrangement. Difficulties had been smoothed as if by magic. Everybody had shown the utmost sympathy, and been prompt with the assistance required. The officers of the Expedition were kept fully employed from morning to evening at laborious tasks connected with the repacking of the ammunition for Emin Pasha's force.

Before concluding these entries, I ought to mention the liberal assistance rendered to the Relief Expedition by Sir John Pender, K.C.M.G., and the Eastern Telegraph Company. All my telegrams from Egypt, Aden and Zanzibar, amounting in the aggregate to several hundred words were despatched free, and as each word from Zanzibar to Europe ordinarily costs eight shillings per word, some idea of the pecuniary value of the favour conferred may be obtained. On my return from Africa this great privilege was again granted, and as I received a score of cablegrams per day for several days, and answers were expected, I should speedily have paid dearly for the fortunate rescue of Emin Pasha, and most probably my stirring career had ended in the Bankruptcy Court had not Sir John Pender and Sir James Anderson quickly reassured me. Among the contributors to the Relief Fund to a very generous amount I therefore may fairly place the names of Sir John Pender and Sir James Anderson in behalf of the Eastern Telegraph Company. I should also state that they were prepared to lend me the Telegraph steamer at Zanzibar to convey my force of carriers and soldiers to the Congo had there been any difficulty in the way of engaging the B.I.S.N. Company's s.s. *Madura.*

Chapter 3

BY SEA TO THE CONGO RIVER

The following private letter to a friend will explain some things of general interest: –

S.S. *Madura,* March 9th., 1887,
Near Cape of Good Hope.
My Dear —,
Apart from the Press letters which are to be published for the benefit of the Relief Fund, and which will contain all that the public ought to know just now, I shall have somewhat to say to you and other friends.

The Sultan of Zanzibar received me with unusual kindness, much of which I owe to the introduction of Mr. William Mackinnon and Sir John Kirk. He presented me with a fine sword, a shirazi blade I should say, richly mounted with gold, and a magnificent diamond ring, which quite makes Tippu-Tib's eyes water. With the sword is the golden belt of His Highness, the clasp of which bears his name in Arabic. It will be useful as a sign, if I come before Arabs, of the good understanding between the Prince and myself; and if I reach the Egyptian officers, some of whom are probably illiterate, they must accept the sword as a token that we are not traders.

You will have seen by the papers that I have taken with me sixty-one soldiers – Soudanese. My object has been to enable them to speak for me to the Soudanese of Equatoria. The Egyptians may affect to disbelieve firmans and the writing of Nubar, in which case these Soudanese will be pushed forward as living witnesses of my commission.

I have settled several little commissions at Zanzibar satisfactorily. One was to get the Sultan to sign the concessions which Mackinnon tried to obtain a long time ago. As the Germans have magnificent territory east of Zanzibar, it was but fair that England

PORTRAIT OF TIPPU-TIB.

should have some portion for the protection she has accorded to Zanzibar since 1841. The Germans appeared to have recognized this, as you may see by the late Anglo-German Agreement. France had already obtained an immense area in West Africa. All the world had agreed (to constitute the domain of King Leopold, on which he had spent a million sterling, as the Independent State of the Congo. Portugal, which is a chronic grumbler, and does little, and that little in a high-handed, illiberal manner, has also been graciously considered by the European Powers; but England, which had sent out her explorers, Livingstone, Burton, Speke, Grant, Baker, Keith Johnston, Thomson, Elton, &c., had obtained nothing, and probably no people had taken such interest in the Dark Continent, or had undergone such sacrifices in behalf of the aborigines, as the English. Her cruisers for the last twenty years had policed the ocean along the coast to suppress slave-catching; her missions were twenty-two in number, settled between East and West Africa. This concession that we wished to obtain embraced a portion of the East African coast, of which Mombasa and Melindi were the principal towns. For eight years, to my knowledge, the matter had been placed before His Highness, but the Sultan's signature was difficult to obtain.

Arriving at Zanzibar, I saw the Sultan was aging, and that he had not long to live.[6] Englishmen could not invest money in the reserved "sphere of influence" until some such concessions were signed.

"Please God," said the Sultan, "we shall agree; there will be no further doubt about the matter." But his political anxieties are wearing him fast, and unless this matter is soon completed it will be too late.

The other affair was with Tippu-Tib. He had actually in his possession three Krupp shells, unloaded, which he had brought with him from Stanley Fails, on the Upper Congo, to Zanzibar, to exhibit to his friends as the kind of missiles which the Belgians pelted his settlements with – and he was exceedingly wroth, and nourished a deep scheme of retaliation. It took me some time to quiet his spasms of resentment. People very furious must be allowed time to vent their anger. When he had poured out his indignation some time, I quietly asked him if he had finished, saying, in a bland way, that I knew well how great and powerful he was, etc., and I told him that it was scarcely fair to blame all the Europeans and King Leopold because an officer at Stanley Falls had been pleased to heave Krupp shells at his settlements; that this trouble had been caused by the excess of zeal of one man in defending a slave woman who had sought his protection, in the same way that Rashid, his nephew, had been carried away by the fury of youth to defend his rights. The Governor of the Congo State was absent

---

6. Seyyid Barghash died six months later.

nearly 1500 miles down the river, and Tippu-Tib, the owner of the settlements, was several hundred miles eastward on the way to Zanzibar. Now I look upon this affair as the result of a match between one young white man and a young Arab. The gray heads are absent who would have settled the trouble without fighting: youths are always "on their muscle," you know.

"Do you know," I continued, "that that station has given us a great deal of trouble. We sent Amelot, you remember. Well, he just left the station without orders, and died somewhere near Nyangwé; then the next, Gleerup, a Swede, followed suit, and travelled across Africa instead; then we sent Deane, and for a change he would have war with the Arabs. King Leopold is not to blame for all this. It is a difficult thing to get men who are always wise, and understand thoroughly what their orders are. If King Leopold had sent Deane to fight you, he would not have sent him with thirty men, you may be sure."

"Now, look here. He proposes that you try your hand at governing that station. He will pay you every month what he would pay an European officer. There are certain little conditions that you must comply with before you become Governor."

Tippu-Tib opened his eyes and snapped them rapidly, as his custom is, and asked, "Me?"

"Yes, you. You like money; I offer you money. You have a grudge against white men being there. Well, if you do your work rightly there will be no need for any white men, except him whom we shall have to place under you, to see that the conditions are not broken."

"Well, what are they?"

"You must hoist the flag of the State. You must allow a Resident to be with you, who will write your reports to the King. You must neither trade in slaves, nor allow anybody else to trade in them below Stanley Falls. Nor must there be any slave-catching; you understand. Such trade as you make in ivory, gums, rubber, cattle, and anything else, you may do as much as you please. But there is to be no pillaging native property of any description whatever below your station. A monthly allowance will be paid into the hands of your Agent at Zanzibar. Don't answer right away. Go and discuss it with your friends, and think of what I offer you. My ship sails on the third day. Give me your answer to-morrow."

A favourable answer was given, a proper agreement was drawn up before the Consul-General, and we both signed.

I made another, agreement with him about the engagement of careers to carry ammunition to Lake Albert from the Congo. If there is no ivory I shall be indebted to Tippu-Tib for the sum of £3,600. But there must be some, as both Emin Pasha and Dr. Junker declare there is a large store of it. At the same time I shall not risk the Expedition for the sake of the ivory.

In consideration of these services which Tippu-Tib has solemnly contracted to perform, I permitted him free passage for himself and ninety-six of his kinsmen from Zanzibar to the Congo, with board included. I also undertook the responsibility of conveying the entire party safely to Stanley Falls, thus incurring not a small expense, but which if faithfully performed will be amply paid for by the services mentioned in the articles of agreement. These negotiations with Tippu-Tib also ensure for us a peaceful march from the Congo through his territory, a thing that would have been by no means possible without him – as his various hordes of raiders will be widely scattered throughout the region; and it is scarcely likely that we should be allowed to pass in peace, resenting, as they must naturally do, their late rupture with Deane. Having bound Tippu-Tib to me I feel somewhat safe against that constant fear of desertion of the Zanzibaris. No Arab will now persuade the people to desert, as is their custom when a white man's Expedition passes near their settlements. Tippu-Tib dare not countenance such proceedings in this case.

The *Madura* is a comfortable steamer. On the *Oriental* and *Navarino* we were uncomfortably crowded. Tween decks abreast of the boilers is rather a hot place for the people; but we have had agreeable weather, and the men have preferred to stow themselves in the boats, and among the donkeys, and on deck, to the baking heat below.

Two hours from Zanzibar, what is called a "shindy" took place between the Zanzibaris and Soudanese. For a short time it appeared as though we should have to return to Zanzibar with many dead and wounded. It rose from a struggle for room. The Soudanese had been located directly in the way of the Zanzibaris, who, being ten times more numerous, required breathing space. They were all professed Moslems, but no one thought of their religion as they seized upon firewood and pieces of planking to batter and bruise each other. The battle had raged some time before I heard of it. As I looked down the hatchway the sight was fearful – blood freely flowed down a score of faces, and ugly pieces of firewood flew about very lively. A command could not be heard in that uproar, and some of us joined in with shillelaghs, directing our attacks upon the noisiest. It required a mixture of persuasiveness and sharp knocks to reduce the fractious factions to order, especially with the Soudanese minority, who are huge fellows. The Soudanese were marched out of their place and located aft, and the Zanzibaris had all the forward half of the ship to themselves. After we had wiped the blood and perspiration away I complimented the officers, especially Jephson, Nelson, and. Bonny, for their share in the fray. They had behaved most gallantly. The result of the scrimmage is ten broken arms, fifteen serious gashes with spears on the face and head, and contusions on shoulders and backs not worth remark, and several abrasions of the lower limbs.

Surgeon Parke has been very busy vaccinating the entire community on board ship. Fortunately I had procured a large supply of lymph for this purpose, because of the harsh experience of the past.

We also divided the people into seven companies of about ninety men each.

I have ordered my Agent to send me 200 loads of various goods to meet the Expedition at Msalala, south end of Lake Victoria. They will be sent about October or November, 1887, arriving at Msalala in February or March, 1888, because if everything proceeds as I should wish, we shall be somewhere near there not very long after that date.

I have been in the company of my officers since I left Aden, and I have been quietly observing them. I will give you a sketch of them as they appear to me now.

Barttelot is a little too eager, and will have to be restrained. There is abundance of work in him, and this quality would be most lovely if it were always according to orders. The most valuable man to me would be he who had Barttelot's spirit and "go" in him, and who could come and ask if such and such a work ought to be done. Such a course suggests thoughtfulness and willingness, besides proper respect.

There is a great deal in Mounteney Jephson, though he was supposed to be effeminate. He is actually fierce when roused, and his face becomes dangerously set and fixed. I noted him during the late battle aboard, and I came near crying out "Bravo, Jephson!" though I had my own stick, "big as a mast," as the Zanzibaris say, to wield. It was most gallant and plucky. He will be either made or marred if he is with this Expedition long enough. Captain Nelson is a fine fellow, and without the ghost of a hobby; he is the same all round, and at all hours.

Stairs, of the Royal Engineers, is a splendid fellow, painstaking, ready, thoughtful, and industrious, and is an invaluable addition to our staff.

Jameson is still the nice fellow we saw; there is not an atom of change in him. He is sociable and good.

Bonny is the soldier. He is not initiative. He seems to have been under a martinet's drill.

March 16th, 1887.

At Cape Town, Tippu-Tib, after remarking the prosperity and business stir of the city, and hearing its history from me, said that he formerly had thought all white men to be fools.

"Really," I said; "Why?"

"That was my opinion."

"Indeed! and what do you think of them now?" I asked.

"I think they have something in them, and that they are more enterprising than Arabs."

"What makes you think so, particularly now?"

"Well, myself and kinsmen have been looking at this town, these big ships and piers, and we have thought how much better all these things appear compared to Zanzibar, which was captured from the Portuguese before this town was built, and I have been wondering why we could not have done as well as you white people. I begin to think you must be very clever."

"If you have discovered so much, Tippu-Tib, you are on the high road to discover more. The white men require a deal of study before you can quite make them out. It is a pity you never went to England for a visit."

"I hope to go there before I die."

"Be faithful to us on this long journey, and I will take you there, and you will see more things than you can dream of now."

"Inshallah! if it is the will of *Allah* we shall go together."

On the 18th March the *Madura* entered the mouth of the Congo River, and dropped her anchor about 200 yards abreast of the sandy point, called Banana.

In a few minutes I was in the presence of Mr. Lafontaine Ferney, the chief Agent of the Dutch Company, to whom our steamer was consigned. Through some delay he had not been informed of our intending to arrive as soon. Everybody professed surprise, as they did not expect us before the 25th, but this fortunate accident was solely due to the captain and the good steamer. However, I succeeded in making arrangements by which the Dutch Company's steamer *K. A. Nieman* – so named after a fine young man of that name, who had lately died at St. Paul de Loanda – would be placed at my disposal, for the transport to Mataddi of 230 men next day.

On returning to the ship, I found my officers surrounding two English traders, connected with the British Congo Company of Banana. They were saying some unpleasant things about the condition of the State steamers. "There is a piece of the *Stanley* on shore now, which will give you an idea of that steamer. The *Stanley* is a perfect ruin, we are told. However, will you leave the Pool? The State has not one steamer in service. They are all drawn up on the banks for repairs, which will take months. We don't see how you are to get away from here under six weeks! Look at that big steamer on the sands! she has just come out from Europe; the fool of a captain ran her on shore instead of waiting for a pilot. She has got the sections of a steamer in her hold. The *Heron* and *Belgique,* both State steamers, have first, of course, to float that steamer off. You are in for it nicely, we can tell you."

Naturally, this news was very discouraging to our officers, and two of them hastened to comfort me with the disastrous news. They were not so well acquainted with the manners of the "natives" of the Lower Congo as I was. I only marveled why they had not been politely requested to accompany their new acquaintances to the cemetery, in order that they might have the exquisite gratification of exhibiting the painted headboards, which record the deaths of many fine young men, as promising in appearance as they.

I turned to the Agent of the British Congo, and requested permission to charter his steamer, the *Albuquerque.* The gentleman graciously acceded. This assured me transport for 140 men and 60 tons cargo. I then begged that he and his friend would negotiate for the charter of the large paddle boat the *Serpa Pinto.* Their good offices were entirely successful, and before evening I knew that we should leave Banana Point with 680 men and 160 tons cargo on the next day. The State steamer *Heron,* I was told, would not be able to leave before the 20th.

On the 19th the steamers *K. A. Kieman, Albuquerque,* and *Serpa Pinto,* departed from Banana Point, and before night had anchored at Ponta da Lenha. The next day the two former steamers steamed straight up to Mataddi. The *Serpa Pinto* hauled into the pier at Boron, to allow me to send an official intimation of the fact that the new Governor of Stanley Falls was aboard, and to receive a hurried visit from two of the Executive Committee charged with the administration of the Congo State.

We had but time to exchange a few words, but in that short time they managed to inform me that there was a "famine in the country"; that "the villages along the road to the Pool were abandoned"; that "the Stanley was seriously damaged"; that "the Mission steamers Peace and Henry Reed were in some unknown parts of the Upper Congo"; that "the En Evant was on shore without machinery or boiler;" that "the A. I. A. was 500 miles above Stanley Pool"; and that "the Royal was perfectly rotten;" and had not been employed for a year; in fact, that the whole of the naval stock promised did not exist at all except in the imagination of the gentlemen of the Bureau at Brussels; and, said one, who seemed to be the principal of the Executive Committee, with deliberate emphasis: "The boats were only to assist you if they could be given without prejudice to the service of the State."

The gruff voice of the Portuguese captain of the *Serpa Pinto* ordered the gentlemen on shore, and we proceeded on our way up the Congo.

My thoughts were not of the pleasantest. With my flotilla of fifteen whale boats I might have been independent; but there was an objection to the Congo route, and therefore that plazas abandoned. We had no sooner adopted the East Coast route than the Sovereign of the Congo State invited Expedition to pass through his territory; the Germans had murmured, and the French Government protested at the idea of our marching through East Africa. When it was too late to order the flotilla of whale boats from Forrest and Son we then accepted the Congo route, after Stipulating for transport up the Lower Congo, for porterage to Stanley Pool, and the loan of the steamers on the Upper Congo which were now said to be wrecked, rotten, or without boilers or engines, or scattered inaccessible. In my ears rang the cry in England: "Hurry up, or you may be too late!" and singing through my memory were the words of Junker: "Emin will be lost unless immediate aid be given him;" and Emin's appeal for help; for, if denied, "we shall perish."

"Well, the aspect of our work is ominous. It is not my fault, and what we have to do is simple enough. We have given our promise to strive Our level best. It is no time for regret, but to struggle and "steer right onward." Every article of our verbal bond, having accepted this responsibility, we must perform, and it is the manner of this performance that I now propose to relate.

I shall not delay the narration to give descriptions of the route overland to the Pool, or of the Upper Congo and its banks, as these have been sufficiently treated of in 'Through the Dark Continent,' and 'The Congo and the Founding of its Free State'; and I now propose to be very brief with the incidents of our journey to Yambuya, at the head of navigation on the Aruwimi.

Chapter 4

TO STANLEY POOL

On the 21st of March the Expedition debarked at the landing-place of the Portuguese trading-house of Señor Joda Ferrier d'Abren, situate at Mataddi, at a distance of 108 miles from the Atlantic. As fast as the steamers were discharged of their passengers and cargo they cast off to return to the seaport of Banana, or the river port below.

About noon the Portuguese gunboat *Kacongo* hove in sight. She brought Major Barttelot, Mr. Jephson, and a number of Soudanese and Zanzibaris; and soon after the state steamer *Heron* brought up the remainder of the cargo left on board the *Madura.*

We set up the tents, stored the immense quantity of rice, biscuits, millet, salt, hay, etc., and bestirred ourselves like men with unlimited work before us. Every officer distinguished himself – the Zanzibaris showed by their celerity that they were glad to be on shore.

Our European party now consisted of Messrs. Barttelot, Stairs, Nelson, Jephson, Parke, Bonny, who had voyaged with me from Aden, Mr. Walker, an engineer, who had joined us at the Cape, Mr. Ingham, an ex-Guardsman, who was our Congo Agent for collection of native carriers, Mr. John Rose Troup, who had been despatched to superintend native porterage to the Pool from Manyanga, and a European servant.

On the following day 171 porters, carrying 7 boxes biscuits = 420 lbs., 157 bags of rice = 10,205 lbs., and beads, departed from Mataddi to Lukungu as a reserve store for the Expedition on arrival. There were 180 sacks of 170 lbs. each = 30,600 lbs. besides, ready to follow or precede us as carriers offered themselves, and which were to be dropped at various places *en route,* and at the Pool. Couriers were also sent to the Pool with request to the Commandant to hurry up the repairs of all steamers.

On the second day of arrival, Mr. Ingham appeared with 220 carriers, engaged at a sovereign per load for conveying goods to the Pool. Lieutenant Stairs practised with the Maxim automatic gun, which fired 330 shots per minute, to the great admiration of Tippu-Tib and his followers.

On the 25th the trumpets sounded in the Soudanese camp at 5.15 A.M. By 6 o'clock tents were folded, the companies were ranged by their respective captains, and near each company's stack of goods, and by 6.15 A.M. I marched out with the vanguard, behind which streamed the Expedition, according to their company, in single file, bearing with us 466 separate "charges" or porter-loads of ammunition, cloth, beads, wire, canned provisions, rice, salt, oil for engines, brass rods, and iron wire. The setting out was admirable, but after the first hour of the march the mountains were so steep and stony, the sunshine was so hot, the loads so heavy, the men so new to the work after the glorious plenty on board the

MAXIM AUTOMATIC GUN.

Madura, and we ourselves were in such an overfed condition, that the Expedition straggled in the most disheartening manner to those not prepared for such a sight. Arriving at the first river, the Mpozo, the *Advance* was already jointed, and we were ferried over to the other bank by fifties, and camped.

The Soudanese were a wretched sight. The Somalis were tolerable, though they had grumbled greatly because there were no camels. The former showed remarkably bad temper. Covered with their hooded great-coats, they had endured a terrible atmosphere, and the effects of heat, fatigue, and little worries were very prominent.

The next day we camped in the grounds of Palaballa, belonging to the Livingstone Inland Mission, and were most hospitably treated by Mr. Clarke, the superintendent, and ladies. As our men were so new to their work, we halted the next day. By the officers' returns I found that nine had died since leaving Zanzibar, and seventeen were so ill that we were compelled to leave them at Palaballa to recuperate.

We resumed the march on the 28th, and reached Maza Mankengi. On the road Mr. Herbert Ward was met, and volunteered as a member of the Expedition. He was engaged, and sent to Mataddi to assist Mr. Ingham with the native transport. Mr. Ward had been of late years in the service of the Congo State, and previously had wandered in New Zealand and Borneo, and was always regarded by me as a young man of great promise.

We were in camp by noon of the 29th at Congo la Lemba, on the site of a place I knew some years ago as a flourishing village. The chief of it was then in his glory, an undisputed master of the district. Prosperity, however, spoiled him, and he began to exact tolls from the State caravans. The route being blocked by his insolence, the State sent a force of Bangalas, who captured and beheaded him. The village was burnt, and the people fled elsewhere. The village site is now covered with tall grass, and its guava, palm, and lemon-trees are choked with reeds.

There was a slight improvement in the order of the march, but the beginning of an Expedition is always a trying time. The Zanzibaris carry 65 lbs. of ammunition, 9 lbs. per rifle, four days' rations of rice, and their own kit, which may be from 4 to 10 lbs. weight of cloth and bedding mats. After they have become acclimated this weight appears light to them; but during the first month we have to be very careful not to make long marches, and to exercise much forbearance.

A heavy rain detained us the early part of next day, but soon after nine we moved on and reached the Luiu River. It was a terribly fatiguing march. Until midnight the people came streaming in, tired, footsore, and sour. The officers slept m my tent, and supped on biscuits and rice.

Near the Mazamba Wood we passed Baron yon Rothkirch supervising a party of Kabindas, who were hauling the *Florida's* shaft. At the rate of progress they would probably reach the Pool about August next; and at the Bembezi Ford a French trader was met descending with a fine lot of ivory tusks.

We passed the Mangola River on the 31st, when I was myself disabled by a fit of sickness from indulging in the guavas of Congo la Lemba, and on the 1st April we travelled to Banza Manteka. At the L. I. Mission Mr. and Mrs. Richards most kindly entertained us. At this place a few years' mission work has produced a great Change. Nearly all the native population had become professed Christians, and attended Divine service punctually with all the fervour of revivalists. Young men whom I had known as famous gin-drinkers had become sober, decent men, and most mannerly in behaviour.

I received three letters from up river, one from Troup at Manyanga, Swinburne at Kinshassa, and Glave at Equator Station, all giving a distressing account of the steamers *Stanley, Peace, Henry Reed,* and *En Avant.* The first is damaged throughout according to my informants, the Mission steamers require thorough overhauling, the *En Avant* has been reduced to a barge. Mr. Troup suggests that we carry a lighter or two from Manyanga to the Pool, a thing utterly impossible. We were already overloaded because of the rice we carried to feed nearly 800 people through the starving country. In order to lighten our work slightly Messrs. Jephson and Walker were despatched with our steel boat, the *Advance,* by the Congo to Manyanga.

We passed by the Lunionzo River on the 3rd, and the next day camped on the site of the abandoned village of Kilolo. During the march I passed a Soudanese trying to strangle a Zanzibari because the wearied man had slightly touched his shoulder with his box. The spleen the Soudanese show is extremely exasperating, but we must exercise patience yet awhile.

A march of three hours brought us to the Kwilu River, with the usual ups and downs of hills, which tire the caravan. At the river, which is 100 yards wide and of strong current, was a canoe without an owner. We took possession of it, and began to cross the Advance Company by tens.

The opportunity afforded by the ferriage was seized by me to write appealing letters to the Commandant at Stanley Pool to interpret the orders of the Minister of the Interior, Strauch, according to the generous spirit expressed by King Leopold when he invited us to seek Emin Pasha *viâ* the Congo. Another was directed to the Rev. Mr. Bentley, of the Baptist Mission, requesting him to remember the assistance I gave the Baptists in 1880-84, and to be prepared to lend the steamer *Peace* that I might hurry the Expedition away from the poverty-stricken region around Stanley Pool. Another was despatched to Mr. Billington, superintendent of the *Henry Reed,* in similar terms, reminding him that it was I who had given them ground at Stanley Pool. Another to the Commandant of Lukungu Station, requesting him to collect 400 carriers to lighten the labours of my men.

On reaching Mwembi the 6th April, I was particularly struck with the increase of demoralization in the caravan. So far, in order not to press the people. I had been very quiet, entrusting the labour of bringing the stragglers to the younger men, that they might become experienced in the troubles which beset Expeditions in Africa; but the necessity of enforcing discipline was particularly demonstrated on this march. The Zanzibaris had no sooner pitched the tents of their respective officers than they rushed like madmen among the neighbouring villages, and commenced to loot native property, in doing which one named Khamis bin Athman was shot dead by a plucky native. This fatal incident is one of these signal proofs that discipline is better than constant forbearance, and how soon even an army of licentious, insubordinate, and refractory men would be destroyed.

It had probably been believed by the mass of the people that I was rather too old to supervise the march, as in former times; but on the march to Vombo, on the 7th, everyone was undeceived, and the last of the lengthy caravan was in camp by 11 A.M., and each officer enjoyed his lunch at noon, with his mind at ease for duty done and a day's journey well made. There is nothing more agreeable than the feeling one possesses after a good journey briefly accomplished. We are assured of a good day's rest; the remainder of the day is our own to read, to eat, to sleep, and be luxuriously inactive, and to think calmly of the morrow; and there can scarcely be anything more disagreeable than to know that, though the journey is but a short one, yet relaxation of severity permits that cruel dawdling on the road in the suffocating high grass, or scorched by a blistering sun – the long line of carriers is crumpled up into perspiring fragments – water far when most needed; not a shady tree near the road; the loads robbed and scattered about over ten miles of road: the carriers skulking among the reeds, or cooling themselves in groves at a distance from the road: the officers in despair at the day's near close, and hungry and vexed, and a near prospect of some such troubles to recur again to-morrow and the day after. An unreflecting spectator hovering near our line of march might think we were unnecessarily cruel; but the application of a few cuts to the confirmed stragglers secure eighteen hours' rest to about 800 people and their Officers, save the goods from being robbed – for frequently these dawdlers lag behind purposely for such intentions – and the day ends happily for all, and the morrow's journey has no horrors for us.

On the 8th the Expedition was welcomed at Lukungu Station by Messrs. Francqui and Dessauer. These hospitable Belgians had of their own impulse gathered four days' rations for our 800 people, of potatoes, bananas, brinjalls, Indian corn, and palm nuts.

No sooner had we all assembled than the Soudanese gathered in a body to demand more food. In fifteen days they had consumed each one 40 lbs. of biscuit and rice; and they announced their intention of returning to the Lower Congo if more rations were not served out. The four days' rations of vegetables they disdained to touch. I had resolved to be very patient; and it was too early yet to manifest even the desire to be otherwise. Extra rations of rice and biscuits were accordingly served out.

Fortunately for me personally there were good officers with me who could relieve me of the necessity of coming into conflict with willful fellows like these sulky obstinate Soudanese. I reserved for myself the *rôle* of mediator between exasperated whites and headstrong undisciplined blacks. Provided one is not himself worn out by being compelled throughout the day to shout at thick-headed men, it is a most agreeable work to extenuate offences and soothe anger. Probably the angry will turn away muttering that we are partial; the other party perhaps thirsts for more sympathy on its side; but the mediator must be prepared to receive a rub or two himself.

Thinking that there would be less chance of the Soudanese storming so furiously against the Zanzibaris on the road, I requested Major Barttelot to keep his Soudanese a day's march ahead of the Zanzibaris.

It will not be surprising that we all felt more sympathy for the loaded Zanzibaris. These formed our scouting parties, and foragers, and food purveyors; they pitched our tents, they collected fuel, they carried the stores; the main strength of the Expedition consisted of them; without them the Europeans and Soudanese, if they had been ten times the number, would have been of no use at all for the succour of Emin. The Soudanese carried nothing but their rifles, their clothing, and their rations. By the time they would be of actual utility we should be a year older; they might perhaps fail us when the hour of need came, but we hoped not; in the meantime, all that was necessary was to keep them moving on with as little trouble as possible to themselves, the Zanzibaris, and us. The Major, however, without doubt was sorely tempted. If he was compelled to strike during these days, I must admit that the Soudanese were uncommonly provoking. Job would have waxed wrathful, and become profane.

The heat was terrible the day we left Lukungu – the 10th. The men dropped down on all sides; chiefs and men succumbed. We overtook the Soudanese again, and the usual scuffling and profanity occurred as an unhappy result.

On Easter Monday, the 11th, the Soudanese Company was stricken down with fever, and lamentation was general, and all but two of the Somalis were prostrated. Barttelot was in a furious rage at his unhappy Company, and expressed a wish that he had been doing Jephson's duty with the boat. I received a letter from Jephson in the evening, wherein he wrote that he wished to be with us, or anywhere rather than on the treacherous and turbulent Congo.

The following day saw a foundering caravan as we struggled most wretchedly into camp. The Soudanese were miles from each other, the Somalis were all ill; one of those in the boat with Mr. Jephson had died. Liebig and meat soups had to be prepared in sufficient quantities to serve out cupfuls to each weakened man as he staggered in.

Lutete's was reached the next day, and the experiences of the march were similar. We suffer losses on every march – losses of men by desertion, by illness, of rifles, boxes of canned provisions, and of fixed ammunition.

At Nselo, on the Inkissi River, we encountered Jephson, who has seen some novelties of life during his voyage up the Congo rapids to Manyanga.

The sun has commenced to paint our faces a vermilion tint, for I see in each officer's face two inflamed circles glowing red and bright under each eye, and I fancy the eyes flash with greater brilliancy. Some of them have thought it would be more picturesque, more of the ideal explorer type, to have their arms painted also, and have bared their milk-white arms until they seem bathed in flame.

The 16th April we employed in ferrying the Expedition across the Inkissi River, and by 5.30 P.M. every soul was across, besides our twenty donkeys and herd of Cape goats.

During the ferriage sonic hot words were exchanged between Salim, son of Massoud, a brother-in-law of Tippu-Tib, and Mr. Mounteney Jephson, who is the master of the boat. Salim, since he has married a sister of Tippu-Tib, aspires to be beyond censure; his conceit has made him abominably insolent. At Mataddi's he chose to impress his views most arrogantly on Lieutenant Stairs; and now it is with Mr. Jephson, who briefly told him that if he did not mind his own business he would have to toss him into the river. Salim savagely resented this, until Tippu-Tib appeared to ease his choler.

At the next camp I received some more letters from Stanley Pool. Lieutenant Liebrichts, the commissaire of the Stanley Pool district, wrote that the steamer *Stanley* would be at my disposition, and also a lighter! The *En Avant* would not be ready for six weeks.

Another was from Mr. Billington. who declined most positively to lend the Henry *Reed.*

One of my most serious duties after a march was to listen to all sorts of complaints – a series of them were made on this day. A native robbed by a hungry Zanzibari of a cassava loaf required restitution; Binza, the goat-herd, imagined himself slighted because he was not allowed to participate in the delicacy of goat tripe, and solicited my favour to obtain for him this privilege; a Zanzibari weakling, starving amidst a well-rationed camp and rice-fed people, begged me to regard his puckered stomach, and do him the justice to see that he received his fair rations from his greedy chief. Salim, Tippu-Tib's henchman, complained that my officers did not admire him excessively. He said, "They should remember he no Queen man now he Tippu-Tib's brudder-in-law" (Salim was formerly an interpreter on board a British cruiser). And there were charges of thefts of a whinstone, a knife, a razor, against certain incorrigible purloiners.

At our next camp on the Nkalama River, which we reached on the 18th April, I received a letter by a courier from Rev. Mr. Bentley, who informed me that no prohibition had been received by him from England of the loan of the Baptist mission steamer *Peace,* and that provided I assured him that the Zanzibaris did nothing contrary to missionary character, which he as a missionary was desirous of maintaining, that he would be most happy to surrender the *Peace* for the service of the "Emin Pasha Relief Expedition." Though very grateful, and fully impressed with his generosity, in this unnecessary allusion to the Zanzibaris, and to this covert intimation that we are responsible for their excesses, Mr. Bentley has proved that it must have cost him a struggle to grant the loan of the *Peace.* He ought to have remembered that the privilege he obtained of building his stations at Leopoldville, Kinshassa. and Lukolela was gained by the labours of the good-natured Zanzibaris, who though sometimes tempted to take freedoms, were generally well behaved, so much so that the natives preferred them to the Houssas, Kabindas, Kru-boys, or Bangalas.

On the 19th we were only able to make a short march, as each day witnessed a severe downpour of rain, and the Luila near which we camped had become dangerously turbulent.

On the 20th we reached Makoko's village. The Zanzibaris were observed to be weakening rapidly. They have been compelled to live on stinted rations lately, and their habit of indulging in raw manioc is very injurious. A pound of rice per day is not a large ration for working men, but if they had contrived to be contented on this scanty but wholesome fare for a while they would not be in a robust condition, it is true, but there certainly would be less illness. During this march from the Lower Congo we had consumed up to date 27,500 lbs. of rice – about 13 tons – so that the resources of the entire region had been severely taxed to obtain this extra carriage The natives having fled front the public paths, and our fear that the Zanzibaris, if permitted to forage far from the camp, would commit depredations, have been the main cause of their plucking up the poisonous manioc tubers, and making themselves wretchedly sick. There were about a hundred men on this date useless as soldiers or carriers.

Arriving at Leopoldville on the 21st to the great delight of all, one of my first discoveries was the fact that the *Stanley,* a small lighter, our steel boat the *Advance,* and the mission steamer *Peace* were the only boats available for the transport of the Expedition up the Congo. I introduce the following notes from my diary: –

Leopoldville, April 22nd. – We are now 845 miles from the sea in view of Stanley Pool, and before us free from rapids are about 1100 miles of river to Yambuya on the Aruwimi whence I propose resuming the land journey to Lake Albert.

Messrs. Bentley and Whitley called on me to-day. We spoke concerning the *Peace.* They said the vessel required many repairs. I insisted that the case was urgent. They finally decided after long consultation that the repairs could be finished by the 30th.

In the afternoon I took Major Barttelot and Mr. Mounteney Jephson into my confidence, and related to them the difficulties that we were in, explained my claims on the consideration of the missionaries and the urgent necessity of an early departure from the foodless district, that provisions were so scarce that the State were able to procure only 60 full rations for 146 people, and that to supply the others the State officers had recourse to hunting the hippopotami in the Pool, and that we should have to pursue the same course to eke out the rice. And if 60 rations can only be procured for 146 people by the State authorities, how were we to supply 750 people? I then directed them to proceed to Mr. Billington and Dr. Sims, and address themselves to the former principally – inasmuch as Dr. Sims was an unsuccessful applicant for a position on this Expedition – and explain matters fairly to him.

They were absent about an hour and a half, and returned to me crestfallen – they had failed. Poor Major! Poor Jephson!

Monsieur Liebrichts, who had formerly served with men the Congo at Bolobo, was now the Governor of the Stanley Pool district. He dined with me this evening and heard the story as related by Major Barttelot and Mr. Mounteney Jephson. Nothing was kept back from him. He knew much of it previously. He agreed heartily with our views of things and acknowledged that here was great urgency. Jephson said, "I vote we seize the *Henry Reed.*"

"No, my friend Jephson. We must not be rash. We must give Mr. Billington time to consider, who would assuredly understand how much his mission was indebted to me, and would see no difficulty in chartering this steamer at double the price the Congo State paid to him. Those who subsist on the charity of others naturally know how to be charitable. We will try again to-morrow, when I shall make a more formal requisition and offer liberal terms, and then if she is not conceded we must think what had best be done under the circumstances."

April 23rd. – Various important matters were attended to this morning. The natives from all parts in this neighbourhood came to revive acquaintance, and it was ten o'clock before I was at liberty.

Ngalyema was somewhat tedious with a long story about grievances that he had borne patiently, and insults endured without plaint. He described the change that had come over the white men, that of late they had become more imperious in their manner, and he and other chiefs suspecting that the change boded no good to them had timidly absented them-selves from the stations, the markets had been abandoned, and consequently food had become scarce and very dear.

Having given my sympathy to my old friends I called Barttelot and Jephson and read to them a statement of former kindnesses shown to the 'Livingstone Inland Mission.' "When you have spoken, request in the name of charity and humanity, and all good feeling, that Mr. Billington allow me to offer liberal terms for the charter of the *Henry Reed* for a period of sixty days."

Barttelot was inspired to believe that his eloquence would prevail, and asked permission to try in his way once more.

"Very good, Major, go, and success attend you."

"I'm sure I shall succeed like a shot," said the Major confidently.

The Major proceeded to the Mission House, and Mr. Jephson accompanied him as a witness of the proceedings. Presently I received a characteristic note from the Major, who wrote that he had argued ineffectually with the missionaries, principally with Mr. Billington, but in the presence of Dr. Sims, who sat in a chair contenting himself with uttering remarks occasionally.

Lieutenant Liebrichts was informed of the event, and presented himself, saying that this affair was the duty of the State.

Monsieur Liebrichts, who is undoubtedly one of the most distinguished officers in the Congo State, and who has well maintained the high character described in a former book of mine, devoted himself with ardour to the task of impressing Mr. Billington with the irrationality of his position, and of his obstinacy in declining to assist us out of our difficulties in which we had been placed by the fault of circumstances. To and fro throughout the day he went demanding, explaining, and expostulating, and finally after twelve hours prevailed on Mr. Billington to accept a charter upon the liberal terms offered – namely, £100 per month.

April 24th. – Mustered Expedition and discovered we are short of 57 men, and 38 Remington rifles. The actual number now is 737 men and 496 rifles. Of billhooks, axes, shovels, canteens, spears, &c., we have lost over 50 per cent. – all in a twenty-eight days' march.

Some of the men, perhaps, will return to their duties, but if such a large number deserts 3000 miles from their native land, what might have been expected had we taken the East Coast route. The Zanzibar head-men tell me with a cynical bitterness that the Expedition would have been dissolved. They say, "These people from the clove and cinnamon plantations of Zanzibar are no better than animals – they have no sense of feeling. They detest work, they don't know what silver is and they have no parents or homes. The men who have homes never desert, if they did they would be so laughed at by their neighbours that they could *not* live." There is a great deal of truth in these remarks, but in this Expedition are scores of confirmed bounty-jumpers who are only awaiting opportunities, hi inspecting the men to-day I was of the opinion that only about 150 were free men, and that all the remainder were either slaves or convicts.

Mr. J. S. Jameson has kindly volunteered to proceed to shoot hippopotami to obtain meat. We are giving 1 lb. of rice to each man – just half rations. For the officers and our Arab guests I have a flock of goats, about thirty in number. The food presents from the various chiefs around have amounted to 500 men's rations and have been very acceptable.

Capt. Nelson is busy with the axemen preparing fuel for the steamers. The *Stanley* must depart to-morrow with Major Barttelot and Surgeon Parke's companies, and debark them at a place above the Wampoko, when they will then march to Mswata. 1 must avail myself of every means of leaving Stanley Pool before we shall be so pinched by hunger that the men will become uncontrollable.

April 25th. – The steamer *Stanley,* steamed up river with 153 men under Major Barttelot and Surgeon Parke.

I paid a visit to Kinshassa to see my ancient secretary, Mr. Swinburne, who is now manager of an Ivory Trading Company, called the "Sanford Exploring Company." The hull of his steamer, *Florida,* being completed, he suggested that if we assisted him to launch her he would be pleased to lend her to the Expedition, since she was of no use to anybody until her machinery and shaft came up with Baron yon Rothkirch, who probably would not arrive before the end of July. I was only too glad, and a number of men were at once ordered up to begin the operations of extending the slip to the river's edge.

Our engineer, Mr. John Walker, was detailed for service on the *Henry Reed,* to clean her up and prepare her for the Upper Congo.

One Soudanese and one Zanzibari died to-day.

April 27th. – Thirteen Zanzibaris and one Soudanese, of those left behind from illness, at stations on the way have arrived. They report having sold their rifles and sapper's tools!

April 28th. – Struck camp and marched Expedition overland to Kinshassa that I might personally superintend launching of hull of steamer, *Florida,* which we hope to do the day after to-morrow, when the ship is finished. We are being hospitably entertained meanwhile by Mr. Antoine Greshoff, of the Dutch Company, and Mr. Swinburne of the Sanford Company.

April 29th. – In camp at Kinshassa under the baobabs. The steamers *Stanley* and *Henry Reed,* towing-barge *En Avant* arrived.

April 30th. – The hull of the *Florida* was launched this morning. Two hundred men pulled her steadily over the extended slip into the river. She was then taken to the landing-place of the Dutch Company and fastened to the steamer *Stanley.*

Each officer was furnished with the plan of embarkation, and directed to begin work of loading the steamers according to programme. The following orders were also issued: –

The Officers commanding companies in this Expedition are –

E.M. Barttelot, Major No. 1 Comapny, Soudanese

W.G. Stairs, Captain No. 2 Co., Zanzibaris

R.H. Nelson, Captain No. 3 Co., Zanzibaris

A.J. Mounteney Jephson, Captain No. 4 Co., Zanzibaris

J.S. Jameson, Captain No. 5 Co., Zanzibaris

John Rose Troup, Captain No. 6 Co., Zanzibaris

T.H. Parke, Captain and Surgeon No. 7 Co., Somalis and Zanzibaris.

Mr. William Bonny takes charge of transport and riding animals and. live stock, and assists Surgeon Parke when necessary.

"Each officer is personally responsible for the good behaviour of his company and the condition of arms and accoutrements."

"Officers will inspect frequently cartridge-pouches of their men, and keep record to prevent sale of ammunition to natives or Arabs."

"For trivial offences – a slight corporal punishment only can be inflicted, and this as seldom as possible. Officers will exercise discretion in this matter, and endeavour to avoid irritating the men, by being too exacting, or showing unnecessary fussiness."

"It has been usual for me to be greatly forbearing – let the rule be, three pardons for one punishment."

"Officers will please remember that the labour of the men is severe, their burdens are heavy, the climate hot, the marches fatiguing, and the rations poor and often scanty. Under such conditions human nature is extremely susceptible, therefore punishments should be judicious, not vexatious, to prevent straining patience too much. Nevertheless discipline must be taught, and when necessary enforced for the general well-being."

"Serious offences affecting the Expedition generally will be dealt with by me."

"While on shipboard one officer will be detailed to perform the duties of the day. He must see to the distribution of rations, ship cleaned, and that no fighting or wrangling occurs, as knifing soon follows unless checked, that the animals arc fed and watered regularly. For all petty details apply to the senior officer, Major Barttelot."

Chapter 5

FROM STANLEY POOL TO YAMBUYA

As I have already expatiated at large upon the description of scenes of the Upper Congo, I intend to expunge altogether any impressions made on us according to our varying moods during our river voyage of about 1100 miles to Yambuya. I will confine myself to the incidents.

The days passed quickly enough. Their earlier hours presented to us every morning panoramas of forest-land, and myriads of forest isles, and broad channels of dead calm water so beshone by the sun that they resembled rivers of quicksilver. In general one might well have said that they were exceedingly monotonous, that is if the traveller was moving upward day by day past the same scenes from such a distance as to lose perception of the details. But we skirted one bank or the other, or steered close to an island to avail ourselves of the deep water, and therefore were saved from the tedium of the monotony.

Seated in an easy-chair scarcely 40 feet from the shore, every revolution of the propeller caused us to see new features of foliage, bank, trees, shrubs, plants, buds and blossoms. We might be indifferent to, or ignorant of the character and virtues of the several plants and varied vegetation we saw, we might have no interest in any portion of the shore, but we certainly forgot the lapse of time while observing the outward forms, and were often kindled into livelier interest whenever an inhabitant of the air or of the water appeared in the field of vision. These delightful views of perfectly calm waters, and vivid green forests with every sprig and leaf still as death, and almost unbroken front line of thick leafy bush sprinkled with butterflies and moths and insects, and wide rivers of shining water, will remain longer in our minds than the stormy aspects which disturbed the exquisite repose of nature almost every afternoon.

From the middle of March to the middle of May was the rainy season, and daily, soon after 2 P.M., the sky betokened the approach of a lowering tempest; the sun was hidden by the, dark portents of storms, and soon after the thunderbolts rent the gloom, lightning blazed through it, the rain poured with tropical copiousness, and general misery prevailed and the darkness of the night followed.

Nature and time were at their best for us. The river was neither too high nor too low. Were it the former we should have had the difficulty of finding uninundatcd ground; had it been the latter we should have been tediously delayed by the shallows. We were permitted to steer generally about 40 yards from the left bank, and to enjoy without interruption over 1000 miles of changing hues and forms of vegetable life, which for their variety, greenness of verdure, and wealth and scent of flowers, the world cannot equal. Tornadoes were rare during the greater portion of the day, whereby we escaped many terrors and perils; they occurred in the evening or the night oftener, when we should be safely moored to the shore. Mosquitoes, gadflies, tsetse, and gnats were not so vicious as formerly. Far more than half the journey was completed before we were reminded of their existence by a few incorrigible vagrants of each species. The pugnacious hippopotami and crocodiles were on this occasion well-behaved. The aborigines were modest in their expectations, and in many instances they gave goats, fowls, and eggs, bananas and plantains, and were content with "chits" on Mr. John Rose Troup, who would follow us later. Our health was excellent, indeed remarkably good, compared with former experiences; whether the English were better adapted physically, or whether they declined to yield, I know not, but I had fewer complaints on this than on any previous expedition.

On the 1st of May the start up the Congo was commenced with the departure of the *Henry Reed* and two barges, with Tippu-Tib and 96 followers and 35 of our men. Soon after her followed the *Stanley* and her consort the *Florida,* with 336 people, besides 6 donkeys, and cargoes of goods; and half-an-hour later the *Peace* attempted to follow, with 135 passengers on board; but the good wishes of the people on shore had scarcely died away, and we were breasting the rapid current, when her rudder snapped in two. Her captain commanded the anchors to be dropped, which happened to be over exceedingly rugged ground where the current was racing six knots. The boat reeled to her beam ends, the chains tore her deck, and as the anchors could not be lifted, being foul among the rocks below, we had to cut ourselves loose and to return to, Kinshassa landing-place. Captain Whitley and Mr. David Charters the engineer set to to repair the rudder, and at 8 P.M. their task was completed.

The next morning we had better fortune, and in due time we reached Kimpoko at the head of the Pool, where the other steamers awaited us.

The *Peace* led the advance up river on the 3rd; but the *Stanley* drew up, passed us, and reached camp an hour and a half ahead of us. The *Henry Reed* was last because of want of judgment on the part of her captain.

The *Peace* was spasmodic. She steamed well for a short time, then suddenly slackened speed. We waited half an hour for another spurt. Her boiler was a system of coiled tubes, and her propellers were enclosed in twin cylindrical shells under the stern, and required to be driven at a furious rate before any speed could be obtained. She will probably give us great trouble.

As soon as we camped, which we generally did about 5 P.M., each officer mustered his men, for wood cutting for the morrow's fuel. This was sometimes very hard work, and continued for hours into the night. The wood of dead trees required to be sought by a number of men and conveyed to the landing-place for the cutter. For such a steamer as the *Stanley* it would require fifty men to search for and carry wood for quite two hours; it would require a dozen axemen to cut it up into 30-inch lengths for the grates. The *Peace* and *Henry Reed* required half as many axes and an equal amount of time to prepare their fuel. It must then be stored on board the steamers that no delay might take place in the morning, and this required some more work before silence, which befits the night, could be obtained, and in the meantime the fires were blazing to afford light, and the noise of crashing, cutting, and splitting of logs continued merrily.

The good-for-nothing *Peace* continued to provoke us on the 4th May. She was certainly one of the slowest steamers any shipbuilder could build. We halted every forty-five minutes or so to "oil up," and sometimes had to halt to clear out the cylinders of the propellers, had to stop to raise steam, to have the grate cleared out of charcoal, while five minutes after raising steam up to 60°, she fell to 40°, and then 35°, and the poor miserable thing floated down stream at the rate of a knot an hour. We lost seven days at Stanley Pool through her; a day was lost when the rudder broke; we were fated to be belated.

The next day, the 5th, we made fast to the landing-place of Mswata. The Major and Dr. Parke had arrived four days previously. They had prepared quantities of fuel, and had purchased a large pile of provisions – loaves of bread from the manioc root and Indian corn.

On the 6th the Major and his companions received orders to march their men to Kwamouth, and await the steamer. The *Stanley* was ordered to proceed to Bolobo, debark her passengers, and descend to Kwamouth to convey Barttelot and men, while we reorganized companies at Bolobo.

On the 7th we observed the *Stanley* steamer ashore on the left bank near Chumbiri, and proceeding to her to inquire into the delay discovered that she was badly injured by running on a rocky reef. The second section had been pierced in four separate places and several rivets knocked out and others loosened. We therefore set to with the engineers of all the other steamers to repair her, but Messrs. Charters and Walker, both Scotchmen, were the most effective at the repairs. We cut up some old sheet iron oil drums, formed plates of them, and screwed them in from the outside. This was very delicate labour, requiring patience and nicety of touch, as there were two feet of water in the hold, and the screws required to be felt to place the nuts on, as well as the punching of holes through the bottom of the steamer. The engineer was up to his waist in water, and striking his chisel through an element that broke the blow, then there was the preparation of the plate to correspond with the holes in the steamer, spreading the minium, then a layer of canvas, and another layer of minium. When everything was ready for fixing the iron plate, a diver was sent down, the iron plate with its canvas patch and minium layers in one hand, and the end of a string attached to a hole in the plate in the other hand. The diver outside had to feel for the corresponding hole in the steamer, and the engineer up to his hips in water within the held felt for the end of the twine, which when found, was drawn in gently, and the plate carefully guided, Or the bolt was slipped in, and the engineer placed the nut on. For hours this tedious work went on, and by evening of the 7th, one large rent in the steel hull had been repaired; the 8th and 9th were passed before the steamer was able to continue her voyage.

On the 10th the *Stanley* caught the asthmatic *Peace* up, and passed us in company with the *Henry Reed*. A few hours later the *Peace* sulked altogether, and declined to proceed. Only 30 lbs. steam could be maintained. We were therefore compelled to make fast to the shore. At this period Mr. Charters' face possessed more interest than anything else in the world. We hung on his words as though they were decrees of Fate. He was a sanguine and cheerful little man, and he comforted us exceedingly. He was sure we would arrive in Bolobo in good time, though we did not appear to be proceeding very rapidly while tied to the shore.

The next day we tried again, starting at 4 A.M., resolved to distinguish ourselves. For an hour the *Peace* behaved nobly, but finally she showed symptoms of relapse. The steam descended lower and lower, and could not retain 5 lbs., and we therefore cast anchor. At 10 A.M. the case appearing hopeless, I despatched Mr. Ward in the whale boat to obtain assistance from the *Henry Reed,* and at eight at night she appeared and anchored sixty yards from us, and all the day we had been idly watching the dark brown current flow by, anchored in mid-stream at least 500 yards from either shore or island, seeing nothing but hippopotami, grassy clumps, weeds, and debris of woods floating by. On the 12th we arrived ignominiously at Bolobo in tow of the *Henley Reed.*

When the traveller reaches Uyanzi such a thing as famine is scarcely possible, and one of the best river ports for abundance and variety of food is Bolobo. Here, then, after reaching a district where the people could recuperate and forget the miseries of limited rations endured since leaving Lukungu, was the place to form the Relief Expedition into two columns.

It was decided that as the force could not be transported on one voyage to the Upper Congo, that the healthiest men should be selected to proceed to Yambuya, and that the weakly should remain in Bolobo as a portion of Major Barttelot's column under Messrs. Herbert Ward, and William Bonny, until the *Stanley* should return from Yambuya. We had started from England with the cry of "urgency" in our ears and memories, and it behooved us to speed on as well as circumstances would permit in obedience to the necessity, trusting that the rear column would be able to follow on our tracks some six or seven weeks later.

We accordingly selected 125 men who appeared weakest in body, and left them at Bolobo to fatten up on the bananas and excellent native bread and fish that were easily procurable here. The *Stanley* in the meantime had descended to Kwamouth with Major Barttelot, Dr. Parke, and 153 men.

The vexed question was also settled here as to who should take charge of the rear column. It being the most important post next to mine, all eyes were naturally directed to the senior officer, Major Barttelot. It was said that he had led a column of a thousand men from Kosseir on the Red Sea to Keneh on the Nile, and that he had distinguished himself in Afghanistan and in the Soudan Campaign. If these facts were true, then undoubtedly he was the fittest officer for the office of commanding the rear column. Had there been a person of equal rank with him, I should certainly have delegated this charge to another, not because of any known unfitness, but because he was so eager to accompany the advance column. On reflecting on the capacities and rank of the other gentlemen, and their eagerness being too well known to me, I informed the Major that I could not really undertake the responsibility of appointing youthful lieutenants to fill a post that devolved on him by rank, experience, and reputation.

"One more steamer like the *Stanley* would have done it, Major, completely," I said, cheerfully, for the young officer was sorely depressed. "Only 125 men and a cargo of goods left of the Expedition. All the rest are on board comfortably. If you can discover some better person than yourself to take your place between here and Yambuya, I would gladly know him. I hope you will not take it too much to heart. For what does it matter after all? You who bring up the rear are as much entitled to credit as we in the advance. If Tippu-Tib will only be faithful, you will only be six weeks behind us, and you may overtake us, for we shall be naturally delayed a great deal, finding the track and boring our way through all kinds of obstacles. You will follow an indicated path, and frequently you may be able to make two of our marches in one day. If Tippu-Tib does not join us, you will be master of your own column, and you will be so occupied with your task that the days will slip by you fast enough. And I tell you another thing for your comfort, Major; there is plenty of work ahead of us, wherein you shall have the most important part. Now tell me, who would you wish for your second?"

"Oh, I would rather leave it to you."

"Nay, I would prefer you would select some one friend as your companion, to share your hopes and thoughts. We all of us have our partialities, you know."

"Well, then, I choose Jameson."

"Very well, Mr. Jameson shall be appointed. I will speak to him myself. I will then leave Mr. Rose Troup, who is a capital fellow, I have reason to believe, and young Ward and Bonny. Both Troup and Ward speak Swahili, and they will be of vast service to you."

In this manner the matter was arranged, and on the 15th of May the flotilla resumed the up-river voyage, conveying 511 persons of the Expedition, and Tippu-Tib and ninety of his followers.

We made a fair journey on the 16th, the repairs on the *Peace* having greatly improved her rate of progress, and on the 19th made fast to the shore near the Baptist Mission of Lukolela, though the *Stanley* did not make her appearance until late on the 19th.

We halted on the 20th at Lukolela, to purchase food for our journey to Equator Station, and we were extremely grateful for the kind hospitality shown to us by the missionaries at this station.

On the 24th of May we arrived at Equator Station, now owned by the Sanford Company, which was represented by Mr. E. J. Glare, a young and clever Yorkshireman. Captain Van Gele was also here, with five Houssa soldiers lately returned from a futile effort to ascend the Mobangi higher than Mr. Grenfell, the missionary, had succeeded in doing some months previously.

We reached Bangala Station on the 30th May. This place was now a very large and prosperous settlement. There was a garrison of sixty men and two Krupps, for defence. Bricks were made, of excellent quality; 40,000 had already been manufactured. The establishment was in every way very creditable to Central Africa. The chief, Van Kirkhoven, was absent at Langa-Langa. He had lately succeeded in releasing twenty-nine Houssa soldiers from slavery. During the escape of Deane from Stanley Falls, these Houssas had precipitately retreated into a canoe, and had floated as far as Upoto when they were captured as runaways by the natives of the district.

Among other good qualities of Bangala, there is a never-failing supply of food. The station possessed 130 goats and a couple of hundred fowls, which supplied the officers with fresh eggs. Ten acres were green with a promising rice crop. The officers enjoyed wine of palm and banana, and fermented beer made of sugar-cane, and exceedingly potent I found the latter to be.

At Bangala I instructed Major Barttelot to proceed with Tippu-Tib and party direct to Stanley Falls, having first taken out thirty-five Zanzibaris from the boats, and replaced them with forty Soudanese, that none of the Zanzibaris might become acquainted with the fact that Stanley Falls was but a few days' march from Yambuya.

With the exception of certain irregularities in the behaviour of the steamer *Stanley,* which by some mysterious manoeuvres disappeared amid intricate passages, on the plea that sufficient fuel of a right quality could be found, we steamed up to the Aruwimi River without any incident, and arrived at our ancient camp, opposite the Basoko villages, on June 12th.

The Basoko were the countrymen of Baruti, or "Gunpowder," who had been captured by Karema when a child, in 1883, and had been taken to England by Sir Francis de Winton, with a view of impressing on him the superiority of civilized customs. From Sir Franciscare Baruti passed into mine, and here we were at last in view of his natal village and tribe, from which he had been absent six years. Seeing Baruti eyeing with excessive interest the place of his birth, he was encouraged by me to hail the Basoko, and invite them to visit us. My previous attempts at winning the confidence of these forest natives had been failures, though in time I was sure there would be no difficulty. For a long period it had been an interesting question to me why aborigines of the forest were more intractable and coy than natives of the open country. The same methods had been applied, the dangling of some bright or gaudy article of barter, the strings of beads of dazzling colour, suspended patiently, the artful speech, the alluring smile and gesture, all were resorted to for long hours, but always ending with disappointment and postponement to a more leisurely occasion. But the reason is that the forest has been always a handy fastness for retreat, the suspicion of the stranger, and the convenient depth of trackless woods plead strongly against some indefinite risk. The least advance causes a precipitate backward movement until he gains the limits of the forest, and then he stands to take a last survey, and finally disappears into the gloom with an air of "It won't do, you know; you can't come over me." Whereas in the open country the native has generally some coign of vantage, some eminence, a tree or an anthill, from the crest of which he has taken his observations, and been warned and informed of the character of the strangers, in the forest the stranger meets the tenant of the woods abruptly; he has advanced out of the unknown, with purpose unfathomed. Surprise is in the face of one, terror marks the face of the other.

Baruti hailed, and the canoes advanced towards us with a tediously slow process, but finally they approached within easy hearing, he recognized some of the canoe-men, and informed them that they had no cause for fear. He asked for a person whose name he uttered, and the wild men hallooed the word with splendid lung-power across the river, until some one responded, and embarked in a canoe and approached. This turned out to be Baruti's elder brother. Baruti demanded to know how his brother fared, after so many years of absence. The brother eyed him vacantly, could not recognize any feature in him, and grunted his doubt.

Baruti mentioned the name of his parents, that of his father, and afterwards that of his mother. Great interest now manifested itself in his brother's face, and he skillfully drew his canoe nearer.

"If you are my brother, tell me some incident, that I may know you."

"Thou hast a scar on thy arm – there, on the right. Dost thou not remember the crocodile?"

This was enough; the young, broad-chested native gave a shout of joy, and roared out the discovery to his countrymen on the further bank, and Baruti for the first time shed tears. The young fellow drew near to the ship, forgot his fears of the strangers, and gave Baruti a frantic hug, and the other canoes advanced to participate in the joy of the two restored brothers.

In the evening Baruti was offered his choice of staying in his village among his tribe, or of following our adventures; at the same time he was advised not to leave us, as life among the Basoko would be very insecure with the Arabs in such close proximity as Stanley Falls.

The lad appeared to think so too, and so declined to be restored to his native land and tribe; but a day or two after reaching Yambuya he altered his mind, came into my tent in the dead of night armed himself with my Winchester rifle and a brace of Smith and Wesson revolvers, a supply of rifle and revolver cartridges, took possession of a silver road-watch, a silver pedometer, a handsome belt with fitted pouches, a small sum of money, and, possessing himself of a canoe, disappeared down river to some parts unknown, most probably to his tribe. At any rate, we have never seen or heard of him since. Peace be with him!

On the 15th of June we arrived opposite Yambuya villages, situated on the left bank of the Aruwimi, 96 miles above the confluence of the Aruwimi and the Congo.

Chapter 6

AT YAMBUYA

We were now over 1300 miles from the sea. Opposite to us
were the villages which we hoped, with the goodwill of the natives,
to occupy temporarily as a depôt for the men and stores left at
Bolobo and Leopoldville, 125 men and about 600 porter-loads of
impedimenta; if not with the natives' goodwill by fair purchase of
the privilege, then by force.

On an exploring visit in 1883 I had attempted to conciliate
them without any permanent result. We had a very serious object in
view now. In prospective we saw only the distant ports of the Nile
and the Albert Nyanza, defended by men ever casting anxious
glances to every cardinal point of the compass, expectant of relief
as they must by this time be well informed by our couriers from
Zanzibar; but between us and them was a broad region justly
marked with whiteness on the best maps extant. Looking at that
black wall of forest which had been a continuous bank of tall
woods from Bolobo hitherto, except when disparted by the majestic
streams pouring their voluminous currents to the parent river, each
of us probably had his own thoughts far hidden in the recesses of
the mind. Mine were of that ideal Governor in the midst of his garrisons, cheering and encouraging his valiant soldiers, pointing with
hand outstretched to the direction whence the expected relief would
surely approach if it were the will of God, and in the distance
beyond I saw in my imagination the Mahdist hordes advancing
with frantic cries and thrilling enthusiasm crying out, "Yallah, Yallah," until from end to end of the swaying lines the cry was heard
rolling through the host of fervid and fanatical warriors, and on the
other sides multitudes of savages vowed to extermination biding

their time, and between them and us was this huge area of the unknown without a track or a path.

Ammunition was served out by the captains of the companies, and instructions were issued to them to hay, steam up on board their respective steamers that we might commence the first most important move preparatory to marching towards the Albert Nyanza.

At six o'clock in the morning of the 16th of June the *Peace* glided from her berth until she was abreast o the *Stanley,* and when near enough to be heard, I requested the officers to await my signal. Then, steaming gently across the river, we attempted to soothe the fears and quiet the excitement of the natives by remaining abreast of the great crowd that stood upon the bluffy bank fifty feet above us, regarding us with wonder and curiosity. Our interpreter was well able to make himself understood, for the natives of the lower Aruwimi speak but one language. After an hour's interchange of compliments and friendly phrases, they were induced to send a few of the boldest down to the river's edge, and by a slight movement of the helm the current pushed the steamer close to the bank, where another hour was passed in entreaty and coaxing on our part, denials and refusals on the other. We succeeded in the purchase of one of their knives for a liberal quantity of beads! Encouraged by this, we commenced to negotiate for leave to reside in their village for a few weeks at a price in cloth, beads, wire, or iron, but it was met with consistent and firm denial for another hour.

It was now nine o'clock, my throat was dry, the sun was getting hot, and I signaled to the steamer *Stanley* to come across and join us, and when near enough, according to agreement, a second signal caused the steam whistles to sound, and under cover of the deafening sounds, pent up as they were by the lofty walls of the forest, both steamers were steered to the shore, and the Zanzibaris and Soudanese scrambled up the steep sides of the bluff like monkeys, and when the summit was gained not a villager was in sight.

We found Yambuya settlement to consist of a series of villages of conical huts extending along the crest of the bank, whence far-reaching views of the Aruwimi up and down stream could be obtained. The companies were marched to their respective quarters. Guards were set at the end of every path leading out. Some of the men were detailed to cut wood for a palisade, others to collect fuel, and several squads were despatched to ascertain the extent of the fields and their locality.

In the afternoon two natives from a village below Yambuya made their appearance with a flattering confidence in their demeanour. They belonged to the Baburu tribes, to which these various fragments of tribes between Stanley Falls and the Lower Aruwimi belong. They sold us a few bananas, were well paid in return, and invited to return with more food, and assurance was given that they need be under no alarm.

On the next day men were sent to collect manioc from the fields, others were sent to construct a palisade, a ditch was traced, workers were appointed to dig a trench for sinking the stockade poles, woodcutters were sent to work to prepare to load the steamers with fuel, that with their weakened crews they might not be surprised on their return journey to the Pool, and everywhere was life and activity.

Several captures were made in the woods, and after being shown everything, the natives were supplied with handfuls of beads to convey the assurance that no fear ought to be entertained of us and no harm done to them.

On the 19th fuel sufficient had been cut for six days' steaming for the *Stanley* with which she could proceed to Equator Station. A cheque was drawn for £50 in favour of the Captain, and another for a similar amount for the engineer, on Ransom, Bouverie & Co., and both were handed in their presence to Mr. Jameson to be presented to them on their return from Stanley Pool, provided they safely reached Yambuya about the middle of August. A valuable jewel was sent to Lieutenant Liebrichts as a token of my great regard for him. The *Stanley* left next morning with my letters to the Emin Relief Committee.

The *Peace* was detained for the sake of accompanying her consort, the *Henry Reed,* which was now hourly expected from Stanley Falls according to the instructions given to Major Barttelot, as she ought to have reached us on the 19th.

In a wild country like this, cannibals in the forest on either hand, and thousands of slave raiders in such a close vicinity as Stanley Falls, we were naturally prone to suspect the occurrence of serious events, if one's expectations were not promptly and punctually realized. Major Barttelot had passed the mouth of the Aruwimi on the 11th inst. in command of the steamer *Henry Reed,* conveying Tippu-Tib and party to a settlement from which an English commandant and garrison had been precipitately ousted. True, the Arab chief had been very confident in his manner, and earnest in the assurance that in nine days after arriving at his settlement he would present himself at Yambuya with 600 carriers in accordance with his agreement, and I was loth to believe that he was in any way responsible for this detention of the Major. Yet the Major should have reached Stanley Falls on the 13th, on the evening of the 14th he should have been at the mouth of the Aruwimi again, and on the 16th at Yambuya; that is, provided the Major was gifted with the spirit of literal performance and permitted nothing to tempt him to delay. It was now the 21st. The officers were confident that nothing had occurred but the delays natural to circumstances of existence in Africa, but hourly I found myself straying to the edge of the bluff sweeping the view down river with my glass.

On the 22nd my uneasiness was so great that I penned an order to Lieutenant Stairs to take fifty of the best men, and the Maxim machine gun, to proceed down river on the morning of the 23rd with the *Peace* to search for the *Henry Reed,* and if all other eventualities mentioned and explained had not transpired to proceed to Stanley Falls. On arriving before this settlement if the vessel was seen at the landing-place, and his friendly signals as he advanced were not responded to, he was to prepare everything for assault and re-capture of the steamer, and to hurry back to me with the news if unsuccessful.

At 5 P.M., however, the Zanzibaris rang out the welcome cry of "Sail ho!" Barttelot was safe, no accident had occurred. Tippu-Tib had not captured the vessel, the Soudanese had not mutinied against the Major, the natives had not assaulted the sleeping camp by night, the steamer had not been sunk by a snag nor had she been run aground, and the boat for which we were morally responsible to the Mission was in as good order and condition as when she left Stanley Pool. But in Africa it is too wearing to be the victim of such anxieties.

The Major had been simply detained by various mischances – fighting with natives, palaver with Tippu-Tib and men, &c. &c.

Two days later the steamers *Peace* and *Henry Reed* were loaded with fuel and despatched homeward down river, and we had severed the last link with civilization for many a month to come.

On this day I delivered the following letter of instructions to Major Barttelot, and a copy of it to Mr. J. S. Jameson his second in command.

June 24th, 1887.

To Major Barttelot, &c., &c., &c.

Sir – As the senior of those officers accompanying me on the Emin Pasha Relief Expedition, the command of this important post naturally devolves on you. It is also for the interest of the Expedition that you accept this command, from the fact that your Soudanese company, being only soldiers, and more capable of garrison duty than the Zanzibaris, will be better utilized than on the road.

The steamer Stanley left Yambuya on the 22nd of this month for Stanley Pool. If she meets with no mischance she ought to be at Leopoldville on the 2nd of July. In two days more she will be loaded with about 500 loads of our goods, which were left in charge of Mr. J. R. Troup. This gentleman will embark, and on the 4th of July I assume that the Stanley will commence her ascent of the river, and arrive at Bolobo on the 9th. Fuel being ready, the 125 men in charge of Messrs. Ward and Bonny, now at Bolobo, will embark, and the steamer will continue her journey. She will be at Bangala on the 19th of July, and arrive here on the 31st of July. Of course, the lowness of the river in that month may delay her a few days, but, having great confidence in her captain, you may certainly expect her before the 10th of August.[7]

---

7.   She arrived on the 14th of August. Had been detained a few days by running on a snag.

It is the non-arrival of these goods and men which compel me to appoint you as commander of this post. But as I shall shortly expect the arrival of a strong reinforcement of men,[8] greatly exceeding the advance force which must, at all hazards, push on to the rescue of Emin Pasha, I hope you will not be detained longer than a few days after the departure of the Stanley on her final return to Stanley Pool in August.

Meantime, pending the arrival of our men and goods, it behooves you to be very alert and wary in the command of this stockaded camp. Though the camp is favourably situated and naturally strong, a bravo enemy would find it no difficult task to capture if the commander is lax in discipline, vigour, and energy. Therefore I feel sure that I have made a wise choice in selecting you to guard our interests here during our absence.

The interests now entrusted to you are of vital importance to this Expedition. The men you will eventually have under you consist of more than an entire third of the Expedition. The goods that will be brought up are the currency needed lot transit through the regions beyond the Lakes; there will be a vast store of ammunition and provisions, which are of equal importance to us. The loss of these men and goods would be certain ruin to us, and the Advance Force itself would need to solicit relief in its turn. Therefore, weighing this matter well, I hope you will spare no pains to maintain order and discipline in your camp, and make your defences complete, and keep them in such a condition, that however brave an enemy may be he can make no impression on them. For this latter purpose I would recommend you to make an artificial ditch 6 feet wide, 3 feet deep, leading from the natural ditch, where the spring is round the stockade. A platform, like that on the southern side of the camp, constructed near the eastern as well as the western gate, would be of advantage to the strength of the camp. For remember, it is not the natives alone who may wish to assail you, but the Arabs and their

---

8.　Tippu-Tib's 600 carriers.

followers may, through some cause or other, quarrel with you and assail your camp.

Our course from here will be due east, or by magnetic compass east by south as near as possible. Certain marches that we may make may not exactly lead in the direction aimed at. Nevertheless, it is the south-west corner of Lake Albert, near or at Kavalli. that is our destination. When we arrive there we shall form a strong camp in the neighbourhood, launch our boat, and steer for Kibero, in Unyoro, to hear from Signor Casati, if he is there, of the condition of Emin Pasha. If the latter is alive, and in the neighbourhood of the Lake, we shall communicate with him, and our after conduct must be guided by what we shall learn of the intentions of Emin Pasha. We may assume that we shall not be longer than a fortnight with him before deciding on our return towards the camp along the same road traversed by us.

We will endeavour, by blazing trees and cutting saplings along our road, to leave sufficient traces of the route taken by us. We shall always take, by preference, tracks leading eastward. At all crossings where paths intersect, we shall hoe up and make a hole a few inches deep across all paths not used by us, besides blazing trees when possible.

It may happen, should Tippu-Tib have sent the full number of adults promised by him to me, viz., 600 men (able to carry loads), and the Stanley has arrived safely with the 125 men left by me at Bolobo, that you will feel yourself sufficiently competent to march the column, with all the goods brought by the Stanley, and those left by me at Yambuya, along the road pursued by me. In that event, which would be very desirable, you will follow closely our route, and before many days we should most assuredly meet. No doubt you will find our boreas intact and standing, and you should endeavour to make your marches so that you could utilise these as you marched. Better guides than those boreas of our route could not be made. If you do not meet them in the course of two days' march, you may rest assured that you are not on our route.

It may happen, also, that though Tippu-Tib has sent some men, he has not sent enough to carry the goods with your own force. In that case you will, of course, use your discretion as to what goods you can dispense with to enable you to march. For this purpose you should study your list attentively.

1st. Ammunition, especially fixed, is most important.
2nd. Beads, brass wire, cowries and cloth, rank next.
3rd. Private luggage.
4th. Powder and caps.
5th. European provisions.
6th. Brass rods as used on the Congo.
7th. Provisions (rice, beans, peas, millet, biscuits).

Therefore you must consider, after rope, sacking, tools, such as shovels (never discard an axe or bill-hook), how many sacks of provisions you can distribute among your men to enable you to march – whether half your brass rods in the boxes could not go also, and there stop. If you still cannot march, then it would be better to make two marches of six miles twice over, if you prefer marching to staying for our arrival, than throw too many things away.

With the Stanley's final departure from Yambuya, you should not fail to send a report to Mr. William Mackinnon, c/o Gray, Dawes and Co., 13, Austin Friars, London, of what has happened at your camp in my absence, or when I started away eastward; whether you have heard of or from me at all when you do expect to hear, and what you purpose doing. You should also scud him a true copy of this order, that the Relief Committee may judge for themselves whether you have acted, or propose to act, judiciously.

Your present garrison shall consist of 80 rifles, and from 40 to 50 supernumeraries. The Stanley is to bring you within a few weeks 50 more rifles and 75 supernumeraries, under Messrs. Troup, Ward and Bonny.

I associate Mr. J. S. Jameson with you at present. Messrs. Troup, Ward and Bonny, will submit to your authority. In the ordinary duties of the defence, and the conduct of the camp or of the march, there is only one chief, which is yourself; but, should any vital step be proposed to be taken, I beg you will take the voice of Mr. Jameson also. And when Messrs. Troup and Ward are here, pray admit them to your confidence, and let them speak freely their opinions.

I think I have written very clearly upon everything that strikes me as necessary. Your treatment of the natives, I suggest, should depend entirely upon their conduct to you. Suffer them to return to the neighbouring villages in peace, and if you can in any manner by moderation, small gifts occasionally of brass rods, &c., hasten an amicable intercourse, I should recommend you doing so. Lose no opportunity of obtaining all kinds of information respecting the natives, the position of the various villages in your neighbourhood, &c., &c.

I have the honour to be, your obedient servant,

Henry M. Stanley.
Commanding Expedition.

The Major withdrew to read it, and then requested Mr. Jameson to make a few copies.

About two o'clock the Major returned to me and asked for an interview, He said he desired to speak with me concerning Tippu-Tib.

"I should like to know, sir, something more regarding this Arab. When I was delayed a few days ago at the Falls, you were pleased to deliver some rather energetic orders to Lieutenant Stairs.

It strikes me that you are exceedingly suspicious of him, and if so, I really cannot see why you should have anything to do with such a man."

"Well, sir, I shall be pleased to discuss him with you, or any other subject," I replied.

"Three days before your steamer was sighted coming up river, I must confess to have been very anxious about you. You were in command of a steamer which belonged to other parties to whom we were pledged to return her within a certain time. You had a company of forty soldiers, Soudanese, as your escort. The vessel was well fitted and in perfect order. We knew the time you ought to have occupied, provided no accident occurred, and as your instructions were positively to depart from Stanley Falls, as soon as the cow promised by our friend Ngalyema was aboard, and if she was not forthcoming within an hour you were to slip away down river. Assuming that no accident happened and that you obeyed orders, you should have been here on the evening of the 16th, or on the 17th at the latest. You did not arrive until 5 P.M. on the 22nd.

"We have no telegraphs here, or posts. As we could gain no intelligence of you, my anxiety about you created doubts. As one day after another passed, doubts became actual dread that something unaccountable had occurred. Had you struck a snag, run aground, like the *Stanley* and *Royal* did, as almost all steamers do, had you been assaulted by natives in the night like Captain Deane in the A.I.A. at Bunga, had your Soudanese mutinied as they threatened to do at Lukungu, had you been shot as a Soudanese regiment shot all their white officers in the Soudan once, had you been detained by force because Tippu-Tib had been over persuaded to do by those young fire-eaters of Arabs at the Falls, had you quarreled with those young fellows, the two Salims, as Stairs and Jephson did below Stanley Pool. If not, what had occurred? Could I, could anybody suggest anything else?"

"But I was obliged —"

"Never mind, my dear Major, say no more about it. Don't think of defending yourself. I am not mentioning these things to complain of you, but replying to your question. All is well that ends safely.

"Now as to Tippu-Tib. I have nothing to do with Tippu-Tib, but from necessity, for your sake as well as mine. He claims this as his territory. We are on it as his friends. Supposing we had not made agreement with him, how long should we be left to prepare for the march to the Albert, or how long would you be permitted to remain here, before you had to answer the question why you were on his territory? Could I possibly leave you here, with my knowledge of what they are capable of – alone? With eighty rifles against probably 3000, perhaps 5000 guns? Why, Major, I am surprised that you who have seen Stanley Falls, and some hundreds of the Arabs should ask the question?

"You have accompanied Tippu-Tib and nearly a hundred of his followers from Zanzibar. You have seen what boyish delight they took in their Weapons, their Winchesters, and valuable double-barreled rifles. You know the story of Deane's fight at Stanley Falls. You know that Tippu-Tib is vindictive, that his fiery nephews would like a fight better than peace. You know that he meditated war against the Congo State, and that I had to pass on a relief mission through a portion of his territory. Why, how can you – grown to the rank of Major – ask such questions, or doubt the why and wherefore of acts which are as clear as daylight?

"Our transport the *Madura* was in Zanzibar harbour. The owner of this district, as he calls himself, was preparing munitions against all white men on the Congo, resenting and resentful. Would it have been prudent for me to have left this man in such a state? That he prepared for war against the State did not materially affect me, but that he intended doing so while I had to pass through his territory, and in his neighbourhood on a humane mission was everything. Therefore I was as much interested in this affair of patching up a peace between the Congo State and King Leopold as His Majesty himself was, and more so indeed.

"And I suppose you will ask me next how does it affect your personal interests? Have you not told me over and over again that you are burning to accompany us, that you would infinitely prefer marching to waiting here? And is it not understood – according to your letter of instructions – that failing Tippu-Tib's appearance with his 600 carriers, you are to make double-stages, or triple-stages rather than stay at Yambuya?

"Look at these pencilled calculations on this paper – nay, you can keep it, if you please. They represent what you can do with your own men, and what you can do assuming that Tippu-Tib really keeps to the letter of his contract.

"Now I have grounded my instructions principally on your impetuous answer to me at Bolobo. 'By Jove! I will not stay a day at Yambuya after I get my column together!'

"See here! The letter says – 'It may happen that Tippu-Tib has sent some men, but not sent enough; therefore, you know, use your discretion; dispense with No. 7, provisions, such as rice, beans, peas, millet, biscuits. See how many sacks of provisions you can issue out to your men – they will eat them fast enough, 1 warrant you.

"It goes on – 'If you still cannot march, then it would be better to make marches of six miles twice over – that is, to go one march of six miles, and then return to fetch another lot, and march forward again. Such as my work wan on the Congo, when with 68 men I made 33 round trips on the stretch of 52 miles to take 2000 loads – 5 immense wagons and make a wagon road, building bridges, etc.' That pencilled paper in your hand informs you how many miles you can do in this fashion in six months.

"But this is how my pact with Tippu-Tib affects you personally. If Tippu-Tib performs his contract faithfully, then on the arrival of the *Stanley* with Messrs. Ward, Troup, and Bonny, and their men, you can set out from Yambuya within a day or two, and perhaps overtake us, or on our return from the Albert we shall meet before many days.

"Now which would you personally prefer doing? Travelling backwards and forwards from camp to camp, twice, or perhaps thrice, or have Tippu-Tib with 600 carriers to help your 200 carriers, and march at a swinging pace through the woods on our track, straight for the Albert Nyanza?"

"Oh, there is not a doubt of it. I should prefer marching straight away and try and catch up with you. Naturally."

"Well, do you begin to understand why I have been sweet, and good, and liberal to Tippu-Tib? Why I have given him free passage and board for himself and followers from Zanzibar to Stanley Falls? Why I have shared the kid and the lamb with him?"

"Quite."

"Not quite yet, I am afraid, Major, otherwise you would not have doubted me. There is still a serious reason.

"Assuming, for instance, that I had not brought Tippu-Tib here, that the Arabs at Stanley Falls were not wrathy with white men for Deane's affair, or that they would fear attacking you. They had but to affect friendship with you, sell you goats and food, and then tell your Zanzibaris that their settlement was but six or seven days away – where they had plenty of rice and fish and oil to tempt three-fourths of your men to desert in a few days, while you were innocently waiting for the Bolobo contingent; and no sooner would the other fellows have reached here than they would hear of the desertion of their comrades for the Falls, and follow suit either wholesale or by twos and threes, sixes and tens, until you would have been left stranded completely. Is it not the fear of this deser-tion that was one of the reasons I chose the Congo? Having Tippu-Tib as my friend and engaged to me, I have put a stop to the possi-bility of any wholesale desertion.

"Let these reasons sink into your mind, Major, my dear fellow. Yet withal, your column may be ruined if you are not very careful. Be tender and patient with your people, for they are as skittish as young colts. Still, it was with these people, or men like them, that I crossed Africa – followed the course of the Congo to the sea, and formed the Congo State."

"Well, now, say do you think Tippu-Tib will keep his contract, and bring his 600 people?" asked the Major.

"You ought to know that as well as I myself. What did he say to you before you left him?"

"He said he would be here in nine days, as he told you at Ban-gala. Inshallah!" replied the Major, mimicking the Arab.

"If Tippu-Tib is here in nine days, it will be the biggest wonder I have met."

"Why?" asked the Major, looking up half wonderingly.

"Because to provide 600 carriers is a large order. He will not be here in fifteen days or even twenty days. We must be reasonable with the man. He is not an European – taught to be rigidly faithful to his promise. Inshallah! was it he said? To-morrow – Inshallah means the day after – or five days hence, or ten days. But what does it matter to you if he does not come within twenty days? The *Stanley* will not be here until the 10th, or "perhaps the middle of August; that will be about seven weeks – forty-two days – hence, He has abundance of time. What do you want to look after 600 men in your camp doing nothing, waiting for the steamer? Idle men are mischievous. No, wait for him patiently until the *Stanley* comes, and if he has not appeared by that time he will not come at all."

"But it will be a severe job for us if he does not appear at all, to carry 500 or 600 loads with 200 carriers, to and fro, backwards and forwards, day after day!"

"Undoubtedly, my dear Major, it is not a light task by any means. But which would you prefer; stay here, waiting for us to return from the Albert, or to proceed little by little – gaining something each day – and be absorbed in your work?"

"Oh, my God! I think staying here for months would be a deuced sight the worse."

"Exactly what I think, and, therefore, I made these calculations for you. I assure you, Major, if I were sure that you could find your way to the Albert, I would not mind doing this work of yours myself; and appoint you commander of the advance column, rather than have any anxiety about you."

"But tell me, Mr. Stanley, how long do you suppose it will be before we meet?"

"God knows. None can inform me what lies ahead here, or how far the forest extends inland. Whether there are any roads, or what kind of natives, cannibals, incorrigible savages, dwarfs, gorillas. I have not the least idea. I wish I had; and would give a handsome sum for the knowledge even. But that paper in your hand, on which I have calculated how long it will take me to march to the Albert Nyanza, is based on this fact. In 1874 and 1875 I travelled 720 miles in 103 days. The distance from here to the Albert Nyanza is about 330 geographical miles in a straight line. Well, in 1874-75, I travelled 330 geographical miles – Bagamoyo to Vinyata, in Ituru, in 64 days; from Lake Uhimba to Ujiji, 330 miles, in 54 days. These were, of course, open countries, with tolerably fair roads, whereas this is absolutely unknown. Is it all a forest? – then it will be an awful work. How far does the forest reach inland? A hundred two hundred – three hundred miles? There is no answer. Let us assume we can do the journey to the Albert in three months; that I am detained a fortnight, and that I am back in three months afterwards. Well, I shall meet you coming toward me, if Tippu-Tib is not with you, the latter part of October or November. It is all down on that paper.

"But it is immaterial. The thing has to be done. We will go ahead, we, will blaze the trees, and mark our track through the forest for you. We will avail ourselves of every advantage – any path easterly will suit me until I bore through and through it, and come out on the plains or pastureland. And where we go, you can go. If we can't go on, you will hear from us somehow. Are you now satisfied?"

"Perfectly," he replied. "I have it all here," touching his forehead – "and this paper and letter will be my reminders. But there is one thing I should like to speak about, it refers to something you said to me in London."

"Ah, indeed. What was said that was in any way peculiar?" I asked.

"Well" – here there was a little hesitation – "do you remember when Mr. —, of the India Office, introduced me to you? The words you used sounded strangely, as though someone had been warning you against me."

"My dear Barttelot, take my word for it, I don't remember to have heard the name of Barttelot before I heard your name. But you interest me. What could I have possibly said that was any way peculiar to cling to your memory like this? I remember the circumstance well."

"The fact is," he said, "you said something about 'forbearance,' which reminded me that I had heard that word before, when General — pitched into me about punishing a Somali mutineer in the desert during the Soudan campaign. I was all alone with the Somalis when they turned on me, and I sprang upon the ringleader at last when there was no other way of reducing them to order and pistolled him, and at once the Somalis became quiet as lambs. I thought that General —, who is not remarkable for goodwill to me, had mentioned the affair to you."

"Indeed, I never heard the story before, and I do not understand how General — could have warned me, considering he could not have known you were going to apply for membership. It was your own face which inspired the word forbearance. Your friend introduced you to me as a distinguished officer full of pluck and courage; upon which I said that those qualities were common characteristics of British officers, but I would prefer to hear of another quality which would be of equal value for a peculiar service in Africa – and that was forbearance. You will excuse me now, I hope, for saying that. I read on your face immense determination and something like pugnacity. Now, a pugnacious fellow, though very useful at times, you know, is not quite so useful for an expedition like this – which is to work in an atmosphere of irritability – as a man who knows not only how and when to fight, but also how to forbear. Why, a thousand causes provoke irritation and friction here between himself and fellow-officers, his own followers and natives, and frequently between himself and his own person. Here is bad food always, often none at all, a miserable diet at the best, no stimulant, incessant toil and worry, intense discomfort, relaxed muscles, weariness amounting to fainting, and, to cap all, dreadful racking fevers, urging one to curse the day he ever thought of Africa. A pugnacious man is naturally ill-tempered, and unless he restrains his instincts, and can control his impulses, he is in hot water every minute of his existence, and will find cross rubs with every throb of his heart. To be able to forbear, to keep down rigorously all bitter feelings, to let the thoughts of his duty, his position, plead against the indulgence of his passions. Ah, that quality, while it does not diminish courage, prevents the waste of natural force; but I don't wish to preach to you, you know what I mean.

"And now to close – one word more about Tippu-Tib. Do you see that Maxim out there with its gaping muzzle? I regard Tippu-Tib somewhat as I do that. It is an excellent weapon for defence. A stream of bullets can be poured out of it, but it may get jammed, and its mechanism become deranged from rust or want of good oil. In that event we rely on our Reining-tons, and Winchester Repeaters. If Tippu-Tib is disposed to help us – he will be a most valuable auxiliary – failure becomes impossible, we shall complete our work admirably. If he is not disposed, then we must do what we can with our own men, and goodwill covers a multitude of errors.

"Do you remember that in 1876 Tippu-Tib broke his contract with me, and returned to Nyangwe, leaving me alone. Well, with about 130 of my own men, I drove my way down the Congo despite his sneer. You said you met Dr. Lenz, the Austrian traveller, at Lamu, after having failed to reach Emin Pasha. Why did he fail? He relied on Tippu-Tib alone; he had no private reserve of force to fall back upon. You have over 200 carriers and 50 soldiers, besides servants and efficient companions. On the Congo work I was promised a contingent of natives to assist me. Only a few came, and those deserted; but I had a faithful reserve of sixty-eight men – they were the fellows who made the Congo State. You remember my letter to the *Times,* where I said, 'We do not want Tippu-Tib to assist us in finding Emin Pasha. We want him to carry ammunition, and on his return to bring away ivory to help pay the expenses of the Mission.' Then, as a last proof of how I regard Tippu-Tib, do not forget that written order to Lieutenant Stairs a few days ago, to rake his settlement with the machine gun upon the least sign of treachery. You have read that letter. You ought to know that the gage of battle is not thrown in the face of a trusted friend.

"Now, Major, my dear fellow, don't be silly. I know you feel sore because you are not to go with us in the advance. You think you will lose some *kudos.* Not a bit of it. Ever since King David, those who remain with the stuff, and those who go to the war, receive the same honours. Besides, I don't like the word 'kudos.' The kudos impulse is like the pop of a ginger-beer bottle, good for a V.C. or an Albert medal, but it effervesces in a month of Africa. It is a damp squib, Major. Think rather of Tennyson's lines: –

Not once or twice in our fair island story
Has the path of duty been the way to glory.

"There, shake hands upon this, Major. For us the word is 'Right Onward'; for you 'Patience and Forbearance.' I want my tea. I am dry with talking."

On the 25th the stockade was completed all round the camp, the ditch was approaching completion. Barttelot superintended the works on one side; Jephson, in shirt-sleeves, looked over another.

Nelson was distributing the European provisions – share and share alike; our Doctor, cheery, smiling, anxious as though he were at a surgical operation, was constructing a gate, and performed the carpenter's operation in such a manner that I wrote in my diary that evening, "He is certainly one of the best fellows alive." Jameson was busy copying the letter of instructions. Stairs was in bed with a severe bilious fever.

A Soudanese soldier, as innocent as a lamb cropping sweet grass before a fox's covert, trespassed for the sake of loot near a native village, and was speared through the abdomen. It is the second fatal case resulting from looting. It will not be our last. We place a Soudanese on guard; his friend comes along, exchanges a word or two with him, and passes on, with the completest unconsciousness of danger that can be imagined. If not slain outright, he returns with a great gash in his body and a look of death in his face. The Zanzibari is set to labour at cutting wood or collecting manioc; he presently drops his task utters an excuse for withdrawing for a moment – a thought glances across his vacuous mind, and under the impulse he hastes away, to be reported by-and-by as missing.

On the 26th I drew out a memorandum for the officers of the Advance Column, of which the following is a copy: –

We propose to commence our march the day after to-morrow, the 28th of June, 1887.

The distance we have to traverse is about 330 geographical miles in an air line – or about 550 miles English, provided we do not find a path more than ordinarily winding.

If we make an average of ten miles per day we ought to be able to reach the Albert within two months.

In 1871 my Expedition after Livingstone performed 360 English miles in 54 days — about 6 1/2 miles per day.

In 1874 my Expedition across Africa performed 360 English miles in 64 days, viz, from Bagamoyo to Vinyata = 5 3/4 miles per day.

In 1874-75 the same Expedition reached Lake Victoria from Bagamoyo 720 miles distance in 103 says = 7 miles per day.

In 1876 the same Expedition traversed 360 miles, the distance from Lake Uhimba to Ujiji in 59 days = 6 1/10 miles per day.

Therefore if we travel the distance to Kavalli, say 550 miles at an average of 6 miles per day, we should reach Lake Albert about the last day of September.

A conception of the character of more than half of the country to be traversed may be had by glancing at our surroundings. It will be a bush and forested country with a native path more or less crooked, connecting the various settlements of the tribes dwelling in it.

The track now and then will be intersected by others connecting the tribes north of our route and those south of it.

The natives will be armed with shields, spears and knives, or with bows and arrows.

As our purpose is to march on swiftly through the country, we take the natives considerably by surprise. They cannot confederate or meet us in any force, because they will have no time. Whatever hostilities we may meet will be the outcome of impulse, and that naturally an angry one. Officers must therefore be prompt to resist these impulsive attacks, and should at all times now see that their Winchester magazines are loaded, and their bearers close to them. Side arms should not be dispensed with on any account.

The order of the march will be as follows:

At dawn the reveille will sound as usual.

First by the Soudanese trumpeter attached to No. 1 Company.

Second by the bugle attached to Captain Stairs's Company, No. 2 – Captain Stairs.

Third by the trumpeter attached to the No. 3 Company – Captain Nelson. Fourth by the drummer attached to Captain Jephson's No. 4 Company. Officers will feed early on coffee and biscuit, and see that their men are also strengthening themselves for the journey.

At 6 A.M. the march of the day will begin, led by a band of 50 pioneers armed with rifles, bill-hooks, and axes, forming the advance guard under myself.

The main body will then follow after 15 minutes, led by an officer whose turn it is to be at the head of it, whose duty will be specially to see that he follows the route indicated by "blazing" or otherwise.

This column will consist of all bearers, and all men sick or well who are not detailed for rear guard. The major part of three companies will form the column. Close to the rear of it, keeping well up, will be the officer whose turn it is to maintain order in rear of the main body.

The rear guard will consist of 30 men under an officer selected for the day to protect the column from attacks in the rear. These men will not be loaded with anything beyond their private kits. No member of the Expedition must be passed by the rear guard. All stragglers must be driven on at all costs, because the person left behind is irretrievably lost.

At the head of the main body will be the head-quarter tents and private luggage, immediately succeeding the officer in command. This officer will also have to be on the alert for signals by trumpets, to communicate them to those in the rear, or be ready to receive signals from the front and pass the word behind.

The advance guard will *"blaze"* the path followed, cut down obstructing creepers, and, on arrival at camp, set to at once for building the boma or bushfence. As fast as each company

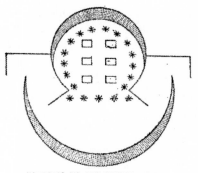

DIAGRAM OF OUR FOREST CAMPS.

arrives, assistance must be given for this important work of defence. No camp is to be considered complete until it is fenced around by bush or trees. Those unemployed in this duty will erect tents. The boma must be round with two gates well masked by at least five yards of bush. The diameter of the camp should be about 250 feet. Tents and baggage piled in the centre, the huts will range around a inner circle of about 200 feet in diameter. The above relates only to circumstances attending the transit of a caravan through dangerous country, unattended by more than the troubles naturally arising from the impulsive attacks of savages.

The pulse of the country which we shall traverse will be felt by the advance guard, of course. If the obstacles in the front are serious, and threaten to be something more than a mere impulse, or temporal messages will be sent to the main body announcing their character. Wherever practicable we shall camp in villages, if the natives have deserted them, for the sake of obtaining food, but such villages must be rendered defensive at once. Officers should remember that it is in the nature of their black soldiers, Soudanese, Somalis or Zanzibaris, to be thoughtless and indifferent, to scatter themselves about in the most heedless manner. They must take my assur-

ance that more lives are lost in this manner than by open warfare. Therefore their men's lives I consider are in the hands of their officers, and the officer who will not relax his energy and rigid enforcement of orders until everything is made snug and tight for the night, will be the most valuable assistant in this Expedition for me. Arriving at the intended halting place for the night, if a village, the officer should first cast his eyes about for lodgment of his people; select such as will be uniform with those already occupied by the preceding company, and those to be occupied by the succeeding company or companies; then turn to and destroy all those lying without the occupied circle, or use their timbers, all material in the vicinity to defend his quarters from night attack by fire or spear. A cue will be given when and how to do things by the conduct of the advance guard, but the officer must not fail to ascertain what this cue is, nor wait to be told every petty detail. He must consider himself as the Father of his Company, and act always as a wise leader should act.

At all such village camps, Lieutenant Stairs will see to the nightly guards being placed at the more accessible points, every company serving out details as may be necessary.

During the first week we will not attempt any very long marches, that the people and ourselves may be broken in gently, but after a fourth of the distance has been made the marches will sensibly lengthen, and I anticipate that, before the half of the journey has been performed, we shall be capable of making wonderful progress.

Further memoranda will be furnished when necessary.

(Signed)
Henry M. Stanley.
Commanding Expedition.
June 26th, 1887.

I close this chapter with a quotation from my diary made on the last evening.

"*Yambuya, June* 27th. – Our men claimed a holiday to-day because it had been deferred until the steamers were despatched, and the camp was fortified for the protection of the garrison. Numbers of things had also to be done. Companies had to be re-organized, since several had sickened since leaving Bolobo, the weak had to be picked out, and the four companies selected for the march ought to be in as perfect condition as possible. our pioneer's tools required numbering. Out of one hundred bill-hooks there were only twenty-six, out of one hundred axes there were left twenty-two, out of one hundred hoes there were only sixty-one, out of one hundred shovels there were but sixty-seven. All the rest had been stolen, and sold to the natives or thrown away. It is a trying work to look after such reckless people.

'Three hundred and eighty-nine souls will march to-morrow – God permitting – into the absolutely unknown. From a native I have heard of names of tribes, or sections of tribes, but of their strength or disposition I know nothing.

Yesterday we made blood-brotherhood with one of the chiefs of Yambuya. As the Major was Commandant of the post, he went bravely through the ceremony, which was particularly disgusting. On the flowing blood a pinch of dirty salt was placed, and this had to be licked. The chief performed his part as though he loved it. the Major looked up and saw the cynical faces of his friends and was mortified.

"'To ensure peace!'

"'Even so,' replied the Major, and sacrificed his taste.

"These forest natives have not been able to win any great regard from me yet. They are cowardly, and at the same time vicious. They lie oftener than any open country folk. I do not credit any statement or profession made by them. At the same time I hope that after better acquaintance there will be a change. This chief received a liberal gift from the hand of the Major, and in return he received a fortnight-old chick and a feathered bonnet of plaited cane. The oft-promised goat and ten fowls had not yet been seen. And the blood of a Soudanese soldier has been spilled, and we have not avenged it. We are either so poor in spirit, or so indifferent to the loss of a man, that a stalwart soldier, worth twenty of these natives, can be slain unavenged. Not only that, but we entreat them to come often and visit us, for they have fish and goats, fowls, eggs, and what not to sell of which we would be buyers. This perhaps will go on for some weeks more.

"It is raining to-night, and the morrow's march will be an uncomfortable one. Stairs is so sick that he cannot move, and yet he is anxious to accompany us. It is rather rash to undertake carrying a man in his condition, though, if death is the issue, it comes as easy in the jungle as in the camp. Dr. Parke has made me exceedingly uncomfortable by saying that it is enteric fever. I lean to bilious fever. We shall put him in a hammock and trust for a favourable issue."

The Advance Force will consist of: –

No. 1 company = 113 men and boys, 99 rifles
No. 2 company = 90 men and boys, 85 rifles
No. 3 company = 90 men and boys, 87 rifles
No. 4 company = 90 men and boys, 86 rifles
Officers -
Self
Stairs
Nelson
Jephson
Parke
European servant
Total of 389 men and 357 rifles

The garrison of Yambuya consists of: –

Soudanese = 44 men, 44 rifles
Zanzibaris = 71 men, 38 rifles
Barttelot's servants = 3 men
Jameson's servants = 2 men
Sowahis = 5 men
Sick men = 2 men
Barttelot personally = 1 man, 3 rifles
Jameson = 1 man, 2 rifles

Total of 129 men, 87 rifles

Contingent at Bolobo to be joined to garrison of Yambuya: –

Zanzibaris = 128 men and boys, 52 rifles
John Rose Troup
Herbert Ward
William Bonny
Total of 131 men, 52 rifles

Advance force = 389 men, 357 rifles
Yambuya garrison = 129 men, 87 rifles
Bolobo, Kinshassa, &c. = 131 men, 52 rifles
Total of 649 men, 496 rifles

Loss of men from Zanzibar to Yambuya = 57 men, 28 rifles
Total of 706 men and 524 rifles.

Chapter 7

TO PANGA FALLS

As African road generally is a foot-track tramped by travel to exceeding smoothness and hardness as of asphalt when the season is dry. It is only twelve inches wide from the habit of the natives to travel in single file one after another. When such a track is old it resembles a winding and shallow gutter, the centre has been trodden oftener than the sides – rain-water has rushed along and scoured it out somewhat – the sides of the path have been raised by humus and dust, the feet of many passengers have brushed twigs and stones and pressed the dust aside. A straight path would be shorter than the usual one formed by native travel by a third in every mile on an average. This is something like what we hoped to meet in defiling out of the gate of the intrenched camp at Yambuya, because during four preceding Expeditions into Africa we had never failed to follow such a track for hundreds of miles. Yambuya consisted of a series of villages. Their inhabitants must have neighbours to the Eastward as well as to the Southward or Westward. Why not?

We marched out of the gate, company after company in single file. Each with its flag, its trumpeter or drummer, each with its detail of supernumeraries, with fifty picked men as advance guard to handle the billhook and axe, to cut saplings, "blaze," or peel a portion of the bark of a tree a hand's-breadth, to sever the leaves and slash at the rattan, to remove all obtrusive branches that might interfere with the free passage of the hundreds of loaded porters, to cut trees to lay across streams for their passage, to form zeribas or bomas of bush and branch around the hutted camp at the end of the day's travel. The advance guard are to find a path, or, if none can be found, to choose the thinnest portions of the jungle and tunnel through without delay, for it is most fatiguing to stand in a heated atmosphere with a weighty load on the head. If no thinner jungle can be found, then through anything, however impenetrable it may appear; they must be brisk – chop-chop – as we say, or an ominous murmur will rise from the impatient carriers behind. They must be clever and intelligent in woodcraft; a greenhorn, or as we call him "goee-goee," must drop his bill-hook, and take the bale or box. Three hundred weary fellows are not to be trifled with, they must be brave also – quick to repel assault – arrows are poisonous, spears are deadly – their eyes must be quick to search the gloom and shade, with sense alert to recognition, and ready to act on the moment. Dawdlers and goee-goees are unbearable; they must be young, lithe, springy – my 300 behind me have no regard for the ancient or the corpulent – they would be smothered with chaff and suffocated with banter. Scores of voices would cry out, "Wherein lies this fellow's merit? Is it all in his stomach? Nay, it is in his wooden back – tut – his head is too big for a scout. He has clearly been used to hoeing. What does the field hand want on the Continent? You may see he is only a Banian slave! Nay, he is only a Consul's freed man! Bosh! he is a mission boy." Their bitter tongues pierce like swords through the armour of stupidity, and the bill-hooks with trenchant, edges are wielded most manfully, and the bright keen axes flash and sever the saplings, or slice a broad strip of bark from a tree, and the bush is pierced, and the jungle gapes open, and fast on their heels continuously close presses the mile-long caravan.

This is to be the order, and this the method of the march, and I have stood observing the files pass by until the last of the rear guard is out of the camp, and the Major and Jameson and the garrison next crowd out to exchange the farewell.

"Now, Major, my dear fellow, we are in for it. Necks or nothing! Remember your promise and we shall meet before many months."

"I vow to goodness. I shall be after you sharp. Let me once get those fellows from Bolobo and nothing shall stop me."

"Well, then, God bless you – keep a stout heart – and Jameson – old man – the same to you."

Captain Nelson, who heard all this, stepped up in his turn to fake a parting grasp, and I strode on to the front, while the Captain placed himself at the head of the rear guard.

THE KIRANGOZI, OR FOREMOST MAN.

The column had halted at the end of the villages or rather the road that Nelson the other day had commenced.

"Which is the way, guide?" I asked to probably the proudest soul in the column – for it is a most exalted position to be at the head of the line. He was in a Greekish costume with a Greekish helmet à la Achilles.

"This, running towards the sunrise," he replied. "How many hours to the next village?" "God alone knows," he answered.

"Know ye not one village or country beyond here?" "Not one; how should I?" he asked.

This amounted to what the wisest of us knew. "Well, then, set on in the name of God, and God be ever with us. Cling to any track that leads by the river until we find a road."

"Bismillah!" echoed the pioneers, the Nubian trumpets blew the signal of "move on," and shortly the head of the column disappeared into the thick bush beyond the utmost bounds of the clearings of Yambuya.

This was on the 28th day of June, and until the 5th of December, for 160 days, we marched through the forest, bush and jungle, without ever having seen a bit of greensward of the size of a cottage chamber floor. Nothing but miles and miles, endless miles of forest, in various stages of growth and various degrees of altitude, according to the ages of the trees, with varying thickness of undergrowth according to the character of the trees which afforded thicker or slighter shade. It is to the description of the march through this forest and to its strange incidents I propose to confine myself for the next few chapters, as it is an absolutely unknown region opened to the gaze and knowledge of civilized man for the first time since the waters disappeared and were gathered into the seas, and the earth became dry land. Beseeching the reader's patience, I promise to be as little tedious as possible, though there is no other manuscript or missal, printed book or pamphlet, this spring of the year of our Lord 1890, that contains any account of this region of horrors other than this book of mine.

With the temperature of 86° in the shade we travelled along a path very infrequently employed, which wound under dark depths of bush. It was a slow process, interrupted every few minutes by the tangle. The bill-hooks and axes, plied by fifty men, were constantly in requisition; the creepers were slashed remorselessly, lengths of track one hundred yards or so were as fair as similar extents were difficult.

At noon we looked round the elbow of the Aruwimi, which is in view of Yambuya, and saw above, about four miles, another rapid with its glancing waters as it waved in rollers in the sunshine; the rapids of Yambuya were a little below us. Beneath the upper rapids quite a fleet of canoes hovered about it. There was much movement and stir, owing, of course, to the alarm that the Yambu-yas had communicated to their neighbours. At 4 P.M. we observed that the point we had gazed at abreast of the rapids consisted of islands. These were now being crowded with the women and children of Yankondé, whom as yet we had not seen. About a hundred canoes formed in the stream crowded with native warriors, and followed the movements of the column as it appeared and disappeared in the light and into the shadows, jeering, mocking, and teasing.

The head of the column arrived at the foot of a broad cleared road, twenty feet wide and three hundred yards long, and at the further end probably three hundred natives of the town of Yankondé stood gesticulating, shouting, with drawn bows in their hands. In all my experience of Africa I had seen nothing of this kind. The pioneers halted, reflecting, and remarking somewhat after this manner: "What does this mean? The pagans have carved a broad highway out of the bush to their town for us, and yet there they are at the other end, ready for a fight! It is a trap, lads, of some kind, so look sharp."

With the bush they had cut they had banked and blocked all passage to the forest on either side of the road for some distance. But, with fifty pairs of sharp eyes searching around above and below, we were not long in finding that this apparent highway through the bush bristled with skewers six inches long sharpened at both ends, which were driven into the ground half their length, and slightly covered with green leaves so carelessly thrown over them that we had thought at first these strewn leaves were simply the effect of clearing bush.

Forming two lines of twelve men across the road, the first line was ordered to pick out the skewers, the second line was ordered to cover the workers with their weapons, and at the first arrow shower to fire. A dozen scouts were sent on either flank of the road to make their way into the village through the woods. We had scarcely advanced twenty yards along the cleared way before volumes of smoke broke out of the town, and a little cloud of arrows came towards us, but falling short. A volley was returned, the skewers were fast being picked out, and an advance was steadily made until we reached the village at the same time that the scouts rushed out of the underwood, and as all the pioneers were pushed forward the firing was pretty lively, under cover of which the caravan pressed through the burning town to a village at its eastern extremity, as yet unfired.

Along the river the firing was more deadly. The very noise was sufficient to frighten a foe so prone as savages to rely on the terrors of sound, but unfortunately the noise was as hurtful as it was alarming. Very many, I fear, paid the penalty of the foolish challenge. The blame is undoubtedly due to the Yambuyas, who must have invented fables of the most astounding character to cause their neighbours to attempt stopping a force of nearly four hundred rifles.

It was nearly 9 P.M. before the rear-guard entered camp. Throughout the night the usual tactics were resorted to by the savages to create alarm and disturbance, such as vertically dropping assegais and arrows heavily tipped with poison, with sudden cries, whoops, howls, menaces, simultaneous blasts of horn-blowing from different quarters, as though a general attack was about to be made. Strangers unacquainted with the craftiness of these forest satyrs might be pardoned for imagining that daylight only was required for our complete extermination. Some of these tactics I knew before in younger days, but there was still something to be gleaned from the craft of these pure pagans. The camp was surrounded by sentries, and the only orders given were to keep strict silence and sharpen their eyesight.

In the morning a narrow escape was reported. A man had wakened to find a spear buried in the earth, penetrating his sleeping cloth and mat on each side of him, slightly pinning him to his bedding. Two were slightly wounded with arrows.

We wandered about for ten minutes or so looking for a track next morning, and at last discovered one leading through a vast square mileage of manioc fields, and at the little village of Bahunga, four miles S.E. of Yankonde, we gladly rested, our object being not to rush at first setting out after a long river voyage, but to accustom the people little by little to the long journey before them.

On the 30th we lit on a path which connected a series of fourteen villages, each separate and in line, surrounded by their respective fields, luxuriant with crops of manioc, or, as some call it, the cassava. We did not fail to observe, however, that some disaster had occurred many months before, judging from the traces. The villages we passed through were mostly newly built, in the sharp, conical – candle-extinguisher – or rather four-angled spiry type; burnt poles, ruins of the former villages, marked the sites of former dwellings. Here and there were blazings on trees, and then I knew that Arabs and Manyuema must have visited here – probably Tippu-Tib's brother.

The following day our march was through a similar series of villages, twelve in number, with a common, well-trodden track running from one to another. In this distance sections of the primeval forest separated each village; along the track were pitfalls for sonic kind of large forest game, or bow-traps fixed for small animals, such as rabbits, squirrels, rats, small monkeys. In the neighbourhood of each village the skewers were plentiful in the ground, but as yet no hurt had been received from them.

Another serious inconvenience of forest travel was experienced on this day. Every fifty yards or so a great tree, its diameter breast high, lay prostrate across the path over which the donkeys had to be assisted with a frequency that was becoming decidedly annoying. Between twenty and fifty of these had to be climbed over by hundreds of men, not all of whom were equally expert at this novel travelling, and these obstructions by the delays thus occasioned began to be complained of as very serious impediments. The main approaches to the many villages were studded with these poisoned skewers, which made every one except the booted whites tread most gingerly. Nor could the Europeans be altogether indifferent, for, slightly leaning, the skewer was quite capable of piercing the thickest boot-leather and burying the splinters of its head deep in the foot – an agony of so dreadful a nature that was worth the trouble of guarding against.

At 3 P.M. we camped near some pools overhung by water lilies far removed from a village, having had three wounded during the traverse through the settlements.

This morning, about three hours before dawn, the camp was wakened by howls, and loud and continued horn-blowing. These were shortly after hushed, and the voices of two men were heard so clear and distinct that many like myself attempted to pierce the intense darkness in the vain effort to see these midnight orators.

The first Speaker said, "Hey, strangers, where are you going?"

The Parasite echoed, "Where are you going?"

Speaker. This country has no welcome for you.

Parasite. No welcome for you.

Speaker. All men will be against you.

Parasite. Against you.

Speaker. And you will be surely slain.

Parasite. Surely slain.

Speaker. Ah-ah-ah-ah-ah-aah.

Parasite. Ah-ah-aaah.

Speaker Ooh-ooh-ooh-ooh-ooooh.

Parasite. Ooh-ooh-ooooooh.

This parasite was such a palpable parasite, with such a sense of humour – that it raised such a chorus of laughter so sudden, startling, and abrupt, that scared speaker and parasite away in precipitate haste.

At dawn of the 2nd, feeling somewhat uneasy at the fact that the track which brought us to these pools was not made by man but by elephants, and feeling certain that the people had made no provision of food beyond the day, I sent 200 men back to the villages to procure each a load of manioc. By the manner these men performed this duty, the reflection came into my mind that they had little or no reasoning faculties, and that not a half of the 389 people then in the camp would emerge out of Africa. They were now brimful of life and vitality – their rifles were perfect, their accoutrements were new, and each possessed 10 rounds of cartridges. With a little care for their own selves and a small portion of prudence, there was no reason why they should not nearly all emerge safe and sound, but they were so crude, stolid, unreasoning, that orders and instructions were unheeded, except when under actual supervision, and, to supervise them effectually, I should require 100 English officers of similar intelligence and devotion to the four then with me. In the meantime they will lose their lives for trifles which a little sense would avoid, and until some frightful calamity overtakes them I shall never be able thoroughly to impress on their minds that to lose life foolishly is a crime.

A party of scouts were also sent ahead along the track to observe its general direction, and, about the same time that the foragers returned, the scouts returned, having captured six natives in the forest. They belonged to a tribe called the Babali, and were of a light chocolate in hue, and were found forming traps for game.

As we endeavoured to draw from them some information respecting the country to which the track led, they said, "We have but one heart. Don't you have two," which meant, Do not speak so fairly to us if you mean any harm to us, and like all natives they asserted strongly that they did not eat human meat, but that the custom was practised by the Babanda, Babali, Babukwa tribes, occupying the bank of the Aruwimi above Yancondé.

Soon after this interview with the natives, Dr. Parke, observing the bees which fluttered about, had mentioned to one of his brother officers that he did not think they stung at all, upon which at the same moment a vicious bee settling in his neck drove its sting into it to punish him for his scornful libel. He then came to me and reported the fact as a good joke, whereupon a second bee attacked and wounded him almost in the same spot, drawing from him an exclamation of pain. "By Jove! but they do sting awfully, though." "Just so," said I; "nothing like experience to stimulate reason."

After distributing the manioc, with an injunction to boil the roots three times in different waters, we resumed the march at 1 P.M. and camped at 4 o'clock.

The next day left the track and struck through the huge towering forest and jungly undergrowth by compass. My position in this column was the third from the leader, so that I could direct the course. In order to keep a steady movement, even if slow, I had to instruct the cutters that each man as he walked should choose an obstructing lliané, or obtrusive branch of bush, and give one sharp cut and pass on – the two head men were confining themselves to an effective and broad "blaze" on the trees, every ten yards or so, for the benefit of the column, and, as the rear party would not follow us for perhaps two months, we were very particular that these "blazes" should be quite a hand's-breadth peel of bark.

Naturally penetrating a trackless wild for the first time the march was at a funereal pace, in some places at the rate of 400 yards an hour, in other more open portions, that is of less undergrowth, we could travel at the rate of half, three-quarters, and even a mile per hour – so that from 6.30 A.M. to 11 A.M. when we halted for lunch and rest, and from 12.30 P.M., to 3 o'clock or 4 P.M. in from six to seven hours per day, we could make a march of about five miles. On the usual African track seen in other regions we could have gone from fourteen to eighteen miles during the same time. Therefore our object was to keep by settlements, not only to be assured of food, but in the hope of utilizing the native roads. We shall see later how we fared.

At 4 P.M. of this day we were still on the march, having passed through a wilderness of creeks, mud, thick scum-faced quagmires green with duckweed into which we sank knee-deep, and the stench exhaled from the fetid slough was most sickening. We had just emerged out of this baneful stretch of marshy ground, intersected by lazy creeks and shallow long stream-shaped pools, when the forest became suddenly darkened, so dark that I could scarcely read the compass, and a distant murmur increasing into loud soughing and wrestling and tossing of branches and groaning of mighty trees warned us of the approach of a tempest. As the ground round about was most uninviting, we had to press on through the increasing gloom, and then, as the rain began to drip, we commenced to form camp. The tents were hastily pitched over the short scrubby bush, while bill-hooks crashed and axes rang, clearing a pace for the camp. The rain was cold and heavily dripped, and every drop, large as a dollar on their cotton clothes, sent a shiver through the men. The thunder roared above, the lightning flashed a vivid light of fire through the darkness, and still the weary hungry caravan filed in until 9 o'clock. The rain was so heavy that fires could not be lit, and until three in the morning we sat huddled and crouching amid the cold, damp, and reeking exhalations and minute spray. Then bonfires were kindled, and around these scores of laming pyramids the people sat, to be warmed into hilarious animation, to roast the bitter manioc, and to till the gnawing pain of their stomachs.

On the 4th we struck N. by E., and in an hour heard natives singing in concert afar off. We sent scouts ahead to ascertain what it meant. We presently heard firing which seemed to approach nearer. We mustered the men in the nearest company, stacked goods and deployed them as skirmishers. Then messengers came and reported that the scouts had struck the river, and, as they were looking upon it, a canoe advanced into view with its crew standing with drawn bows and fixed arrows, which were flown at them at once, and compelled the scouts to fire. We then resumed the march, and at 8 A.M. we were on the river again, in time to see a line of native canoes disappearing round a bend on the opposite bank, and one canoe abandoned tied to the bank with a goat.

Observing that the river was calm and free from rapids, and desirous of saving the people from as much labour as circumstances would offer, the steel boat sections were brought up to the bank, and Mr. Jephson, whose company had special charge of the *Advance,* commenced to fit the sections together. In an hour the forty-four burdens, which the vessel formed, had been attached together and fitted to their respective places and launched. As the boat weighed forty-four loads and had a capacity of fifty loads, and at least ten sick, we could then release ninety-eight people from the fatigue of bearing loads and carrying Lieutenant Stairs, who was stir very ill. Mr. Jephson and crew were despatched across river and the goat secured.

As the *Advance* was in the river, it was necessary for the column to cling to the bank, not only for the protection of the boat, but to be able to utilize the stream for lessening labour. Want of regular food, lack of variety, and its poor nutritive qualities, coupled with the urgency which drove us on, requiring long marches and their resulting fatigue, would soon diminish the strength of the stoutest. A due regard for the people therefore must be shown, and every means available for their assistance must he employed. Therefore, the boat keeping pace with the column, we travelled up-stream until 3 P.M. and camped.

On the 5th the boat and column moved up, as on the day previous, and made six-and-half miles. The river continued to be from 500 to 800 yards wide. The bank was a trifle more open than in the interior, though frequently it was impossible to move before an impenetrable mass of jungle had been tunneled to allow our passage under the vault of close network of branch and climber, cane, and reed above. At 2.30 we reached the village of Bukanda. We had come across no track, but had simply burst out of the bush and a somewhat young forest with a clearing. In the middle of the clearing by the river side was the village. This fact made me think, and it suggested that if tracks were not discoverable by land, and as the people were not known to possess the power of aerial locomotion, that communication was maintained by water.

We had reason to rejoice at the discovery of a village, for since the 2nd the caravan subsisted on such tubers of manioc as each man took with him on that date. Had another day passed without meeting with a clearing we should have suffered from hunger.

It was evening before the boat appeared, the passage of rapids and an adventure with a flotilla of eleven canoes had detained her. The canoes had been abandoned in consequence, and the commander of the boat had secured them to an island. One was reported to be a capacious hollow log, capable of carrying nearly as much as the boat. Since the river was the highway of the natives, we should be wise to employ the stream, by which we should save our men, and carry our sick as well as a reserve of food. For we had been narrowly brought to the verge of want on the last day, and we were utter strangers in a strange land, groping our way through darkness. The boat was sent back with an extra crew to secure the canoe and paddle her up to our camp.

Of course Bukanda had been abandoned long before we reached it – the village of cone huts was at our disposal – the field of manioc also. This custom also was unlike anything I had seen in Africa before. Previously the natives may have retired with their women, but the males had remained with spear and target, representing ownership. Here the very fowls had taken to flight. It was clearly a region unsuitable for the study of ethnology.

At noon of the 6th we defiled out of Bukanda refurnished with provisions, and two hours later were in camp in uninhabited space. We had devoted the morning to cleaning and repairing rifles – many of whose springs were broken.

Some facts had already impressed themselves upon us. We observed that the mornings were muggy and misty – that we were chilly and inclined to be cheerless in consequence; that it required some moral courage to leave camp to brave the cold, damp, and fogginess without, to brave the mud and slush, to ford creeks up to the waist in water; that the feelings were terribly depressed in the dismal twilight from the want of brightness and sunshine warmth; and the depression caused by the sombre clouds and dull grey river which reflected the drear daylight. The actual temperature on these cold mornings was but seventy to seventy-two degrees – had we judged of it by our cheerlesness it might have been twenty degrees less.

The refuse heaps of the little villages were large and piled on the edge of the bank. They were a compost of filth, sweepings of streets and huts, peelings of manioc, and often of plantains with a high heap of oyster-shells. Had I not much else to write about, an interesting chapter on these composts, and the morals, manners, and usages of the aborigines might be written. Just as Owen could prefigure an extinct mammoth of the dead ages from the view of a few bones, the history of a tribe could be developed by me out of these refuse heaps. Reveling in these fetid exhalations were representatives of many insect tribes. Columns of ants wound in and out with more exact formation than aborigines could compose themselves, flies buzz in myriads over the heaps, with the murmur of enjoyment, butterflies which would have delighted Jameson's soul swarmed exulting in their gorgeous colours, and a perfect cloud of moths hovered above all.

The villages of the Bakuti were reached on the 7th, after seven hours' slow marching and incessant cutting. I occupied a seat in the boat on this day and observed that the banks were from six to ten feet above the river on either side, that there were numerous traces of former occupation easily detected despite the luxuriance of the young forest that had grown up and usurped the space once occupied by villages and fields; that either wars or epidemics had disturbed the inhabitants twenty years ago, and that as yet only one crocodile had been seen on the Aruwimi, and only one hippo, which I took to be a sure sign that there was not much pasture in this region.

As the rowers urged the boat gently up the stream, and I heard the bill-hooks and axes carving away through bush and brake tangle and forest without which scarcely a yard of progress could be made, I regretted more than ever that I had not insisted on being allowed to carry out my own plan of having fifteen whale-boats. What toil would have been saved, and what anxiety would have been spared me.

On the 9th we gained, after another seven hours' toiling and marching, the villages of the Bakoka. Already the people began to look jaded and seedy. Skewers had penetrated the feet of several, ulcers began to attract notice by their growing virulence, many people complained of curious affections in the limbs. Stairs was slowly recovering.

We had passed so many abandoned clearings that our expedition might have been supported for weeks by the manioc which no owner claimed. It was very clear that internecine strife had caused the migrations of the tribes. The Bakoka villages were all stockaded, and the entrance gates were extremely low.

The next day we passed by four villages all closely stockaded, and on the 10th came to the rapids of Gwengweré. Here there were seven large villages bordering the rapids and extending from below to above the broken water. All the population had fled probably to the opposite main, or to the islands in mid-river, and every portable article was carried away except the usual wreckage of coarse pottery, stools, and benches, and back rests. The stockades were in good order and villages intact. In one large village there were 210 conical huts, and two square sheds used for public assemblies and smithies. This occupied a commanding bluff sixty feet above the river, and a splendid view of a dark grey silver stream, flanked by dense and lofty walls of thickest greenest vegetation, was obtained.

Lieutenant Stairs was fast recovering from his long attack of bilious fever; my other companions enjoyed the best of health, though our diet consisted of vegetables, leaves of the manioc and herbs bruised and made into patties. But on this day we had a dish of weaver-birds furnished by the Doctor, who with his shot-gun bagged a few of the thousands which had made their nests on the village trees.

On the 11th we marched about a mile to give the canoe-men a chance to pole their vessels through the rapids and the column a rest. The day following marched six geographical miles, the river turning easterly, which was our course. Several small rapids were passed without accident. As we were disappearing from view of Gwengweré, the population was seen scurrying from the right bank and islands back to their homes, which they had temporarily vacated for our convenience. It seemed to me to be an excellent arrangement. It saved trouble of speech, exerted possibly in useless efforts for peace and tedious chaffer. They had only one night's inconvenience, and were there many caravans advancing as peaceably as we were, natural curiosity would in time induce them to come forward to be acquainted with the strangers.

Our people found abundant to eat in the fields, and around the villages. The area devoted to cultivation was extensive: plantains flourished around the stockades; herbs for potage were found in little plots close to the tillages; also sufficient tobacco for smoking, and pumpkins for dessert, and a little Indian corn; but, alas, we all suffered from want of meat.

There were few aquatic birds to be seen. There were some few specimens of divers, fish eagles, and kingfishers. Somewhere, at a distance, a pair of ibis screamed; flocks of parrots whistled and jabbered in vain struggles to rob the solitude of the vast trackless forest of its oppressive silence; whip-poor-wills, and sunbirds, and weavers aided them with their varied strains; but insects, and flies, and moths were innumerable.

On the 12th we moved up as usual, starting at 6.30 A.M., the caravan preceding the boat and its consorts. Though proceeding only at the rate of a mile and a half per hour, we soon overhauled the struggling caravan, and passed the foremost of the pioneers. At 10 A.M. we met a native boy, called Bakula, of about fifteen years, floating down river on a piece of a canoe. He sprung aboard our boat with alacrity, and used his paddle properly. An hour later we rounded the lowest point of a lengthy curve, bristling with numerous large villages. The boy volunteer who had dropped to our aid from the unknown, called the lower village Bandangi, the next Ndumba, and the long row of villages above, the houses of the Banalya tribe. But all were deserted. We halted at Bandangi for lunch, and at 2 P.M. resumed our journey.

An hour's pull brought us to the upper village, where we camped. Our river party on this day numbered forty men; but, as we landed, we were lost in the large and silent village. I had counted thirteen villages – one of these numbered 180 huts. Assuming that in this curve there were 1300 huts, and allowing only four persons to each hut, we have a population of 5200.

At 5.30 appeared the advance guard of the column, and presently a furious tempest visited us, with such violent accompaniments of thunder and lightning as might have been expected to be necessary to clear the atmosphere charged with the collected vapours of this humid region – through which the sun appeared daily as through a thick veil. Therefore the explosive force of the electric fluid was terrific. All about us, and at all points, it lightened and shattered with deafening explosions, and blinding forks of flame, the thick, sluggish, vaporous clouds. Nothing less than excessive energy of concentrated electricity could have cleared the heavy atmosphere, and allowed the inhabitants of the land to see the colour of the sky, and to feel the cheering influence of the sun. For four hours we had to endure the dreadful bursts; while a steady stream of rain relieved the surcharged masses that had hung incumbent above us for days. While the river party and advance guard were housed in the upper village, the rear guard and No. 4 Company occupied Bandangi, at the town end of the *crescent,* and we heard them shooting minute guns to warn us of their presence; while we vainly, for economical reasons, replied with the tooting of long ivory horns.

Such a large population naturally owned exclusive fields of manioc, plantations of bananas, and plantains, sugar-cane, gardens of herbs, and Indian corn, and as the heavy rain had saturated the ground, a halt was ordered.

By nine o'clock the rear guard was known to have arrived by Nelson's voice crying out for "chop and coffee" – our chop consisted of cassava cakes, a plantain or so roasted, and a mess of garden greens, with tea or coffee. Flesh of goat or fowl was simply unprocurable. Neither bird nor beast of any kind was to be obtained. Hitherto only two crocodiles and but one hippo had been discovered, but no elephant, buffalo, or antelope or wild hog, though tracks were numerous. How could it be otherwise with the pioneers' shouts, cries, noise of cutting and crushing, and pounding of trees, the murmur of a large caravan? With the continuous gossip, storytelling, wrangling, laughing or wailing that were mainrained during the march, it was simply impossible. Progress through the undergrowth was denied without a heavy knife, machete, or bill-hook to sever entangling creepers, and while an animal may have been only a few feet off on the other side of a bush, vain was the attempt to obtain view of it through impervious masses of vegetation.

In our boat I employed the halt for examining the islands near Bandangi. We discovered lengthy heaps of oyster-shells on one island, one of which was sixty feet long, ten feet wide, and four feet high; we can imagine the feasts of the bivalves that the aborigines enjoyed during their picnics, and the length of time that had elapsed since the first bivalve had been eaten. On my return I noticed through a bank-slip in the centre of the curve a stratum of oyster-shell buried three feet under alluvium.

Our native boy Bakula, informed us that inland north lived the Baburu, who were very different from the river tribes, that up river, a month's journey, would be found dwarfs about two feet high, with long beards; that he had once journeyed as far as Panga where the river tumbled from a height as high as the tallest tree, that the Aruwimi was now called Lui by the people of the left bank, but that to the Baburu on the right bank it was known as the Luhali. Bakula was an exceptionally crafty lad, a pure cannibal, to whom a mess of human meat would have been delectable. He was a perfect mimic, and had by native cunning protected himself by conforming readily to what he divined would be pleasing to the strangers by whom he was surrounded. Had all the native tribes adopted this boy's policy our passage through these novel lands would have been as pleasant as could be desired. I have no doubt that they possessed all the arts of craft which we admired in Bakula, they had simply not the courage to do what an accident had enabled him to carry out.

From Chief Bambi's town of the Banalya we moved to Bungangeta villages by river and land on the 15th. It was a stern and sombre morning, gloomy with lowering and heavy clouds. It struck me on this dull dreary morning, while regarding the silent flowing waters of the dark river and the long unbroken forest frontage, that nature in this region seems to be waiting the long expected trumpet-call of civilization – that appointed time when she shall awake to her duties, as in other portions of the earth. I compared this waiting attitude to the stillness preceding the dawn, before the insect and animal life is astir to fret the air with its murmur, before the day has awakened the million minute passions of the wilds; at that hour when even Time seems to be drowsy and nodding, our inmost thoughts appear to be loud, and the heart throbs to be clamorous. But when the young day peeps forth white and gray in the East the eyelids of the world lift up. There is a movement and a hum of invisible life, and all the earth seems wakened from its brooding. But withal, the forest world remains restful, and Nature bides her day, and the river shows no life; unlike Rip Van Winkle, Nature, despite her immeasurably long ages of sleep, indicates no agedness, so old, incredibly old, she is still a virgin locked in innocent repose.

What expansive wastes of rich productive land lie in this region unheeded by man! Populous though the river banks are, they are but slightly disturbed by labour – a trifling grubbing of parts of the foreshore, a limited acreage for manioc, within a crater-like area in the bosom of the dark woods, and a narrow line of small cotes, wherein the savages huddle within their narrow circumference.

One of my amusements in the boat was to sketch the unknown course of the river – for as the aborigines disappeared like rats into their holes on one's approach I could gain no information respecting it. How far was it permissible for me to deviate from my course? By the river I could assist the ailing and relieve the strong. The goods could be transported and the feeble conveyed. Reserves of manioc and plantain could also be carried. But would a somewhat long curve, winding as high as some forty or fifty geographical miles north of our course, be compensated by these advantages of relief or the porters, and the abundance of provisions that are assuredly found on the banks? When I noted the number of the sick, and saw the jaded condition of the people, I felt that if the river ascended as far as 2° N., it was infinitely preferable to plunging into the centre of the forest.

The temperature of the air during the clouded morning was 75°, surface of the river 77°. What a relief it was to breathe the air of the river after a night spent in inhaling the close impure air in the forest by night!

On the 16th we possessed one boat and five canoes, carrying seventy-four men and 120 loads, so that with the weight of the boat sections, half of our men were relieved of loads, and carried nothing every alternative day. We passed by the mouth of a considerable affluent from the south-east, and camped a mile above it. The temperature rose to 94° in the afternoon, and as a consequence rain fell in torrents, preceded by the usual thunder roars and lightning flashes. Until 1 P.M. of the 17th the rain fell unceasingly. It would have been interesting to have ascertained the number of inches that fell during these nineteen hours' rain-pour. Few of the people enjoyed any rest; there was a general wringing of blankets and clothes after it ceased, but it was some hours before they recovered their usual animation. The aborigines must have been also depressed, owing to our vicinity, though if they had known what wealth we possessed, they might have freely parted with their goats and fowls for our wares.

The column camped at 3 P.M. opposite the settlement of Lower Mariri. Besides their immense wooden drums, which sounded the alarm to a ten-mile distance, the natives vociferated with unusual powers of lung, so that their cries could be heard a mile off. The absence of all other noises lends peculiar power to their voices.

The Somalis, who are such excellent and efficient servants in lands like the Masai, or dry regions like the Soudan, are perfectly useless in humid regions. Five of them declined to stay at Yambuya, and insisted on accompanying me. Since we had taken to the river I had employed them as boatmen, or rather did employ them when they were able to handle a paddle or a pole, but their physical powers soon collapsed, and they became mere passengers. On shore, without having undergone any exertion, they were so prostrated after a two hours' river voyage, that they were unable to rig shelter against rain and damp, and as they were thievish the Zanzibaris refused to permit them to approach their huts. The result was that we had the trouble each day to see that a share of food even was doled out to them, as they would have voluntarily starved rather than cut down the plantains above their heads.

From opposite Lower Mariri we journeyed to a spot ten miles below the Upper Mariri on the 18th. The canoes had only occupied 4 h. 15 m., but the land column did not appear at all.

On the 19th I employed the boat and canoe crews to cut a road to above a section of the rapids of Upper Mariri. This was accomplished in 2½ hours. we returned to camp in 45 minutes. Our pace going up was similar to that of the caravan, consequently an ordinary day's travel through the forest would be six miles. On returning to camp formed the column, and marched it to the end of our paths; the boat and canoes were punted up the rapids without accident, and in the afternoon the people foraged for food at a village a mile and a half above camp with happy results. On the 20th the advance column marched up and occupied the village.

About two hours after arrival some of the natives of Mariri came in a canoe and hailed us. We replied through Bakula, the native boy, and in a short time were able to purchase a couple of fowls, and during the afternoon were able to purchase three more. This was the first barter we had been able to effect on the Aruwimi. Mariri is a large settlement abounding in plantains, while at our village there were none. Two men, Charlie No. 1 and Musa bin Juma disappeared on this day. Within twenty-three days we had not lost a man.

No casualty had as yet happened, and good fortune, which had hitherto clung to us, from this date began to desert us. We were under the impression that those men had been captured by natives, and their heedless conduct was the text of a sermon preached to the men next morning when they were mustered for the march. It was not until thirteen months later that we knew that they had deserted, that they had succeeded in reaching Yambuya, and had invented the most marvelous tales of wars and disasters, which, when repeated by the officers at Yambuya in their letter to the Committee, created so much anxiety. Had I believed it had been possible that two messengers could have performed that march, we certainly had availed ourselves of the fact to have communicated authentic news and chart of the route to Major Barttelot, who in another month would be leaving his camp as we believed. From the village opposite Upper Mariri we proceeded to S. Mupé, a large settlement consisting of several villages, embowered in plantations. The chiefs of Mupé are Mbadu, Alimba, and Mangrudi.

On the 22nd Surgeon Parke was the officer of the day, and was unfortunate enough to miss the river, and strike through the forest in a wrong direction. He finally struck a track on which the scouts found a woman and a large-eyed, brown-coloured child. The woman showed the route to the river, and was afterwards released. Through her influence the natives of N. Mupé on the right bank were induced to trade with us, by which we were enabled to procure a dozen fowls and two eggs.

The bed of the river in this locality is an undisturbed rock of fine-grained and hard, brick-coloured sandstone. This is the reason that the little rapids, though frequent enough, present but little obstacles to navigation. The banks at several places rose to about forty feet above the river, and the rock is seen in horizontal strata in bluffy form, in many instances like crumbling ruins of cut stone.

The sign of peace with these riverine natives appears to be the pouring of water on their heads with their hands. As new-comers approached our camp they cried out, "We suffer from famine, we have no food, but up river you will find plenty, Oh, 'monomopote'! (son of the sea)." "But we suffer from want of food, and have not the strength to proceed unless you give us some," we replied. Whereupon they threw us fat ears of Indian corn, plantains, and sugar-cane. This was preliminary to a trade, in doing which these apparently unsophisticated natives were as sharp and as exorbitant as any of the Wyyanzi on the Congo. The natives of Mupé are called Babé.

Trifles, such as empty sardine boxes, jam and milk cans, and cartridge cases, were easily barterable for sugar-cane, Indian corn, and tobacco. A cotton handkerchief would buy a fowl, goats were brought to our view, but not parted with. They are said to be the monopoly of chiefs. The natives showed no fixed desire for any specialty but cloth – gaudy red handkerchiefs. We saw some cowries among them, and in the bottom of a canoe we found a piece of an infantry officer's sword nine inches long. We should have been delighted to have heard the history of that sword, and the list of its owners since it left Birmingham. But we could not maintain any lengthy conversation with them, our ignorance of the language, and their excitability prevented us from doing more than observing and interchanging words relating to peace and food with them. We can accept the bit of sword blade as evidence that their neighbours in the interior have had some contact with the Soudanese.

Neither in manners, customs or dress was there any very great difference between these natives and those belonging to the upper parts of the Upper Congo. Their head-dresses were of basket work decorated with red parrot feathers, monkey skin caps of grey or dark fur, with the tails drooping behind. The neck, arm and ankle ornaments were of polished iron, rarely of copper, never of brass.

They make beautiful paddles, finely carved like a long pointed leaf. "Senneneh" was the peaceful hail as in Manyuema, Uregga and Usongora, above Stanley Falls. The complexion of these natives is more ochreous than black. When a body of them is seen on the opposite bank, there is little difference of colour between their bodies and the reddish clayey soil of the landing-place. Much of this is due to the Camwood powder, and with this mixed with oil they perform their toilet. But protection from sunshine considerably contributes to this light colour. The native boy, Bakula, for instance, was deprived of this universal cosmetic made of Camwood, and he was much lighter than the average of our Zanzibaris.

On the 24th, Mr. Jephson led the van of the column, and under his guidance we made the astonishing march of seven and a half geographical miles – the column having been compelled to wade through seventeen streams and creeks. During these days Jephson exhibited a marvelous vigour. He was in many things an exact duplicate of myself in my younger days, before years and hundreds of fevers had cooled my burning blood. He is exactly of my own height, build and weight and temperament. He is sanguine, confident, and loves hard work. He is simply indefatigable, and whether it is slushy mire or a muddy creek, in he enters, without hesitation, up to his knees, waist, neck or overhead it is all the same. A sybarite, dainty and fastidious civilization, a traveller and labourer in Africa, he requires to be restrained and counseled for his own sake. Now these young men, Stairs, Nelson and Parke, are very much in the same way. Stairs is the military officer, alert, intelligent, who understands a hint, a curt intimation, grasps an idea firmly and realises it to perfection. Nelson is a centurion as of old Roman times, he can execute because it is the will of his chief; he does not stay to ask the reason why; he only understands it to be a necessity, and his great vigour, strength, resolution, plain, good sense is at my disposal, to act, suffer or die; and Parke, noble, gentle soul, so tender and devoted, so patient, so sweet in mood and brave in temper, always enduring and effusing comfort as he moves through our atmosphere of suffering and pain. No four men ever entered Africa with such qualities as these. No leader ever had cause to bless his stars as I.

On this day Jephson had two adventures. In his usual free, impulsive manner, and with swinging gait he was directing the pioneers – crushing through the jungle, indifferent to his costume, when he suddenly sank out of sight into an elephant pit! We might have imagined a playful and sportive young elephant crashing through the bushes, rending and tearing young saplings, and suddenly disappearing from the view of his more staid mamma. Jephson had intelligence, however, and aid was at hand, and he was pulled out none the worse. It was a mere amusing incident to be detailed in camp and to provoke a laugh.

He rushed ahead of the pioneers to trace the course to be followed, and presently encountered a tall native, with a spear in his hand, face to face. Both were so astonished as to be paralysed, but Jephson's impulse was that of a Berserker. He flung himself, unarmed, upon the native, who, eluding his grasp, ran from him, as he would front a lion, headlong down a steep bank into a creek,

Jephson following. But the clayey soil was damp and slippery, his foot slipped, and the gallant Captain of the *Advance* measured his length face downwards with his feet up the slope, and such was his impetus that he slid down to the edge of the creek. When he recovered himself it was to behold the denizen of the woods, hurrying up the opposite bank and casting wild eyes at this sudden pale-faced apparition who had so disturbed him as he brooded over the prospect of finding game in his traps that day.

Our camp on this day was a favourite haunt of elephants from time immemorial. It was near a point round which the river raced with strong swirling currents. A long view of a broad silent river is seen upward, and one of a river disparted by a series of islands below.

On the 25th Captain Nelson led the column, Jephson was requested to assist me with the long narrow canoes laden with valuable goods, and to direct some of the unskillful 'lubbers' who formed our crews. The boat led the way anchored above the dangerous and swirly point, and cast the manilla rope to the canoe crew, who, hauling by this cord drew the canoes to quiet water. Then rowing hard against the strong currents, at 11 A.M. we caught the head of the caravan gathered on the bank of a wide and dark sluggish creek, the Rendi, which lazily flowed out of dark depths of woods. By one o'clock the ferriage was completed, and the column resumed its march, while we, on the river, betook ourselves to further struggles with the dangerous waves and reefs of what is now called Wasp Rapids, from the following incident.

These rapids extended for a stretch of two miles. Above them were the villages which became the scene of a tragic strife, as will be learned later in a subsequent chapter, and these settlements were the dear objects of our aims in order to obtain shelter and food.

Our first efforts against the rapids were successful. The current was swift and dangerous, breaking out into great waves now and then. For the first half-hour we were successful. Then began a struggle, rowing on one side hard and the starboard side crew grasping at overhanging bushes, two men poling, two men on the decked bow, with boat-hooks outstretched with their fangs ready to snatch at saplings for firm hold. I steered. We advanced slowly but steadily, a narrow rushing branch between rocky islets, and the bank was before us which raced over a reef, showing itself in yard square dots of rock above the waves. We elected to ascend this as in view of a capsize there was less fear of drowning. With noble spirits braced for an exciting encounter, we entered it. Eager hands were held out to catch at the branches, but at the first clutch there issued at this critical moment an army of fierce spiteful wasps and settled on our faces, hands, and bodies, every vulnerable spot, and stung us with the venom of fiends. Maddened and infuriated by the burning stings, battling with this vicious enemy, beset by reefs, and rocks, and dangerous waves, and whirling vortexes, we tore on with tooth and nail, and in a few minutes were a hundred yards above the awful spot. Then, clinging to the trees, we halted to breathe and sympathise with each other, and exchange views and opinions on the various stings of insects, bees, hornets, and wasps.

One asked my servant with a grim smile, "Did you say the other day that you believed there was much honey in these brown paper nests of the wasps? Well, what do you think of the honey now? Don't you think it is rather a bitter sort?" This raised a general laugh. We recovered our good temper, and resumed our work, and in an hour reached the village which the land party had occupied. The canoes' crews, who followed us, seeing the battle with the wasps, fled across river, and ascended by the right bank. But the Somalis and Soudanese, more trustful in Allah, bravely followed our track, and were dreadfully stung; still, they were consoled by being able to exult over the Zanzibaris, the leader of which was Uledi, of the "Dark Continent."

"Oh," I remarked to Uledi, "it is not a brave thing you have done this day – to fly away from wasps."

"Oh, sir," he replied, "naked manhood is nowhere in such a scrape as that. Wasps are more dangerous than the most savage men."

The native settlement on the left bank is called Bandeya; the one facing opposite consists of the villages of the Bwamburi. North of the Bwamburi, a day's march, begins the tribes of the Ababua and the Mabodé, who have a different kind of architecture from the steeply conical huts prevailing among the riverine tribes. The Mabodé are said to possess square houses with gable roofs, the walls are neatly plastered, and along the fronts are clay verandahs.

On the 26th we halted to rest and recuperate. Those of us who were attacked by the wasps suffered from a fever; the coxswain of the boat was in great distress. The following day the chief of the Bwamburi came over to pay us a visit, and brought us as a gift a month old chick, which was declined on the ground that we should feel we were robbing him were we to accept such a gift, from a professedly poor man. His ornaments consisted of two small ivory tusks planed flat and polished, which hung suspended from a string made of grass encircling his neck. His head-dress was a long-haired monkey skin. We exchanged professions of amity and brotherhood, and commenced the march, and camped opposite Mukupi, a settlement possessing eight villages, on the 28th.

Two sturdy prisoners imparted to us strange information of a large lake called "No-uma," as being situated somewhere in the neighbourhood of a place called Panga. It was said to be many days' journey in extent. In the centre was a large island, so infested with serpents that natives dreaded to go near it; that from it flowed the Nepoko into the Nowellé, the name now given to the Aruwimi. After several days' march we discovered that the lake story was a myth, and that the Nepoko did not flow from the left bank of the Aruwimi.

Our camp on the 29th was opposite My-yui, a series of villages embowered amongst banana groves on the right bank. It was not long before we struck an acquaintance with this tribe. We quickly recognized a disposition on the part of the aborigines to be sociable. A good report of our doings had preceded us. Trade commenced very pleasantly. Our people had cowries, beads, and brass rods, besides strange trifles to exchange for food. When the land column arrived, prices advanced somewhat, owing to the greater demand. It was reported that there were no settlements between our camp opposite My-yui and Panga; that we should be nine days performing the journey through the forest.

The next morning the bartering was resumed, because we wished to prepare provisions for several days; new ration currency had already been distributed to each man. But we were astonished to find that only three ears of Indian corn were given on this day for a brass rod twenty-eight inches in length, of the thickness of telegraph wire. At Bangala such a brass rod would have purchased five days' provisions per man in my clays, and here was a settlement in the wilds where we could only obtain three ears of corn! For one fowl four brass rods were demanded. Cowries were not accepted; beads they declined. The men were ravenously hungry; there were nine days' wilderness ahead. Wasp rapids was the nearest place below. We, expostulated, but they were firm. The men then began to sell their cartridge-pouches for two plantains each. They were detected selling their ammunition at the rate of one cartridge for an ear of corn; a tin canteen purchased two. Bill-hooks and axes went next, and ruin stared us in the face. The natives were driven away; one of Mugwye's (the chief's) principal slaves was lifted out of his canoe by a gigantic Zanzibari, and word was sent to the natives that if there were no fair sales of food made as on the first day, that the prisoner would be taken away, and that we should cross over and help ourselves.

Having waited all the afternoon for the reappearance of food, we embarked at dawn on the 31st with two full companies, entered My-yui, and despatched the foragers. By 3 P.M. there was food enough in the camp for ten days In the afternoon of the 1st of August, the advance column was encamped opposite Mambanga. The river party met with an accident. Careless Soudanese were capsized, and one of the Zanzibari steersmen disobeying orders shoved his canoe under the branchy trees which spread out from the bank to the distance of fifty feet; and by the swift current was driven against a submerged branch, and capsized, causing a loss of valuable property some of them being fine beads, worth four shillings a necklace. Six rifles were also lost.

The first death in the advance column occurred on the 2nd August, the 36th day of departure from Yambuya, which was a most extraordinary immunity considering the hardship and privations to which we were all subjected. Could we have discovered a settlement of bananas on the other bank, we should certainly have halted to recuperate for many days. A halt at this period of four or five days at a thriving settlement, would have been of vast benefit to all of us, but such a settlement had not been found, and it was necessary for us to march and press on until we could discover one.

We traversed a large village that had been abandoned for probably six months before we reached it, and as it was the hour of camping, we prepared to make ourselves comfortable for the evening. But as the tents were being pitched, my attention was called to the cries made by excited groups, and hastening to the scene, heard that there was a dead body almost covered with mildew in a hut. Presently the discovery of another was announced and then another. This sufficed to cause us to hastily pack up again and depart from the dead men's village, lest we might contract the strange disease that had caused the abandonment of the village.

One of our poor donkeys, unable to find fitting sustenance in the region of trees and jungle, lay down and died. Another appeared weak and pining for grass, which the endless forest did not produce.

Opposite our camp on this day was the mouth of the Ngula River, an affluent on the north side. Within the river it appeared to be of a width of fifty yards.

On the 3rd two hills became visible, one bearing E.S.E., the other S.E. by E. 1/2 E., as we moved up the river. We camped at the point of a curve in the centre of which were two islands. Paying a visit to one of them we found two goats, at which we were so rejoiced, that long before evening one was slaughtered for the officers, and another to make broth for the sick. A flock of a hundred would have saved many a life that was rapidly fading away.

The next day we arrived at Panga or the Nepanga Falls, about which we, had heard so much from Bakula, the native boy.

The falls are fully thirty feet high, though at first view they appear to he double that height, by the great slope visible above the actual fall. They extend over a mile in length from the foot of the falls, to above the portage. They are the first serious obstacles to navigation we had encountered. They descend by four separate branches, the largest of which is 200 yards wide. They run by islets of gneissic rock, and afford cover to the natives of Panga, who when undisturbed, live upon a large island called Nepanga, one mile long and 300 yards wide, situated 600 yards below the Falls. This island contains three villages numbering some 250 huts of the conical type. There are several settlements inland on both banks. The staple food consists of plantains, though there are also fields of manioc.

An unfortunate Zanzibari, as though he had vowed to himself to contribute largely to our ruin, capsized his canoe as he approached Nepanga, by which we lost two boxes of Maxim ammunition, five boxes of cowries, three of white beads, one of fancy beads, one box fine copper wire, cartridge pouches and seven rifles.

All things are savage in this region. No sooner had a solitary hippo sighted us than he gave chase, and nearly caught us. He was punished severely, and probably received his death wound. The fowls of Nepanga declined to be caught on the island of Nepanga, but evaded the foragers by flight into the jungle; the goats were restless, and combative, and very wild. Altogether we captured twelve, which gave us some hopes of being able to save some of our sick people. A few fish were obtained in the weirs and basket-nets.

The results of 3 days' foraging on islands, right and loft banks were 250 lbs. of Indian corn, 18 goats, and as many fowls, besides a few branches of plantains, among 383 people. A number of villages and settlements were searched, but the natives do not appear to possess a sufficiency of food. They were said to be at war with a tribe called the Engwedde, and instead of cultivating live on banana stalks, mushrooms, roots, herbs, fish, and snails and caterpillars, varying this extraordinary diet by feeding on slain humanity. In such a region there were no inducements to stay, and we accordingly commenced the business of portage. Stairs' Company was detailed for clearing the canoe track, and to strew it with branches placed athwart the road. No. 3 and 4 Companies hauled the canoes, and No. 1 Company carried the whale-boat bodily overland to the sound of wild music and song, and by the end of the 6th, after a busy day, we were encamped above the great Falls of Panga.

Chapter 8

FROM PANGA FALLS TO UGARROWWA'S

In full view of this last camp there was an island in mid-river distant about two miles, that resembled a water battery, and a village lying low, apparently level with the face of the river. on exploring it on the 7th – by no means an easy task, so strong was the current sweeping down the smooth dangerous slope of river towards Panga – it appeared to have been originally a flat rocky mass of rock a few inches-above high river, with inequalities on its surface which had been filled in with earth carried from the left bank. It measured 200 feet in length by about ninety feet in width, to which a piscatorial section of a tribe had retreated and built 60 cone huts, and boarded it round about with planks cut out of a light wood out of the forest and wrecked canoes. At this period the river was but six inches below the lowest surface of the island.

Another serious accident occurred on this day during the journey from above Panga Falls to Nejambi Rapids.

A witless, unthinking canoe coxswain took his canoe among the branches in broken water, got entangled, and capsized. Nine out of eleven rifles were recovered; two cases of gunpowder were lost. The Zanzibaris were so heedless and lubberly among rapids that I felt myself growing rapidly aged with intense anxiety while observing them. How headstrong human nature is prone to be. I had ample proofs daily. My losses, troubles, and anxieties rose solely from the reckless indifference to instructions manifested by my followers. On land they wandered into the forest, and simply disappeared, or were stabbed or pierced with arrows. So far we had lost eight men and seventeen rifles.

On the 8th the caravan had hauled the canoes past Nejambi Rapids, and was camped a few miles below Utiri. The next day we reached the villages, where we found the architecture had changed. The houses were now all gable-roofed and low, and each one surrounded by strong, tall, split log palisades, six feet long, nine inches by four inches wide and thick, of the rubiacæ wood. Constructed in two lines, a street about twenty feet ran between them. As I observed them I was impressed with the fact that they were extremely defensible even against rifles. A dozen resolute men in each court of one of these villages armed with poisoned arrows might have caused considerable loss and annoyance to an enemy.

On the 10th we halted, and foragers were despatched in three different directions with poor results, only two days' rations being procurable. One man, named Khalfan, had been wounded in the wind-pipe by a wooden arrow. The manner he received the wound indicates the perfect indifference with which they receive instructions. While Khalfan examined the plantains alcove, a native stood not twenty feet away and shot him in the throat with a poisoned arrow. The arrow wound was a mere needlepoint puncture, and Dr. Parke attended to him with care, but it had a fatal consequence a few days later.

The 11th was consumed by the river party in struggling against a wild stretch, five miles long, of rapids, caused by numerous reefs and rocky islets, while the land column wound along the river bank on a passable track which led them to Engwedde, where we rejoined them on the 12th. Our day's rate having been broken by the rapids, foragers were again despatched to collect food, and succeeded in procuring three days' rations of plantains. On the 13th we marched to Avisibba, or Aveysheba, a settlement of five large villages, two of which were situate on the upper side of Ruku Creek.

The river column was the first to occupy the villages above the Ruku. A fine open street ran between two rows of low huts, each hut surrounded by its tall palisades. There was a promising abundance in the plantain groves about. The untouched forest beyond looked tall, thick, and old. From the mouth of the creek to the extremity of the villages there was a hundred yards' thickness of primeval forest, through which a native path ran. Between the village and the Aruwimi was a belt of timber fifty yards wide. While the ferriage was progressing across the creek, the boat-crew was searching eagerly and carefully among the scores of courts for hidden savages, and with rifles projecting before them were burrowing into the plantain groves, and outside the villages. When the column was across I had a murder case to inquire into. For on the 12th, at Engwedde, one of our Zanzibaris had been killed with a rifle bullet outside of camp, and it was supposed that some vengeful ruffian in the column had shot him. Meantime, I had suggested to two head men to take forty scouts and re-cross the creek, to explore if there were any opportunities for foraging on the next day to the south-west, of the creek. My little court had just sat down for the inquiry, and a witness was relating his evidence, when the rifles were heard firing with unusual energy. Lieutenant Stairs mustered some fifty men, and proceeded on the double-quick to the river. Under the impression that ninety breech-loaders were quite sufficient we resumed the investigation, but as volley after volley rang out, with continued cracking of scouts' rifles, the Doctor, Nelson, and myself hastened to the scene with a few more men. The first person I saw was Lieutenant Stairs, with his shirt torn open, and blood streaming from an arrow-wound in the left breast, about the region of the heart, and I heard a pattering on the leaves around me, and caught a glimpse of arrows flying past. After consigning our poor friend to Parke's care I sought for reformation. There were numbers of men crouching about, and firing in the most senseless fashion at some

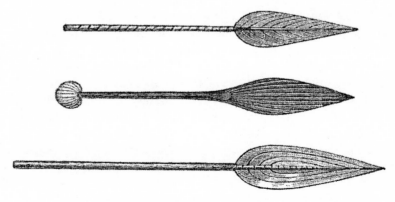

LEAF-BLADED PADDLE OF AVISIBBA.

suspicious bushes across the creek. There were certainly obstinate savages hidden behind them, but I failed to get a glimpse of one.

The creek I soon found lay between us. I was told that as the boat was crossing the crock a body of natives had suddenly issued on the other side and shot their arrows into them; that surprised by the discharge they had crouched in the bottom of the boat to escape the arrows, and had paddled the boat back to the landing-place with their hands. They had then picked up their rifles and blazed away at them. Simultaneously Lieutenant Stairs had rushed in among them and fired at the enemy, who were of a bolder kind than any they had yet met. In a short time he had received an arrow in the breast, which he had torn off while retreating, and five other men had been punctured. Almost as soon as I had finished receiving these particulars, I saw for the first time a dark shadow creep along the ground between two bushes, and fired into the centre of it, and a curiously weird wail responded to it. Two minutes later the arrows had ceased their patter among the leaves. Having posted a strong guard of the best shots along the bank to observe any movement on the opposite bank of the creek, the rest of the people were withdrawn.

In the evening some scouts that had searched in the woods inland returned with a flock of seven goats. They had discovered the crossing-place, and had suddenly opened fire on a small column going either to the assistance of the enemy or coming from their direction.

On the 14th, at dawn, pushed over the creek two companies to hunt up the enemy that had done us such damage; a company was also sent, under Captain Nelson, to the forest inland. In a few minutes we heard a volley, and a second, and then incessant rifle fire, showing that the enemy were of a resolute character. There were some crack shots in No. I Company, but it was scarcely possible to do much damage in a thick bush against a crafty enemy, who knew that they possessed most dangerous weapons, and who were ignorant of the deadly force of the pellets that searched the bushes. About 300 rounds had been fired, and silence followed. Four only of these had been fatal, and our party received four wounds from arrows smeared over freshly with a copal-coloured substance. One dead body was brought to me for examination. The head had a crop of long hair banded by a kind of coronet of iron; the neck had a string of iron drops, with a few monkey teeth among them. The teeth were filed into points. The distinguishing mark of the body appears to form double rows of tiny cicatrices across the chest and abdomen. The body was uncircumcised Another dead body brought

A HEAD-DRESS OF AVISIBBA WARRIORS.

to the landing-place had a necklace of human teeth, and a coronet of shining plated iron, and the forehead and several wristlets of the same metal, polished; on the left arm was the thick pad of silk cotton covered with goat skin, to protect the arm from the bow string.

After the natives had been chased away on all sides from the vicinity, the people commenced to forage, and succeded in bringing to Avisibba during the day sufficient plantains to give eighty per man – four days' rations.

Lieutenant Stairs' wound was one-fifth of an inch in diameter, an inch and a quarter below the heart, and the pointed head of the arrow had penetrated an inch and a half deep. The other men were wounded in the wrists, arms, and one in the fleshy part of the back. At this period we did not know what this strange copal-coloured substance was with which the points had been smeared, nor did we know what were its peculiar effects when dry or wet; all that the Doctor could do at this time was to inject water in the wounds and cleanse them. The "old hands" of the Zanzibaris affirmed it was poison extracted from the India rubber (Landolphia) by boiling; that the scum after sufficient boiling formed the poison.

A native declared that it was made of a species of arum, which, after being bruised, was boiled; that the water was then poured out into another pot, and boiled again until it had left a strong solution, which was mixed with fat, and this was the substance on the arrows. The odour was acrid, with a suspicion of asafœtida. The men proved its deadly properties by remarking that elephants and all big game were killed by it. All these stories caused us to be very anxious, but our ignorance was excessive, I admit. We could only look on with wonder at the small punctures on the arms, and express our opinion that such small wounds could not be deadly, and hope, for the sake of our friend Stairs and our nine wounded men, that all this was mere exaggeration.

The arrows were very slender, made of a dark wood, twenty-four inches long, points hardened by slow baking in the warm atmosphere above the hut fires; at the butt end was a slit, in which a leaf was introduced to guide the flight; the sharp points were as sharp as needles, and half an inch from the point began a curving line of notches for about two inches. The arrow heads were then placed in the prepared and viscid substance, with which they

CORONETED AVISIBBA WARRIOR—HEAD-DRESS.

were smeared; large leaves were then rolled round a sheaf before they were placed in the quiver. Another substance was pitch black in colour, and appeared more like Stockholm tar when fresh, but had a very disagreeable smell. In a quiver there would be nearly a hundred arrows. When we observed the care taken of these arrows, rolled up in green leaves as they were, our anxiety for our people was not lessened.

The bow is of stubborn hard brown wood, about three feet long; the string is a broad strip of rattan carefully polished. To experiment with their power I drove one of the wooden arrows, at six feet distance, through two sides of an empty biscuit tin. At 200 yards' distance was a tall tree. I drove an arrow, with full force, over the top of the highest branch and beyond the tree. It dawned on us all then that these wooden arrows were not the contemptible things we had imagined. At a short distance we judged, from what we saw, that the stiff spring of this little bow was sufficient to drive

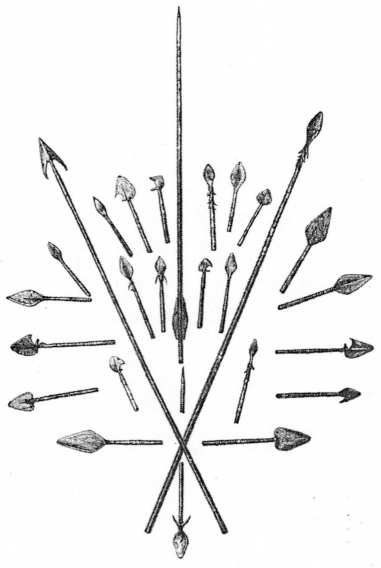

WOODEN ARROWS OF THE AVISIBBA.

(*From a photograph.*)

one of these slender arrows clean through a human body. At 120 paces I have been able to miss a bird within an inch with one of them.

At noon on the 15th of August the land column filed out of the palisaded villages of Avisibba led by Mr. Jephson, the officer of the day. As a captive had informed us that there were three cataracts ahead not tier off, I instructed Mr. Jephson that he must follow the river and halt at the first convenient spot about 2.30 P.M.; that I would halt the river column, now consisting of the boat and fourteen canoes, until the rear guard under Captain Nelson had quite left the settlement; but as the canoes would proceed faster than the land caravan, I would probably overtake him, and camp at the first fit place I could find after an hour's row, in which event he would proceed until he found us. The instructions were also repeated to the leading men of the pioneers.

I ought to have stated that our start at noon was occasioned by the delay caused by the discovery at the morning muster that five men were absent. They ultimately turned up at 10 o'clock; but this perpetual straying away without leave was most exasperating, and had drawn a lecture from me, though this was not uncommon in those stupid early days of training.

The Zanzibaris persisted in exhibiting an indifference to danger absolutely startling, not from bravery, or from ignorance of fear, but from an utter incapacity to remember that danger existed, and from a stupid unconsciousness as to how it affected them. Animals are indebted to instinct as a constant monitor against danger, but these men appeared to possess neither instinct nor reason, neither perception nor memory. Their heads were uncommonly empty. The most urgent entreaties to beware of hidden foes, and the most dreadful threats of punishment failed to impress on their minds the necessity they were under of being prudent, wary, and alert to avoid the skewers in the path, the lurking cannibal behind the plantain stalk, the cunning foe lying under a log, or behind a buttress, and the sunken pit, with its pointed pales at the bottom. When the danger fronted them it found them all unprepared. A sudden shower of arrows sent them howling abjectly out of reach or under shelter; and if the arrows were only followed by a resolute advance, resistance, by reason of excess of terror, would be impossible. An unexpected show of dauntlessness in a native compelled from them a ready recognition of his courage. On the road they sneaked into the woods to avoid the rear guard, but flew screaming with terror if a prowling savage suddenly rose before them with uplifted spear. They roved far singly or by twos amongst the villages, as looting was dear to their hearts; but should they meet the wild owners of them, they were more apt to throw the deadly rifle down on the ground than to use it. They strayed through the plantain grove with magnificent unconcern, but if they heard the whiz of an arrow they collapsed nervelessly and submitted to their fate. With an astounding confidence they scattered along the road, and stretched the line of the column to 3 miles in length, but at sight, of natives all sense was lost save that of cowardly fear. Out of 370 men at this time in the camp there were clearly 250 of this description, to whom rifles were of no use save as a clumsy, weighty club, which they would part with for a few ears of corn, or would willingly exchange for a light walking staff if they dared.

The day previous the Zanzibari head men, urged by their friends, had appeared before me in a body, and demanded to be despatched to forage without any officers, as the officers, they said, bored them with their perpetual orders of "Fall in, fall in." "Why," said they, "who can gather bananas if they are continually watched and told to 'Fall in, fall in?'"

"Very true," said I, "the thing is impossible. Let me see what you can do by yourselves. The banana plantations are but a quarter of an hour's distance. I shall expect you all back within an hour."

After such an exposition of character as the above it will not be wondered, that, each man having cleared from my presence, forgot all his promises, and wandered according to his wont. A flock of sheep or a herd of swine could not have gone further astray. After fourteen hours' absence the 200 foragers had returned save five. These five had departed no one knew where until 10 A.M. of this day.

Ah, those early days! Worse were to come, and then, having become purified by suffering, and taught by awful experience, they became Romans!

But to return to Jephson. We pulled up stream – after seeing that every one was clear of the settlement of Avisibba – at the rate of a knot and a half an hour, and at 2.45, having discovered a convenient camp, halted for the night. We waited in vain for Mr. Jephson, and the column fired signal guns, rowed out into the stream, and with a glass searched the shore up and down, but there was no sign of camp-fire, or smoke above the woods, which generally covered the forest as with a fog in still weather, no sound of rifle-shot, blare of trumpet, or human voice. The caravan, we thought, must have found a fine track, and proceeded to the cataracts ahead.

On the 16th the river column pulled hard up stream, passed Mabengu villages, came up to a deep but narrow creek flowing from the south bank into the Nevva, as the Aruwimi was now called, looked anxiously up stream, and an hour later we had reached the foot of Mabengu Rapids. On the right bank, opposite to where we selected a camping-place, was a large settlement – that of Itiri. Then, having, as yet, met no traces of the absent column, I sent boat's crew up the creek to search for traces of fording. After ascending several miles up the creek, the boat's crew returned unsuccessful; then I despatched it back again to within half-an-hour's distance of Avisibba, and at midnight the boat returned to announce their failure to find any traces of the missing.

On the 17th the boat's crew, with "Three O'clock," the hunter (Saat Tato), and six scouts, were sent to our camping-place of the 15th, with orders for the hunter and his six scouts to follow the path observed there – inland – until they had struck the trail of the column, then to follow the trail and overtake them, trod return with them to the river. On the boat's return, the coxswain informed me that they had seen the trail about 7 miles (3 hours' march). I concluded that Mr. Jephson had led his column south, instead of E. by N. and E. N. E., according to course of river, and that Saat Tato would overtake them, and return next day.

Our condition at the river camp was this. We had thirty-nine canoemen and boatmen, twenty-eight sick people, three Europeans, and three boys, and one of the Europeans (Lieutenant Stairs) was suffering from a dangerous wound, and required the constant care of the surgeon. One man had died of dysentery at Avisibba. We had a dying idiot in camp, who had become idiotic some days before. We had twenty-nine suffering from pleurisy, dysentery, incurable debility, and eight suffering from wounds. One called Khalfan was half strangled with the wound in his windpipe, another called

Saadi, wounded in the arm, appeared dangerously ill, his arm was swollen, and gave him great pain. Out of the thirty-nine available I had despatched three separate parties in different directions to scout for news of the missing column, lest it was striking across some great bend to reach the river a long distance higher up, while we, unable to stir, were on the other side of the curve. Across the river the people of Itiri, perceiving we were so quiet on our side of the river, seemed to be meditating an attack, and only two miles below on our bank was the large settlement of Mabengu, from whose inhabitants we might hear at any moment, while our little force of thirty-nine men, scattered in various directions, were searching for the missing 300. But the poet said that it became

"No man to nurse despair;
But in the teeth of clenched antagonisms
To follow the worthiest till he die."

I quote from my diary of August 18th.

The idiot fell asleep last night. His troubles are over, and we have buried him.

I wonder if Tennyson were here, who wrote such noble lines, what he would think of our state. A few days ago I was chief of 370 men, rich in goods, munitions of war, medicines, and contented with such poor comforts as we had, and to-day I have actually only eighteen men left fit for a day's march, the rest have vanished. I should be glad to know where.

If 389 picked men, such as we were when we left Yambuya, are unable to reach Lake Albert, how can Major Barttelot with 250 men make his way through this endless forest. We have travelled, on an average, 8 hours per day for forty-four days since leaving Yambuya. At two miles per hour we ought, by this date, to have arrived on the Lake shore, but, instead of being there, we have accomplished just a third of the distance. The poet says we must not "nurse despair," for to do that is to lie down and die, to make no effort, and abandon hope.

Our wounded take considerable time to heal. The swelling is increasing, the wounds are most painful, not one has yet proved fatal, but they are all quite incapacitated from duty.

The fifth rain of this month began at 8 A.M. Had we not enough afflictions without this perpetual rain? One is almost tempted to think that the end is approaching. The very "flood gates of heaven" seem opened, and nature is dissolving. Such a body of rain is falling that the view of all above is obscured by the amazing fall of rain-drops. Think of the countless numbers of leaves in this forest, and that every leaf drops ten to twenty times per minute, and that from the soaking ground rises a grey cloud of minute rain in vapour, and that the air is full of floating globules of water and flying shreds of leaves! And add to all this the intense fall of rain as the blast comes bearing down the top, and whips drowning showers on us, and sways the countless branches, and rushes wailing through the glades with such force, as though it would wrench the groaning trees out of the earth. The moaning and groaning of the forest is far from comforting, and the crashing and fall of mighty trees is far from assuring, but it is a positive terror when the thunder rumbles above, and its sounds reverberating through the aisles and crooked corridors of the forest, and the blazing lightning darts spitefully hither and thither its forky tongues and sheets of flame, and explodes over our heads with overwhelming and deafening shocks. It would be a vast relief for our sick and wounded to be free of such sounds. An European battle has no such variety. And throughout the day this has continued unceasingly. It is now about the tenth hour of the day. It is scarcely possible daylight will ever appear again, at least so I judge from the human faces steeped in misery. Their owners appear stupefied by terror, woe, sickness, loss of friends, hunger, rain and thunder, and general wretchedness. They may be seen crouching under plantain-leaf sheds, native shields, cotton shelters, straw mats, earthen and copper pots above their heads, even saddles, tent canvass covers, blankets, each body wreathed in blue vapour, self-absorbed with speechless anguish. The poor asses with their ears drawn back, inverted eyes and curving backs, captive fowls with drooping crests represent abject discomfort. Alas! the glory of this earth is quite extinguished. When she finally recovered her beauty, and her children assumed their proud bearing, and the growing lakes and increasing rivers were dried up, and how out of chaos the sun rose to comfort the world again I know not. My own feeling of misery had so exhausted me that a long sleep wrapped me in merciful oblivion.

August 19th. – Still without news of land caravan. The scouts have returned without having seen any traces of the missing. Two of the wounded men are doing very badly. Their sufferings appear to be terrible.

August 20th. – Still without news of caravan. Young Saadi wounded by a poisoned arrow on the morning of the 14th, is attacked with tetanus, and is in a very dangerous condition. Wherefore I take it to be a vegetable poison. Khalfan's neck and spine have become rigid. I have given both morphine by injection, but the doses though double, that is in half grains, do not appear to ease the sufferers much. Stairs is just the same as yesterday, neither worse nor better. The wound is painful, still he has appetite, and enjoys sleep. I fear the effect on him of knowing what the other patients are undergoing.

It is strange that out of 300 people and 3 officers, not one has sense enough to know that he has lost the road, and that the best way of recovering it would be to retrace their steps to Avisibba and try again.

August 21st. – Poor Khalfan wounded in the windpipe on the 10th instant, and the young fellow Saadi hurt on the morning of the 14th; both died in the night, after intolerable agonies – one at 4 A.M., Saadi about midnight. Khalfan's wound was caused by a poisoned arrow; but the poison must have been laid on the arrow some days before it was used. He had been daily getting weaker from abstinence from food, because of pain. The wound did not seem dangerous; it had closed up, externally, and there were no signs of inflammation; but the poor fellow complained he could not swallow. He had subsisted on liquid food made of plaintain flour gruel. On the 8th day his neck became rigid and contracted; he could not articulate, but murmur; the head was inclined forward, the abdomen was shrunk, and on his face lines of pain and anxiety became fixed. Yesterday he had some slight spasms. I gave two injections of half a grain hypodermically, which relieved him for an hour, but, not much accustomed to treat patients with morphia, I feared giving larger doses. Saadi was punctured on the right forearm, midway between wrist and elbow – a mere wound, such as a coarse stocking needle would have made. The wound was sucked by a comrade; it was syringed with warm water and dressed, but on the morning of the fourth day he was attacked with tetanus of so severe a kind that his case was hopeless from our sheer inability to relieve him from the frightful spasms. Morphia injections rendered him slightly somnolent; but the spasms continued, and Saadi died on the 11th hour after receiving the wound. I am inclined to think that the arrow was smeared for the fight of the 14th the night previous.

A third man died of dysentery before noon, making the fourth death in this camp.

At 5 P.M. the caravan arrived. Its sufferings have been great from mental distress. There have been three deaths also in the land column. Maruf, punctured in shoulder, died of tetanus on the night of the 19th, 24 hours earlier than Saadi. This may have been due to the travel accelerating the action of the poison. One man named Ali was shot by an iron-barbed arrow, and died of internal hæmorrhage, the arrow having pierced the liver. Another succumbed to dysentery immediately after the heavy rain which had afflicted us on the 18th; thus we have had seven fatal cases since the 14th. We have several others, in whom life is flickering. The column brought in two others wounded by arrows. The wounds are much inflamed, and exude a gangrenous matter.

Lieut. Stairs still appears hearty, and appears as though he was recovering, despite the influence these many deaths might have on his nerves. The surgeon having appeared, I feel an intense relief. I hate to see pain, and take no delight in sick men's groans. I feel pleasure in ministering to their needs only when conscious I can cure.

We have now about 373 in camp, but 60 of them appear fitter for a hospital than to continue our wandering life; but in this savage region not even rest and food can be secured for the weary souls.

A few more days of this disheartening work, attending on the sick, looking at the agonies of men dying from lockjaw, listening to their muffled screams, observing general distress and despondency, from hunger, and the sad anxiety caused by the unaccountable absence of their brothers and comrades, with the loss of 300 men impending over me must, have exercised a malign influence over myself, I am conscious of the insidious advance of despair towards me. Our food has been bananas or plantains, boiled or fried, our other provisions being re-tarred for perhaps an extreme occasion which may present itself in the near future. The dearest passion of my life has been, I think, to succeed in my undertakings; but the last few days have begun to fill me with a doubt of success in the present one.

What the feelings of the officers have been I have not heard yet; but the men have frankly confessed that they have been delivered from a hell.

The following note has just been placed in my hands: –

August 1887.

Dear Sir,

Saat Taro reached us at 3 P.M. yesterday with your order to follow him. We at once recrossed the river (the creek which the boat's crew had searched) and hope to reach you tonight. I can understood how great your anxiety must have been, and deeply regret having caused it.

I have the honour to be,

&c., &c., &c.
A. M. Jephson.

On the 22nd we moved camp to the foot of the highest Mabengu Rapids, and on the following day proceeded above the rapids.

I then took the opportunity of mustering the people. The following returns tell their own tale: –

	Healthy	Sick	Dead	Loads
Company No. 1	80	6	4	43
Capt. Stairs, No. 2	69	14	5	50

	Healthy	Sick	Dead	Loads
Capt. Nelson, 3	67	16	4	72
Capt. Jephson, 4	63	21	3	72
Europeans	6			
Boys	12			
Soudanese	10			
Somalis	6			
Cooks	2			
Donkey Boy	1			
Sick	57			
	373			
Dead	16			
Total	389			

The experiences of the column during its wanderings appeared to confirm me in my impressions theft the Aruwimi in this region of rapids was not so much utilized by the natives as it was below. Large settlements had been discovered inland; the scouts had traversed the forest by several well-trodden tracks which led from the river to the interior. The river banks were not so populous, the settlements were now generally a little way inland, and along the river bank was a perceptible path which materially assisted us. Ever since leaving Utiri we had noted this fact. On the 24th we travelled a few miles, and camped below Avugadu Rapids, near a rich plantain grove, and the next day passed the rapids and formed a comfortable camp in a somewhat open portion of the forest, haunted by fishermen. On the 26th the column oil land swung along at a good rate, while we had a long stretch of undisturbed river, and had to pull hard to keep pace with them until both columns met in one of the largest villages of the Avejeli tribe established in front of the Nepoko mouth.

This latter river, of which Dr. Junker was the first to inform us, and which he had crossed far up, tumbled into the Aruwimi, now called the Itiri, by a series of cascades, over reefs of shaly rock, from an altitude of 40 feet. The mouth was about 300 yards wide, narrowing to about 250 yards above the cascade. The natives had staked a considerable distance of the reef, to which to attach their large funnel-shaped baskets for the reception of the fish washed down the rapids. The colour of the Nepoko was of chocolate, that of the Itiri was of tea and milk.

Had I known that one week later I should have encountered Arabs, and their desperate bands of Manyuema, there is no doubt that I should have endeavoured to put a degree of latitude between the centre of their influence and our route. Even as it was, I mentally debated a change of route, from some remarks made to me by Binza (Dr. Junker's Monbuttu boy), who suggested that it were better to travel through lands inhabited by "decent men," to such a horrid region infested by peoples who did not deserve the name of men applied to them, and that the Momvu tribes were sure of according a welcome to those who could show in return that they appreciated hospitality. Binza was most enticing in his descriptions of the Momvu nation. But food with the Avejeli was abundant and various, and we hoped that a change had come over the land. For ever since we had observed a difference in the architecture of the native dwellings, we had observed a change for the better in the diet of the people. Below Panga Falls the aborigines principally subsisted on manioc, and on the different breads, puddings, cakes, and porridges to which they converted these tubers. It will not be forgotten, perhaps, that tapioca is made out of manioc, or cassava. But above Panga Falls manioc had been gradually replaced by plantain groves and the plantain is a much more excellent edible than manioc for an expedition, and the groves had been clearly growing into higher importance, therefore we hoped that happier days were in store for us. There were also fields of Indian corn, manioc, yams, and colocassia, plots of tobacco for the smokers, and to our great joy we came across many fowls. A halt was ordered that the sorely-tried people might recuperate.

In their very excusable eagerness for meat, the Zanzibaris and Soudanese were very reckless. No sooner was a fowl sighted than there was a general scramble for it; some reckless fellows used their rifles to shoot the chickens, and many a cartridge was expended uselessly for which due punishment was frequently awarded. The orders were most positive that no ammunition was to be wasted, and the efforts made to detect all breaches of these orders were most energetic, but when did a Zanzibar obey orders when away from his employer's eye? The indiscriminate shooting of this day resulted in the shooting of one of the brave band of hard-working pioneers. A bullet from a Winchester struck trim in the foot, the bones of which were pulverized and its amputation became imperative. Surgeon Parks performed the operation in a most skilful and expeditious manner, and as the good surgeon was most resolute when "one of his cases" required care – this unfortunate[9] young man had to be lifted in and out by eight men, must needs have the largest share of a canoe that nothing might offend the tender wound, and of necessity required and received the most bounteous supply of the best food and to have servants to wait upon him – in short, such a share of good things and ready services that I often envied him, and thought that for a sixpence in addition I would not mind exchanging places with him.

Of course another severe lecture followed, and there were loud protestations that they would all pay implicit attention in the future, and of course before the next lay every promise was forgotten. There is much to be said for these successive breaches of promise. They believe the mind from vast care and all sense of responsibility. No restraint burdens it, and an easy gladness brightens the face. Why should a man, being an animal, continually fetter himself with obligations as though he were a moral being to be held accountable for every idle word uttered in a gushing moment?

On the 28th the river column consisting now of the *Advance* steel boat and sixteen canoes, pushed up river to a camp five miles above Avejeli. The land party was left far behind, for they were struggling through a series of streams and creeks, and buried in

---

9.   Was he very unfortunate? I paid Ugarrowwa for thirteen months' board, sent him to Stanley Falls, thence down the Congo and by sea to Madeira, *viâ* the Cape to Zanzibar, where he arrived in a state well described by "as fat as butter."

depths of suffocatingly close bush, and did not arrive until the next day at noon, when they were urged to proceed about two hours higher, whither we followed them.

We arrived at the foot of a big cataract on the 30th, and by observation ascertained that we had reached halfway to the Albert Lake, Kavalli being in 30° 30' and Yambuya in 25° 3 1/2'. Our camp on this day was in about 27° 47'.

We had 163 geographical miles in an air line to make yet, which we could never accomplish within 64 days as we had performed the western half of the route. The people were in an impoverished state of body, and mentally depressed, ulcers were raging like an epidemic, anemia had sapped their vitality. They were told the half-way camp was reached, but they replied with murmurs of unbelief. They asked, "How can the master tell? Will that instrument show him the road? Will it tell him which is the path? Why does it not tell us, then, that we may see and believe? Don't the natives know their own country better? Which of them has seen grass? Do they not all say that all the world is covered with trees and thick bush? Bah – the master talks to us as though we were children and had no proper perception."

The morning of the evil date, August 31st, dawned as on other days. It struggled through dense clouds of mist, and finally about 9 o'clock the sun appeared, pale, indistinct, a mere circle of lustreless light. But in the meantime we were hard at our frequent task of cutting a broad highway through the bush and forest, through which the boat could be carried bodily by 60 men, standing underneath; the crew of the flotilla were wrestling with the mad waters, and shoving their vessels up steep slopes of a racing river.

The highway was finished in an hour, and a temporary camp was located above. The canoes began to arrive. I left the Doctor to superintend the pioneers bearing the boat, but he presently returned to report that the boat could not be lifted. I retraced my steps to oversee the operation personally. I had succeeded in conveying it half way when my European servant came running at a mad pace, crying out as he ran: "Sir, oh, sir, Emin Pasha has arrived."

"Emin Pasha!"

"Yes, sir. I have seen him in a canoe. His red flag, like ours (the Egyptian), is hoisted up at the stern. It is quite true, sir!"

Of course we bounded forward; the boat was dropped as though it was red hot. A race began, master and man striving for the lead. In the camp the excitement was also general. It was owing, we soon heard, to the arrival of nine Manyuema, who served one called Uledi Balyuz, known to natives by the name of Ugarrowwa, and who was reported to be settled about eight marches up river, and commanding several hundred armed men.

The Arabs were, then, so far inland on the Upper Aruwimi, and I had flattered myself that I had heard the last of these rovers! We were also told that there were fifty of them camped six miles above on their way, by orders of Ugarrowwa, to explore the course of the river, to ascertain if communication with Stanley Falls could be obtained by the unknown stream on whose banks they had settled.

We imparted the information they desired, whereupon they said they would return to their camp and prepare for a hospitable reception on the morrow. The Zanzibaris were considerably elated at the news, for what reason may shortly be seen.

The first absconder was one Juma, who deserted with half a hundredweight of biscuit that night.

On the 1st September, in the early morning, we were clear of the rapids, and, rowing up in company with the caravan, were soon up at the village where the Manyuema were said to be camped. At the gate there was a dead male child, literally hacked to pieces; within the palisades was a dead woman, who had been speared. The Manyuema had disappeared. It seemed to us then that some of our men had damped their joy at the encounter with us, by suggesting that. the slaves with them might probably cause in us a revulsion of feeling. Suspicion of this caused an immediate change in their feelings. Their fears impelled them to decamp instantly. Their society was so much regretted, however, that five Zanzibaris, taking five loads, four of ammunition and one of salt, disappeared.

We resumed our journey, and halted at the base of a another series of rapids.

The next day Saat Tato, having explored the rapids, reported encouragingly, and expressed his confidence that without much difficulty these could also be surmounted. This report stimulated the boatmen to make another trial. While the river column was busy in its own peculiar and perilous work, a search party was despatched to hunt news of the missing men, and returned with one man, a box of ammunition, and three rifles. The search party had discovered the deserters in the forest, with a ease of ammunition open, which they were distributing. In trying to surround them, the deserters became alarmed and scudded away, leaving three of their rifles and a case behind them.

On the 3rd of September five more deserted, carrying away one ease of Remington cartridges, one ease of Winchester cartridges, one box of European provisions, and one load of fine Arab clothing, worth £50. Another was detected with a box of provisions open before him, having already abstracted a tin of sago, one tin of Liebig, a tin of butter, and one of milk. Ten men had thus disappeared in a couple of days. At this rate, in sixty days the Expedition would be ended. I consulted the chiefs, but I could gain no encouragement to try what extreme measures would effect. It was patent, however, to the dullest that we should be driven to resort to extremities soon to stop this wholesale desertion and theft. Since leaving Yambuya we had lost forty-eight rifles and fifteen cases of Maxim, Winchester, and Remington ammunition.

The day following four men deserted, and one was caught in the act of desertion. The people were accordingly mustered, and sixty men, suspected of being capable of desertion, as no head man would guarantee their fidelity, were rendered helpless by abstracting the mainsprings of the rifles, which we took and locked up. Demoralisation had set in rapidly since we had met the Manyuema. Nothing was safe in their hands. Boxes had been opened, cloth had been stolen, beads had been pilfered, much ammunition had been taken out of the cases, and either thrown, or secreted as a reserve, by the way.

On September 5th we camped near Hippo Broads, so called because the river was fine and broad, and a large herd of hippopotami were seen. The site of our resting place was an abandoned clearing, which had become the haunts of these amphibiæ, and exquisite bits of greensward caused us to imagine for a moment that possibly the open country was not far. Foragers returned after a visit, into the interior, on both banks, with four goats and a few bananas, numbers of roast rats, cooked beetles, and slugs. On the 6th we reached a cataract opposite the Bafaido settlement, where we obtained a respectable supply of plantains. The day following we dragged our canoes over a platform of rock, over a projecting ledge of which the river tumbled 10 feet.

From the Bafaido cataract we journeyed along a curving river to Avakubi Rapids, and formed a camp at the landing-place. A path led hence into the interior, which the hungry people soon followed. While scouring the country for food, a woman and child were found, who were brought to me to be examined. But the cleverest interpreter was at, fault. No one understood a syllable of the meaningless babble.

Some more rapids were reached the next day. We observed that the oil-palm flourished throughout this section.

Palm nuts were seen in heaps near each village. We even discovered some palms lately planted, which showed some regard for posterity. Achmet, the Somali, who had insisted on leaving Yambuya, in accompanying us had been a passenger ever since we had struck the river above Yankondé, was reported to be dying. He was said to suffer from melanosis. Whatever the disease might be, he had become singularly emaciated, being a literal skeleton covered lightly with skin.

From this camp we rounded a point, passed over a short winding course of river, and in an hour approached in view of an awful raging stream choked by narrow banks of shale. The outlook beyond the immediate foreview was first of a series of rolling waves whirling and tossed into spray, descending in succeeding lines, and a great fall of about 30 feet, and above that a steep slope of wild rapids, and the whole capped with mist, and tearing down tumultuously towards us.

This was appalling considering the state of the column. There were about 120 load in the canoes, and between fifty and sixty sick and feeble people. To leave these in the woods to their fate was impossible, to carry the loads and advance appeared equally so; yet to drag the canoes and bear the boat past such a long stretch of wild water appeared to be a task beyond our utmost powers.

Leaving the vessels below the falls and rapids, I led the Expedition by land to the destroyed settlement of Navabi, situated near a bend of the Itiri (Aruwimi) above the disturbed stream, where we established camp. The sick dragged themselves after the caravan, those too feeble and helpless to travel the distance were lifted up and borne to the camp. Officers then mustered the companies for the work of cutting a broad highway through the bush and hauling the canoes. This task occupied two whole days, while No. 1 Company foraged far and near to obtain food, but with only partial success. Navabi must have been a remarkable instance of aboriginal prosperity once. It possessed groves of the elais and plantain, large plots of tobacco and indian corn; the huts under the palms looked almost idyllic; at least so we judged from two which were left standing, and gave us a bit of an aspect at once tropical, pretty, and apparently happy. Elsewhere the whole was desolate. Some parties, which we conjectured belonged to Ugarrowwa, had burnt the settlement, chopped many of the palms down, leveled the banana plantations, and strewed the ground with the bones of the defenders. Five skulls of infants were found within our new camp at Navabi.

On the 12th, as we resumed our journey, we were compelled to leave five men who were in an unconscious state and dying. Achmet, the Somali, whom we had borne all the way from Yambuya, was one of them.

From Navabi we proceeded to the landing place of Memberri, which evidently was a frequent haunt of elephants. One of these not far off was observed bathing luxuriously in the river near the right bank. Hungry for meat, I was urged to try my chance. On this Expedition I had armed myself with the Express rifles of 577-bore, which Indian sportsmen so much applaud. The heavy 8-bores were with Major Barttelot and Mr. Jameson. I succeeded in planting six shots in the animal at a few yards distance, but to no purpose except to unnecessarily wound him.

At Memberri we made a muster, and according to returns our numbers stood: –

August 23rd ....373 men.
September 12th.....................................343 men.

14 deserted and 16 deaths; carriers 235 loads 227; sick 58.

Added to these eloquent records every member of the Expedition suffered from hunger, and the higher we ascended the means for satisfying the ever-crying want of food appeared to diminish, for the Bakusu and Basongora slaves, under the Manyuema head men of Ugarrowwa, had destroyed the plantations, and either driven the populations to unknown recesses in the forest or had extirpated them.

On the following day we reached Amiri Falls. The previous day the head man, Saadi, had been reproached for leaving one named Makupeté to return along the track to search for a box of ammunition that was reported to be missing, whereupon Saadi took the unwise resolution of proceeding to hunt up Makupeté. Then one, Uledi Manga, disgusted with the severe work and melancholy prospect before us, absconded with another box of ammunition.

We had only three Zanzibari donkeys left. Out of the six with which we had started from Yambuya, one of the three, probably possessed with a presentiment that the caravan was doomed, took it into his head that it was better to return before it was too late, and deserted also. Whither he went no one knew. It is useless to search in the forest for a lost man, donkey, or article. Like the waves divided by a ship's prow uniting at the stern, so the forest enfolds past finding within its deep shades whatsoever enters, and reveals nothing.

Near a single old fishing hut our camp was pitched on the 15th. The river after its immense curve northward and eastward now trended south-easterly, and we had already reached S. Lat. 1° 24' from 1° 58'.

Having been in the habit of losing a box of ammunition per diem for the last few days, having tried almost every art of suppressing this robbery, we now had recourse to lashing the boxes in series of eights, and consigning each to the care of a head man, and holding him responsible for them. This we hoped would check the excuse that the men disappeared into the forest under all kinds of wants.

On the 16th of September, while halting for the midday rest and lunch, several loud reports of musketry were heard up-river. I sent Saat Tato to explore, and in half-an-hour we heard three rifle-shots announcing success; and shortly after three canoes besides our own appeared loaded with men in white dresses, and gay with crimson flags. These came, so they reported, to welcome us in the name of Ugarrowwa, their chief, who would visit my evening camp. After exchanging compliments, they returned up-river, firing their muskets and singing gaily.

At the usual hour we commenced the afternoon march, and at 4 P.M. were in camp just below Ugarrowwa's station. At the same time a roll of drums, the booming of many muskets, and a flotilla of canoes, announced the approach of the Arab leader. About 50 strong, robust fellows accompanied him, besides singers and women, every one of whom was in prime condition of body.

The leader gave his name as Ugarrowwa, the Zanzibar term for "Lualaba," or native name of "Ruarawwa," known formerly as Uledi Balyuz (or the Consuls Uledi). He had accompanied Captains Speke and Grant, 1860-3, as a tent-boy, and had been left or had deserted in Unyoro. He offered as a gift to us two fat goats and about 40 lbs. of picked rice, a few ripe plantains, and fowls.

Upon asking him if there was any prospect of food being obtained for the people in the vicinity of his station, he admitted, to our sorrow, that his followers in their heedless way had destroyed everything, that it was impossible to cheek them because they were furious against the "pagans" for the bloody retaliation and excesses the aborigines had committed against many and many of their countrymen during their search for ivory.

Asked what country we were in, he replied that we were in Bunda, the natives of which were Babunda; that the people on the north bank in the neighbourhood of his station were called Bapai or Bavaiya.

He also said that his raiders had gone eastward a month's journey, and had seen from a high hill (Kassololo?), a grassy country extending to the eastward.

Further information was to the effect that his caravan, 600 strong, had left the Lualaba at Kibongés (above Leopold R.), and that in nine moons he had travelled the distance of 370 geographical miles, about a N.E. course, throughout continuous forest without having seen as much grass as would cover the palm of his hand; that he had only crossed one river, the Lindi, before he sighted the Ituri, as the Aruwimi was now called; that he had heard from Arab traders that the Lulu (Lowwa) rose from a small lake called the Ozo, where there was a vast quantity of ivory.

Four days higher Ugarrowwa possessed another station manned with 100 guns, near the Lenda river, a tributary of the Aruwimi, which entered it from the south bank. His people had sown rice, of which he had brought us some, and onions; but near each settlement was a waste, as it was not policy to permit such "murderous pagans" to exist near them, otherwise he and his people's lives were not safe. He had lost about 200 men of the Bakusu and Basangora tribes, and many a fine Manyuema headman. One time he had lost 40, of whom not one had returned. He had an Arab guest at his station who had lost every soul out of his caravan.

I observed a disposition on his part to send some men with me to the Lake, and there appeared to be no difficulty in housing with him my sick men for a consideration – to be hereafter agreed upon.

On the 17th we proceeded a short distance to encamp opposite Ugarrowwa's station.

In the afternoon I was rowed across in my boat to the Arab settlement, and was hospitably received. I found the station to be a large settlement, jealously fenced round with tall palisades and short planks lashed across as screens against chance arrows. In the centre, facing the river, was the house of the chief, commodious, lofty, and comfortable, the walls of which were pierced for musketry. It resembled a fort with its lofty and frowning walls of baked clay. On passing, through a passage which separated Ugarrowwa's private apartments from the public rooms, I had a view of a great court 60 feet square, surrounded by buildings and filled with servants. It suggested something baronial in its busy aspect, the abundant service, the great difference of the domestics, amplitude of space, and plenty. The place was certainly impregnable against attack, and, if at all spiritedly defended, a full battalion would have been necessary to have captured this outpost of a slave trader.

I was informed that the river for many days' march appeared to flow from the eastward; that the Ihuru, a considerable distance up, flowed from the northward and joined the Ituri, and that, besides the Lenda, there was another affluent called the Ibina, which entered from the south.

Somewhere higher up also, – vaguely given as ten days' by others twenty days' march, – another Arab was settled who was called Kilonga-Longa, though his real name was also Uledi.

At this settlement I saw the first specimen of the tribe of dwarfs who were said to be thickly scattered north of the Ituri, from the Ngaiyu eastward. She measured thirty-three inches in height, and was a perfectly formed young woman of about seventeen, of a glistening and smooth sleekness of body. Her figure was that of a miniature coloured lady, not wanting in a certain grace, and her face was very prepossessing. Her complexion was that of a quadroon, or of the colour of yellow ivory. Her eyes were magnificent, but absurdly large for such a small creature – almost as large as that of a young gazelle; full, protruding, and extremely lustrous. Absolutely nude, the little demoiselle was quite possessed, as though she were accustomed to be admired, and really enjoyed inspection. She had been discovered near the sources of the Ngaiyu.

Ugarrowwa, having shown me all his treasures, in-eluding the splendid store of ivory he had succeeded in collecting, accompanied me to the boat, and sent away with me large trays of exquisitely cooked rice, and an immense bowl full of curried fowl, a dish that I am not fond of, but which inspired gratitude in my camp.

Our landing-place presented a lively scene. The sellers of bananas, potatoes, sugar-cane, rice, flour of manioc, and fowls clamoured for customers, and cloths and beads exchanged hands rapidly. This is the kind of life which the Zanzibaris delight in, like almost all other natives, and their happy spirits were expressed in sounds to which we had long been strangers.

Early this morning I had sent a canoe to pick up any stragglers that might have been unable to reach camp, and before 3 P.M. five sick men, who had surrendered themselves to their fate, were brought in, and shortly after a muster was held. The following were the returns of men able to march: –

No. 1 Company, 69 men 4 chiefs
No. 2, 57 men 4 chiefs
No. 3, 60 men 4 chiefs
No. 4, 61 men 4 chiefs
Cooks, 3
Boys, 9
Europeans, 6
Soudanese, 6

Total 271 men 16 chiefs
Minus 56 sick = 327
Departed from Yambuya, 389
Loss by desertion and death, 62

The boat and canoes were manned, and the sick transported to the Arab settlement, arrangements having been made for boarding them at the rate of five dollars each per month until Major Barttelot should appear, or some person bearing an order from me.

It will be remembered that we met Ugarrowwa's men on the 31st of August, one day's march from Avejeli, opposite the Nepoko mouth. These men, instead of pursuing their way down river, had returned to Ugarrowwa to inform him of the news they had received from us, believing that their mission was accomplished. It was Ugarrowwa's wish to obtain gunpowder, as his supply was nearly exhausted. Major Barttelot possessed two and a quarter tons of this explosive, and, as reported by us, was advancing up river, but as he had so much baggage it would take several months before he could arrive so far. I wished to communicate with Major Barttelot, and accordingly I stipulated with Ugarrowwa that if his men continued their way down river along the south or left bank until they delivered a letter into his hands, I would give him an order for three hundredweight of powder. He promised to send forty scouts within a month, and expressed great gratitude. (He actually did send them, as he promised, between the 20th and 25th of October. They succeeded in reaching Wasp Rapids, 165 miles from Yambuya, whence they were obliged to return, owing to losses and the determined hostility of the natives.)

Our Zanzibari deserters had been deluded like ourselves. Imagining that Ugarrowwa's people had continued their journey along some inland route westward, they had hastened westward in pursuit to join them, whereas we discovered they had returned eastward to their master. The arrangements made with Ugarrowwa, and the public proclamation of the man himself before all, would, I was assured, suffice to prevent further desertion.

We were pretty tired of the river work with its numerous rapids, and I suggested to Ugarrowwa that I should proceed by land; the Arab, however, was earnest in dissuading me from that course, as the people would be spared the necessity of carrying many loads, the sick having been left behind, and informed me that his information led him to believe that the river was much more navigable above for many days than below.

Chapter 9

UGARROWWA'S TO KILONGA LONGA'S

Once more the Expedition consisted of picked men. My mind was relieved of anxiety respecting the rear column, and of the fate which threatened the sick men. We set out from Ugarrrowa's station with 180 loads in the canoes and boat, forty-seven loads to be carried once in four days by alternate companies. The Arabs accompanied us for a few hours on the 19th to start us on our road and to wish us success in our venture.

We had scarcely been all collected in our camp, and the evening was rapidly becoming dusky, when a canoe from Ugarrowwa appeared with three Zanzibaris bound as prisoners. Inquiring the cause of this, I was astonished to find that they were deserters whom Ugarrowwa had picked up soon after reaching his station. They had absconded with rifles, and their pouches showed that they had contrived to filch cartridges on the road. I rewarded Ugarrowwa with a revolver and 200 cartridges. The prisoners were secured for the night, but before retiring I debated carefully as to what method was best to deal with these people. If this were permitted to proceed without the strongest measures, we should in a short time be compelled to retrace our steps, and all the lives and bitter agonies of the march would have been expended ill vain.

In the morning "all hands" were mustered, and an address was delivered to the men in fitting words, to which all assented; and all agreed that we had endeavoured our utmost to do our duty, that we had all borne much, but that the people on this occasion appeared to be all slaves, and possessed no moral sense whatever. They readily conceded that if natives attempted to steal our rifles, which were "our souls," we should be justified in shooting them dead, and that if men, paid for their labour, protected and treated kindly, as they were, attempted to cut our throats in the night, were equally liable to be shot.

"Well then," said 1, "what are these doing but taking our arms, and running away with our means of defence. You say that you would shoot natives, if they stood in your way preventing your progress onward or retreat backward. What are these doing? For if you have no titles left, or ammunition, can you march either forward or backward?"

"No," they admitted.

"Very well, then, you have condemned them to death.

One shall die to-day, another to-morrow, and another the next day, and from this day forward, every thief and deserter who leaves his duty and imperils his comrades' lives shall die."

The culprits were then questioned as to who they were. One replied that he was the slave of Farjalla-bill Ali – a headman in No. 1 company; another that he was the slave of a Banyan in Zanzibar, and the third that he was the slave of an artizan at work in Unyanyembé.

Lots were cast, and he who chose the shortest paper of three slips was the one to die first. The lot fell upon the slave of Farjalla, who was then present. The rope was heaved over a stout branch. Forty men at the word of command lay hold of the rope and a noose was cast round the prisoner's neck.

"Have you anything to say before the word is given?"

He replied with a shake of the head. The signal was given, and the man was hoisted up. Before the last struggles were over, the Expedition had filed out of camp leaving the rearguard and river column behind. A rattan was substituted in place of our rope, the body was secured to the tree, and within fifteen minutes the camp was abandoned.

We made good progress on this day. A track ran along the river which greatly assisted the caravan. In passing through we searched and found only ten bunches of miniature plantains. We formed camp an hour's distance from the confluence of the Lenda and Ituri.

Another noble tusker was bathing opposite the river, and Captain Nelson, with a double-barreled rifle, similar to my own, myself, and Saat Taro the hunter, crossed over and floated down within fifteen yards of the elephant. We fired three bullets simultaneously into him, and in a second had planted two more, and yet with all this lead fired at vital parts the animal contrived to escape. From this time we lost all confidence in these rifles. We never bagged one head of game with the Expresses during the entire Expedition. Captain Nelson sold his rifle for a small supply of food to Kilonga-Longa some time afterwards, and I parted with mine as a gift to Antari, King of Ankori, nearly two years later. With the No. 8 or No. 10 Reilly rifle I was always successful, therefore those interested in such things may avail themselves of our experience.

As the next day dawned and a grey light broke through the umbrageous coping of the camp I despatched a boy to call the head chief Rashid.

"Well, Rashid, old man, we shall have to execute the other man presently. It will soon be time to prepare for it. What do you say?"

"Well, what can we do else than kill those who are trying to kill us? If we point to a pit filled at the bottom with pointed pales and poisoned skewers, and tell men to beware of it, surely we are not to blame if men shut their ears to words of warning and spring in. On their own heads let the guilt lie."

"But it is very hard after all. Rashid bin Omar, this forest makes men's hearts like lead, and hunger has driven their wits out of their heads; nothing is thought of but the empty belly and crying stomach. I have heard that when mothers are driven by famine they will sometimes eat their children. Why should we wonder that the servant runs away from his master when he cannot feed him?"

"That is the truth as plain as sunshine. But if we have to die let us all die together. There are plenty of good men here who will give you their hearts whenever you bid them do it. There are others – slaves of slaves – who know nothing and care for nothing, and as they would fly with what we need to make our own lives sure, let them perish and rot. They all know that you, a Christian, are undergoing all this to save the sons of Islam who are in trouble near some great sea, beyond here; they profess Islam, and yet would leave the Christian in the bush. Let them die."

"But supposing, Rashid, we could prevent this breakup and near ruin by some other way not quite so severe as to hang them up until they are dead; what would you say?"

"I would say, sir, that all ways are good, but, without doubt, the best is that which will leave them living to repent."

"Good, then, after my coffee the muster will be sounded. Meanwhile, prepare a long rattan cable double it over that stout branch yonder. Make a good noose of a piece of that new sounding line. Get the prisoner ready, put guards over him, then when hear the trumpet tell these words in the ears of other chiefs, 'Come to me, and ask his pardon, and will give it you.' I shall look to you, and ask if you have anything to say; that will be your signal, do you like it?"

"Let it be as you say, The men will answer you."

In half-an-hour the muster signal sounded; the companies formed a square enclosing the prisoner. A long rattan cable hung suspended with the fatal noose attached to a loop; it trailed along the ground like an immense serpent. After a short address, a man advanced and placed the noose around the neck; a company was told off to hoist the man upward.

"Now, my man, have you anything to say to us before you join your brother who died yesterday?"

The man remained silent, and scarcely seemed conscious that I spoke. I turned round to the head man. "Have you anything to say before I pass the word?"

Then Rashid nudged his brother chiefs, at which they all rushed up, and threw themselves at my feet, pleading forgiveness, blaming in harsh terms the thieves and murderers, but vowing that their behaviour in future would be better if mercy was extended for this one time.

During this scene the Zanzibaris' faces were worth observing. How the eyes dilated and the lips closed, and their cheeks became pallid, as with the speed of an electric flash the same emotion moved them!

"Enough, children! take your man, his life is yours. But see to it. There is only one law in future for him who robs us of a rifle, and that is death by the cord."

Then such a manifestation of feeling occurred that I was amazed – real big tears rolled down many a face, while every eye was suffused and enlarged with his passionate emotions. Caps and turbans were tossed into the air. Rifles were lifted,, and every right arm was up as they exclaimed "Until the white cap is buried none shall leave him! Death to him who leaves Bula Matari! Show the way to the Nyanza! Lead on now – now we will follow!"

Nowhere have I witnessed such affecting excitement except in Spain – perhaps when the Republicans stormily roared their sentiments, after listening to some glorious exhortations to stand true to the new faith in Libertad, Igualdad, and Fraternidad!

The prisoner also wept, and after the noose was flung aside, knelt down and vowed to die at my feet. We shook hands and I said, "It is God's work, thank Him."

Merrily the trumpet blared once more, and at once rose every voice, "By the help of God! By the help of God!" The detail for the day sprang to their posts, received their heavy load for the day, and marched away rejoicing as to a feast. Even the officers smiled their approval. Never was there such a number of warmed hearts in the forest of the Congo as on that day.

The land and river columns reached the Lenda within an hour, and about the same time. This was apparently a deep river about a hundred yards wide. On the west side of the confluence was a small village, but its plantain groves had been long ago despoiled of fruit. Soon after the ferriage was completed the men were permitted to scour the country in search of food; some on the north bank, and others on the south bank, but long before night they all returned, having been unable to find a morsel of any kind of edible.

On the 22nd, while pursuing our way by river and by land as usual, I reflected that only on the 18th I had left fifty-six invalids under the care of an Arab; yet on observing the people at the muster, I noticed that there were about fifty already incapacitated by debility. The very stoutest and most prudent were pining under such protracted and mean diet. To press on through such wastes unpeopled by the ivory hunters appeared simply impossible, but on arriving at Umeni we had the good fortune to find sufficient for a full day's rations, and hope again filled us.

The following day, one man, called "Abdallah the humped," deserted. We on the river were troubled with several rapids, and patches of broken water, and in discharging cargo, and hauling canoes, and finally we came in view of a fall of forty feet with lengths of rapids above and below.

One would have thought that by this time the Ituri would have become an insignificant stream, but when we saw the volume of water precipitated over the third large cataract, we had to acknowledge that it was still a powerful river.

The 24th was passed by us in foraging, and cutting highway to above the rapids and disconnecting boat sections for transport. The pioneers secured a fair quantity of plantains, the three other companies nothing. The obstructions to this cataract consisted of reddish schistose rock.

On the next day we were clear of the third cataract and halted at an old Arab encampment. During this day no new supply of food was obtained.

The day following we reached another series of rapids, and after a terrible day's work unloading and reshipping several times, with the fatigues and anxiety incurred during the mounting of the dangerous rapids, we reached camp opposite Avatiko.

How useful the boat and canoes were to us may be imagined from the fact that it required us to make three round trips to carry 227 loads. Even then it occupied all the healthy men until night. The people were so reduced by hunger, that over a third could do no more than crawl. I was personally reduced to two bananas on this day from morning to night. But some of our Zanzibaris had found nothing to subsist on for two entire days, which was enough to sap the strength of the best. A foraging party of No. 1 Company crossed the river to Avatiko settlement, and found a small supply of young fruit, but they captured a woman who stated that she knew and could guide us to plantains as large as her arms.

The 27th of September was a halt. I despatched Lieutenant Stairs to explore ahead along the river, and 180 men across river to forage for food, with our female captive as guide. The former returned to report that no village had been seen, and to detail an exciting encounter he had had with elephants, from which it appeared he had a narrow escape. The Zanzibaris came back with sufficient plantains to distribute from sixty to eighty per man. If the people had followed our plan of economising the food, we should have had less suffering to record, but their appetites were usually ungovernable. The quantity now distributed impartially, ought to have served them for from six to eight days, but several sat up all night to eat, trusting in God to supply them with more on peremptory demand.

On the 30th the river and land parties met at lunch time. This day the officers and myself enjoyed a feast. Stairs had discovered, a live antelope in a pit, and I had discovered a mess of fresh fish in a native basket-net at the mouth of a small creek. In the afternoon we camped at a portion of the river bank which showed signs of its being used as a landing near a ferry. Soon after camping we were startled by three shots. These indicated the presence of Manyuema, and presently about a dozen fine-looking men stalked into the camp. They were the followers of Kilonga-Longa, the rival of Ugarrowwa in the career of devastation to which these two leaders had committed themselves.

The Manyuema informed us that Kilonga-Longa's settlement was but five days' journey, and that as the country was uninhabited it would be necessary to provide rations of plantains which could be procured across river, and that still a month's journey lay between us and the grass land. They advised us to stay at the place two days to prepare the food, to which we were very willing to agree, the discovery of some kind of provisions being imperative.

During the first day's halt, the search for food was unsuccessful, but on the second day at early dawn a strong detachment left for the north bank, under Lieutenant Stairs and Surgeon Parke. In the afternoon the foragers returned with sufficient plantains to enable us to serve out forty to each man. Some of the most enterprising men had secured more, but extreme want had rendered them somewhat unscrupulous, and they had contrived to secrete a small reserve.

On the 3rd of October, soon after leaving our camp in the morning, we entered into a pool-like formation, surrounded by hills rising from 250 to 600 feet above the river, and arriving at the end saw a crooked, ditch-like, and very turbulent stream. The scenery reminded us of a miniature Congo canon, banked as it was with lines of lofty hills. A presentiment warned us that we were about to meet more serious obstacles than any we had yet met. We progressed, however, upward about three miles, but the difficulties of advance were so numerous that we were unable to reach the caravan camp.

On the 4th we proceeded about a mile and a half, and crossed the Expedition to the north bank, as we had been told that the Manyuema settlement of Ipoto was situated on that side. The Manyuema had disappeared, and three of our deserters had accompanied them. Two men had also died of dysentery. We experienced several narrow escapes; a canoe was twice submerged, the steel boat was nearly lost, and the severe bumping she received destroyed the rate of our chronometers, which hitherto had been regular. I should have abandoned the river on this day, but the wilderness, the horrible, lonely, uninhabited wilderness, and the excessive physical prostration and weakness of the people, forbade it. We hoped and hoped that we should be able to arrive at some place where food and rest could be obtained, which appeared improbable, except at Kilonga-Longa's settlement.

The next day we arrived, at 10 A.M., after a push through terribly wild water, at a sharp bend curving eastward from N.E., distinguished by its similarity of outline on a small scale to Nsona Mambo, of the Lower Congo. Stepping on shore before we had gone far within the bend, and standing on some lava-like rock, I saw at a glance that this was the end of river navigation by canoes. The hills rose up to a bolder height, quite 600 feet; the stream was contracted to a width of twenty-five yards, and about a hundred yards above the point on which I stood, the Ihuru escaped, wild and furious, from a gorge; while the Ituri was seen descending from a height in a series of cataracts, and, both uniting at this point, and racing madly at the highest pitch and velocity, bellowed their uproar loudly amongst the embanking and sombre forest heights.

I sent messengers across the river to recall the caravan which was under the leadership of Stairs, and on their return recrossed the people to the south bank.

On the morning of the 6th of October our state and numbers were 271 in number, including white and black. Since then two had died of dysentery, one from debility, four had deserted, and one man was hanged. We had therefore 263 men left. Out of this number fifty-two had been reduced to skeletons, who first, attacked by ulcers, had been unable to forage, and to whom through their want of economising what rations had been distributed, had not sufficient to maintain them during the days that intervened of total want.

These losses in men left me 211 still able to march, and as among these there were forty men non-carriers, and as I had 227 loads, it followed that when I needed carriage, I had about eighty loads more than could be carried. Captain Nelson for the last two weeks had also suffered from a dozen small ulcers, which had gradually increased in virulence. On this day then, when the wild state of the river quite prohibited further progress by it, he and fifty-two men were utterly unfit and incapable of travel.

It was a difficult problem that now faced us. Captain Nelson was our comrade, whom to save we were bound to exert our best force. To the fifty-two black men we were equally bound by the most solemn obligations; and dark as was the prospect around us, we were not so far reduced but that we entertained a lively hope that we could save them. As the Manyuema had reported that their settlement was only five days' journey, and we had already travelled two days' march, then probably the village or station was still three days ahead of us. It was suggested by Captain Nelson that if we despatched intelligent couriers ahead, they would be enabled to reach Kilonga-Longa's settlement long before the column. As this suggestion admitted of no contradiction, and as the head men were naturally the most capable and intelligent, the chief of the head men and five others were hastened off, and instructed at once to proceed along the south bank of the river until they discovered some landing place, whence they must find means to cross the Ituri and find the settlement, and obtain an immediate store of food.

Before starting officers and men demanded to know from me whether I believed the story of Arabs being ahead. I replied that I believed most thoroughly, but that it was possible that the Manyuema had underestimated the distance to gratify or encourage us and abate our anxiety.

After informing the unfortunate cripples of our intention to proceed forward until we could find food that we might not all be lost, and send relief as quickly as it could be obtained, I consigned the fifty-two men, eighty-one loads, and ten canoes in charge of Captain Nelson – bade him be of good cheer, and hoisting our loads and boat on our shoulders, we marched away.

No more gloomy spot could have been selected for a camp than that sandy terrace, encompassed by rocks and hemmed in narrowly by those dark woods, which rose from the river's edge to the height of 600 feet, and pent in the never-ceasing uproar created by the writhing and tortured stream and the twin cataracts, that ever rivaled each other's thunder. The imagination shudders at the hapless position of those crippled men, who were doomed to remain inactive, to listen every moment to the awful sound of that irreconcilable fury of wrathful waters, and the monotonous and continuous roar of plunging rivers, to watch the leaping waves, coiling and twisting into changing columns as they ever wrestled for mastery with each other, and were dashed in white fragments of foam far apart by the ceaseless force of driven currents; to gaze at the dark, relentless woods spreading upward and around, standing perpetually fixed in dull green, mourning over past ages, past times, and past generations; then think of the night, with its palpable blackness, the dead black shadows of the wooded hills, that eternal sound of fury, that ceaseless boom of the cataracts, the indefinite forms born of nervousness and fearfulness, that misery engendered by loneliness and creeping sense of abandonment; then will be understood something of the true position of these poor men.

And what of us trudging up these wooded slopes to gain the crest of the forest uplands, to tramp on and on, whither we knew not, for how long a time we dared not think, seeking for food with the double responsibility weighing us down for these trustful, brave fellows with us, and for those, no less brave and trustful, whom we had left behind at the bottom of the horrible cañon!

As I looked at the poor men struggling wearily onward it appeared to me as though a few hours only were needed to ensure our fate. One day, perhaps two days, and then life would ebb away. How their eyes searched the wild woods for the red berries of the phrynia, and the tartish, crimson, and oblong fruit of the amoma! How they rushed for the flat beans of the forest, and gloated over their treasures of fungi! In short, nothing was rejected in this severe distress to which we were reduced except leaves and wood. We passed several abandoned clearings; and some men chopped down pieces of banana stalk, then searched for wild herbs to make potage, the bastard jack fruit, or the *fenessi,* and other huge fruit became dear objects of interest as we straggled on.

"Return we could not, nor
Continue where we were; to shift our place
Was to exchange one misery with another.
And every day that came, came to decay
A day's work in us."

On the 7th of October we began at 6.30 A.M. to commence that funereal pace through the trackless region on the crest of the forest uplands. We picked up fungi, and the *matonga* wild fruit, as we travelled, and after seven hours' march we rested for the day. At 11 A.M. we had halted for lunch at the usual hour. Each officer had economised his rations of bananas. Two were the utmost that I could spare for myself. My comrades were also as rigidly strict and close in their diet, and a cup of sugarless tea closed the repast. We were sitting conversing about our prospects, discussing the probabilities of our couriers reaching some settlement on this day, or the next, and the time that it would take them to return, and they desired to know whether in my previous African experiences I had encountered anything so grievous as this.

"No, not quite so bad as this," I replied. "We have suffered, but not to such an extremity. Those nine days on the way into Ituru were wretched. On our flight from Bumbiré we certainly suffered much hunger, and also while floating down the Congo to trace its course our condition was much to be pitied; but we had a little of something, and at least large hope. The age of miracles is past, it is said, but why should they be? Moses drew water from the rock at Horeb for the thirsty Israelites. Of water we have enough and to spare. Elijah was fed by ravens at the brook Cherith, but there is not a raven in all this forest. Christ was ministered unto by angels. I wonder if any one will minister unto us?"

Just then there was a sound as of a large bird whirring through the air. Little Randy, my fox-terrier, lifted up a foot and gazed inquiringly; we turned our heads to see, and that second the bird dropped beneath the jaws of Randy, who snapped at the prize and held it fast, in a vice as of iron.

"There, boys," I said, "truly the gods are gracious. The age of miracles is not past," and my comrades were seen gazing in delighted surprise at the bird, which was a fine fat guinea fowl. It was not long before the guinea fowl was divided, and Randy, its captor, had his lawful share, and the little doggie seemed to know that he had grown in esteem with all men, and we enjoyed our prize each with his own feelings.

On the next day, in order to relieve the boat-bearers of their hard work, Mr. Jephson was requested to connect the sections together, and two hours after starting on the march came opposite an inhabited island. The advance scouts seized a canoe and bore straight on to the island, to snatch in the same unruly manner as Orlando, meat for the hungry.

"What would you, unruly men?"

"We would have meat! Two hundred stagger in these woods and reel with faintness."

The natives did not stand for further question, but vanished kindly, and left their treasures of food. We received as our share two pounds of Indian corn and half-a-pound of beans. Altogether about twenty-five pounds of corn were discovered, which was distributed among the people.

In the afternoon I received a note from Mr. Jephson, who was behind with the boat: "For God's sake, if you can get any food at the village send us some."

We despatched answer to Jephson to hunt up the wounded elephant that I had shot, and which had taken refuge on an island near him, and in reply to his anxious letter, a small handful of corn.

On the 9th of October 100 men volunteered to go across river and explore inland from the north bank with a resolute intention not to return without food of some kind. I went up river with the boat's crew, and Stairs down river to strike inland by a little track in the hope that it might lead to some village; those who were too dispirited to go far wandered southward through the woods to search for wild fruit and forest beans. This last article was about four times the size of a large garden bean, encased in a brown leathery rind. At first we had contented ourselves with merely skinning it and boiling it, but this produced sickness of the stomach. An old woman captured on the island was seen to prepare a dish of these beans by skinning them and afterwards cleaning the inner covering, and finally scraping them as we would nutmegs. Out of this floury substance she made some patties for her captor, who shouted in ecstasies that they were good. Whereupon everybody bestirred themselves to collect the beans, which were fairly plentiful. Tempted by a "lady finger" cake of this article that was brought to me, I ventured to try it, and found it sufficiently filling, and about as palatable as a mess of acorns. Indeed, the flavour strongly reminded me of the acorn. The fungi were of several varieties, some pure and perfect mushrooms, others were of a less harmless kind; but surely the gods protected the miserable human beings condemned to live on such things. Grubs were collected, also slugs from the trees, caterpillars, and white ants – these served for meat. The *mabengu* (nux vomica) furnished the dessert, with *fenessi* or a species of bastard jack fruit.

The following day some of the foragers from across the river returned bringing nothing. They had discovered such emptiness on the north bank as we had found on the south bank; but "Inshallah!" they said, "we shall find food either to-morrow or the next day."

In the morning I had eaten my last grain of Indian corn, and my last portion of everything solid that was obtainable, and at noon the horrid pains of the stomach had to be satisfied with something. Some potato leaves brought me by Wadi Khamis, a headman, were bruised fine and cooked. They were not bad, still the stomach ached from utter depletion. Then a Zanzibari, with his face aglow with honest pride, brought me a dozen fruit of the size and colour of prize pear, which emitted a most pleasant fruity odour. He warranted them to be lovely, and declared that the men enjoyed them, but the finest had been picked out for myself and officers. He had also brought a pattie made out of the wood-bean flour which had a rich custardy look about it. With many thanks I accepted this novel repast, and I felt a grateful sense of fullness. In an hour, however, a nausea attacked me, and I was forked to seek my bed. The temples presently felt as if constricted by an iron band, the eyes blinked strangely, and a magnifying glass did not enable me to read the figures of Norie's Epitome. My servant, with the rashness of youth, had lunched bravely on what I had shared with him of the sweetly-smelling pear-like fruit, and consequently suffered more severely. Had he been in a little cockle boat on a mad channel sea he could scarcely have presented a more flabby and disordered aspect than had been caused by the forest pears.

Just at sunset the foragers of No. 1 Company, after an absence of thirty-six hours, appeared from the N. bank, bringing sufficient plantains to save the Europeans from despair and starvation; but the men received only two plantains each, equal to four ounces of solid stuff, to put into stomachs that would have required eight pounds to satisfy.

The officers Stairs, Jephson, and Parke, had been amusing themselves the entire afternoon in drawing fanciful menus, where such things figured as: –

> Filet de boeuf en Chartreuse.
> Petites bouchées aux huitres de Ostende.
> Bécassines rôties a` la Londres.

Another had shown his Anglo-Saxon proclivities for solids such as: –

> Ham and eggs and plenty of them,
> Roast beef and potatoes unlimited,
> A weighty plum pudding.

There were two of the foragers missing, but we could not wait for them. We moved from this starvation camp to one higher up, a distance of eleven miles.

A man of No. 3 Company dropped his box of ammunition into a deep affluent and lost it. Kajeli stole a box of Winchester ammunition and absconded. Salim stole a case containing Emin Pasha's new boots and two pairs of mine, and deserted. Wadi Adam vanished with Surgeon Parke's entire kit. Swadi, of No. 1 Company, left his box on the road, and departed himself to parts unknown. Bull-necked Uchungu followed suit with a box of Remington cartridges.

On the 12th of October we marched four-and-a-half miles, E. by S. The boat and crew were far below, struggling in rapids. We wished now to cross the river to try our fortune on the N. bank. We searched for a canoe, and saw one on the other side, but the river was 400 yards wide, and the current was too strong against the best swimmers in their present state of debility.

Some scouts presently discovered a canoe fastened to an island only forty yards from the south bank, which was situate a little above our halting place. Three men volunteered, among whom was Wadi Asman, of the Pioneers, a grave man, faithful, and of much experience in many African lands. Twenty dollars reward was to be the prize of success. Asman lacked the audacity of Uledi, the coxswain of the "advance," as well as his bold high spirit, but was a most prudent and valuable man.

These three men chose a small rapid for their venture, that they might obtain a footing now and then on the rocks. At dusk two of them returned to grieve us with the news that Asman had tried to swim with his Winchester on his back, and had been swept by the strong current into a whirlpool, and was drowned.

We were unfortunate in every respect; our chiefs had not yet returned, we were fearing for their fate, strong men deserted. Our rifles were rapidly decreasing in number. Our ammunition was being stolen. Feruzi, the next best man to Uledi as a sailor, soldier, carrier, good man and true, was dying from a wound inflicted on the head by a savage's knife.

The following day was also a halt. We were about to cross the river, and we were anxious for our six chiefs, one of whom was Rashid bin Omar, the "father of the people," as he was called. Equipped with only their rifles, accoutrements and sufficient ammunition, such men ought to have travelled in the week that had elapsed since our departure from Nelson's camp over a hundred miles. If they, during that distance, could not discover the Manyuema settlement, what chance had we, burdened with loads, with a caravan of hungry and despairing men, who for a week had fed on nothing but two plantains, berries, wild fruit, and fungi? Our men had begun to suffer dearly during this protracted starvation. Three had died the day before.

Towards evening Jephson appeared with the boat, and brought a supply of Indian corn, which sufficed to give twelve cupfuls to each white. It was a reprieve from death for the Europeans.

The next day, the 15th, having blazed trees around the camp, and drawn broad arrows with charcoal for the guidance of the head men when they should return, the Expedition crossed over to the north bank and camped on the upper side of a range of hills. Feruzi Ali died of his wound soon after.

Our men were in such a desperately weak state, that I had not the heart to command the boat to be disconnected for transport, as had a world's treasure been spread out before them, they could not have exhibited greater power than they were willing to give at a word. I stated the case fairly to them thus: –

"You see, my men, our condition in brief is this. We started from Yambuya 389 in number and took 237 loads with us. We had 80 extra carriers to provide for those who by the way might become weak and ailing. We left 56 men at Ugarrowwa's Settlement, and 52 with Captain Nelson. We should have 271 left, but instead of that number we have only 200 to-day, including the chiefs who are absent. Seventy-one have either died, been killed, or deserted. But there are only 150 of you fit to carry anything, and therefore we cannot carry this boat any further. I say, let us sink her here by the riverside, and let us press on to get food for ourselves and those with Captain Nelson, who are wondering what has become of us, before we all die in these woods. You are the carriers of the boat – not we. Do you speak, what shall be done unto her?"

Many suggestions were made by the officers and men, but Uledi of 'Through the Dark Continent,' always Uledi – the ever faithful Uledi, spoke straight to the purpose. "Sir, my advice is this. You go on with the caravan and search for the Manyuema, and I and my crew will work at these rapids, and pole, row, or drag her on as we can. After I have gone two days up, if I do not see signs of the Manyuema I will send men after you to keep touch with you. We cannot lose you, for a blind man could follow such a track as the caravan makes."

This suggestion was agreed by all to be the best, and it was arranged that our rule of conduct should be as Uledi sketched out.

We separated at 10 A.M., and in a short time I had my first experience among the loftier hills of the Aruwimi valley. I led the caravan northward through the trackless forest, sheering a little to the north east to gain a spur, and using animal tracks when they served us. Progress was very slow, the undergrowth was dense; berries of the phrynium and fruit of the Amomum *fenessi* and nux vomica, besides the large wood beans and fungi of all sorts, were numerous, and each man gathered a plentiful harvest. Unaccustomed to hills for years, our hearts palpitated violently as we breasted the steep-wooded slopes, and cut and slashed at the obstructing creepers, bush and plants.

Ah, it was a sad night, unutterably sad, to see so many men struggling on blindly through that endless forest, following one white man who was bound whither none knew, whom most believed did not know himself. They were in a veritable hell of hunger already! What nameless horrors awaited them further on none could conjecture? But what matter, death comes to every man soon or late! Therefore we pushed on and on, broke through the bush, trampled down the plants, wound along the crest of spurs zigzagging from north-east to north-west, and descending to a bowl-like valley by a clear stream, lunched on our corn and berries.

During our mid-day halt, one Umari having seen some magnificent and ripe *fenessi* at the top of a tree thirty feet high, essayed to climb it, but on gaining that height, a branch or his strength yielded and he tumbled headlong upon the heads of two other men who were waiting to seize the fruit. Strange to say, none of them were very seriously injured. Umari was a little lame in the hip and one of those upon whom he fell complained of a pain in the chest.

At 3.30 after a terrible struggle through a suffocating wilderness of arums, amoma, and bush, we came to a dark amphitheatral glen and at the bottom found a camp just deserted by the natives, and in such hot haste that they had thought it best not to burden themselves with their treasures. Surely some divinity provided for us always in the most stressful hours. Two bushels of Indian corn, and a bushel of beans awaited us in this camp.

My poor donkey from Zanzibar showed symptoms of surrender. Arums and amoma every day since June 28th were no fit food for a dainty Zanzibar ass, therefore to end his misery I shot him. The meat was as carefully shared as though it were the finest venison, for a wild and famished mob threatened to defy discipline. When the meat was fairly served a free fight took place over the skin, the bones were taken up and crushed, the hoofs were boiled for hours, there was nothing left of my faithful animal but the spilled blood and hair; a pack of hyænas could not have made a more thorough disposal of it. That constituent of the human being which marks him as superior to all others of the animal creation was so deadened by hunger that ore' men had become merely carnivorous bipeds, inclined to be as ferocious as any beast of prey.

On the 16th we crossed through four deep gorges one after another, through wonderful growths of phrynia. The trees frequently bore *fenessi* nearly ripe, one foot long and eight inches in diameter. Some of this fruit was equal to pineapple, it was certainly wholesome. Even the rotten fruit was not rejected. When the *fenessi* were absent, the wood-bean tree flourished and kindly sprinkled the ground with its fruit. Nature seemed to confess that the wanderers had borne enough of pain and grief. The deepest solitudes showed increasing tenderness for the weary and long-suffering. The phrynia gave us their brightest red berries, the amoma furnished us with the finest and ripest scarlet fruit, the *fenessi* were in a state of perfection, the wood-beans were larger and fatter, the streams of the wood glens were clear and cold; no enemy was in sight, nothing was to be feared but hunger, and nature did its best with her unknown treasures, shaded us with her fragrant and loving shades, and whispered to us unspeakable things sweetly and tenderly.

During the mid-day halt the men discussed our prospects. They said, with solemn shaking of their heads, "Know you that such and such a man is dead? that the other is lost! another will probably fall this afternoon! the rest will perish to-morrow!" The trumpet summoned all to their feet, to march on, and strive, and press forward to the goal.

Half-an-hour later the pioneers broke through a growth of amoma, and stepped on a road. And lo! on every tree we saw the peculiar "blaze" of the Manyuema, a discovery that was transmitted by every voice from the head to the rear of the column, and was received with jubilant cheers.

"Which way, sir?" asked the delighted pioneers. "Right turn of course," I replied, feeling far more glad than any, and fuller of longings for the settlement that was to end this terrible period, and shorten the misery of Nelson and his dark followers.

"Please God," they said, "to-morrow or the next day we shall have food," which meant that after suffering unappeasable hunger for 336 hours, they could patiently wait if it pleased God another thirty-six or sixty hours more.

We were all frightfully thin, the whites not so much reduced as our coloured men. We thought of the future and abounded with hope, though deep depression followed any inspection of the people. We regretted that our followers did not have greater faith in us. Hunger followed by despair killed many. Many freely expressed their thoughts and declared to one another plainly that we knew not whither we were marching. And they were not far wrong, for who knew what a day might bring forth in unexplored depths of woods. But as they said, it was their fate to follow us, and therefore they followed fate. They had fared badly and had suffered greatly. It is hard to walk at all when weakness sets in through emptiness; it is still worse to do so when burdened with sixty pounds weight. Over fifty were yet in fair condition; 150 were skeletons covered with ashy grey skins, jaded and worn out, with every sign of wretchedness printed deep in their eyes, in their bodies and movements. These could hardly do more than creep on and moan, and shed tears and sigh. My only dog "Randy," alas! how feeble he had become! Meat he had not tasted – except with me of the ass's meat – for weeks. Parched corn and beans were not fit for a terrier, and *fenessi* and *mabengu,* and such other acid fruit he disdained, and so he declined, until he became as gaunt as the pariah of a Moslem. Stairs had never failed me. Jephson every now and then had been fortunate in discoveries of grain treasures, and always showed an indomitable front, and Parke was ever striving, patient, cheerful and gentle. Deep, deep down to undiscovered depths our life in the forest had enabled me to penetrate human nature with all its endurance and virtues.

Along the track of the Manyuema it was easy to travel. Sometimes we came to a maze of roads; but once the general direction was found, there was no difficulty to point to the right one. It appeared to be well travelled, and it was clearer every mile that we were approaching a populous settlement. As recent tracks became more numerous, the bush seemed more broken into, with many a halt and many wayward strayings. Here and there trees had been lopped of their branches. Cording vines lay frequently on the track; pads for native carriers had often been dropped in haste. Most of the morning was expended in crossing a score of lazy, oozy fillets, which caused large breadths of slime-covered swamp. Wasps attacked the column at one crossing, and stung a man into high fever, and being in such an emaciated condition there was little chance of his recovery. After a march of seven miles south-east-wardly we halted on the afternoon of the 17th.

The night was ushered by a tempest which threatened to uproot the forest and bear it to the distant west, accompanied by floods of rain, and a severe cold temperature. Nevertheless, fear of famishing drove us to begin the march at an early hour on the following day. In about an hour and-a-half we stood on the confines of a large clearing, but the fog was so dense that we could discern nothing further than 200 feet in front. Resting awhile to debate upon our course, we heard a sonorous voice singing in a language none of us knew, and a lusty hail and an argument with what appeared to be some humour. As this was not a land where aborigines would dare to be so light-hearted and frivolous, this singing we believed could proceed from no other people than those who knew they had nothing to fear. I fired a Winchester rapidly in the air. The response by heavy-loaded muskets revealed that these were the Manyuema whom we had been so long seeking, and scarcely had their echoes ceased their reverberations than the caravan relieved its joy by long continued hurrahs.

We descended the slope of the clearing to a little valley, and from all sides of an opposite slope were seen lines of men and women issuing to welcome us with friendly hails. We looked to the right and left and saw thriving fields, Indian corn, rice, sweet potatoes, and beans. The well-known sounds of Arab greeting and hospitable tenders of friendship burst upon our ears; and our hands were soon clasped by lusty huge fellows, who seemed to enjoy life in the wilds as much as they could have enjoyed it in their own lands. These came principally from Manyuema, though their no less stout slaves, armed with percussion muskets and carbine, echoed heartily their superiors' sentiments and professions.

We were conducted up the sloping clearing through fields of luxuriant gram, by troops of men and youngsters who were irrepressibly frolicsome in their joy at the new arrivals and dawning promise of a holiday. On arrival at the village we were invited to take our seats in deep shady verandahs where we soon had to answer to hosts of questions and congratulations. As the caravan filed past us to its allotted quarters which men were appointed to show, numerous were the praises to God, uttered by them for our marvelous escapes from the terrible wilderness that stretched from their settlement of Ipoto to the Basopo Cataract, a distance of 197 miles, praises in which in our inmost hearts each one of our sorely tried caravan most heartily joined.

Chapter 10

WITH THE MANYUEMA AT IPOTO

This community of ivory hunters established at Ipoto had arrived, five months previous to our coming, from the banks of the Lualaba, from a point situated between the exits of the Lowwa and the Leopold into the great river. The journey had occupied them seven-and-a-half months, and they had seen neither grass nor open country, nor even heard of them during their wanderings. They had halted a month at Kinnena on the Lindi, and had built a station-house for their Chief Kilonga-Longa, who, when he had joined them with the main body, sent on about 200 guns and 200 slave carriers to strike further in a north-easterly direction, to discover some other prosperous settlement far in advance of him, whence they could sally out in bands to destroy, burn and enslave natives m exchange for ivory. Through continual fighting, and the careless-ness which the unbalanced mind is so apt to fall into after one or more happy successes, they had decreased in number within seven-and-a-half months into a force of about ninety guns. On reaching the Lenda River they had heard of the settlements of Ugarrowwa, and sheered off the limits of his raiding circle to obtain a centre of their own, and, crossing the Lenda, they succeeded in reaching the south bank of the Ituri, about south of their present settlement at Ipoto.

As the natives would not assist them over the river to the north bank, they cut down a big tree and with axe and fire hollowed it into a sizeable canoe which conveyed them across to the north bank to Ipoto. Since that date they had launched out on one of the most sanguinary and destructive careers to which even Tippu-Tib's or Tagamoyo's career offer but poor comparison. Towards the Lenda and Ihuru Rivers, they had leveled into black ashes every settlement, their rage for destruction had even been vented on the plaintain groves, every canoe on the rivers had been split into pieces, every island had been searched, and into the darkest recesses, whither a slight track could be traced, they had penetrated with only one dominating passion, which was to kill as many of the men and capture as many of the women and children as craft and cruelty would enable them. However far northward or eastward these people had reached, one said nine days' march, another fifteen days; or wherever they had gone they had done precisely as we had seen between the Lenda River and Ipoto, and reduced the forest land into a howling wilderness, and throughout all the immense area had left scarcely a hut standing.

What these destroyers had left of groves and plantations of plaintain and bananas, manioc, and corn-fields, the elephant, chimpanzee, and monkeys had trampled and crushed into decaying and putrid muck, and in their places had sprung up, with the swiftness of mushrooms, whole hosts of large-leafed plants native to the soil, briars, calamus and bush, which the natives had in times past suppressed with their knives, axes and hoes. With each season the bush grew more robust and taller, and a few seasons only were wanted to cover all traces of former habitation and labour.

From Ipoto to the Lenda the distance by our track is 105 miles. Assume that this is the distance eastward to which their ravages have extended, and northward and southward, and we have something like 44,000 square miles. We know what Ugarrowwa has done from the preceding pages, what he was still doing with all the vigour of his mind, and we know what the Arabs in the Stanley Falls are doing on the Lumami and what sort of devil's work Mumi Muhala, and Bwana Mohamed are perpetrating around Lake Ozo, the source of the Lulu, and, once we know where their centres are located, we may with a pair of compasses draw great circles round each, and park off areas of 40,000 and 50,000 square miles into which half-a-dozen resolute men, aided by their hundreds of bandits, have divided about three-fourths of the Great Upper Congo Forest for the sole purpose of murder, and becoming heirs to a few hundred tusks of ivory.

At the date of our arrival at Ipoto, there were the Manyuema headmen, physically fine stalwart fellows, named Ismailia,

Khamisi, and Sangarameni, who were responsible to Kilonga-Longa, their chief, for the followers and operations entrusted to their charge. At alternate periods each set out from Ipoto to his own special sub-district. Thus, to Ismailia, all roads from Ipoto to Ibwiri and east to the Ituri were given as his special charge. Khamisi's area was along the line of the Ihuru, then east to Ibwiri, to Sangarameni all the land east and west between the Ibina and Ihuru affluents of the Ituri. Altogether there were 150 fighting men, but only about 90 were armed with guns. Kilonga-Longa was still at Kinnena, and was not expected for three months yet.

The fighting men under the three leaders consisted of Bakusu, Balegga, and Basongora, youths who were trained by the Manyuema as raiders in the forest region, in the same manner as in 1876, Manyuema youths had been trained by Arabs and Waswahili of the east coast. We see in this extraordinary increase in number of raiders in the Upper Congo basin the fruits of the Arab policy of killing off the adult aborigines and preserving the children. The girls are distributed among the Arab, Swahili and Manyuema harems, the boys are trained to carry arms and are exercised in the use of them. When they are grown tall and strong enough they are rewarded with wives from the female servants of the harem, and then are admitted partners in these bloody ventures. So many parts of the profits are due to the great proprietor, such as Tippu-Tib, or Said bin Abed, a less number becomes the due of the headmen, and the remainder becomes the property of the bandits. At other times large ivories, over 35 lbs. each, become the property of the proprietor, all over 20 lbs. to 35 lbs. belong to the headmen, scraps, pieces and young ivory are permitted to be kept by the lucky finders. Hence every member of the caravan is inspired to do his best. The caravan is well armed and well manned by the proprietor, who stays at home on the Congo or Lualaba river indulging in rice and pilaf and the excesses of his harem, the headmen, inspired by greed and cupidity, become ferocious and stern, the bandits fling themselves upon a settlement without mercy to obtain the largest share of loot, of children, flocks, poultry, and ivory.

All this would be clearly beyond their power if they possessed no gunpowder. Not a mile beyond their settlements would the Arabs and their followers dare venture. It is more than likely that if gunpowder was prohibited entry into Africa there would be a general and quick migration to the sea of all Arabs from inner Africa, as the native Chiefs would be immeasurably stronger than any combination of Arabs armed with spears. What possible chance could Tippu-Tib, Abed bin Salim, Ugarrowwa and Kilonga-Longa have against the Basongora and Bakusu? How could the Arabs of Ujiji resist the Wajiji and Warundi, or how could those of Unyamyembé live among the bowmen and spearmen of Unyamwezi?

There is only one remedy for these wholesale devastations of African aborigines, and that is the solemn combination of England, Germany, France, Portugal, South and East Africa, and Congo State against the introduction of gunpowder into any part of the Continent except for the use of their own agents, soldiers, and employés, or seizing upon every tusk of ivory brought out, as there is not a single piece nowadays which has been gained lawfully. Every tusk, piece and scrap in the possession of an Arab trader has been steeped and dyed in blood. Every pound weight has cost the life of a man, woman or child, for every five pounds a hut has been burned, for every two tusks a whole village has been destroyed, every twenty tusks have been obtained at the price of a district with all its people, villages and plantations. It is simply incredible that, because ivory is required for ornaments or billiard games, the rich heart of Africa should be laid waste at this late year of the nineteenth century, signalized as it has been by so much advance, that populations, tribes and nations should be utterly destroyed. Whom after all does this bloody seizure of ivory enrich? Only a few dozens of half-castes, Arab and Negro, who, if due justice were dealt to them, should be made to sweat out the remainder of their piratical lives in the severest penal servitude.

On arriving in civilization after these terrible discoveries, I was told of a crusade that had been preached by Cardinal Lavigerie, and of a rising desire in Europe to effect by force of arms in the old crusader style and to attack the Arabs and their followers in their strongholds in Central Africa. It is just such a scheme as might have been expected from men who applauded Gordon when he set out with a white wand and six followers to rescue all the garrisons of the Soudan, a task which 14,000 of his countrymen, under one of the most skilful English generals, would have found impossible at that date. We pride ourselves upon being practical and sensible men, and yet every now and then let some enthusiast – whether Gladstone, Gordon, Lavigerie or another – speak, and a wave of Quixotism spreads over many lands. The last thing I heard in connection with this mad project is that a band of 100 Swedes, who have subscribed £25 each, are about to sail to some part of the East Coast of Africa, and proceed to Tanganika to commence ostensibly the extirpation of the Arab slave-trader, but in reality to commit suicide.

However, these matters are not the object of this chapter. We are about to have a more intimate acquaintance with the morals of the Manyuema, and to understand them better than we ever expected we should.

They had not heard a word or a whisper of our Headmen whom we had despatched as couriers to obtain relief for Nelson's party, and, as it was scarcely possible that a starving caravan would accomplish the distance between Nelson's Camp and Ipoto before six active and intelligent men, we began to fear that among the lost men we should have to number our Zanzibari chiefs. Their track was clear as far as the crossing-place of the 14th and 15th December. It was most probable that the witless men would continue up the river until they were overpowered by the savages of some unknown village. Our minds were never free from anxiety respecting Capt. Nelson and his followers. Thirteen days had already elapsed since our parting. During this period their position was not worse than ours had been. The forest was around them as it was around us. They were not loaded down as we were. The most active men could search about for food, or they could employ their canoes to ferry themselves over to the scene of the forage of the 3rd December, one day's journey by land, or an hour by water. Berries and fungi abounded on the crest of the hills above their camp as in other parts. Yet we were anxious, and one of my first duties was to try and engage a relief party to take food to Nelson's camp. I was promised that it should be arranged next day.

For ourselves we received three goats and twelve baskets of Indian corn, which, when distributed, gave six ears of corn per man. It furnished us with two good meals, and many must have felt revived and refreshed, as I did.

On the first day's halt at Ipoto we suffered considerable lassitude. Nature either furnishes a stomach and no food, or else furnishes a feast and robs us of all appetite. On the day before, and on this, we had fed sumptuously on rice and pilaf and goat stew, but now we began to suffer from many illnesses. The masticators had forgotten their office, and the digestive organs disdained the dainties, and affected to be deranged. Seriously, it was the natural result of over-eating; corn mush, grits, parched corn, beans and meat are solids requiring gastric juice, which, after being famished for so many days, was not in sufficient supply for the eager demand made for it.

The Manyuema had about 300 or 400 acres under corn, five acres under rice, and as many under beans. Sugar-cane was also grown largely. They possessed about 100 goats – all stolen from the natives. In their store-huts they had immense supplies of Indian corn drawn from some village near the Ihuru, and as yet unshucked. Their banana plantations were well stocked with fruit. Indeed the condition of every one in the settlement was prime.

It is but right to acknowledge that we were received on the first day with ostentatious kindness, but on the third day something of a strangeness sprang up between us. Their cordiality probably rose from a belief that our loads contained some desirable articles, but unfortunately the first-class beads that would have sufficed for the purchase of all their stock of corn were lost by the capsizing of a canoe near Panga Falls, and the gold braided Arab burnooses were stolen below Ugarrowwa, by deserters. Disappointed at not receiving the expected quantity of fine cloth or fine beads, they proceeded systematically to tempt our men to sell everything they possessed, shirts, caps, daoles, waist cloths, knives, belts, to which, being their personal property, we could make no objection. But the lucky owners of such articles having been seen by others less fortunate, hugely enjoying varieties of succulent food, were the means of inspiring the latter to envy and finally to theft. The unthrifty and reckless men sold their ammunition, accoutrements, bill hooks, ramrods, and finally their Remington Rifles. Thus, after escaping the terrible dangers of starvation and such injuries as the many savage tribes could inflict on us, we were in near peril of becoming slaves to the Arab slaves.

Despite entreaties for corn, we could obtain no more than two ears per man per day. I promised to pay triple price for everything received, on the arrival of the rear column, but with these people a present possession is better than a prospective one. They professed to doubt that we had cloth, and to believe that we had travelled all this distance to fight them. We represented on the other hand that all we needed were six ears of corn per day during nine days' rest. Three rifles disappeared. The Headmen denied all knowledge of them. We were compelled to reflect that, if it were true, they suspected we entertained sinister intentions towards them, that surely the safest and craftiest policy would be to purchase our arms secretly, and disarm us altogether, when they could enforce what terms they pleased on us.

On the 21st six more rifles were sold. At this rate the Expedition would be wrecked in a short time, for a body of men without arms in the heart of the great forest, with a host of men to the eastward and a large body to the westward depending upon them, were lost beyond hope of salvation. Both advance and retreat were equally cut off, and no resource would be left but absolute submission to the chief who chose to assert himself to be our master or Death. Therefore I proposed for my part to struggle strongly against such a fate, and either to provoke it instantly, or ward it off by prompt action.

A muster was made, the five men without arms were sentenced to twenty-five lashes each and to be tied up. After a considerable fume and fuss had been exhibited, a man stepped up, as one was about to undergo punishment and begged permission to speak.

"This man is innocent, sir." "I have his rifle in my hut, I seized it last night from Juma (one of the cooks), son of Forkali, as he brought it to a Manyuema to sell. It may be Juma stole it from this man. I know that all these men have pleaded that their rifles have been stolen by others, while they slept. It may be true as in this case." Meantime Juma had flown, but was found later on hiding in the corn fields. He confessed that he had stolen two, and had taken them to the informer to be disposed of for corn, or a goat, but it was solely at the instigation of the informer. It may have been true, for scarcely one of them but was quite capable of such a course, but the story was lame, and unreasonable in this case and was rejected.

Another now came up and recognized Juma as the thief who had abstracted his rifle – and having proved his statement and confession having been made – the prisoner was sentenced to immediate execution, which was accordingly carried out by hanging.

It now being proved beyond a doubt that the Manyuema were purchasing our rifles at the rate of a few ears of corn per gun, I sent for the head men, and make a formal demand for their instant restitution, otherwise they would be responsible for the consequences. They were inclined to be wrathy at first. They drove the Zanzibaris from the village out into the clearing, and there was every prospect of a fight, or as was very probable, that the Expedition was about to be wrecked. Our men, being so utterly demoralized, and utterly broken in spirit from what they had undergone, were not to be relied on, and as they were ready to sell themselves for corn – there was little chance of our winning a victory in ease of a struggle. It requires fullness of stomach to be brave. At the same time death was sure to conclude us in any event, for to remain quiescent under such circumstances tended to produce an ultimate appeal to arms. With those eleven rifles, 3000 rounds of ammunition had been sold. No option presented itself to me than to be firm in my demand for the rifles; it was reiterated, under a threat that I would proceed to take other means – and as a proof of it they had but to look at the body hanging from a tree, for if we proceeded to such extremities as putting to death one of our own men, they certainly ought to know that we should feel ourselves perfectly prepared to take vengeance on those who had really caused his death by keeping open doors to receive stolen property.

After an hour's storming in their village they brought five rifles to me, and to my astonishment pointed the sellers of them. Had it not been impolitic in the first place to drive things to the extreme, I should have declined receiving one of them back before all had been returned, and could I have been assured of the aid of fifty men I should have declared for a fight; but just at this juncture Uledi, the faithful coxswain of the *Advance,* strode into camp, bringing news that the boat was safe at the landing-place of Ipoto and of his discovery of the six missing chiefs in a starving and bewildered state four miles from the settlement. This produced a revulsion of feelings. Gratitude for the discovery of my lost men, the sight of Uledi

– the knowledge that after all, despite the perverseness of human nature, I had some faithful fellows, left me for the time speechless.

Then the tale was told to Uledi, and he undertook the business of eradicating the hostile feelings of the Manyuema, and pleaded with me to let bygones be bygones on the score that the dark days were ended, and happy days he was sure were in store for us.

"For surely, dear master," he said, "after the longest night comes day, and why not sunshine after darkness with us? I think of how many long nights and dark days we pulled through in the old times when we pierced Africa together, and now let your heart be at peace. Please God we shall forget our troubles before long."

The culprits were ordered to be bound until morning. Uledi, with his bold frank way, sailed straight into the affections of the Manyuema headmen. Presents of corn were brought to me, apologies were made and accepted. The corn was distributed among the people, and we ended this troublesome day, which had brought us all to the verge of dissolution, in much greater content than could have been hoped from its ominous commencement.

Our long wandering chiefs who were sent as heralds of our approach to Ipoto arrived on Sunday the 23rd. They surely had made but a fruitless quest, and they found us old residents of the place they had been despatched to seek. Haggard, wan and feeble from seventeen days feeding on what the uninhabited wilderness afforded, they were also greatly abashed at their failure. They had reached the Ibina River which flows from the S.E., and struck it two days above the confluence with the Ituri; they had then followed the tributary down to the junction, had found a canoe and rowed across to the right bank, where they had nearly perished, from hunger. Fortunately Uledi had discovered them in time, had informed them of the direction of Ipoto, and they had crawled as they best could to our camp.

Before night, Sangarameni, the third head man, appeared from a raid with fifteen fine ivories. He said he had penetrated a twenty days' journey, and from a high hill had viewed an open country all grass land.

Out of a supply I obtained on this day I was able to give two ears of corn per man, and to store a couple of baskets for Nelson's party. But events were not progressing smoothly, I could obtain no favourable answer to my entreaty for a relief party. One of our men had been speared to death by the Manyuema on a charge of stealing corn from the fields. One had been hanged, twenty had been flogged for stealing ammunition, another had received 200 cuts from the Manyuema for attempting to steal. If only the men could have reasoned sensibly during these days, how quickly matters could have been settled otherwise!

I had spoken and warned them with all earnestness to "endure, and cheer up," and that there were two ways of settling all this, but that I was afraid of them only, for they preferred the refuse of the Manyuema to our wages and work. The Manyuema were proving to them what they might expect of them; and with us the worst days were over; all we had to do was to march beyond the utmost reach of the Manyuema raids, when we should all become as robust as they. Bah! I might as well have addressed my appeals to the trees of the forest as unto wretches so sodden with despair.

The Manyuema had promised me three several times by this day to send eighty men as a relief party to Nelson's camp, but the arrival of Sangarameni, and misunderstandings, and other trifles, had disturbed the arrangements.

On the 24th firing was heard on the other side of the river, and, under the plea that it indicated the arrival of Kilonga-Longa, the relief caravan was again prevented from setting out.

The next day, those who had fired, arrived in camp, and proved to be the Manyuema knaves whom we had seen on the 2nd of October. Out of fifteen men they had lost one man from an arrow wound. They had wandered for twenty-four days to find the track, but having no other loads than provisions these had lasted with economy for fifteen days, but for the last nine days they had subsisted on mushrooms and wild fruit.

On this evening I succeeded in drawing a contract, and getting the three headmen to agree to the following: –

"To send thirty men to the relief of Captain Nelson, with 400 ears of corn for his party.

"To provide Captain Nelson and Surgeon Parke, and all sick men unable to work in the fields, with provisions, until our return from Lake Albert.

"The service of a guide from Ipoto to Ibwiri, for which they were to be paid one bale and a half of cloth on the arrival of the rear column."

It was drawn up in Arabic by Rashid, and in English by myself, and witnessed by three men.

For some fancy articles of personal property I succeeded in purchasing for Mr. Jephson and Capt. Nelson 250 ears of Indian corn, and for 250 pistol cartridges I bought another quantity, and for an ivory-framed mirror from a dressing-case purchased two baskets full; for three bottles of ottar of roses obtained three fowls, so that I had 1000 ears of corn for the relieving and relieved parties.

On the 26th Mr. Mounteney Jephson, forty Zanzibaris, and thirty Manyuema slaves started on their journey to Nelson's camp. I cannot do better than introduce Mr. Jephson's report on his journey.

Arab Settlement at Ipoto,
November 4th, 1887.

Dear Sir,

I left at midday on October 26th, and arrived at the river and crossed over with 30 Manyuema and 40 Zanzibaris under my charge the same afternoon and camped on landing. The next morning we started off early and reached the camp, where we had crossed the river, when we were wandering about in a starving condition in search of the Arabs, by midday the signs and arrow heads we had marked on the trees to show the chiefs we had crossed were still fresh. I reached another of our camps that night. The next day we did nearly three of our former marches. The camp where Feruzi Ali had got his death wound, and where we had spent three such miserable days of hunger and anxiety, looked very dismal as we passed through it. During the day we passed the skeletons of three of our men who had fallen down and died from sheer starvation, they were grim reminders of the misery through which we had so lately gone.

On the morning of the 29th I started off as soon as it was daylight, determining to reach Nelson that day and decide the question as to his being yet alive. Accompanied by one man only, I soon found myself far ahead of my followers. As I neared Nelson's camp a feverish anxiety to know his fate possessed me, and I pushed on through streams and creeks, by banks and bogs, over which our starving people had slowly toiled with the boat sections. All were passed by quickly to-day, and again the skeletons in the road testified to the trials through which we had passed. As I came down the hill into Nelson's camp, not a sound was heard but the groans of two dying men in a hut close by, the whole place had a deserted and woe-begone look. I came quietly round the tent and found Nelson sitting there; we clasped hands, and then, poor fellow! he turned away and sobbed, and muttered something about being very weak.

Nelson was greatly changed in appearance, being worn and haggard looking, with deep lines about his eyes and mouth. He told me his anxiety had been intense, as day after day passed and no relief came; he had at last made up his mind that something had happened to us, and that we had been compelled to abandon him. He had lived chiefly upon fruits and fungus which his two boys had brought in from day to day. Of the fifty-two men you left with him, only five remained, of whom two were in a dying state. All the rest had either deserted him or were dead.

He has himself given you an account of his losses from death and desertion. I gave him the food you sent him, which I had carefully watched on the way, and he had one of the chickens and some porridge cooked at once, it was the first nourishing food he had tasted for many days. After I had been there a couple of hours my people came in and all crowded round the tent to offer him their congratulations.

You remember Nelson's feet had been very bad for some days before we left him, he had hardly left the tent the whole time he had been here. At one time he had had ten ulcers on one foot, but he had now recovered from them in a great measure and said he thought he would be able to march slowly. On the 30th we began the return march. I gave out most of the loads to the Manyuema and Zanzibaris, but was obliged to leave thirteen boxes of ammunition and seven other loads, these I buried, and Parke will be able to fetch them later on.

Nelson did the marches better than I expected, though he was much knocked up at the end of each day. On the return march we crossed the river lower down and made our way up the right bank and struck your old road a day's march from the Arab camp. Here again we passed more skeletons, at one place there were three within 200 yards of each other.

On the fifth day, that is November 3rd, we reached the Arab camp, and Nelson's relief was accomplished. He has already picked up wonderfully in spite of the marching, but he cannot get sleep at night and is still in a nervous and highly strung state; the rest in the Arab camp will, I trust, set him up again. It is certain that in his state of health he could not have followed us in our wanderings in search of food, he must have fallen by the way.

I am &c., &c.
(Signed) A.J. Moutneney Jephson.

The following are the reports of Captain Nelson and Surgeon Parke.

Arab Village, Ipete,
6th November, 1887.

Dear Sir,

"Mr. Jephson arrived at my camp on the 29th October with

the men for the loads and with the food you sent for me. Many thanks for the food, it was badly needed. He will tell you what state he found me in and of the few men still alive.

You left me on the 6th October last; on the morning of the 9th I got up a canoe and sent Umari and thirteen of the best men I could find (they were all very bad) over the river to look for food. On the 8th Assani (No. 1 Company) came to me and said that he had returned from the column sick. Same day Uledi's brother came into camp, told me he had lost the road while looking for bananas, near the camp, where we met the Manyuema. On the 10th I found that Juma, one of Stairs' chiefs, had cleared in the night with ten men, and stolen a canoe and gone down river. On the 11th I counted the men and could only find seventeen (I had fifty-two the first day); the rest had gone away either after the column or down river. On the 14th one man died. Umari returned with very few bananas, about enough for two days; however, they were very welcome, as I had nothing but herbs and fungi to eat up to this time. On the 15th another man died, and I found that Saadi (No. 1.) with some other men had come into camp in the night and stolen the canoe (Umari had re-crossed the river in) and gone down river. On the 17th Umari went away with twenty-one men to look for food; 19th, man died; 22nd, two men died; 23rd, man died; 29th, two men died; Jephson arrived; 30th, one man died; we left camp on way here. Umari had not returned; he, however, if alive, will come on here, I feel sure, but how many men with him I cannot tell, perhaps five or six may reach here with him. With the exception of the few bananas I got from Umari I lived entirely on herbs, fungi, and a few mabengu. I had ten ulcers on my left leg and foot and so was unable to look for food myself and was kept alive entirely by my two boys and little Baruk, one of my company, and Abdalla, a man Stairs left with me. I was very weak when Jephson arrived. Now, however, I feel a little better. We arrived at the village on the 3rd November, the chief Ismail brought me the day I came a very small quantity of coarse meal and two small dried fish, about enough for one meal.

Yesterday, no food having come for two days, we sent for it, and after a good deal of trouble Ismail sent us a little meal. At present I am living on my clothes; we get hardly anything from the Chief. Today Dr. Parke and I went to the Chief, with Hamis Part as interpreter, and talked to him about food. He told us that no arrangement had been made by you for my food, and that he was feeding the Doctor and me entirely from his own generosity, and he refused to feed our boys, three in number (fewer we cannot possibly do with), as you never told him to do so.

I have the honour to be,

&c., &c.
R. H. Nelson.

Arab Camp, Ipoto,
November 6th, 1887.

My Dear Mr. Stanley,

Captain Nelson and Mr. Jephson arrived here on the 3rd inst. a few of the Zanzibaris and Manyuema men getting in with their loads the previous day. Of all those men left at Nelson's camp, only five have arrived here, the remaining live ones were away on a foraging tour with Umari, when the relief party arrived. It is very likely that some of them may find their way here; if so, I shall get Ismaili to allow them to work for their food. Nelson staggered into camp greatly changed in appearance, a complete wreck after the march, his features shrunken and pinched, and a frame reduced to half its former size. I have done the best I could for him medically, but good nourishing food is what he

*requires to restore him to his health; and I regret to say that
my experience here and the conversation which we had to-
day with Ismaili goes to show that we shall have to exist on
scanty fare. Since you left, I have had some flour and corn
from the chiefs, but this was generally after sending for it
several times. By a lucky accident I got a goat, most of which
I distributed amongst the sick men here, for I am informed by
Ismaili, through H. Part, that only those who work in the
field get food, and there are some here who certainly cannot
do so; therefore they are trusting to the generosity of the
other men, who get five heads of corn each day they work.
Both Nelson and myself have much trouble in getting food
from Ismaili for ourselves, and he has refused to feed our
boys, who are absolutely necessary to draw water, cook,
&c., &c., although I have reduced mine to one.*

*Nelson and myself went and saw him to day (Hamis Part,
interpreter), and Ismaili stated that you had told the chiefs
that a big Mzungu was to come (Nelson), and he would make
his own arrangements about food and that I was here living
on his (Ismaili's) generosity, as no arrangements had been
made for me. I reminded him of the conversation you had
with him in your tent the evening you called me down and
gave me your gold watch, and I said that you had told me
that you had made a written arrangement with the chiefs that
both Nelson and myself should be provisioned. We both told
him that we did not want goats and fowls, but simply what he
can give us. Not having seen any agreement, I could not
argue further, but asked to see the document, so that we
might convince him; this he said he could not do, as Hamis,
the Chief, had it, and he was away, and would not return for
two months. He however sent us up some corn shortly afterwards. This is a very unhappy state of affairs for us who
shall have to remain here for so long a time. Nelson has sold
much of his clothes, and out of my scanty supply (my bag
having been lost on the march), I have been obliged to make
a further sale so as to provide ourselves with sufficient food.*

We shall get along here as best we can, and sacrifice much to keep on friendly terms with the Arabs, as it is of such essential importance. I sincerely hope you will have every success in attaining the object of the Expedition, and that we shall all have an opportunity of meeting soon and congratulating Emin Pasha on his relief.

With best wishes, &c.,

(Signed) T. H. Parke,
A.M.D.

Arab Village, Ipoto,
10th November, 1887.

Dear Sir,

I am sorry to have to tell you that several attempts have been made to rob the hut, and last night unfortunately they managed to get a box of ammunition out of Parke's tent while we were having dinner; also one attempt to burn the hut, which happily I frustrated, owing to my not being able to sleep well. We have spoken to the Chief Ismail about the thieving: he says it is done by Zanzibaris and not by his people; but if there were no sale for the cartridges they would not be stolen. It is of course most unfortunate. Since Jephson left, the enormous quantity of forty small heads of Indian corn has been given to us by Ismail; this is of course quite absurd; as we cannot live on it, we get herbs, with which we supplement our scanty fare.

Uledi returned this afternoon and goes on to-morrow, and by him I send this letter.

With kindest regards to you, Sir, Stairs and Jephson.

I have the honour to be, &c., &c.,

(Signed) R. H. Nelson.

P.S. – Just as I finished this letter the Chief sent us a little meal, which evidently was done so that Uledi who was waiting for the letter could tell you that we were getting plenty (!!) of food.

H.M. Stanley, Esq.
Commanding E. P. R. Expedition.

On the evening of the 26th Ismaili entered my hut, and declared that he had become so attached to me that he would dearly love to go through the process of blood-brotherhood with me. As I was about to entrust Captain Nelson and Surgeon Parke and about thirty sick men to the charge of himself and brother chiefs, I readily consented, though it was somewhat *infra dig.* to make brotherhood with a slave, but as he was powerful in that bloody gang of bandits, I pocketed my dignity and underwent the ceremony. I then selected a five-guinea rug, silk handkerchiefs, a couple of yards of crimson broadcloth, and a few other costly trifles. Finally I made another written agreement for guides to accompany me to the distance of fifteen camps, which he said was the limit of his territory, and good treatment of my officers, and handed to him a gold watch and chain, value £49 in London, as pledge of this agreement, in presence of Surgeon Parke.

The next day after leaving Surgeon Parke to attend to his friend Nelson and twenty-nine men, we left Ipoto with our reduced force to strive once more with the hunger of the wilderness.

Chapter 11

THROUGH THE FOREST
TO MAZAMBONI'S PEAK

We marched for two hours to Yumbu, and in four and a quarter hours on the following day to Busindi.

We were now in the country of the Balessé. The architecture was peculiar. Its peculiarity consisted in a long street flanked by a long low wooden building, or rather planked building, on either side, 200, 300, or 400 feet long. At first sight one of these villages appeared like a long gable-roofed structure sawn in exact half along the ridge of the roof, and as if each half house had been removed backward for a distance of 20 or 30 feet, and then along the inner sides been boarded up, and pierced with low doors, to obtain entrance into independent apartments. The light wood of the Rubi-acæ affords good material for this kind of house. A sizeable tree, 1 foot 18 inches, or 2 feet in diameter, is felled, and the log is cut into short pieces from four to six feet in length; the pieces are easily split by hard wedges, and with their small neat adzes they contrive to shape the plank smooth, tolerably even, and square. They are generally an inch or an inch and a quarter thick. For what is called the ceiling or inner boarding, the boards are thinner and narrower. When a sufficient number of boards and planks are ready, the inner ceiling is lashed to the uprights, frequently in as neat a fashion as a carpenter's apprentice might do it with saw, nails and hammer; on the outer side of the uprights are lashed the thicker planks, or broad slabs, the hollow between the inner and outer frame is then stuffed with the phrynia, or banana leaves. The wall facing the street may be 9 feet high, the back wall facing the forest or clearing is 4 or 4½ feet high, the width of the house varies from 7 to 10 feet. Alto-

gether it is a comfortable and snug mode of building, rather dangerous in ease of fire, but very defensible, with trifling labour.

Another peculiarity of the Balessé is the condition of their
clearings, and some of these are very extensive, quite a mile and a
half in diameter, and the whole strewn with the relics, debris, and
timber of the primeval forest. Indeed I cannot compare a Balessé
clearing to anything better than a mighty abattis surrounding the
principal village, and over this abattis the traveller has to find his
way. As one steps out of the shadow of the forest, the path is at
first, may be, along the trunk of a great tree for 100 feet, it then
turns at right angles along a great branch a few feet; he takes a few
paces on the soil, then finds himself in front of a massive prostrate
tree-stem 3 feet in diameter or so; he climbs over that, and presently finds himself facing the outspreading limbs of another giant,
amongst which he must creep, and twist, and crawl to get footing
on a branch, then from the branch to the trunk, he takes a half turn
to the right, walks along the tree from which, increasing in thickness, he must soon climb on top of another that has fallen across
and atop of it, when after taking a half-turn to the left, he must follow, ascending it until he is 20 feet above the ground, When he has
got among the branches at this dizzy height, he needs judgment,
and to be proof against nervousness. After tender, delicate balancing, he places his foot on a branch – at last descends cautiously
along the steep slope until he is 6 feet from the ground from which
he must jump on to another tapering branch, and follow that to
another height of 20 feet, then along the monster tree, then down to
the ground; and so on for hours, the hot, burning sun, and the close,
steamy atmosphere of the clearing forcing the perspiration in
streams from his body. I have narrowly escaped death three times
during these frightful gymnastic exercises. One man died where he
fell. Several men were frightfully bruised. Yet it is not so dangerous with the naked feet, but with boots in the early morning, before
the dew is dried, or after a rain, or when the advance-guard has
smeared the timber with a greasy clay, I have had six falls in an
hour. The village stands in the centre. We have often congratulated
ourselves on coming to a clearing at the near approach to camping-
time, but it has frequently occupied us one hour and a half to reach
the village. It is a most curious sight to see a caravan laden with

heavy burdens walking over this wreck of a forest, and timbered clearing. Streams, swamps, watercourses, ditches are often twenty to twenty-five feet below a tapering slippery tree, which crosses them bridge-like. Some men are falling, some are tottering, one or two have already fallen, some are twenty feet above the ground, others are on the ground creeping under logs. Many are wandering

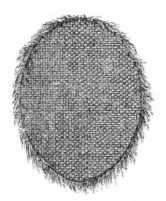 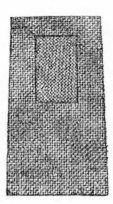

SHIELDS OF THE BALESSÉ.

among a maze of branches, thirty or more may be standing on one delicate and straight shaft, a few may be posted like sentries on a branch, perplexed which way to move. All this, however, is made much harder, and more dangerous, when, from a hundred points, the deadly arrows are flying from concealed natives, which, thank Heaven, were not common. We have been too cautious for that kind of work to happen often, though we have seldom been able to leave one of these awful clearings without having some man's foot skewered, or some one lamed.

On the 29th we marched to Bukiri or Myyulus, a distance of nine miles in six hours.

A few natives having been tormented and persecuted to submission to the Manyuema, greeted us with cries of "Bodo! Bodo! Ulenda! Ulenda!"; greetings which they accompanied with a flinging motion of the hand, as though they jerked "Away! away!"

The chief was styled Mwam. They wore much polished iron-work, rings, bells, and anklets, and appeared to be partial to many leglets made of calamus fibre, and armlets of the same material, after the manner of Karagwé and Uhha. They cultivate maize, beans, plantains, and bananas, tobacco, sweet potatoes, yams, brinjalls, melons, gourds. Their goats are fine, and of good size. Fowls are plentiful, but fresh eggs are rare.

Among some of these villages there is generally a dome hut of ample size, after the manner of Unyoro, with double porches.

The following day we halted, during which the Manyuema guides took particular care to show our people that they should have no doubt of their contempt for them. They would not allow them to trade with the natives for fear some desirable article would be lost to themselves, they also vociferated at them loudly if they were seen proceeding to the clearing to cut plantains. As I told them, they did not advance in their favour in the least by abandoning the whites, and turning a deaf ear to our adjurations to be manly and faithful. A word, or even a defiant look, was visited with a sharp cut on the naked body with a rattan from slave boys of the six Manyuema guides with us. What awful oaths of vengeance were uttered for all these indignities they suffered!

On the 31st we came across the first village of Dwarfs, and, during the day, across several empty settlements belonging to them. We marched nine miles in five and a quarter hours, and camped in a dwarfs village in the woods.

Stealing continued steadily. On examining the pouches, there was one cartridge out of three pouches The cartridges were lost, of course! Hilallah, a boy of sixteen, deserted back to Ipoto with my cartridge pouch, and thirty cartridges in it. A man who carried my satchel ran away with seventy-five Winchester cartridges.

The next day we entered the extensive clearing and large settlement of Mambungu's or Nebassé.

Khamis, the chief of the guides, left Ipoto on the 31st, and arrived at this place with seven men, according to agreement with Ismaili, my Manyuema brother.

The track which we followed has enabled us to increase our rate of progress per hour. Along the river bank, by dint of continued work, and devoting seven, eight, nine hours – sometimes ten hours – we could travel from 3 to 7 miles. We were now enabled to make 1 1/2 to 1 3/4, and even 2 miles per hour; but the pace was still retarded by roots, stumps, climbers, llianes, convolvuli, skewers, and a multitude of streams, and green-scummed sinks. We could rarely proceed a clear hundred yards without being ordered to halt by the pioneers.

Each day towards evening the clouds gathered, the thunder reverberated with awful sounds through the echoing forest; lightning darted hither and thither, daily severing some tree-top, or splitting a mighty patriarch from crown to base, or blasting some stately and kingly tree; and the rain fell with a drowning plenty which chilled and depressed us greatly in our poor blooded and anæmic state. But during the march, Providence was gracious; the sun shone, and streamed in million beams of soft light through the woods, which brightened our feelings, and caused the aisles and corridors of the woods to be of Divine beauty, converted the graceful thin tree-shafts into marbly-grey pillars, and the dew and raindrops into sparkling brilliants; cheered the invisible birds to pour out, with spirit, their varied repertory of songs; inspired parrot flocks to vent gleeful screams and whistlings; roused hosts of monkeys to exert their wildest antics; while now and then some deep, bass roar in far-away recesses indicated a family of *soko* or chimpanzees enjoying some savage sport.

The road from Mambungu's, eastward, was full of torments, fears, and anxieties. Never were such a series of clearings as those around Mambungu, and the neighbouring settlement of Njalis. The trees were of the largest size, and timber enough had been eat to build a navy; and these lay, in all imaginable confusion, tree upon tree, log above log, branches rising in hills above hills; and amongst all this wild ruin of woods grew in profusion upon profusion bananas, plantains, vines, parasites; ivy-like plants, palms, calamus, convolvuli, etc., through which the poor column had to burrow, struggle, and sweat, while creeping, crawling, and climbing, in, through, and over obstacles and entanglements that baffle description.

On the 4th November we were 13 3/4 miles from Mambungu's in the settlement of Ndugubisha, having passed, in the interval, through five deserted forest villages of pigmies. On this day I came near smiling – for I fancied I observed the dawn of happier days foretold by Uledi. Each member of the caravan received one ear of corn, and 15 plantains as rations.

Fifteen plantains and one ear of corn make a royal ration compared to two ears of corn, or a handful of berries, or a dozen fungus. It was not calculated, however, to make men too cheerful, though our people were naturally light-hearted and gay.

"But never mind, my boys," I said, as I doled the spare diet to the hungry creatures; "the morning is breaking; a week more, and then you shall see the end of your troubles."

Verbal reply was not given to me; only a wan smile lightened the famine-sharpened features. Our officers had borne these privations with the spirit ascribed by Caesar to Antony, and as well as though they were to the manner born. They fed on the flat wood beans of the forest, on the acid wild fruit and strange fungus, with the smiling content of Sybarites at a feast. Yet one of them paid £1,000 for this poor privilege, and came near being thought too dainty for rough African life. They had been a living example to our dark followers, many of whom had probably been encouraged to strive for existence by the bright, hopeful looks our officers wore under our many unhappy afflictions.

On the following day we crossed the watershed between the Ihuru and Ituri rivers, and we now plunged into cool streams flowing to leftward, or towards the Ihuru. Hills rose to the right and left in wooded cones and ridgy mounts, and after a march of nine and three-quarter miles, we halted for the night at West Indekaru, at the base of a hill whose top rose 600 feet above the village. Another short march brought us to a village perched half-way up a tall mount, which may be designated as East Indekaru, and by aneroid we were 4,097 feet above the ocean. From this village we enjoyed a first view of our surroundings. Instead of crawling like mighty bipeds in the twilight, 30 fathoms below the level of the white light of the day, compelled to recognize our littleness, by comparison with the giant columns and tall pillar-like shafts that rose by millions around us, we now stood on the crest of a cleared mount, to look upon the leafy world below us. One almost felt as if walking over the rolling plain of leafage was possible, so compact and unbroken was the expanse, extending to a lovely pale blueness as the eyesight followed it to the, furthest limits of distinctness – away, far away to an unknown distance the forest tops spread round about a variegated green of plushy texture, broad red patches of tree flowering, and rich russety circles of leaves, not unfrequent. How one envied the smooth, easy flight of the kites and white-collared eagles, sailing gracefully without let or hindrance through the calm atmosphere! Ah! that we had the wings of kites, that we might fly and be at rest from these incorrigibly wicked Manyuema! Whose wish was that? Indeed, I think we all of us shared it, more or less.

On the 7th, while we halted on the mount, the Manyuema monopolizing the village, and our men in the bush, unworthy to be near their nobility, there was a little storm between Saat Tato (Three o'clock), the hunter, and Khamis, the chief of the Manyuema guides. It threatened, from the sound of words, to explode hurtfully at one time. Khamis slapped him in the face. Both were tall men, but Saat Tato was two inches taller, a good soldier, who had seen service in Madagascar and with Sultan Barghash as a sergeant, but who, from his habits of getting drunk by the third hour of each day, was nicknamed "Three o'clock," and dismissed, he was an excellent man, faithful, strong, obedient, and an unerring shot. Given the benefits of twenty-five pounds of food, Saat Tato, at a hint, would have smilingly taken hold of Khamis, and snapped his vertebrae across his knee with the ease that he would have broken a spear staff. I observed Saat Taro closely, for it must be remembered that it had become fully impressed on my mind that my men were quite too broken-spirited. Saat Taro looked at him a second severely; then, lifting his forefinger, said to Khamis, "It is well, but I should like to see you repeat that blow a little time hence, after I have a little food in me, and filled this stomach of mine. Strike me again, do; I can bear it."

Advancing, and touching Khamis on the shoulder, I said, "Khamis, do not do that again. I do not allow even my officers to strike my men like that."

The ill-humour was increasing, and, little as the Manyuema imagined, they were assisting me to restore the spirit of the Zanzibaris by their cruelty. There were signs that the Christians would prevail after all. The mutual affection expressed between the Moslem coreligionists at the altar of which our men were ready to sacrifice our lives and liberties and their own freedom, had been cooled by the cruelty, perverseness, and niggardliness of the Manyuema. All we had to do was to watch it, bear patiently, and be ready.

To our great comfort Khamis confessed that West Indekaru was the utmost limit of his master Ismaili's territory.

We, however, were not to part from him until we reached Ibwiri.

We marched eleven miles on the 8th of November through a much more open forest, and we could see further into the interior. The road was better, so much so that our rate of marching increased to two miles per hour. The gritty and loamy soil had absorbed the rain, and walking became pleasant. The llianes were not so riotously abundant, only a strong creeper now and then requiring severance. At several places there were granite outcroppings of a colossal size, which were a novelty and added a kind of romantic and picturesque interest to the woods, darkly suggestive of gitanos, bandits, or pigmies.

A march of nine and a half miles on the 9th of November took us to a Pigmies' camp. Until noon a mist had hung over the land. Towards the latter part of the tramp we passed through several lately deserted villages of the dwarfs, and across eight streams. Khamis, the guide, and his followers, and about half-a-dozen of the pioneers proceeded to Ibwiri, which was only one and a half mile distant, and on the next day we joined them. This was one of the richest and finest clearings we had seen since leaving Yambuya, though had the Expedition been despatched eight months earlier, we should have found scores in the same prosperous condition. Here was a clearing three miles in diameter abounding in native produce, and hitherto unvisited by the Manyuema. Almost every plantain stalk bore an enormous branch of fruit, with from fifty to one hundred and forty plantains attached. Some specimens of this fruit were twenty-two inches long, two and a half inches in diameter, and nearly eight inches round, large enough to furnish Saat Tato the hunter, with his long desired full meal. There was an odour of ripe fruit pervading the air, and as we climbed over the logs and felt our way gingerly along the prostrate timber, I was often asked by the delighted people to note the bunches of mellow fruit hanging temptingly before their eyes.

Before reaching the village Murabo, a Zanzibari headman, whispered to me that there were five-villages in Ibwiri, and that each hut in every village was more than a fourth full of Indian corn, but that Khamis and his Manyuema had been storing corn in their own huts, which, according to right of preemption, they had reserved for themselves.

On entering the street of the village, Khamis met me with the usual complaints about the wickedness of the "vile Zanzibaris." Looking down on the ground I saw many a trail of corn which went to corroborate Murabo's story, and as Khamis proposed that the Expedition should occupy the western half of the village, and he and his fifteen Manyuema would occupy the eastern half, I ventured to demur to the proposition on the ground that as we had departed out of his master's territory we claimed all the land to the eastward, and would in future dispense with any suggestion as to what we should do, and that furthermore not a grain of corn, nor plantain, banana, or any other native product in the land would leave the country without my permission. He was told, no people on earth could have borne so uncomplainingly such shames, affronts, and insults as had been put upon the Zanzibaris, and that in future they should be permitted to resent all such injuries as they best knew how. Khamis assented submissively to all this.

The first thing after storing goods, and distributing the men to their quarters, was to give fifty ears of corn per man, and to arrange with the natives as to our future conduct towards one another.

Within an hour it was agreed that the western half of the Ibwiri clearing should be granted to us for foraging; that the eastern half, from a certain stream, should be the reserve of the natives. Khamis, the Manyuema, was also induced to enter into the pact. In return for a packet of brass rods, Boryo, the principal chief of the Balessé of the district, presented us with five fowls and a goat.

This was a great day. Since August 31st not one follower of the Expedition had enjoyed a full meal, but now bananas, plantains ripe and green, potatoes, herbs, yams, beans, sugar-cane, corn, melons in such quantities were given them that were they so many elephants they could not have exhausted the stock provided for them in less than ten days. They could gratify to the full the appetite so long stinted and starved.

As we were compelled to wait for Mr. Jephson and some sixty Zanzibaris – forty of the relief party, boat's crew, and convalescents from Ipoto – the good effect of this abundance would be visible in a few days. It was also one of those settlements we had been anxiously searching for as a recuperating station. On this date the men were hideous to look upon, because of their gaunt nakedness. They were naked, for they had stripped themselves to obtain food from the slaves of the Manyuema at Ugarrowwa's and Ipoto; of flesh they had none, for they had been reduced to bones by seventy-three days of famine and thirteen days of absolute want; of strength they had but little, and they were ill-favoured in every respect; their native colour of oiled bronze had become a mixture of grimy black and wood ashes; their rolling eyes betrayed signs of disease, impure blood, and indurated livers; that beautiful contour of body, and graceful and delicate outlines of muscles – alas, alas! – were all gone. They more befitted a charnel-house than a camp of men bound to continually wear fighting accoutrements.

Khamis, the Manyuema guide, offered the next morning to proceed east to search out the road from Ibwiri, for, as he informed me, Boryo, the chief, had told him of a grass-land being not many days off. He thought that with a few of Boryo's natives, and thirty of our riflemen, he could discover something of interest. Calling Boryo to me, he confirmed, as well as we could understand him, that from a place called Mandé, which he said was only two days' good marching – say forty miles – the grassland could be seen; that herds of cattle came in such numbers to the Ituri river to drink that the river "swelled up." All this chimed with my eager desire to know how far we were from the open country, and as Boryo said he was willing to furnish guides, I called for volunteers. Twenty-eight men came forward, to my surprise, as willing and as eager for new adventures as though they had been reveling in plenty for the last few months. Khamis and his party departed shortly after.

Despite strict prohibition to touch anything on the native reservation of Ibwiri, one of our raiders paid it a visit, and captured nineteen fowls, two of which he had already despatched, the remaining seventeen he had decapitated, but our detectives pounced upon him and his stock, as he and his chum were debating what they should do with the feathers. The flesh and bones did not promise to be any trouble to them. Close by them two men had despatched an entire goat, excepting the head! These facts serve to illustrate the boundless capacity of Zanzibari stomachs.

The natives of Ibwiri had behaved most handsomely, and personally I felt a sense of shame at the ingratitude of my followers. The chief and his family were living with us, and exchanged their greetings of "Bodo, Bodo, ulenda, ulenda," half-a-dozen times a day. Yet our men had undergone such extremes of wretchedness during the last two and a half months that we might have well anticipated some excesses would be committed upon the first opportunity. No other body of men in the wide world that I am acquainted with could have borne such a period of hunger so meekly, so resignedly. Not a grain or a bit of human food discoverable anywhere, their comrades dying at every camp, or falling dead along the track, others less patient plunging into the depths of the wilderness maddened by hunger, leaving them to fare as they might under the burdens of war-munitions, and baggage. Goaded by the protracted hunger, and fierce despair, and loss of trust in their officers, they might have seized their Remingtons and, by one volley, have slain their white chiefs, and fed on them, and shaken off power, and, in a moment, the clutch of authority which, so far as they knew, was only dragging them down to certain doom.

While I pitied the natives who had lost their property when they least deserved it, I could not remove from my memory that extended fast in the area of desolation and forest wilderness stretching between the Basopo Rapids and Ibwiri, on the edge of which we were even now located, or their patient obedience thefts and small practices notwithstanding, their unfaltering fidelity, their kindness to us while we were starving, in bestowing upon us the choicest and finest of the wild fruit they had discovered, and their altogether courageous bearing and noble hopefulness during the terrible days of adversity; all these virtues must needs extenuate their offences, and it was best to await fullness and reflection to assist us in reclaiming them into tractableness and good order. Every mile or two almost of that hungry forest solitude between the Ihuru and Ituri confluence and Ipoto had been marked by the dead bodies of their comrades; there they lay fast mildewing and rotting in the silent gloom, and, but for the fidelity of the survivors, none of those capable of giving intelligent testimony of the stern trials endured during September, October, and the half of November, would have lived to relate the sad and sorrowful details.

The more experience and insight I obtain into human nature, the more convinced do I become that the greater portion of a man is purely animal. Fully and regularly fed, he is a being capable of being coaxed or coerced to exertion of any kind, love and fear sway him easily, he is not averse to labour however severe; but when starved it is well to keep in mind the motto "Cave Canem," for a starving lion over a raw morsel of beef is not so ferocious or so ready to take offence. Rigid discipline, daily burdens, and endless marching into regions of which they were perfectly ignorant, never seemed to gall our men much when their stomachs were pampered, and abundant provender for their digestive organs were provided; but even hanging unto death was only a temporary damper to their inclination to excessive mischief when pinched with hunger. The aborigines also of Ibwiri surrounded by plenty are mild and meek enough through pure sleekness, but the dwarfish nomads of the forest are, I am told, as fierce as beasts of prey, and fight till their quivers are empty.

I received word on the 12th that Khamis, the Manyuema who was supposed to have gone for my gratification to explore the country ahead, and to make friends with the aid of the natives, had, owing to perverseness, been unable to accomplish his mission; that he was greatly disappointed, and that he had been attacked by the natives of East Ibwiri and had lost two men. I sent word to him to return.

The fleas of Ibwiri became so intolerable that in order to obtain rest, I had to set my tent in the open street.

On the 13th of November, while taking an inspection of the village camp, and examining into the condition of the men, I was amazed at the busy scene of eating I beheld. Almost every man was engaged in pounding corn, reducing dried bananas into flour, or grinding mouthfuls of food with their fine teeth, making amends for the compulsory fast of September, October and November.

Khamis returned on the 14th with a large flock of goats obtained from somewhere. He was gracious enough to allow us sixteen head. This inclined us to suspect that the real object of his design was not to explore but to extend the conquests of his master, Ismaili, farther east through our assistance, and to reduce the natives of Ibwiri into the same state of poverty as the neighbourhood of Ipoto, for instance. But though Khamis possessed force sufficient to have accomplished even this last, the silly fellow's greed caused him to behave with such reckless disregard of the poisoned shafts of the natives that he lost three of his men. It seems that as soon as a flock of goats was sighted, Khamis forgot his design to explore, urged his Manyuema to their capture, and retained our people by him. Our men by these tactics returned uninjured without having been engaged in this disgraceful action. Then, as Khamis was returning to our village, mourning the loss of three of his most active comrades, he suddenly met Boryo, the Chief of East Ibwiri, and without a word made him a prisoner. Before reporting to me, Khamis, on arrival, ordered his men to strangle the chief in revenge for the death of his men. Happening to hear of it, I sent a guard to take him by force out of Khamis' hands, and placed him in a hut out of harm's way, and bade Boryo rest quiet until Khamis had departed.

We luxuriated during our days of rest. There had been discovered such an abundance of food that we might safely have rested six months without fear of starving. We enjoyed ripe plantains made into puddings with goats' milk; fritters, patties and bread, sweet potatoes, manioc, yams, herbs, fowls and goat meat without stint. On the evening of this day the *menu* for dinner was –

Kid soup.
Roast leg of kid, and baked sweet potatoes.
Boiled sweet manioc.
Fried bananas.
Sweet cake of ripe plantain.
Plantain fritters.
Goats' milk.

Already I noted a change in the appearance of ourselves and followers. There was certainly more noise, and once or twice I heard an attempt at singing, but as there was a well recognised flaw in the voice, it was postponed to another day.

At 3 P.M. of the 16th Mr. Jephson appeared, having performed his mission of relief most brilliantly. As will be seen by Mr. Jephson's letter descriptive of his success, he had been able to proceed to the relief of Captain Nelson, and to return with him to Ipoto within seven days, after a journey of about a hundred miles. Judging from Captain Nelson's letter, he seemed to have been delivered out of his terrible position to fall into a similar desperate strait in the midst of the plenty of Ipoto.

The next day Khamis and his Manyuema returned homeward without taking leave. I despatched a letter to the officers at Ipoto, sent Khamis' ivory and a present of cloth with it to Indekaru, whence the Manyuema might be able to obtain assistance from their own natives. I was never so dissatisfied with myself as when I was compelled to treat these men thus so kindly, and to allow them to depart without even the small satisfaction of expressing my private opinion of Manyuema in general and of the gang at Ipoto in particular. At all points I was worsted; they compelled a generous treatment from me, and finally trapped me into the obligation of being the carrier of their stolen ivory.

Yet I felt grateful to them somewhat that they had not taken greater advantage of my position. With Captain Nelson and Dr. Parke and about thirty men in their power, they might have compelled a thousand concessions from me, which happily they did not. I hoped that after a season of forbearance divine justice would see fit to place me in more independent circumstances. When the Doctor and Nelson and their sick men were recovered and in my camp, and the 116 loads and boat left at Ipoto been conveyed away, then, and not till then, would I be able to east up accounts, and demand a peremptory and final settlement. The charges were written plainly and fairly, as a memorandum.

Messrs. Kilonga Longa and Co., Ipoto.
To Mr. Stanley, officers and men of the E.P.R. Expedition

November 17th, 1887.
To having caused the starvation to death between the Lenda River and Ibwiri of 67 men: because we had crossed that river with 271 men – and in camp with, those due that shortly there were only 175, and 28 inclusive of Captain Nelson and Dr. Parke – therefore loss of men} 67

To 27 men at Ipoto too feeble to travel, many of whom will not recover.

To spearing to death Mufta Mazinga.................. 1

To flogging one man to death............................ 1

To flogging Ami, a Zanzibari, 200 lashes.

To attempting to starve Captain Nelson and Dr. Parke.

To instigating robbery of two boxes of ammunition.

To receiving thirty stolen Remington rifles.

To various oppressions of Zanzibaris.

To compelling Sarboko to work as their slave.

To various insults to Captain Nelson and Dr. Parke.

To devastating 44,000 square miles of territory.

To butchery of several thousands of natives.

To enslaving several hundreds of women and children.

To theft of 200 tusks of ivory between May, 1887, and October, 1887.

To many murders, raids, crimes, devastations past, present and prospective.

To deaths of Zanzibaris..................................... 69

To mischiefs incalculable!

During the afternoon of the 17th we experienced once again the evils attending our connection with the Manyuema. All Ibwiri and neighbouring districts were in arms against us. The first declaration of their hostilities took place when a man named Simba proceeded to the stream close to the camp to draw water, and received an arrow, in the abdomen. Realizing from our anxious faces the fatal nature of the wound, he cried out his "Buryani brothers!" and soon after, being taken into his hut, loaded a Remington rifle near him, and made a ghastly wreck of features that were once jovial, and not uncomely.

The reflections of the Zanzibaris on the suicide were curious, and best expressed by Sali, the tent boy.

"Think of it, Simba! a poor devil owning nothing in the world, without anything or anybody dear to him, neither name, place, property, or honour, to commit suicide! Were he a rich Arab now, a merchant Hindu, a captain of soldiers, a governor of a district, or a white man who had suffered misfortune, or had been the victim of dishonour or shame, yea, I could understand the spirit of the suicide; but this Simba, who was no better than a slave, an outcast of Unyanyembé, without friends on the face of the earth, save the few poor things in his own mess in this camp, to go and kill himself like a man of wealth! Faugh! pitch him into the wilderness, and let him rot! What right has he to the honour of a shroud and a burial?" This was the sentiment of the men who were once his comrades – though not so forcibly expressed as was done by little Sali in his fierce indignation at the man's presumption.

Early on this morning Lieutenant Stairs and thirty-six rifles were despatched to make a reconnaissance eastward under the guidance of Boryo, and a young Manyuema volunteer, as we had yet a few days to wait for the arrival of several convalescents who, wearied of the cruelties practised at Ipoto on them, preferred death on the road to the horrible servitude of the Manyuema slaves.

On the 19th Uledi, the coxswain of the *Advance* with his boat's crew, arrived, reporting that there were fifteen convalescents on the way. By night they were in the camp.

On the 21st the reconnoitering party under Lieutenant Stairs returned, Boryo still accompanying them; nothing new about the grass land had been obtained, but they reported a tolerably good path leading steadily east ward, which was as comforting news as we could expect. On the 23rd, the last day of our stay at Ibwiri, there was a muster and reorganization: –

No. 1 company, Jephson	80 men
No. 2 company, Stairs	76 men
Soudanese	5
Cooks	3
Boys	6
Europeans	4
Manyuema guide	1
175 men	

Inclusive of Captain Nelson and Dr. Parke there were twenty-eight at Ipoto; we had left to recuperate at Ugarrowwa's fifty-six. Some from Nelson's starvation camp under Umari, the headman, probably ten, might return; so that we reckoned the number of the advance column to be 268 still living out of 389 men who had departed from Yambuya 139 days previously, and put down our loss at 111. We were greatly mistaken, however, for by this date many of the sick at Ugarrowwa's had died, and the condition of the sick at Ipoto was deplorable.

Since our arrival at Ibwiri the majority of our followers had gained weight of body at the rate of a pound per day. Some were positively huge in girth; their eyes had become lustrous, and their skins glossy like oiled bronze. For the last three nights they had ventured upon songs; they hummed their tunes as they pounded their corn; they sang as they gazed at the moon at night after their evening meal. Frequently a hearty laugh had been heard. In the afternoon of this day a sparring match took place between two young fellows, and a good deal of severe thumping was exchanged; they were always "spinning yarns" to interested listeners. Life had come back by leaps and bounds. Brooding over skeletons and death, and musing on distant friends in their far-away island, had been abandoned for hopeful chat over the future, about the not far distant grass land with its rolling savannahs, and green champaigns, abounding in fat cattle; and they dwelt unctuously on full udders and massive humps, and heavy tails of sheep, and granaries of millet and sesame, pots of zogga, pombe, or some other delectable stimulant, and the Lake Haven, where the white man's steamers were at anchor, appeared distinctly in their visions.

They all now desired the march, for the halt had been quite sufficient. There were twenty perhaps to whom another fortnight's rest was necessary, but they all appeared to me to have begun recovery, and, provided food was abundant, their marching without loads would not be hurtful.

At dawn of the bright and sunny day, 24th of November, the Soudanese trumpeter blew the signal with such cheery strains that found a ready response from every man. The men shouted their "Ready, aye ready, Master!" in a manner that more reminded me of former expeditions, than of any day we had known on this. There was no need of the officers becoming exasperated at delays of laggards and the unwilling; there was not a malingerer in the camp. Every face was lit up with hopefulness. A prospective abundance of good cheer invited them on. For two days ahead the path was known by those of the reconnaissance, and the members of the party had, like Caleb and Joshua, expatiated upon the immense and pendent clusters of plantains effusing delicious odours of ripeness, and upon the garden plots of potatoes, and waving fields of maize, &c. Therefore, for once, we were relieved from the anxiety as to who should take this load, or that box; there was no searching about for the carriers, no expostulations nor threats, but the men literally leaped to the goods pile, fought for the loads, and laughed with joy; and the officers faces wore grateful smiles, and expressed perfect content-merit with events.

We filed out of the village, a column of the happiest fellows alive. The accursed Manyuema were behind us, and in our front rose in our imaginations vivid pictures of pastoral lands, and a great lake on whose shores we were to be greeted by a grateful Pasha, and a no less grateful army of men.

In forty-five minutes we arrived at Boryo's village (the chief had been released the day before), a long, orderly arrangement of a street 33 feet wide, flanked by four low blocks of buildings 400 yards in length. According to the doors we judged that fifty-two families had formed Boryo's particular community. The chief's house was recognized by an immense slab of wood four feet wide and six feet long, and two inches thick; its doorway being cut out of this in a diamond figure.

The height of the broad eaves was 10 feet above the ground, and the houses were 10 feet in width, The eaves projected 30 inches in front, and 2 feet over the back walls. Outside of the village extended, over level and high ground, the fields, gardens, and plantations, banked all round by the untouched forest, which looked dark, ominous, and unwelcome. Altogether Boryo's village was the neatest and most comfortable we had seen throughout the valley of the Aruwimi. One hundred yards from the western end ran a perennial and clear stream, which abounded with fish of the silurus kind.

After a short halt we resumed the journey, and entered the forest. Four miles beyond Boryo's we passed over a swamp, which was very favourable to fine growths of the Raphia palm, and soon after lunched. In the afternoon I undertook, as an experiment, to count my paces for an hour, and to measure a space of 200 yards, to find the number of inches to a pace, and found that the average rate in a fair track through the forest was 4800 paces of 26 inches long =

3470 yards per hour. At 3 o'clock we camped in an extensive pigmies' village. The site commanded four several roads, leading to
villages. There is no doubt it was a favourite spot, for the village
common was well tamped and adapted for sport, gossip, and meet-
ings. The bush around the camp was quite undisturbed.

On the 25th, after 8 1/4 miles march, we reached Indemwani.
Our track led along the water-parting between the Ituri and Ihuru
rivers. The village was of oval shape, similar in architecture to
Boryo's. A wealth of plantains surrounded it, and Indian corn,
tobacco, beans, and tomatoes were plentiful. In passing through the
clearing, over a fearful confusion of logs, one of our men toppled
over, and fell and broke his neck.

From Indemwani we moved on the 26th to West Indenduru,
through a most humid land. Streams were crossed at every mile;
moss, wet and dripping, clothed stems from base to top. Even
shrubs and vines were covered with it.

A peculiarity of this day's march was a broad highway, cut and
cleared for 3 miles through the undergrowth, which was terminated
by a large village of the pigmies, but recently vacated. There were
ninety-two huts, which we may take to represent ninety-two families, or thereabouts. There was one hut more pretentious than the
others, which possibly was the chief's house. We had seen now
about twenty villages of the forest pigmies, but as yet we had only
viewed the pretty little woman at Ugarrowwa – the miniature Hebé.

Lieutenant Stairs, during his reconnaissance from Ibwiri, had
reached West Indenduru, and had left the village standing; but
because he had occupied it, the natives had set fire to it after his
departure. We observed also that the Balessé seldom ate of the produce of a field twice, and that a plantain grove, after bearing fruit
once, is abandoned for another; and a corn plot, after being tilled,
sown, and harvested, is left to revert to wilderness. They appear to
be continually planting bananas and preparing ground for corn,
which accounted for the immense clearings we had passed, and for
the thousands of trees that littered the ground in one great ruin. For
the bananas or plantains, they simply cut down the underwood and
plant the young bulbs in a shallow hole, with sufficient earth to
keep it upright. They then cut the forest down, and let the trees lie
where they fall. In six months the Musa bulbs have thriven wonder-

fully under shade and among roots and debris, and grown to 8 feet in height; within a year they have borne fruit. The Indian corn or maize requires sunshine. The trees are cut down well above the buttress, by building scaffolds 10, 15, or even 20 feet high. The logs are cut up, and either split for slabs or lining for the inner and outer walls of their huts, or scooped out for troughs for the manufacture of plantain wine. The branches are piled around the plot to rot; they do not burn them, because that would impoverish the soil, and as the surface is rich in humus, it would burn down to the clay.

Considering what great labour is involved in the clearing of a portion of primeval forest, we were tempted to regard the Balessé as very foolish in burning their villages for such a trivial cause as one night's occupation of them by strangers; but it is an instance of the obstinate sullenness of these people. Boryo's village, for instance, could scarcely be constructed under a twelvemonth. The population of the largest village we saw could not exceed 600 souls; but while we wonder at their prejudices, we must award credit to them for great industry and unlimited patience to produce such splendid results as we observed.

East Indenduru was also an exceedingly well-built village, and extremely clean, though the houses within swarmed with vermin. The street, however, was too narrow for the height of the buildings, and a fire occurring in the night might easily have consumed half the inhabitants. For the huts were higher than at Boryo's, and as the buildings were a few hundred yards in length, and had only one principal exit at the eastern end, the danger of a fire was such that we did not occupy it without having taken many precautions to avoid a possible disaster in what appeared to be a perfect trap.

Field-beans, of a dark variety, were gathered by the bushel, and our men reveled in the juice of the sugar-cane.

We were now in S. Lat. 1° 22 1/2' and south of the watershed, all streams flowing towards the Ituri.

On the 28th we halted in East Indenduru, and sent three separate reconnoitering parties to obtain a knowledge of the general direction of the routes leading out of the settlement. We had tested the task of forming our own track through the forest long enough, and having discovered one which had been of such service to us, we were loth to revert to the tedious labour of travelling through jungles and undergrowth again.

Jephson's party proceeded S.S.E., and finally S., and at noon turned back to report. This road would not do for us. Rashid's party took one leading E.N.E., and finally north, through two small villages, one path returning southerly, another going north-easterly. Continuing his explorations along the latter, he came to a native camp. There was a slight skirmish; the natives fled, and he obtained a prize of nine fat goats, only five of which they brought to camp. This road would not suit us either.

A third search party was led by a famous scout, who discovered one path heading easterly. We resolved to adopt this.

On the 29th we left Indenduru and journeyed to Indepessu by noon, and in the afternoon sheered by a northerly path to the settlement of the Baburu, having accomplished a distance of ten miles in five hours, which was exceedingly fair walking.

On the next morning, after a march of an hour and a half along a tolerably good path, we emerged in front of an extensive clearing of about 240 acres. The trees were but recently cut. This marked the advent of a powerful tribe, or a late removal to new ground of old settlers of some numerical force, resolved upon securing many creature comforts. A captive woman of the Waburu led the way through the middle of this wide abattis, the very sight of which was appalling. An hour later we had crossed this, not without bruised shins and much trembling, and the path then led up an easy ascent up a prolonged span of a hill. The hollows on either side of it showed prodigious groves of plantains and many gardens, ill-kept, devoted to herbs and gourds. Within thirty minutes from the summit of the ascent we had reached an altitude that promised to give us shortly a more extended view than any we had been lately accustomed to, and we pressed gladly upwards, and soon entered a series of villages that followed the slope. A village of these parts always gave us a highway well trodden, from forty to sixty feet wide; in a series of this type of villages we should soon be able to pace a mile. We had passed through several fine separate long blocks of low structures, when the foremost of the advance guard was seen running swiftly down to meet me. He asked me to look towards the sunrise, and, turning my eyes in that direction, they were met by the gratifying sight of a fairly varied scene of pasture-land and forest, of level champaigns and grassy slopes of valleys and hills, rocky knolls and softly rounded eminences, a veritable "land of hills and valleys, that drinketh the rain of heaven." That the open country was well watered was indicated by the many irregular lines of woods which marked the courses of the streams, and by the dumps of trees, whose crowns just rose above their sloping banks.

The great forest in which we had been so long buried, and whose limits were in view, appeared to continue intact and unbroken to the N.E., but to the E. of it was an altogether different region of grassy meads and plains and hills, freely sprinkled with groves, dusters, and thin lines of trees up to certain ranges of hills that bounded the vision, and at whose base I knew must be the goal whither we had for months desired to reach.

This, then, was the long promised view and the long expected exit out of gloom! Therefore I called the tall peak terminating the forested ridge, of which the spur whereon we stood was a part, and that rose two miles E. of us to a height of 4600 feet above the sea, Pisgah, – Mount Pisgah, – because, after 156 days of twilight in the primeval forest, we had first viewed the desired pasturelands of Equatoria.

The men crowded up the slope eagerly with inquiring open-eyed looks, which, before they worded their thoughts, we knew meant "Is it true? Is it no hoax? Can it be possible that we are near the end of this forest hell?" They were convinced themselves in a few moments after they had dropped their burdens, and regarded the view with wondering and delighted surprise.

"Aye, friends, it is true. By the mercy of God we are well nigh the end of our prison and dungeon!" They held their hands far out yearningly towards the superb land, and each looked up to the bright blue heaven in grateful worship, and after they had gazed as though fascinated, they recovered themselves with a deep sigh, and as they turned their heads, lo! the sable forest heaved away to the infinity of the west, and they shook their clenched hands at it with gestures of defiance and hate. Feverish from sudden exaltation, they apostrophised it for its cruelty to themselves and their kinsmen; they compared it to Hell, they accused it of the murder of one hundred of their comrades, they called it the wilderness of fungi and wood-beans; but the great forest which lay vast as a continent before them, and drowsy, like a great beast, with monstrous fur thinly veiled by vaporous exhalations, answered not a word, but rested in its infinite sullenness, remorseless and implacable as ever.

From S.E. to S. extended a range of mountains between 6,000 and 7,000 feet above the sea. One woman captive indicated S.E. as our future direction to the great water that "rolled incessantly on the shore with a booming noise, lifting and driving the sand before it," but as we were in S. Lat. 1°. 22' on the same parallel as Kavalli, our objective point, I preferred aiming east, straight towards it.

Old Boryo, chief of Ibwiri, had drawn with his hand a semicircle from S.E. to N.W. as the course of the Ituri River, and said that the river rose from a plain at the foot of a great hill, or a range of hills. To the S.E. of Pisgah we could see no plain, but a deep wooded valley, and unless our eyes deceived us, the forest seemed to ascend up the slopes of the range as far as its summits. Five months of travel in one continuous forest was surely experience enough; a change would therefore be agreeable, even if we varied but our hardships. This was another reason why I proposed to decline all advice upon the proper path leading to the "great water."

In the village of the Bakwuru, in which we now prepared to encamp, we found sleeveless vests of thick buffalo hide, which our men secured, as fitting armour against the arrows of the tribes of the grass land.

On the 1st of December we retraced our steps down the spur, and then struck along a track running easterly. In a short time we ascended another spur leading up to a terrace below Pisgah peak, where we obtained the highest reading of the aneroid that we had yet reached. We then followed a path leading from the terrace down another spur to the average level. A number of well-defined and trodden roads were crossed, but our path seemed to increase in importance until, at 11.15 A.M., we entered the large village of Iyugu, which, of course, was quite deserted, so quickly do the natives of the forest seem to be apprised of new arrivals. The street of this village was forty feet wide.

We observed a considerable dryness in the woods between Pisgah base and Iyugu, which was a great change from that excessive humidity felt and seen between Indenduru and Ibwiri. The fallen forest leaves had a slightly crispy look about them and crackled under our feet, and the track, though still in primeval shade, had somewhat of the dusty appearance of a village street.

After the noon halt we made a two hours' march to a small village consisting of three conical huts, near which we camped. Though we had travelled over ten miles we might have been hundreds of miles yet from the open country for all we could gather from our surroundings. For they were, as usual, of tail dense woods, of true tropic character, dark, sombrous and high, bound one to the other with creepers and vines, and a thick undergrowth throve under the shades.

We, however, picked up a strange arrow in one of the huts, which differed greatly from any we had as yet seen. It was twenty-eight inches in length, and its point was spear-shaped, and three inches long. Its shaft was a light reed cane, beautifully and finely notched for decoration, a thin triangular-shaped piece of kid leather directed the arrow, instead of a leaf or a piece of black cloth as hitherto. A quiver full of forest-tribe arrows was also found, and they were twenty inches long, and each arrowhead differed from the other, though each was murderously sharp and barbed.

On the 2nd of December, soon after leaving the camp, we lost the native road, and had to pick our way amongst a perplexing number of buffalo and elephant tracks. A stupid fellow, who had been out wandering, had informed us that he had reached the plain the night before, and that he could easily guide us to it. Trusting in him, we soon lost all signs of a track, and began a crooked and erratic course through the woods, as in times past. After nearly three hours' travelling N. by E. we stumbled upon a village, whose conical roofs were thatched with grass. This was a grand discovery, and was hailed with cheers. One fellow literally rushed to the grass and kissed it lovingly. Already there were two characteristics of pasture-land before us, the cone hut and the grass thatch. We halted for a noon rest, and a few young men took advantage of it to explore, and before the halting-time was expired brought to us a bunch of green grass, which was hailed with devout raptures, as Noah and his family may have hailed the kindly dove with the olive branch. However, they reported that the way they had followed led to a swamp, and swamps being a horror to a laden caravan, our afternoon march was made in a S.S.E. direction, which in ninety minutes brought us to Indesura, another village, or rather a district, consisting of several small settlements of cone huts thatched with grass. Here we halted.

Having occasion to repair a roof a man mounted to the top of a house, and looking round languidly was presently seen to lift his hand to his eyes and gaze earnestly. He then roared out loud enough for the entire village to hear, "I see the grassland. Oh, but we are close to it!"

"Nay," said one in reply, mockingly, "don't you also see the lake, and the steamer, and that Pasha whom we seek?"

Most of us were, however, stirred by the news, and three men climbed up to the roofs with the activity of wild cats, others climbed to the tops of trees, while a daring young fellow climbed one which would have tasked a monkey almost, and a chorus of exclamations

CHIEF OF THE IYUGU.

rose, "Aye, verily, it is the truth of God, the open land is close to us, and we knew it not! Why, it is merely an arrow's flight distant! Ah, when we reach it, farewell to darkness and blindness."

As a man went to draw water from the stream close by, an ancient crone stepped out of the bush, and the man dropped his water-pot and seized her. She being vigorous and obstinate, like most of her sex just previous to dotage, made a vigorous defence for her liberty. A Countess of Salisbury could not have been more resolute, but the man possessed superior strength and craft and hauled her into camp. By dint of smiles and coaxing and obsequiously filling a long pipe for her, we learned that we were in Indesura, that the people were called Wanya-Sura, that the villagers quenched their thirst with the waters of the Ituri. "The Ituri?"

"Ay, the Ituri; this stream close by;" that many days east of us was a great broad river, ever so much broader than the Ituri, with canoes as wide as a house (ten feet) which would carry six people (sic); that a few days north there was a mighty tribe called the Banzanza, and east of them another people called the Bakandi, and both of these tribes possessed numerous herds of cattle, and were very valorous and warlike, and who were rich in cattle, cowries, and brass wire.

Our ancient captive, who was somewhat peculiar for her taste in personal decoration by having a wooden disk of the size of an ulster button intruded into the centre of her upper lip, was now seized with another fit of obstinacy and scowled malignantly at all of us except at a bashful smooth-faced youth upon whom she apparently doted, but the foolish youth ascribed the ugliness of agedness to witchcraft, and fled from her.

Indé-sura – and, as we discovered later, all the villages situated on the edge of the forest – was remarkable for the variety and excellent quality of its products. Mostly all the huts contained large baskets of superior tobacco weighing from twenty to fifty pounds each, such quantities, indeed, that every smoker in the camp obtained from five to ten pounds. The crone called it "Taba;" in Ibwiri it was called Tabo. Owing to the imperfect drying it is not fragrant, but it is extremely smokable. Fifty pipefuls a day of it would not produce so much effect on the nerves as one of the article known as Cavendish. But here and there among the leaves there were a few of rich brown colour slightly spotted with nitre which produced a different effect. Two of our officers experimented on a pipeful of this, which they deemed to be superior, and were inconceivably wretched in consequence. When, however, these leaves are picked out, the tobacco is mild and innocuous, as may be judged by the half-pint pipe-bowls peculiar to this region. In every district near the grassland the plant is abundantly cultivated, for the purpose of commerce with the herdsmen of the plains in exchange for meat.

The castor-oil plant was also extensively cultivated. Requiring a supply of castor-oil as medicine, the beans were roasted, and then pounded in a wooden mortar, and we expressed a fair quantity, which proved very effective. We also required a supply for rifles, and their mechanisms, and the men prepared a supply for anointing their bodies – an operation which made them appear fresh, clean, and vigorous.

Having discovered that four of our scouts were strangely absent, I despatched Rashid bin Omar and twenty men in search of them. They were discovered and brought to us next morning, and to my surprise the four absentees, led by the incorrigible Juma Waziri, were driving a flock of twenty fine goats, which the chief scout had captured by a ruse. I had often been tempted to sacrifice Juma for the benefit of others, but the rogue always appeared with such an inoffensive, and crave-your-humble-pardon kind of face, which could not be resisted. He was of a handsome Abyssinian type, but the hypocrisy on his features marred their natural beauty. A Mhuma, Masai, Mtaturu, or Galla must have meat, even more so than the Englishman. It is an article of faith with him, that life is not worth living without an occasional taste of beef. I therefore warned Juma again, and consoled myself with the reflection, that his career as a scout could only be for a brief time, and that he would surely meet natives of craft and courage equal to his own some day.

We had made an ineffectual start on this day, had actually left the village a few hundred yards when we were stopped by the depth of a river forty yards wide and with a current of two and a half miles an hour. The old crone called this the Ituri. Marveling that between Ipoto and Ibwiri a river 400 yards wide could be narrowed to such a narrow stream, we had returned to Indé-sura for a day's halt, and I had immediately after sent Lieutenant Stairs and Mr. Jephson with sufficient escort back along yesterday's path to find a ford across the Ituri.

At 4 P.M. both officers returned to report a successful discovery of a ford a mile and a half higher up the stream, and that they had set foot upon the grassland, in proof of which they held a bunch of fine young succulent grass. Meantime, Uledi and his party had also found another ford waist deep, still nearer Indé-sura.

On the evening of this day a happier community of men did not exist on the face of the round earth than those who rejoiced in the camp of Indé-sura. On the morrow they were to bid farewell to the forest. The green grassy region of which we had dreamed in our dark hours, when slumbering heavily from exhaustion of body and prostration from hunger during the days of starvation, was close at hand. Their pots contained generous supplies of juicy meat; the

PIPES.

messes were roast and boiled fowls, corn mush, plantain flour porridge, and ripe bananas. No wonder they were now exuberantly happy, and all except ten or twelve men were in finer condition than when they had embarked so hopefully for the journey in the port of Zanzibar.

On the 4th of December we filed out of Indé-sura and proceeded to the ford. It was waist deep, and at this place fifty yards wide. Two of the aneroids indicated an altitude of 3050 feet above the ocean – 1850 feet higher than the level of the river at the landing-place of Yambuya, and 2000 feet higher than the Congo at Stanley Pool.

From the Ituri we entered a narrow belt of tall timber on its left bank, and, after waiting for the column to cross, marched on, led by Mr. Mounteney Jephson along a broad elephant track for about 600 yards, and then, to our undisguised joy, emerged upon a rolling plain, green as an English lawn, into broadest, sweetest daylight, and warm and glorious sunshine, to inhale the pure air with an uncontrollable rapture. Judging of the feelings of others by my own, we felt as if we had thrown all age and a score of years away, as we stepped with invigorated limbs upon the soft sward of young grass. We strode forward at a pace most unusual, and finally, unable to suppress our emotions, the whole caravan broke into a run. Every man's heart seemed enlarged and lifted up with boyish gladness. The blue heaven above us never seemed so spacious, lofty, pure, and serene as at this moment. We gazed at the sun itself undaunted by its glowing brightness. The young grass, only a month since the burning of the old, was caressed by a bland, soft breeze, and turned itself about as if to show us its lovely shades of tender green. Birds, so long estranged from us, sailed and soared through the lucent atmosphere; antelopes and elands stood on a grassy eminence gazing and wondering, and then bounded upward and halted snorting their surprise, to which our own was equal; buffaloes lifted their heads in amazement at the intruders on their silent domain, heaved their bulky forms, and trooped away to a safer distance. A hundred square miles of glorious country opened to our view – apparently deserted – for we had not as yet been able to search out the fine details of it. Leagues upon leagues of bright green pasture land undulated in gentle waves, intersected by narrow winding lines of umbrageous trees that filled the hollows, scores of gentle hills studded with dark clumps of thicket, graced here and there by a stately tree, lorded it over level breadths of pasture and softly sloping champaigns; and far away to the east rose some frowning ranges of mountains beyond which we were certain slept in its deep gulf the blue Albert. Until breathlessness forced a halt, the caravan had sped on the double-quick – for this was also a pleasure that had been long deferred.

Then we halted on the crest of a commanding hill to drink the beauty of a scene to which we knew no rival, which had been the subject of our thoughts and dreams for months, and now we were made "glad according to the days wherein we had been afflicted and the period wherein we had seen evil." Every face gloated over the beauty of the landscape and reflected the secret pleasure of the heart. The men were radiant with the fulfillment of dear desires. Distrust and sullenness were now utterly banished. We were like men out of durance and the dungeon free and unfettered, having exchanged foulness and damp for sweetness and purity, darkness and gloom for divine light and wholesome air. Our eyes followed the obscure track, roved over the pasture hillocks, great and small, every bosky islet and swarded level around it, along the irregularities of the forest line that rose darkly funereal behind us, advancing here, receding there, yonder assuming a bay-like canoe, here a cape-like point. The mind grasped the minutest peculiarity around as quick as vision, to cling to it for many, many years. A score of years hence, if we live so long, let but allusion be made to this happy hour when every soul trembled with joy, and praise rose spontaneously on every lip, and we shall be able to map the whole with precision and fidelity.

After examining the contour of the new region before us with the practical view of laying a course free from river or swamp, I led the Expedition N.N.E. to a rocky knoll which was about four miles from us, in order to strike the southern base of a certain hilly range that ran E. by S. from the knoll. I imagined we should then be able to travel over upland, trending easterly, without much inconvenience.

We reached the base of the rock-heap that stood about 300 feet above the valley to our right, then perceiving that the obscure game track we had followed had developed into a native highway running N.E., we struck across the grassy upland to retain our hold upon the crown we had gained, the short young grass enabling us to do so without fatigue. But near noon the tall unburnt grass of last season interrupted our too-easy advance with its tangle of robust stalks of close growth; but we bore on until 12.30, and after an hour of serious exercise halted by the side of a crystal stream for refreshments.

In the afternoon we breasted the opposing grassy slope, and, after an hour and a half of rapid pacing, selected a camp near the junction of two streams, which flowed south-easterly. Relieved from their burdens, a few tireless fellows set out to forage in some villages we had observed far below our line of march in the valley. The suddenness of their descent among the natives provided them with a rich store of fowls, sugar-cane, and ripe branches of bananas. They brought us specimens of the weapons of this new land: several long bows and lengthy arrows; shields of a heavy rectangular form, formed of a double row of tough rods crossed, and tightly bound together with fibre and smeared with some gummy substance. They presented very neat workmanship, and were altogether impenetrable to arrows or spears. Besides shields the natives wore vests of buffalo hide, which appeared to be quite impervious to pistol shots.

Our course as far as the rocky knoll already described was nearly parallel with the edge of the forest, our path varying in distance from it from a half mile to a mile and a half. As a sea or a lake indents its shore, so appeared the view of the line of forest.

The trend of the Ituri that we had crossed, which we must call West Ituri, was E.S.E.. I should have estimated the source of the river to have been distant from the crossing about 25 geographical miles N.N.W.

On the next day we advanced up a long slope of short grass land, and on the crest halted to arrange the column with more order, lest we might be suddenly confronted by an overwhelming force, for we were as yet ignorant of the land, its people, and the habits of those among whom we had dropped so suddenly. Marching forward we chose a slight track that followed the crest leading E. by S., but soon all traces of it were lost. However, we were on a commanding upland, and a score of miles were visible to us in any direction out of which we might select any course. A village was in view N.E. of us, and to it we directed our steps, that we might avail ourselves of a path, for the closely-packed acreages of reedy cane and fifteen-feet-high grass, that we stumbled upon occasionally, were as bad as the undergrowth of the jungle. The very tallest and rankest grass impeded us, and prevented rapid advance. We crossed jungly gullies, on whose muddy ground were impressed the feet of lions and leopards, and finally entered a tract of acacia thorn, which was a sore annoyance, and out of this last we emerged into the millet fields of Mbiri. In a few seconds the natives were warned of our approach, and fled instinctively, and, Parthian-like, shot their long arrows. The scouts dashed across every obstacle, and seized a young woman and a lad of twelve, who were the means of instructing our poor ignorance. No long conversation could be maintained with them, owing to our very imperfect knowledge of any dialect spoken near this region, but a few names of nouns assisted by gestures brought out the fact that we were in the district of Mbiri, that the main road easterly would take us to the Babusessé country, that beyond them lay the Abunguma, all of which naturally we heard with supreme indifference. What did such names convey to dull senses and. blank minds? They had never heard of Shakespeare, Milton, or even of Her Majesty the Queen.

"Had any of them heard of Muta, or Luta Nzige?"

A shake of the head.

"Of Unyoro?"

"Unyoro? Yes. Unyoro lies a great way off," pointing east.

"Of a great water near Unyoro?"

"The Ituri, you mean?"

"No, wider; ever so much wider than the Ituri – as wide as all this plain."

But instead of confining themselves to monosyllables, which we might easily have understood, the wretched woman and boy, anxious to convey too much information, smothered comprehension by voluble talk in their dialect, and so perplexed us that we had recourse to silence and patience. They would show us the way to Babusessé at least.

The mode of hut construction is similar to that seen all over East and Central Africa. It is the most popular. A cone roof occupies two-thirds of the height; one-third is devoted to the height of the walls. Huts of this pattern, scattered amongst the banana groves, are found every few dozen yards. Paths lead from one to the other, and are most baffling to the stranger, who without a local guide must necessarily go astray. To every group of huts there are attached outhouses for cooking sheds, for gossip, to store fuel, and doing chores; also circular grass-walled and thatched little granaries raised a foot or so above the ground as protection against vermin and damp.

Our people obtained a large quantity of ripe plantains and ripe bananas, out of which the aborigines manufacture an intoxicating wine called *marwa*. A few goats were also added to our flock, and about a dozen fowls were taken. All else were left untouched according to custom, and we resumed our journey.

The path was well trodden. Traffic and travel had tamped it hard and smooth. It led S.E. by E. up and down grassy hills and vales. Near noon we halted for refreshments, shaded by fine woods, and close by boomed a loud cataract of the Ituri, we were told. This was rather puzzling. We could not understand how the Ituri, which we had forded the day before, could be roaring over precipices and terraces at this high altitude, and after we had purposely struck away from its valley to avoid it.

A march of an hour and a half in the afternoon, apparently not very far from the river, brought us to the populous district of the Babusessé. The banana plantations were very extensive, reminding me of Uganda, and their deep shades covered a multitude of huts. Fields of millet and sesame, plots of sweet potatoes, occupied the outskirts of these plantations, and there was ample evidence round about that the land was thickly peopled and industriously cultivated.

Before entering the banana shades we repaired our ranks, and marched in more compact order. A strong body of men armed with Winchesters formed the advance guard; a similar number of men armed with Remingtons, under the command of Stairs, closed the rear of the column. But however well cautioned the men were against breaking rank, no sooner had the advance guard passed safely through a dangerous locality than the main body invariably despatched scores of looters into huts and granaries to hunt up booty and fowls, bananas, goats, sugar-cane, and trivial articles of no earthly use. These plantations hid a large number of natives, who permitted the advance to pass because their files were unbroken, and their eyes on the watch, but those straggling looters soon gave the aborigines the opportunity. Some arrows flew well aimed; one pinned a man's arm to his side, another glancing from a rib admonished its owner of his folly. A volley from rifles drove the men away from their covert without harm to any of them.

At the easternmost settlement we camped. There were only two large conical huts and other outhouses in it, and around these the huts for the night were arranged hastily, put up with banana leaves sufficient to shed rain and dew.

At dusk I called the captives to me again, and attempted, during half an hour, to gain a lucid answer to the question as to whether there was a great body of water or great river east of us. When one of the headmen who were assisting us demanded to know which was the largest Nyanza, that of Unyoro, or that of Uganda –

"Nyanza!" cried the native boy – "Nyanza?Ay, the Nyanza lies this way" (pointing east) "and extends that way" (north-east)"a long distance;" and when asked how many "sleeps" intervened between the Babusessé, held up three fingers on his dexter hand, and answered "three."

It was now dark, and we were suddenly startled by a shriek of pain, and a sequent yell singularly weird, and with a note of triumph in it, and in the silence that followed we heard the hurtling of arrows through the banana leaves above our heads.

"Put out the fires! Keep cool. Where are the sentries? Why are they not at their posts?" were the next words uttered.

The natives had stolen on us at the very hour when the camp was least watched, for it was supper-time, and the guards, except on

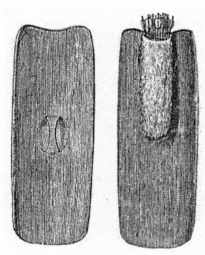

unusual occasions, were permitted to feed before going out on guard duty for the night. We soon ascertained that one arrow had penetrated the thigh of a man named Salim to the depth of four inches, another had pierced the roast leg of a kid before the fire, several others had perforated banana stalks. Salim, after a little coaxing, bravely drew out the shaft until the barbed point was seen, when, with a wrench, I extracted it with a pair of pincers. Eucalyptine was then applied to the wound, and the

SHIELDS OF BABUSESSÉ.

man was sent to his quarters.

Half an hour later, all the guards being now on duty, however, the natives essayed another quarter of the camp, but the rifle-shots rang out quickly in reply, and there was a scamper and a rustle heard. In the distance we heard two rifles fired, and an agonised cry, by which we knew that there were some of our incorrigible looters abroad.

Our force was weak enough, in all conscience, not in numbers, but in real strength, for defence and capacity for bearing ammunition, and these wanderers were always a source of great anxiety to me. It was useless to reason and expostulate; only downright severity restrained them, and as yet, so fresh were we from the horrors of the forest, that I had not the moral courage to apply the screw of discipline; but when I assumed mildness, their own heedless imprudence incurred punishments far more severe than any of us would ever have thought of inflicting.

A heavy rain fell on us during the night, which detained us next morning until eight o'clock. I employed the time in extracting something intelligible respecting the character of the natives in front, but we were all so profoundly ignorant of the language that we could make but little headway. In the endeavour to make herself clear, the woman drew on the ground a sketch of the course of the Ituri. This illustrated one of the strangest facts in African geography that one could imagine. The river was represented as going up to the crest of the watershed, flowing steeply upward parallel with Lake Albert, and finally lifting itself over to be precipitated into the Nyanza! Stupefied by what she said, I kept her by me as we marched out of camp into the open. From the crown of a hill she pointed out, half a mile below, the Ituri River flowing eastward. The stretch in view was an east by south course.

Now here was a deep puzzle. We had crossed from the right bank to the left bank of the Ituri two days previously, in N. Lat. 1° 24': we were now in N. Lat. 1° 28'. Yet the Ituri we saw flowed E. by S. and E.S.S., and my route to Kavalli was obviously south of east.

I declined to perplex myself any more with the problem, or in trying to understand what the woman meant, that the river we had ascended for 600 miles from the Congo flowed to the Nyanza. The only solution possible was that, there were two Ituris, one flowing to the Congo, the other into the Nile basin; but both she and her brother stoutly maintained that there was only one Ituri.

We continued on our journey, following a path which dipped down into the valley. We presently stood on the banks of the stream, and the solution was at hand. It was the main Ituri River, flowing south of west. We are all wise after the event. There was a clumsy, misshapen canoe in the river, and as Saat Taro was an expert canoeist, he was detailed to ferry the caravan over for a reward of 20 dollars. The river was 125 yards broad, about seven feet average depth, with a current of two knots. It was a cataract of this stream whose low thunder we had heard near Mbiri. The natives of Abunguma, on the left side of the river, watched our operations from a hill-top a mile off, with an air of confidence which seemed to say, "All right, friends. When you are through, you will have to reckon with us." Nothing could be done in such an open land as this without "all the world knowing it." The Abunguma shook their spears bravely at us; the Babusessé occupied every prominent point on the right side of the river. It appeared once or twice as if our manhood was about to be tested on an important scale. There was the comfort, however, that, knowing the natives to be alert and active, we could not be surprised on a pasture slope where the grass around the camp was but three inches high. Since we had entered Ibwiri we had fared luxuriously – for Africa. We had enjoyed meat and milk daily. We had lived on fowls, young and dried beans, sugar-cane, sweet potatoes, yams, colocassia, tomatoes, brinjalls, melons, plantains, and bananas. On the people the effect was wonderful. They were men in every respect superior both in body and spirit to the gaunt and craven wretches whom the Arab slaves of Ipoto scourged and speared without more than a mild protest. On the whites also the effect had been most beneficial. Though spare, we were no longer meagre and haggard; a little wine would have completed the cure. A gentle grassy slope, on the next morning, took us, in the course of an hour, to the crown of one of those long undulations so characteristic of this region. It furnished us with another all-round view peculiarly interesting to us. Our intended direction was southeast, as we were bearing for a high conical peak at the end of a range of grass-covered mountains, which afterwards became known to us as Mazamboni's Peak. We dipped down into delightful vales, watered by cool and clear brooks. Close to these were small clusters of native homesteads, with their fields of unripe sorghum, sweet potato, and sugar-cane patches, &c. But the homesteads were all abandoned, and their owners were observing us from the sky-line of every superior hill. Finally we passed an empty cattle zeriba, the sight of which was loudly cheered, and cries of "Ay, the master is right, and every word comes to pass. First will comb the grass-land, then the cattle with brave men to defend them, then hills, then the Nyanza, and lastly the white man. The grass-land we have seen, here is the cattle yard, yonder are the mountains, the brave men and the Nyanza and the white man we shall yet see, please God."

We bore on our way to a valley through which another river rushed and roared. On our left was a rugged line of rocks that rose in huge and detached masses, on the top of which a dozen men might be seated comfortably. Connecting these huge rock masses was a lower line of rocks, more uniform, forming the bare spine of a ridge. At some places we passed so close to the base of this hill that we were within easy stone's throw of the summits. But though we were prepared for a demonstration, the natives remained singularly quiet. The path we followed halted at a suspension bridge across a third "Ituri," which had better be distinguished as East Ituri to prevent misunderstanding. This last river was thirty yards wide, deep and swift as a rapid. Spanned by a bridge of such, fragile make that we could only pass one at a time in safety, it required one hundred and twenty seconds for a single person to cross the ninety-feet span, and the caravan was not on the other side entirely before 6 P.M. As the crossing was in a position of great disadvantage, riflemen had been on the look-out all day.

In the afternoon we saw a fine black cow and her calf issue out of a defile in the rocky ridge just described, and clamours of "Beef, beef – ay, beef, how are you? we have not seen you since we were young!" rose loud. The Abunguma had hidden their cattle among the rocky hills, and these specimens had probably been refractory.

Leaving the picturesque valley of East Ituri on the 8th, we ascended an easy slope to the top of a hill where we obtained a long view of the crooked and narrow valley of the East Ituri, and were able to observe that it came from an east-south-east direction. Shortly after, something more like a plain opened before us, extending over a score of miles to the south, bordered on the north by the stony ridge and valley we had just left behind, while to the eastward rose Mazamboni's mountain range, whose northern end, conspicuous by the tall peak, was our present objective point.

At 9.30 A.M. we had approached several miles nearer this mountain range, and before descending into the valley of a stream-let flowing northward, we observed with wonder that the whole intervening space as far as the mountains was one mass of planta-tions, indicative of a powerful population. Here then, we thought, "will be the tug of war. The Abunguma have left their settlements in order to join this numerous tribe, and meet us with a fitting reception." No more populous settlements had been seen since we had departed from Bangala on the Congo. A suspicion that these were among the confederation of tribes who hemmed in the poor anxious governor of Equatoria also crept into our minds, as we looked upon this huge display of numbers and evidence of wealth and security.

With the view of not provoking the natives, and of preventing the incorrigible looters of the column from the commission of mis-chief, we took a south-east track to skirt the district. We were able to steer our course between the plantations, so that no cover was afforded to an enemy. At 11.30 we had reached the eastern extrem-ity of the district, and then rested for the noon halt and refreshment, under the shadow of a tree whose branches rustled before a strong cool breeze from the Nyanza.

Resuming the march at 1 P.M. we entered the depths of banana plantations, marveling at the great industry evinced, and the neat-ness of the cultivated plots. The conical homesteads were large and partitioned within, as we observed while passing through a few open doorways, by screens of cane grass. Every village was cleanly swept, as though they had been specially prepared for guests. Each banana stalk was loaded with bananas, the potato fields were exten-sive, the millet fields stretched away on either side by hundreds of acres, and the many granaries that had lately been erected mani-fested expectations of a bountiful harvest.

We finally emerged from the corn-fields without being once annoyed. We thought the natives had been cowed by exaggerated reports of our power, or they had been disconcerted by our cautious manoeuvre of leaving a fair open margin between the line of march and the groves; but much to our surprise we encountered no opposition, though large masses of the aborigines covered the eminences bordering our route.

The broad and well-trodden path towards the mountains which we were now rapidly approaching bisected an almost level plain, three miles wide, rich with pasture grass in flower. The Eastern Ituri was not far off on our left flank, and on the other side of it another populous settlement was in view.

At 3 P.M. we arrived at the base of the Mountain of the Peak. Many of its highest points were crowned with clusters of huts. The cotes of the natives were in the folds of the mountain fronting us. The people gathered in large groups on the nearest summits, and when we were near enough the shouts of defiance were uttered with loud and strident voices. We estimated the average height of the hills nearest to us at about 800 feet above the plain, and as the slopes were particularly steep we judged their distance to be between 800 and 1000 yards from us.

Much to our pleasure and relief the path, instead of ascending those steep slopes, skirted their base, and turned east, pursuing the direction we wished being now in, North Lat. 1° 25' 30". A valley unfolded to our view as we rounded the corner of the Peak Range, with a breadth of one to two miles wide, which was clothed with luxuriant sorghum ripening for the sickle. On our right, rising immediately above us, was the north side of Mazamboni's range; to our left, the ground, hidden by crops of grain, sloped gradually to a rapid branch of the East Ituri, and beyond it rose, an easy slope to a broad horse-shoe shaped grassy ridge, studded with homesteads, green with millet and corn, and rich in banana groves. One sweeping view of our surroundings impressed us with the prosperity of the tribe.

On entering this rich crop-bearing valley a chorus of war-cries pealing menacingly above our heads caused us to look up. The groups had already become more numerous, until there were probably 300 warriors with shield, spear, and bow, shaking their flashing weapons, gesturing with shield and spear, crying wrathfully at us in some language. Waxing more ungovernable in action they made a demonstration to descend; they altered their intentions, returned to the summit, and kept pace with us – we along the base, they along the crest of the fore hills, snarling and yelling, shouting and threatening, which we took to be expressive of hate to us, and encouragement to those in the valley.

Issuing out of the first series of cornfields, we heard the war-cries of the valley natives, and comprehended that they were taking position in favourable localities – the hill natives warning and guiding them. It was now near 4 P.M., a time to pick out camp, to make ready for the night in the midst of a population overwhelming in its numbers. Fortunately, close at hand rose the steep hill of Nzera Kum with a spur, whose level top rose a hundred feet above the general face of the valley. It stood like an islet in the valley, distant from the river 500 yards, and from the base of Mazamboni's range 200 yards. From the crest of Nzera Kum we could command a view east and west of all the northern face of the high range, and away over the summit lines of the horse-shoe ridge, across the Ituri branch. Fifty rifles could hold a camp on such a position against a thousand. We hurried up towards it, the warriors on the range slopes converging downward as if divining our intentions; a mass of noisy belligerents hastening towards the line of march from the river banks. The scouts in the advance fired a few solitary shots to clear the front, and we succeeded in reaching the islet hill and scrambled up. The loads were thrown down, a few picked skirmishers were ordered to either flank of the column to assist the rear-guard, others were directed to form a zeriba around the crown of the spur; a body of thirty men was sent to secure water from the river. In half an hour the column was safe on the hill, the zeriba was near completion, there was water for the thirsty, and we had a few minutes to draw breath and to observe from our commanding elevation what were our surroundings. The bird's-eye view was not a bit encouraging. About fifty villages were sprinkled through the valley; plantation after plantation, field after field, village after village met our vision in every direction. What lay on the mountains we did not know. The swarms of lusty-voiced natives on the slopes now numbered over 800. The air seemed filled with the uproar of the shouts.

The mountaineers appeared disposed to try conclusions at once. We were fatigued with the march of 13 miles; the hot sun and weight of burdens had weakened the physical powers of the men. Some of the best, however, were picked out and sent to meet the mountaineers, while we stood and watched to weigh the temper of our opponents. Four of the scouts were foremost. An equal number of the mountaineers, not a whir loth for the encounter, bounded gallantly to meet them. They intuitively felt that the courage of our four men was not of the highest order. They approached to within 100 yards of them, and prepared their bows against the rifles. Our men delivered their fire harmlessly, and then backed; the mountaineers advanced, with fingers on their bow-strings. Our four men fled, while a hundred voices from our camp, looking down upon the scene, execrated them. This was a bad beginning for our side; the natives accepted it as a favourable omen to them, and yelled triumphantly. To check this glow, our riflemen sought cover, and seriously annoyed the natives. Some at the extremity of the hill of Nzera Kum did execution among the mountaineers on the slope of the range opposite, at 400 yards distance; others crept down into the valley towards the river, and obtained a triumph for us; others, again, working round the base of Nzera Kum, effected a diversion in our favour. Saat Tato, our hunter, carried away a cow from her owners, and we thus obtained a taste of beef after eleven months' abstinence. As night fell, natives and strangers sought their respective quarters, both anticipating a busy day on the morrow.

Before turning in for the night, I resumed my reading of the Bible as usual. I had already read the book through from beginning to end once, and was now at Deuteronomy for the second reading, and I came unto the verse wherein Moses exhorts Joshua in those fine lines, "Be strong and of a good courage; fear not, nor be afraid of them: for the Lord thy God, He it is that doth go with thee; He will not fail thee, nor forsake thee."

I continued my reading, and at the end of the chapter closed the book, and from Moses my mind travelled at once to Mazamboni. Was it great fatigue, incipient ague, or an admonitory symptom of ailment, or a shade of spiteful feeling against our cowardly four, and a vague sense of distrust that at some critical time my loons would fly? We certainly were in the presence of people very different from the forest natives. In the open our men had not been tested as they were to-day, and what my officers and self had seen of them was not encouraging. At any rate, my mind was occupied with a keener sense of the danger incurred by us in adventuring with such a small force of cowardly porters to confront the tribes of the grass land than I remember it on any previous occasion. It seemed to me now that I had a more thorough grasp of what might be expected. Whether it followed a larger visual view of land and population, or that I was impressed by the volume of human voices, whose uproar yet seemed to sound in my ears, I know not. But a voice appeared to say, "Be strong and of a good courage; fear not, nor be afraid of them." I could almost have sworn I heard the voice. I began to argue with it. Why do you adjure me to abandon the Mission? I cannot run if I would. To retreat would be far more fatal than advance; therefore your encouragement is unnecessary. It replied, nevertheless, "Be strong and of a good courage. Advance, and be confident, for I will give this people and this land unto thee. I will not fail thee nor forsake thee; fear not, nor be dismayed."

Still – all this in strict confidence – before I slept I may add that though I certainly never felt fitter for a fight, it struck me, that both sides were remarkably foolish, and about to engage in what I conceived to be an unnecessary contest. We did not know even the name of the land or of the people, and they were equally ignorant of our name and of our purpose and motives. I sketched out my plans for the morrow, adjured the sentries to keep strict watch, and in sleep became soon oblivious of this Mazamboni – lord of the mountains and plains.

December 9th was a halt. In the morning we completed our thorn-bush fence, distributed cartridges, and examined rifles. By 9 o'clock the chill of early day retired before the warmth of a hot sun, and shortly after the natives mustered in imposing numbers. War-horns, with the weird notes heard in Usoga and Uganda in 1875, sounded the gathering, and over twenty drums boomed from each mountain top. There were shouts and cries flying in currents from mountain to valley, and back again, for we were quite surrounded. About 11 A.M. some few natives descended close enough for one Fetteh, a man of Unyoro, to distinguish what was said, and he exchanged a hot abuse with them, until there was quite a wordy war. Hearing that one of our people understood the language, I directed the wrathful tongues in the interests of peace, and a more amicable language resulted.

"We on our side," was said, "only fight in defence. You assail us while quietly passing through the land. Would it not be better to talk to each other, and try to understand one another first, and then, if we cannot agree, fight."

"True, those are wise words," a man replied. "Tell us who you are. Where you are from, and where you are going."

"We are of Zanzibar, from the sea, and our chief is a white man. We are bound for the Nyanza of Unyoro."

"If you have a white man with you, let us see him, and we shall believe you."

Lieutenant Stairs promptly stepped out of the zeriba and was introduced by Fetteh.

"Now you tell us who you are," said Fetteh. "What land is this? Who is your chief? And how far is the Nyanza?"

"This land is Undussuma, the chief is Mazamboni. We are Wazamboni. The Ruweru (Nyanza) is reached in two days. It will take you five days. It lies east. There is only one road, and you cannot miss it."

This began the exchange of friendly intercourse. Strangerhood was broken. We then learned that there were two chiefs in Undussuma, one of whom would not be averse to peace, and exchange of friendly gifts, if it were agreeable to us. We gladly assented, and several hours were passed without a hostile cry being heard, or a shot fired, except at the river, the natives on whose shores were obstinate, and declined listening to anything but war proposals.

In the afternoon a message came from Mazamboni saying he would like to see the pattern and quality of our monies. We sent two yards of scarlet uniform cloth, and a dozen brass rods, and a promise was given that early next morning the chief himself would appear and go through the ceremony of brotherhood with me.

The next day we were refreshed after an undisturbed night, and fondly indulged in anticipations that in a few hours, perhaps, our camp would be filled with friendly natives. We had been requested not to depart until a return gift should arrive from Mazamboni. We accordingly had resolved on another day's halt. The morning was still raw and cold, for we were 4,235 feet above the sea. A mist covered the tall mountain tops, and a slight drizzle had set in, which excused our friends from a too early appearance; but at the third hour the mist cleared away, and the outline of the entire range was clear against a pale blue sky. Lieutenant Stairs, Mr. Jephson, and myself, were out at the extreme west end of the spur enjoying the splendid view, admiring the scenery, and wondering when such a beautiful land would become the homesteads of civilized settlers. Stairs thought that it resembled New Zealand, and said that he would not mind possessing a ranch here. He actually went so far as to locate it, and pointed out the most desirable spot. "On that little hill I would build my house" – "Shebang" he called it. I wonder if that is a New Zealand term for a villa – "There I would herd my cattle; my sheep could browse on the mountain slope behind, and–"

But meantime the natives had appeared on the crests of the mountain in lengthy columns, converging towards a common centre – a butt end of a truncated hill – a thousand yards in an air line from where we stood, and a voice like that of a mob orator, clear and harmonious, broke on our ear. It proceeded from a man who, with a few companions, had descended to about 300 feet above the valley. He was ten minutes speaking, and Fetteh had been brought to listen and translate. Fetteh said that he commanded peace in the name of the king; but strange to say, no sooner had the man concluded his speech than loud, responsive yells rose from the valley in a hideous and savage clamour, and then from every mountain top, and from the slopes there was a re-echo of the savage outburst.

We surmised that such forceful yelling could not signal a peace, but rather war; and in order to make sure, sent Fetteh down into the valley below the speaker to ask him. The replies from the natives left us no room to doubt. The two sounds – Kanwana, "peace," and Kurwana, "war," were so similar that they had occasioned Fetteh's error.

"We do not want your friendship," they cried. "We are coming down to you shortly to drive you out of your camp with our herdsmen's staffs." And a treacherous fellow, who had crawled under cover of low bush, came near causing us a severe loss – our interpreter especially having an exceedingly narrow escape. Fetteh picked up the arrows and brought them to us, and delivered his news.

There was then no alternative but to inflict an exemplary lesson upon them; and we prepared to carry it out without losing a moment of time, and with the utmost vigour, unless checked by proffers of amity.

The companies were mustered, and fifty rifles were led out by Lieutenant Stairs towards those obstinate and fierce fellows on the other side of the Ituri branch. A party of thirty rifles were sent under Mr. Jephson to skirmish up the slopes to the left; and twenty picked men were sent with Uledi to make a demonstration to the right. Rashid was ordered with ten men to the top of Nzera-Kum to guard against surprise from that quarter. Jephson and Uledi would be marching to their positions unobserved by the mountaineers, because the crowns of the forehills would obstruct the view, and would approach to them within 200 yards without being seen, while Lieutenant Stairs' company, being further out in the valley, would absorb their attention.

In a few minutes Stairs' company was hotly engaged. The natives received our men with cool determination for a few minutes, and shot their arrows in literal showers; but the Lieutenant, perceiving that their coolness rose from the knowledge that there was a considerable stream intervening between them and his company, cheered his men to charge across the river. His men obeyed him, and as they ascended the opposite bank opened a withering fire which in a few seconds broke up the nest of refractory and turbulent fellows who had cried out so loudly for war. The village was taken with a rush and the banana plantations scoured. The natives broke out into the open on a run, and fled far northward. Lieutenant Stairs then collected his men, set fire to the village, and proceeded to the assault of other settlements, rattling volleys from the company announcing the resistance they met.

Meanwhile, Uledi's party of chosen men had discovered a path leading up the mountain along a spur, and after ascending 500 feet, led his men up into view on the right flank of the mob observing and cheering their countrymen in the valley. The Winchesters were worked most handsomely. At the same time Mr. Jephson's party came out of the left ravine, and together they had such a disastrous effect on the nerves of the natives that they fled furiously up the slopes, Uledi and his men chasing them.

Mr. Jephson, after seeing them in full flight, faced eastward, and pushed on for two miles, clearing every inhabitant out. By 1

P.M. all our men were in camp, with only one man slightly wounded. Every man had behaved wonderfully well; even the four cowards, who had been marked men, had distinguished themselves.

At 2 P.M., the natives in the valley having returned, each party was despatched once again. Stairs led his men across the Ituri branch, and followed the running fugitives far northward, then veered sharply round to join Jephson, who had continued his way eastward. Uledi's scouts were sent up to the very summit of the mountain range; but on observing the immense number of home-steads that dotted it, he prudently halted.

Until the afternoon the contest continued; the natives were constantly on the run, charging or retreating. By evening not one was in sight, and the silence around our camp was significant of the day's doings. The inhabitants were on the mountains or far removed eastward and northward. In the valley around us there was not a hut left standing to be a cover during the night. The lesson, we felt, was not completed. We should have to return by that route. In the natural course of things, if we met many tribes of the quality of this, we should lose many men, and if we left them in the least doubt of our ability to protect ourselves, we should have to repeat our day's work. It was, therefore, far more merciful to finish the affair thoroughly before leaving a tribe in unwhipped insolence in our rear.

The natives must have entertained an idea that we could not fight outside our bush fence, which accounts for their tall talk of driving us out with sticks, and that they were safe on the mountains. We were compelled to root out the idea that they could harm us in any way.

A cow neglected by her owner was burnt in one of the villages close by, and furnished us with a second limited ration of roast beef.

On the 11th it rained again during the early morning, which kept us indoors until 10 A.M. Some natives having then come out to demonstrate their hostility on the mountains, Stairs, Jephson and Uledi led their men up the mountain slopes in three separate small columns to the attack, and made a successful tour among their stronghold. A small flock of goats was captured, and distributed to the men, and our experiences of this day satisfied the natives that they had nothing to gain by fighting.

At one time it appeared as though the day would end with reconciliation, for a native stood on a high hill above our position after all had reached camp, and announced that he had been sent by Mazamboni to say that he received gifts, but that he had been prevented from visiting us according to promise by the clamour of his young men, who insisted on fighting. But now, as many of them had been killed, he was ready to pay tribute, and be a true friend in future.

We replied that we were agreeable to peace and friendship with them, but as they had mocked us, kept our peace presents, and then scornfully called us women, they must purchase peace with cattle or goats, and if they held up grass in their hands they could approach without fear.

It should be mentioned that when the warriors descended the mountain slopes for the fight, every little squad of men was accompanied by a large hound, of somewhat slender build, but courageous, and prompt to attack.

The arms of the Wazamboni consisted of long bows five and a half feet long, and arrows twenty-eight inches long, besides a long sharp spear. Their shields were long and narrow generally, but there were many of the true Uganda type. The arrows were cruelly barbed, and the spear was similar to that of Karagwé, Uhha, Urundi, and Ihangiro.

Chapter 12

ARRIVAL AT LAKE ALBERT, AND OUR RETURN TO IBWIRI

On the 12th December we left camp at dawn without disturbance, or hearing a single voice, and up to 9 A.M. it did not appear
as if anybody was astir throughout the valley. Our road led E. by S.
and dipped down into ravines, and narrow valleys, down which its
tributaries from the mountain range and its many gorges flowed
under depths of jungle, bush, and reed-cane. Villages were seen
nestling amid abundance, and we left them unmolested in the hope
that the wild people might read that when left alone we were an
extremely inoffensive band of men. But at nine o'clock, the chill of
the morning having disappeared, we heard the first war-cries, and
traced them to a large group of villages that crowned a detached
line of hills occupying the foreground of the Undussuma range.
Perceiving that we continued our march without appearing to
notice them, they advanced boldly and hovered on our right flank
and rear.

By 11 A.M. there were two separate bands of natives who followed us very persistently. One had come from the eastward, the
other was formed out of the population of the villages in the valley
that we had left undamaged and intact.

By noon these bands had increased into numerous and frantic
mobs, and some of them cried out, "We will prove to you before
night that we are men, and every one of you shall perish to-day."

At this hour, refreshed by our halt, we resumed the march
through a grassy wilderness. There were no villages in view on
either hand, but the mobs followed us, now and then making dem-
onstrations, and annoying us with their harsh cries and menaces.
An expert shot left the line of march, and wounded two of them at a

range of 400 yards. This silenced them for awhile, as though they were absorbed in wondering what missile could inflict injuries at such a distance. But soon their numbers received fresh accessions, and their audacity became more marked. The rear-guard band presently were heard firing, and possibly with effect; at any rate it was clear they had received a check.

Finally, at 3.30, we came in view of the Bavira villages – the chief of whom is called Gavira – situated on an open plain and occupying both banks of a deep and precipitous ravine hollowed out of the clay by a considerable tributary of the East Ituri. We in the front halted on the eastern bank, as the natives – too tardy to effect anything – came rushing down to prevent the crossing. Loads were at once dropped, skirmishers were despatched from the advance to recross the river, and to assist the rear guard, and a smart scene of battle-play occurred, at the end of which the natives retreated on the full run. To punish them for four hours' persecution of us we turned about and set fire to every hut on either bank, then reforming we hastened up a steep hilly plateau, that rose 200 feet above the plain, to meet the natives who had gathered to oppose us. Long, however before we could reach the summit they abandoned their position and left us to occupy a village in peace. It being now a late hour we camped, and our first duty was to render our quarters safe against a night attack.

It should be observed that up to the moment of firing the villages, the fury of the natives seemed to be increasing, but the instant the flames were seen devouring their homes the fury ceased, by which we learned that fire had a remarkable sedative influence on their nerves.

The village of Gavira's, wherein we slept that night, was 4,657 feet above the sea. It had been a fine day for travel, and a S.E. breeze was most cooling. Without it we should have suffered from the great heat. As the sun set it became very cold; by midnight the temperature was 60°. We had travelled nine miles, and mostly all complained of fatigue from the marching and constant excitement.

On the 13th we set off easterly a little after dawn, in order that we might cover some distance before the aborigines ventured out into the cold raw air of the morning. The short pasture grass was beaded with dew, and wet as with rain. The rear guard, after disarranging our night defences that the natives might not understand the manner of them, soon overtook us, and we left the district in compact order ready for fresh adventures. Until the third hour of the morning we were permitted to travel amid scenes of peaceful stillness. We enjoyed the prospects, had time to note the features of the great plain north of East Ituri, and to admire the multitude of hilly cones that bounded the northern horizon, to observe how the lines of conical hills massed themselves into a solid and unbroken front to the east and west; how to the south of us the surface of the land was a series of great waves every hollow of which had its own particular stream; and how, about five miles off, the mountain range continued from Undussuma East to the Balegga country, whose summits we knew so well, formed itself into baylike curves wherein numerous settlements found water and sweet grass for their cattle and moisture for their millet fields, and finally prolonged itself, rounding northward until its extremity stood east of us. Hence we observed that the direction we travelled would take us before many hours between the northern and southern ranges, to the top of a saddle that appeared to connect them. A group of villages situated on the skyline of this saddle was our objective point at present, until we could take further bearings thence.

But at 9 A.M. the natives began to stir and look around. Every feature of the wide landscape being then free from mist and fog. Our long serpent-like line of men was soon detected and hailed with war-cries, uttered with splendid force of lungs, that drew hundreds of hostile eyes burning with ferocity and hate upon us. Village after village was passed by us untouched, but this, as we experienced the day before, they did not place to our credit, but rather debited us with pusillanimity, all reports of their neighbours notwithstanding. We felt it in our veins that we were being charged with weakness. A crowd of fifty natives stood aside, 300 yards from our path, observant of our conduct. They saw us defile through their settlements with kindly regard for their property, and eyes fixed straight before us, intent on our own business of travel only. Far from accepting this as a proof that there was some virtue in us, they closed behind the column, loudly and imperiously summoned their countrymen to gather together and surround us – a call their countrymen appeared only too willing to obey. As soon as they deemed their numbers strong enough to take the offensive, they charged on the rear guard, which act was instantly responded to by good practice with rifles.

Every half-hour there was a stream at the bottom of its own valley, and a breadth of cane-brake on either side of the brook, which required great caution to keep the impulsive natives at bay.

That group of villages on the skyline already mentioned, connecting the now converging lines of hills to north and south of us, became more and more distinct as we steadily pressed on eastward, and I began to feel a presentiment that before another hour was passed, we should see the Albert Nyanza. But as though there was some great treasure in our front, or as if Emin Pasha and his garrison found himself in the position of Gordon during his last hours at Khartoum, and these were the beleaguering hosts, the natives waxed bolder and more determined, increased in numbers faster, the war-cries were incessantly vociferated from every eminence, groups of men became mobs, and finally we became conscious that a supreme effort was about to be made by them. We cast our eyes about and saw each elevation black with masses of men, while the broad and rolling plain showed lines of figures, like armies of ants travelling towards us.

At 11 A.M. we were near the crest of the last ridge intervening between us and the saddle which we were aiming for, when we caught a view of a small army advancing along a road, which, if continued, would soon cross our track on the other side of the stream that issued from this ridge. The attacking point I felt sure would be a knoll above the source of the stream. The advance guard was about a hundred yards from it, and these were ordered when abreast of the knoll to wheel sharply to the right, and stack goods on its summit, and the word was passed to close files.

As we arrived at the summit of the knoll, the head of the native army, streaming thickly, was at the foot of it on the other side, and without an instant's hesitation both sides began the contest simultaneously, but the rapid fire of the Winchesters was altogether too much for them, for, great as was the power of the united voices, the noise of the Winchesters deafened and confused them, while the fierce hissing of the storm of bullets paralysed the bravest. The advance guard rushed down the slopes towards them, and in a few seconds the natives turned their backs and bounded away with the speed of antelopes. Our men pursued them for about a mile, but returned at the recall, a summons they obeyed with the precision of soldiers at a review, which pleased me more even than the gallantry they had displayed. The greatest danger in reality with half-disciplined men is the inclination to follow the chase, without regard to the design the enemy may have in view by sudden flight. It frequently happens that the retreat is effected for a ruse, and is often practised in Uganda. On this occasion forty men were chasing 500, while 1,500 natives at least were certainly surveying the field on a hill to the right of us, and a similar number was posted to the left of us.

Again we re-formed our ranks, and marched forward in close order as before, but at 12.30 halted for refreshments, with a pretty wide circle around us now, clear of noisy and yelling natives. Our noon halt permitted them to collect their faculties, but though they were undoubtedly sobered by the events of the morning they still threatened us with imposing numbers of the Balegga, Bavira, and Wabiassi tribes.

After an hour's rest the line of march was resumed. We found an exceedingly well-trodden path, and that it was appreciated was evident from the rapid and elastic tread of the column. Within fifteen minutes we gained the brow of the saddle, or rather plateau, as it turned out to be, and, about twenty-five miles away, we saw a dark blue and uniform line of table-land, lifted up into the clouds and appearing portentously lofty. The men vented a murmur of discontented surprise at the sight of it. I knew it was Unyoro, that between us and that great and blue table-land was an immense and deep gulf, and that at the bottom of this gulf was the Albert. For there seemed to be nothing else before us, neither hill, ridge, or elevation, but that distant immense dark blue mass; the eastern slopes of the northern and southern ranges dipped down steeply as it were into a gulf or profoundly deep valley. Our people, on viewing the plateau of Unyoro in the distance, cried out in a vexed manner "Mashallah! but this Nyanza keeps going further and further away from us;" but I cheered them up with, "Keep your eyes open, boys! You may see the Nyanza any minute now," which remark, like many others tending to encourage them, was received with grunts of unbelief.

But every step we now took proved that we were approaching an unusually deep valley, or the Nyanza, for higher and higher rose the Unyoro plateau into view, lower and lower descended the slopes on either hand of our road, until at last all eyes rested on a grey cloud, or what is it, mist? Nay, it is the Nyanza sleeping in the haze, for, looking to the north-eastward it was the colour of the ocean. The men gazed upon the lake fully two minutes before they realised that what they looked upon was water, and then they relieved their feelings with cheers and enthusiastic shouts.

We continued our pace a few minutes longer, until we stood on the verge of the descent from the plateau, and near a small village perched on this exposed situation we made a short halt to take bearings, inspect aneroids, and reflect a little upon our next step.

Though the people were shouting and dancing, and thronging around me with congratulations for having "hit the exact spot so well," a chill came over me, as I thought of the very slight chance there was, in such a country as this, of finding a canoe fit to navigate the rough waters of the Albert. With my glass I scrutinized anxiously the distant shore of the Lake, but I could not see any canoe, neither could I see a single tree in all the long stretch of slope and extended plain of a size suitable for a canoe, and the thought that, after all, our forced march and continual fighting and sacrifice of life would be in vain, struck me for the first time, even while upon every man's lips was the pious ejaculation, "Thank God."

And yet it was just possible we might be able to buy a canoe with brass rods and some red cloth. It would be too hard if our long travels hither were to be quite in vain.

The scene I looked upon was very different to what I had anticipated. I had circumnavigated the Victoria Nyanza and the Tanganika, and I had viewed the Muta Nzigé from a plateau somewhat similar to this, and canoes were procurable on either Lake; and on the Victoria and Tanganika it would not be difficult, after a little search, to find a tree large enough for cutting out a canoe. But I saw here about twenty miles of most barren slopes, rugged with great reeks, and furrowed with steep ravines and watercourses, whose banks showed a thin fringe of miserable bush, and between them were steeply descending sharp and long spurs, either covered with rocky and clayey debris or tall green grass. Between the base of this lengthy fall of slope and the Lake was a plain about five or six miles in breadth, and about twenty miles long, most pleasant to look upon from the great altitude we were on. It resembled a well-wooded park land, but the trees spread out their branches too broadly to possess the desirable stems. They appeared to me to be more like acacia, and thorn-trees and scrub, which would be utterly useless for our purpose.

Our aneroids indicated an altitude of 5,000 feet. The islet marked on Mason's chart as near Kavalli bore E.S.E., magnetic, about six miles from our position. Laying Colonel Mason's chart of the Albert Nyanza before us, we compared it with what was spread so largely and grandly over 2,500 feet below us, and we were forced to bear witness to the remarkable accuracy of his survey. Here and there some trifling islets and two or three small inlets of the Lake into that singular sunken plain which formed the boundary of the Lake as its southerly extremity were observed as omissions.

I had often wondered at Sir Samuel Baker's description of the Albert Nyanza's extension towards the southwest, perhaps oftener after Colonel Mason's mysteriously brusque way of circumscribing its "illimitability," but I can feel pure sympathy with the discoverer now, despite the terrible "cutting off" to which it has been subjected. For the effect upon all of us could not have been greater if the Albert stretched to Khartoum. Whether limited or unlimited, the first view of water and mountain is noble, and even inspiring. Even at its extremity the Lake has a spacious breadth, but as we follow the lines of its mountain banks the breadth widens grandly, the silver colour of its shallow head soon changes into the deep azure of ocean, the continuing expanding breadth, immense girdle of mountains and pale sky, lose their outlines, and become fused into an indefinite blueness at the sea-horizon north-eastward, through which we may vainly seek a limit.

Our point of observation was in N. Lat. 1° 23' 00". The extreme end of the eastern end of the lake bore S.E. magnetic, and the extreme western end bore S.E. and S.E. by S. Between the two extremities there were five inlets, one of which reached two miles further south than any of those observed points.

The table-land of Unyoro maintained an almost uniform level as far as we could see, its terminable point being cut off from view by a large shoulder of mountain, that thrust itself forward from the western range. Southward of the lake and between these opposing heights – that of the table-land of Unyoro on the east, and that of the table-land on the west – extended a low plain which formerly, but not recently, must have been inundated by the waters of the lake, but now was dry firm ground, clothed with sere grass, gently rising as it receded south, and finally producing scrubby wood, acacia and thorn, like the terrace directly below us.

After a halt of about twenty minutes, we commenced the descent down the slopes of the range. Before the rearguard under Lieutenant Stairs had left the spot, the natives had gathered in numbers equal to our own, and before the advance had descended 500 feet, they had begun to annoy the rearguard in a manner that soon provoked a steady firing. We below could see them spread out like skirmishers on both flanks, and hanging to the rear in a long line up the terribly steep and galling path.

While they shot their arrows, and crept nearer to their intended victims, they cried, "*Ku-la-la heh lelo?*" – "Where will you sleep to-night? Don't you know you are surrounded? We have you now where we wanted you."

Our men were not a whir slow in replying, "Wherever we sleep, you will not dare come near; and if you have got us where you wanted us to be, why not come on at once?"

Though the firing was brisk, there was but little hurt done; the ground was adverse to steadiness, and on our side only one was wounded with an arrow, but the combat kept both sides lively and active. Had we been unburdened and fresh, very few of these pestilent fellows would have lived to climb that mountain again.

The descent was continued for three hours, halting every fifteen minutes to repel the natives, who, to the number of forty, or thereabouts, followed us down to the plain.

Half a mile from the base of the mountain we crossed a slightly saline stream, which had hollowed a deep channel, banked by precipitous and in some places perpendicular walls of debris 50 feet high, on either side. On the edge of one of these latter walls we formed a camp, the half of a circle being thus unassailable; the other half we soon made secure with brushwood and material from an abandoned village close by. Having observed that the daring natives had descended into the plain, and knowing their object to be a night attack, a chain of sentries were posted at a distance from the camp, who were well hidden by the grass. An hour after dark the attack was made by the band of natives, who, trying one point after another, were exceedingly surprised to receive a fusillade from one end of the half circle to the other.

This ended a troublous day, and the rest we now sought was well earned.

Inspecting the aneroid on reaching the camping-place, we discovered that we had made a descent of 2,250 feet since we had left our post of observation on the verge of the plateau above.

On the 14th we left the base of the plateau, and marched across the plain that gently sloped for 5 miles to the lake. As we travelled on, we examined closely if among the thin forest of acacia any tree would likely be available for a canoe; but the plain was destitute of all but acacia, thorn-bush, tamarind, and scrub – a proof that the soil, though sufficiently rich for the hardier trees, had enough acrid properties – nitre, alkali, or salts – to prevent the growth of tropical vegetation. We, however, trusted that we should be enabled to induce the natives to part with a canoe, or, as was more likely, probably Emin Pasha had visited the south end of the lake, according to my request, and had made arrangements with the natives for our reception. If not, why ultimately perhaps we should have legitimate excuse for taking a temporary loan of a canoe.

About a mile and a half from the lake we heard some natives cutting fuel in a scrubby wood, not far from the road. We halted, and maintained silence while the interpreter attempted to obtain a reply to his friendly hail. For ten minutes we remained perfectly still, waiting until the person, who proved to be a woman, deigned to answer. Then, for the first time in Africa, I heard as gross and obscene abuse as the traditional fishwoman of Billingsgate is supposed to be capable of uttering. We were obliged to desist from the task of conciliating such an unwomanly virago.

We sent the interpreter ahead with a few men to the village at the lake side, which belonged to a chief called Katonza, and sometimes Kaiya Nkondo, with instructions to employ the utmost art possible to gain the confidence of the inhabitants, and by no means to admit rebuff by words or threats, hostile action only to be accepted as an excuse for withdrawal. We, in the meantime, were to follow slowly, and then halt until summoned, close to the settlement.

The villagers were discovered totally unconscious of our approach and neighbourhood. Their first impulse, on seeing our men, was to fly; but, observing that they were not pursued, they took position on an anthill at an arrow-flight's distance, more out of curiosity than goodwill. Perceiving that our men were obliging, polite, and altogether harmless, they sanctioned the approach of the caravan, and on seeing a white man they were induced to advance near, while assurances of friendliness were being assiduously reiterated. About forty natives mustered courage to draw near for easy parley, and then harangues and counter-harangues, from one side to the other, one party vowing by their lives, by the love of their throats, by the blue sky above, that no harm was intended or evil meditated – that only friendship and goodwill were sought, for which due gifts would be given, the other averring that though their hesitation might be misjudged, and possibly attributed to fear, still they had met – often met – a people called the Wara-Sura, armed with guns like ours, who simply killed people. Perhaps, after all, we were Wara-Sura, or their friends, for we had guns also, in which case they were quite ready to fight the instant they were assured we were Wara-Sura or their allies.

"Wara-Sura! Wara-Sura! What men are these? We never heard of the name before. Whence are they?" &c., &c., and so on unceasingly for three mortal hours in the hot sun. Our cajolings and our winsomest smiles began to appear of effect, but they suddenly assumed moodiness, and expressed their suspicion in the harsh, rasping language of Unyoro, which grated horribly on the hearing. In the end our effort was a complete failure. We had, unknown to ourselves, incurred their suspicion by speaking too kindly of Unyoro and of Kabba Rega, who, we found later, was their mortal enemy. They would not accept our friendship, nor make blood-brotherhood, nor accept even a gift. They would give us water to drink, and they would show the path along the lake.

"You seek a white man, you say. We hear there is one at Kabba Rega's (Casati). Many, many years ago a white man came from the north in a smoke-boat (Mason Bey), but he went away, but that was when we were children. There has been no strange boat on our waters since. We hear of strange people being at Buswa (Mswa), but that is a long way from here. There northward along the lake lies your way. All the wicked people come from there. We never heard any good of men who came in from the Ituri either. The Wara Sura sometimes come from there."

They condescended to show us the path leading along the shore of the lake, and then stood aside on the plain, bidding us, in not unfriendly tones, to take heed of ourselves, but not a single article for their service would they accept. Wondering at their extraordinary manner, and without a single legitimate excuse to quarrel with them, we proceeded on our way meditatively, with most unhappy feelings.

Pondering upon the strange dead stop to that hopefulness which had hitherto animated us, it struck us that a more heartless outlook never confronted an explorer in wild Africa than that which was now so abruptly revealed to us. From the date of leaving England, January 21, 1887, to this date of 14th December, it never dawned on us that at the very goal we might be baffled so completely as we were now. There was only one comfort, however, in all this; there was henceforward no incertitude. We had hoped to have met news of the Pasha here. A governor of a province, with two steamers, life-boats, and canoes, and thousands of people we had imagined would have been known everywhere on such a small lake as the Albert, which required only two days' steaming from end to end. He could not, or he would not, leave Wadelai, or he knew nothing yet of our coming.[10] When compelled through excess of weakness to leave our steel boat at Ipete, we had hoped one of three things: either that the Pasha, warned by me of my coming, would have pre-

---

10. In November, 1887, Emin Pasha wrote to his friend Dr. Felkin: "All well; on best terms with chiefs and people; will be leaving shortly for Kibiro, on east coast of Lake Albert. Have sent reconnoitering party to look out for Stanley, which had to return with no news yet. Stanley expected about December 15th (1887)." We arrived on the 14th.

pared the natives for our appearance, or that we could purchase or make a canoe of our own. The Pasha had never visited the south end of the lake; there was no canoe to be obtained, nor was there any tree out of which one could be made.

Since we had entered the grass land we had expended five cases of cartridges. There remained forty-seven cases with us, besides those at Ipoto in charge of Captain Nelson and Dr. Parke. Wadelai was distant twenty-five days' journey by land, though it was only four by lake. If we travelled northward by land, it was most likely we should expend twenty-five cases in fighting to reach Wadelai, assuming that the tribes were similar to those in the south. On reaching Emin Pasha we should then have only twenty-two left. If we then left twelve cases only with him, we should have only ten to return by a route upon which we had fired thirty eases. Ten cases would be quite as an inadequate supply for us as twelve would be for Emin. This was a mental review of our position as we trudged northward along the shore of the Albert. But hoping that at Kasenya Island, to which we were wending, we might be able to obtain a canoe, I resolved upon nothing except to search for a vessel of some kind for a couple of days, and failing that, discuss the question frankly with my companions.

At our noon halt, a few miles north of Katonza's, the first note of retreat was sounded. The officers were both shocked and grieved.

"Ah, gentlemen," said I, "do not look so. You will make my own regrets greater. Let us look the facts fairly in the face. If the island of Kasenya has no canoe to give us, we must retrace our tracks; there is no help for it. We will devote to-day and to-morrow to the search, but we are then face to face with starvation if we linger longer in this deserted plain. There is no cultivation on this acrid lake terrace, nothing nearer than the plateau. Our principal hope was in Emin Pasha. I thought that he could make a short visit in his steamers to this end of the lake, and would tell the natives that he expected friends to come from the west. What has become of him, or why he could not reach here, we cannot say. But Katonza's villagers told us that they had never seen a steamer or a white man since Mason Bey was here. They have heard that Casati is in Unyoro. Without a boat it means a month's journey to us to find him."

"There is but one way besides retreating that appears feasible to me, and that is by seizing upon some village on the lake shore, and build an entrenched camp, and wait events – say, for the news to reach Unyoro, or Wadelai, or Kabba Rega; and Casati, Emin, or the Unyoro king may become curious enough to send to discover who we are. But there is the food question. These lake villagers do not cultivate. They catch fish and make salt to sell to the people on the plateau for grain. We should have to forage, ascending and descending daily that dreadful mountain slope. For a week or so the natives of the plateau might resist every foraging party, but finally surrender, and emigrate elsewhere to distant parts, leaving a naked land in our possession. You must admit that this would be a most unwise and foolish plan."

"Were our boat here, or could a canoe be procurable by any means, our position would be thus: –We could launch and man her with twenty men, supply them with ten or twelve days' provisions and an officer, and bid the crew 'God speed,' while we could re-ascend to the plateau, seize upon a good position near the edge of the plateau, render it quickly unassailable, and forage north, south, and west in a land abounding with grain and cattle, and keep sentries observing the lake and watching for the signal of fire or smoke. On her arrival, a hundred rifles could descend to the lake to learn the news of Emin Pasha's safety, or perhaps of his departure, viâ Ukedi and Usoga, to Zanzibar. The last is probable, because the latest news that I received from the Foreign Office showed that he meditated taking such a step. But now, as we are without canoe or boat, I feel, though we are but four days by water from Wadelai, that we are only wasting valuable time in searching for expedients, when common-sense bids us be off to the forest, find some suitable spot like Ibwiri to leave our surplus stores, sick men, and convalescents from Ugarrowwa and Ipoto, and return here again with our boat and a few dozen eases of ammunition. In this inexplicable absence of Emin, or any news of him, we should be unwise in wasting our strength, carrying the too great surplus of ammunition, when perhaps the Pasha has departed from his province."

During our afternoon march we travelled along the lake until the island of Kasenya bore from our camping-place 127° magnetic, or about a mile distant, and our observation point on the summit of the plateau bore 289°.

We made a bush fence, and halted at an early hour. The afternoon was likewise spent in considering our position more fully under the new light thrown upon it by the determined refusal of Katonza and his followers to entertain our friendship.

On the morning of the 15th December I sent Lieutenant Stairs and forty men to speak with the people of Kasenya Island, which is about 800 yards from the shore. As the lake is very shallow, the canoe with two fishermen which Lieutenant Stairs hailed could not approach the shore to within several hundred yards. The mud was of unfathomed depth, and none dared to put a foot into it. Along the water's edge the singular wood ambatch thrives, and continues its narrow fringe around the southern extremity of the lake, resembling from a distance an extensive range of fishermen's stakes or a tall palisade. The fishermen pointed out a locality further up the lake where they could approach nearer, and which was their landing-place, the distance they were then at barely allowing the sounds of the voice to be heard. We spent the morning awaiting Lieutenant Stairs, who had considerable difficulty with the mud and swamps. In the afternoon I sent Mr. Jephson and forty men to the landing-place indicated by the natives, which was a low bluff wooded at the summit, with depth of water sufficient for all practical purposes. In reply to a hail a fisherman and his wife came to within a good bow-shot from the shore, and deigned to converse with our party. They said –

"Yes, we remember a smoke-boat came here a long time ago. There was a white man (Colonel Mason) in her, and he talked quite friendly. He shot a hippopotamus for us, and gave it to us to eat. The bones lie close to where you stand, which you may see for yourselves. There are no large canoes on this lake or anywhere about here, for the biggest will but hold two or three people with safety, and no more. We buy our canoes from the Wanyoro on the other side for fish and salt. Will we carry a letter for you to Unyoro? No (with a laugh). No, we could not think of such a thing; that is a work for a chief and a great man, and we are poor people, no better than slaves. Will we sell a canoe? A little canoe like this will carry you nowhere. It is only fit for fishing close to shore in shallow waters like these. Which way did you come here? By the way of the Ituri? Ah! that proves you to be wicked people. Who ever heard of good people coming from that direction? If you were not wicked people you would have brought a big boat with you, like the other white man, and shoot hippos like him. Go your ways – yonder lies your road; but as you go you will meet with people as bad as yourselves, whose work is to kill people. There is no food close to this lake or in all this plain. Fishermen like we have no need of hoes. Look around everywhere and you will not find a field. You will have to go back to the mountains where there is food for you; there is nothing here. Our business is to make salt and catch fish, which we take to the people above, and exchange for grain and beans. This island is Kasenya, and belongs to Kavalli, and the next place is Nyamsassi. Go on. Why do you not go on and try your luck elsewhere? The first white man stopped in these waters one night in his boat, and the next morning he went on his way, and since then we have not seen him or any other."

Go! The inevitable closed around us to fulfil the law that nothing worth striving for can be obtained but by pain and patience. Look where we might, a way to advance was denied to us, except by fighting, killing, destroying, consuming and being consumed. For Unyoro we had no money, or goods fit for Rabba Rega. Marching to Wadelai would only be a useless waste of ammunition, and its want of it would probably prevent our return, and so reduce us to the same helplessness as Emin Pasha was reported to be in. If we cast our eyes lakewards we became conscious that we were bipeds requiring something floatable to bear us over the water. All roads except that by which we came were closed, and in the meantime our provisions were exhausted.

At the evening's council we resolved to adopt the only sensible course left us – that is, to return to Ibwiri, eighteen days' journey from here, and there build a strong stockade, then to send a strong party to Ipoto to bring up the boat, goods, officers, and convalescents to our stockade, and after leaving fifty rifles there under three or four officers, hurry on to Ugarrowwa's settlement, and send the convalescents from there back to Ibwiri, and afterwards continue our journey in search of the Major and the rear column before he and it was a wreck, or marched into that wilderness whence we so narrowly escaped, and then, all united again, march on to this place with the boat, and finish the mission thoroughly, with no anxieties in the rear bewildering or enfeebling us.

The following day, December 16th, a severe rainstorm detained us in camp until 9 A.M. The low hard plain absorbed the water but slowly, and for the first hour we tramped through water up to the knee in some places. We then emerged on a gently rolling plain, where the grass was but three inches high, with clumps of bush and low trees a few score of yards apart, making the whole scene resemble an ornamental park. Arriving at the path connecting the landing-place of Kasenya with the mountain pass by which we descended, we crossed it, keeping parallel to the lake shore, and about a mile and a half from it. Presently herds of game appeared, and, as our people were exceedingly short of provisions, we prepared to do our best to obtain a supply of meat. After some trouble a male kudu fell to my share, and Saat Taro, the hunter, dropped a hartebeest. Two miles beyond the landing-place of Kasenya we halted.

Our object in halting here was to blind the natives of Katonza's, who, we felt sure, would follow us to see if we had moved on, for naturally, having behaved so unruly to us, they might well entertain fears, or at least anxiety, respecting us. At night we proposed to retrace our steps, and follow the road to the foot of the mountain pass, and before dawn commence the steep and stony ascent, and be at the summit before the natives of the table-land above would be astir – as a struggle with such determined people, heavily loaded as we were, was to be avoided if possible.

About 3 P.M., as we were occupied in dividing the game among the hungry people, some native yells were heard, and half a dozen arrows fell into the halting-place. Nothing can give a better idea of the blind stupidity or utter recklessness of these savages than this instance of half a score of them assaulting a well-appointed company of 170 men in the wilderness, any two of whom were more than a match for them in a fight. Of course, having delivered their yells and shot their arrows, they turned sharply about and fled. Probably they knew they could rely upon their speed, for they left our pursuing men far out of sight in an incredibly short time. The ten savages who thus visited us were the same who had affected such solicitude as to come to ascertain if we had lost the road yesterday.

In my rambles after meat during the day, far down the shore of the Lake from the halting-place, I came to vast heaps of bones of slaughtered game. They seem to have been of many kinds, from the elephant and hippopotamus down to the small bush-bok. It is probable that they had been surrounded by natives of the district who, with the assistance of fire, had slaughtered them in heaps within a circle of not more than 300 yards in diameter.

Saat Tato the hunter, after wounding a buffalo, was deterred from following it by the appearance of a full-grown lion, who took up the chase.

The shore of the Lake as it trends North Easterly, increases greatly in beauty. Over a score of admirable camping places were seen by me close by the edge of the Lake, with slopes of white firm sand, over much of which the waves rolled ceaselessly. Behind was a background of green groves isleted amid greenest sward, and game of great variety abounding near by; while a view of singular magnificence and beauty greeted the eye in every direction.

At 5.30 P.M. we gathered together, and silently got into order of march for the base of the mountain. We had three sick people with us, two of them had not yet recovered from the effects of our miserable days in the great forest, another suffered from a high fever incurred in last night's rain-storm.

At 9 P.M. we stumbled upon a village, which confused us somewhat, but the huge mountain, rising like a dark cloud above us, prevented us from retracing our steps, which without it we might well have done, as it was extremely dark. In dead silence we passed through the sleeping village, and followed a path out of it, which, degenerating into a mere trail, was soon lost. For another hour we bore on, keeping our eyes steadily fixed on the darker shadow that rose to the starry sky above us, until at last wearied nature, betrayed by the petulance of the advance guard, demanded a halt and rest. We threw ourselves down on the grass even where we halted, and were soon in deepest slumber, indifferent to all troubles.

At dawn we rose from a deep sleep, drenched with dew and but little refreshed, and gazing up at the immense wall of the table-land that rose in four grand terraces of about 600 feet each, we discovered that we were yet about two miles from the foot of the pass. We therefore pressed forward, and shortly reached the base of the ascent. By aneroids we were 150 feet above the level of the Lake, which was 2400 feet above the sea, and we were 2500 feet below the summit of the saddle, or sunken ridge between the Northern and Southern ranges whose Eastern ends frowned above us.

While the carriers of the expedition broke their fast on the last morsels of meat received from yesterday's hunting, thirty picked men were sent up to seize the top of the ascent, and to keep the post while the loaded caravan struggled upward.

After half-an-hour's grace we commenced ascending up the rocky and rain-scoured slope, with a fervid "Bismillah" on our lips. After the fatiguing night-march, the after-chill of the dew, and drizzling rain and cold of the early morn, we were not in the best condition to climb to a 2500 feet altitude. To increase our discomfort, the Eastern sun shone full on our backs, and the rocks reflected its heat in our faces. One of the sick men in delirium wandered away, another suffering from high bilious fever surrendered and would proceed no further. When we were half-way up twelve natives of Katonza's were seen far below on the plains, bounding along the track in hot chase of the Expedition, with the object of picking up stragglers. They probably stumbled across our sick men, and the ease with which a delirious and unarmed person fell a sacrifice to their spears would, inspire them with a desire to try again. However, Lieutenant Stairs was in charge of the rear guard, and no doubt would give a good account of them if they approached within range.

At the top of the second terrace we found a little stream which was refreshingly cool, for the quartzose rocks and gneissic boulders were scorching. That the column suffered terribly was evident by the manner it straggled in fragments over the slopes and terraced flats, and by the streams of perspiration that coursed down their naked bodies. It was a great relief that our sharp-shooters held the brow of the hill, for a few bold spearmen might have decimated the panting and gasping sufferers.

At the top of the third terrace there was a short halt, and we could command a view far down to the rear of the column, which had not yet reached the summit of the first terrace, and perceived the twelve natives steadily following at about 500 yards' distance, and one by one they were seen to bend over an object, which I afterwards found from the commander of the rear-guard was our second sick man. Each native drove his spear into the body.

Observing their object, it was resolved that their hostility should be punished, and Saat Tato the hunter and four other experts were posted behind some large rocks, between which they could observe without being detected.

In two and three-quarter hours we reached the brow of the plateau, and were standing by the advance-guard, who had done excellent service in keeping the enemy away, and as the rear-guard mounted the height we heard the sharp crack of rifles from the ambushed party, who were avenging the murder of two of their comrades. One was shot dead, another was borne away bleeding, and the ferocious scavengers had fled.

During the short breathing pause the advance-guard were sent to explore the village near by, which, it seems, was the exchange place between the plateau natives and Lakists, and the gratifying news of a rich discovery soon spread through the column. A large store of grain and beans had been found, sufficient to give each man five days' unstinted rations.

At 1 P.M. we resumed our march, after giving positive command that close order should be maintained in order to avoid accidents and unnecessary loss of life. From the front of the column, the aborigines, who had in the interval of the halt gathered in vast numbers, moved away to our flanks and rear. A large party hid in some tall grass through which they supposed we should pass, but we swerved aside through a breadth of short grass. Baffled by this movement they rose from their coverts and sought by other means to gratify their spleenish hate.

In crossing a deep gully near the knoll, which had already witnessed a stirring contest between us, the centre and rear of the column became somewhat confused in the cany grass, and crossed over in three or four broken lines; our third sick man either purposely lagged behind, or felt his failing powers too weak to bear him further, and laid down in the grass, but it is certain he never issued from the gully. We in the advance halted for the column to reform, and just then we heard a storm of triumphant cries, and a body of about 400 exulting natives came leaping down the slopes, infatuated with their noisy rage and indifferent to rear-guards. Doubtless the triumphant cries were uttered when the sick man's fate was sealed. We had lost three! The rush was in the hopes of obtaining another victim. And, indeed, the rear-guard, burdened with loads and harassed, by their duties, seemed to promise one speedily. But at this juncture an expert left the advance and proceeded to take position three hundred yards away from the line of march, and nearer to the exultant natives, who were bounding gleefully towards the tired rear-guard. His first shot laid a native flat, a second smashed the arm of another and penetrated his side. There was an instant's silence, and the advance leaped from their position to assist the rear-guard, who were immediately relieved of their pursuers.

An hour's journey beyond this scene we camped on a tabular hill, which commanded a wide view of rich plains, for the night – footsore and weary beyond any former experience.

On this afternoon I reflected upon the singularity that savages possessing such acute fear of death should yet so frequently seek it. Most men would have thought that the losses which had attended their efforts on the 10th, 11th, 12th, and 13th would deter such as these from provoking strangers who had proved themselves so well able to defend themselves. At one time we had almost been convinced that fire would teach them caution; we had also thought that keeping in a quiet line of march, abstaining from paying heed to their war-cries and their manoeuvres, and only act when they rushed to the attack, were sufficient to give them glimpses of our rule of conduct. But this was the fifth day of our forbearance. We were losing men, and we could ill afford to lose one, for a vast work remained unfinished. We had still to penetrate the forest twice, we had to proceed to Ipoto to carry our boat to the Nyanza, search the shores of the Lake as far as Wadelai – even Dufflé, if necessary – for news of Emin, to return back again to the assistance of Major Barttelot and the rear-column – who were by this time no doubt looking anxiously for help, wearied with their overwhelming task – and again to march through these grass-land tribes to be each time subject to fatal loss through their unprecedented recklessness and courage. I resolved, then, that the next day we should try to find what effect more active operations would have on them, for it might be that, after one sharp and severe lesson and loss of their cattle, they would consider whether war was as profitable as peace.

Accordingly, the next day before dawn I called for volunteers. Eighty men responded with alacrity. The instructions were few –

"You see, boys, these natives fight on the constant run; they have sharp eyes and long limbs. In the work of to-day we white men are of no use. We are all footsore and weary, and we cannot run far in this country. Therefore you will go together with your own chiefs. Go and hunt those fellows who killed our sick men yesterday. Go right to their villages and bring away every cow, sheep, and goat you can find. Don't bother about firing their huts. You must keep on full speed, and chase them out of every cane-brake and hill. Bring me some prisoners that I may have some of their own people to send to them with my words."

Meanwhile we availed ourselves of the halt to attend to our personal affairs. Our shoes and clothing needed repair, and for hours we sat cobbling and tailoring.

At five in the afternoon the band of volunteers returned, bringing a respectable herd of cattle with several calves. Six bulls were slaughtered at once, and distributed to the men according to their companies, who became nearly delirious with happiness.

"Such," said Three O'clock the hunter, "is life in this continent with a caravan. One day we have a feast, and on the next the stomach is craving. Never are two days alike. The people will eat meat now until they are blind, and next month they will thank God if they get as much as a wood-bean." Saat Taro had discovered, like myself, that life in Africa consists of a series of varied sufferings with intervals of short pleasures.

The cold was very great on this high land. Each night since we had entered the grass country we had been driven indoors near sunset by the raw misty weather of the evening, and we shivered with chattering teeth in the extreme chilliness of the young day. On this morning the temperature was at 59° Fahrenheit. The men were stark naked owing to the exactions and extortions of the

Manyuema, and had taken kindly to the leather dresses of the natives, and the bark cloths worn by the aborigines of the forest. After experiencing the extremes of cold to which these open pasture-lands were subject, we no longer wondered at the tardiness shown by the inhabitants to venture out before nine o'clock, and it would have been manifest wisdom for us to have adopted their example, had our task permitted it.

On the 19th December we struck across the rolling plains towards Mazamboni. As we came near Gavira's we were hailed by a group of natives, who shouted out, "The country lies at your feet now. You will not be interfered with any more; but you would please us well if you killed the chief of Undussuma, who sent us to drive you back."

At noon, as we were abreast of the Balegga Hills, two parties of forty men each were observed to be following us. They hailed us finally, and expressed a wish to "look us in the face." As they declined the permission to approach us without arms, they were sharply ordered away, lest we should suspect them of sinister designs. They went away submissively.

In the afternoon we came to the villages of those who had so persistently persecuted us on the 12th. The people were spread over the hills vociferating fiercely. The advance-guard were urged forward, and the hills were cleared, despite the storms of abuse that were poured out by the Balegga.

A few of the captured cattle furnished milk. Our goats also gave an ample supply for tea and coffee, which we were bound to accept as evidence that the heart of Africa could supply a few comforts.

On the 20th our march lay through the rich valley of Undussuma, the villages of which had been fired on the 10th and 11th. Already it had recovered its aspect of populousness and prosperity, for the huts were all built anew, but it was still as death, the inhabitants sitting on the mountains looking down upon us as we marched past. Not being challenged or molested, we passed through in close order amidst a voiceless peace. May it not be that by comparing one day's conduct with another, the now from then, the children of Mazamboni will accept the proffer of friendship which we may make on our return? We felt that the next time we came into the land we should be received with courtesy, if not with hospitality. Thus steadily, in view of hundreds of Mazamboni's warriors, we passed through the renovated valley. The millet was now ripe for the harvest, and with our departure westward, happy days were yet in store for them.

The next day we entered the Abunguma country, and after fording the East Ituri River, camped on the right bank.

The 22nd was a halt – both Lieutenant Stairs and myself were prostrated by ague and footsores; and on the 23rd we marched to the main Ituri River, where we found that the Babusessé had withdrawn every canoe. We proceeded down along the bank to a part of the stream that was islanded. By 2 P.M. of the 24th we had made a very neat and strong suspension bridge from the left bank to an island in midstream, though only two men could travel by it at a time. Uledi, the coxswain of the advance, with a chosen band of thirteen men, swam from the island to the right bank with their rifles over their shoulders, and the gallant fourteen men scoured up and down the banks for canoes, but were unsuccessful. In the meantime a terrible storm of hail as large as marbles beat down our tents, nearly froze the men, and made everybody miserable with cold. The temperature had suddenly fallen from 750 to 52° Fahrenheit. After lasting fifteen minutes the sun shone on a camp ground strewn with hail.

At daylight, Christmas morning, I sent Mr. Jephson and Chief Rashid across the river with instructions to make a raft of banana stalks. It was noon before it was finished, but in the meantime the caravan was passing by the suspension bridge to the island, and the ferriage by raft commenced, taking four men with loads at one trip. In one hour we transported forty men and their loads by these banana stalks. Getting more confident, we sent six men and six loads at one trip, and by 4 P.M. No. 2 Company was safe across. No. 1 Company then turned to haul the cattle from the left bank island, and after the rear-guard had crossed by the bridge, "Three O'clock" laid his bill-hook to the suspension bridge, and with a few strokes destroyed it.

By noon of the 26th the Expedition was across the main Ituri River. Six calves were slaughtered for a Christmas ration of beef. The next day one of our head men died from inflammation of the lungs, caused by a chill caught while halting on the brow of the plateau after the perspiring ascent from the lake plain. By the 29th we had reached Indé-sura; we thence proceeded to the small village of three huts near Iyugu. On the 1st of January, 1888, we camped at Indé-tongo, and the next day passed by a gigantic granite rock in the forest, which sometimes is used by the forest natives as a refuge resort during internecine strife.

On the 6th January we passed by Indé-mwani, and came across the spot whence Msharasha, a Zanzibari, had fallen from a log and broken his neck. The scavengers of the woods – the red ants had eaten the scalp and picked the skull clean, until it resembled a large ostrich egg. The chest of the body was still entire, but the lower limbs were consumed clean. On the next day we entered Ibwiri, and came to Boryo's village; but, alas! for our fond hopes of rendering the village comfortable for occupation, the natives had set fire to their own fine dwell-rags. Fortunately for us, they had taken the precaution to pick out the finest boards, and had stacked many of them in the bush. The large stores of Indian corn had been hastily removed into temporary huts built within the recesses of impervious bush. We set to at once to collect the corn as well as the boards, and before night we had begun the construction of the future Fort Bodo, or the "Peaceful Fort."

Chapter 13

LIFE AT FORT BODO

On arriving at West Ibwiri, about to build Fort Bodo, I felt precisely like a "city man" returning from his holiday to Switzerland or the sea-side, in whose absence piles of business letters have gathered, which require urgent attention and despatch. They must be opened, read, sifted, and arranged, and as he reflects on their import he perceives that there are many serious affairs, which, unless attended to with method and diligence, will involve him in confusion. Our holiday trip had been the direct and earnest march to the Albert Lake, to serve a Governor who had cried to the world, "Help us quickly, or we perish." For the sake of this, Major Barttelot had been allowed to bring up the rear column, the sick had been housed at Ugarrowwa's and Kilonga-Longa's stations, the extra goods had been buried in a sandy caché at Nelson's starvation camp or stored at Ipoto, the boat *Advance* had been disconnected and hidden in the bush, and Nelson and Surgeon Parke had been boarded with the Manyuema, and everything that had threatened to impede, delay, or thwart the march had been thrust aside, or eluded in some way.

But now that the Governor, who had been the cynosure of our imaginations and the subject of our daily arguments, had either departed homeward, or could, or would not assist in his own relief, the various matters thrust aside for his sake required immediate attention. So I catalogued our impending duties thus: –

To extricate Nelson and Parke from the clutches of the Manyuema, also to bring up the convalescents, the *Advance* steel boat, Maxim machine gun, and 116 loads stored at Ipoto.

To construct Fort Bodo, to securely house a garrison; make a clearing; plant corn, beans, tobacco, that the defenders may be secure, fed, and comforted.

To communicate with Major Barttelot by couriers, or proceed myself to him; to escort the convalescents at Ugarrowwa's.

If boat was stolen or destroyed, then to make a canoe for transport to the Nyanza.

If Barttelot was reported to be advancing, to hasten supplies of corn and carriers to his assistance.

And first, the most needful duty was to employ every soul in the building of the stockade, within which the buildings could be constructed at more leisure, and without the necessity of having rifles slung to our shoulders. During our absence the natives had burnt West Ibwiri, and Boryo's fine village was a smoking ruin when we entered. But the finest boards had been stripped off the buildings, and were stacked outside, and the corn had been hastily removed to temporary huts in impervious bush two hundred yards away. These were now invaluable to us.

By the 18th of January the stockade of Fort Bodo was completed. A hundred men had been cutting tall poles, and bearing them to those who had sunk a narrow trench outlining the area of the fort, to plant firmly and closely in line. Three rows of cross poles were bound by strong vines and rattan creepers to the uprights. Outside the poles, again, had been fixed the planking, so that while the garrison might be merry-making by firelight at night, no vicious dwarf, or ferocious aborigine might creep up, and shoot a poisoned arrow into a throng, and turn joy to grief. At three angles of the fort, a tower sixteen feet high had been erected, fenced, and boarded, in like manner, for sentries by night and day to observe securely any movement in the future fields; a banquette rose against the stockade for the defenders to command greater view. For during the months that we should be employed in realizing our stated tasks, the Manyuema might possibly unite to assault the fort, and its defence therefore required to be bullet-proof as well as arrow-proof.

When the stockade was completed, the massive uprights, beams, hundreds of rafters, thousands of climbers, creepers, vines, for the frames of the officers' buildings, storerooms, kitchens, corn-bins, outhouses, piles of phrynia leaves for roofing the houses, had to be collected, and then when the gross work was so far advanced on the evening of the 18th, Lieutenant Stairs was summoned to receive his special instructions, which were somewhat as follows: –

"You will proceed to-morrow with a hundred rifles to Ipoto, to see what has become of Nelson, Parke, and our sick men, and if living to escort every man here. You will also bring the boat *Advance,* and as many goods as possible. The last letters from Nelson and Parke informed us of many unpleasant things. We will hope for the best. At any rate, you have one hundred men, strong and robust as the Manyuema now, and their march to the Albert Lake has made men of them. They are filled with hate of the Manyuema. They go there independent, with corn rations of their own. You may do what you like with them. Now, if Nelson and Parke have no complaints of hostility other than general niggardliness and sulkiness of the Manyuema, do not be involved in any argument, accusation, or reproach, but bring them on. If the boat is safe, and has not been injured, halt but one day for rest, and then hoist her up on your shoulders and carry her here. But if the survivors will prove to you that blood has been shed by violence, and any white or black man has been a victim, or if the boat has been destroyed, then consult with the surviving whites and blacks, think over your plans leisurely, and let the results be what they ought to be, full and final retaliation. That is all, except remember for God's sake that every day's absence beyond a reasonable period necessary for marching there and back, will be dooming us here to that eternal anxiety which follows us on this Expedition wherever we go. It is enough to be anxious for Barttelot, the Pasha, Nelson and Parke and our sick men, without any further addition."

Three cows were slaughtered for meat rations for Stairs' Expedition, each man received 120 ears of corn, goats, fowls, and plaintains were taken for the commander and his two friends, and the party set off for Kilonga-Longa on the 19th.

Stairs' party at muster consisted of – The garrison numbered –
88 men. ....60 men.
6 chiefs.. 3 cooks.
1 officer..4 boys.

```
1 boy........................................................3 whites.
1 cook.
1 Manyema.
98 ....................................................................... 70
```

After the departure of Stairs, I commenced the construction of a corn-bin to store 300 bushels of Indian corn, and to plaster the interior of head-quarters. Jephson busied himself in leveling floor of officers' house. Men carried clay, others rammed and tamped. Some men were on the roofs arranging the large-leaved phrynia one above the other on a kind of trestle frame, others formed ladders, made clay-dough for the walls, doors and windows for the houses, built kitchens, excavated latrines, or dug the ditch – ten feet wide, six feet deep – through a hard yellow clay, that lay under the twenty-four inches of humus and loam of the clearing. When the houses were completed, we made a whitewash out of wood ashes, which gave them a clean and neat appearance.

On the 28th, head-quarters was ready for occupation. We had cleared three acres of land, cut down the bush clean to the distance of 200 yards from the fort, chopped the logs – the lighter were carried away, the heavier were piled up – and fire applied to them, and the next day folded the tents and removed to our mansions, which, as Jephson declared, were "remarkably snug." There was at first a feeling of dampness, but a charcoal fire burning night and day soon baked the walls dry.

To February 6 we extended the clearing, but discovering that natives were prowling about the fort, planting poisoned splinters in the paths, cutting down the bananas, and bent on general mischief, half of the garrison were divided into two parties of patrols, to scour the plantations and the adjoining forest. On this day's explorations several camps of dwarfs were found at the distance of a mile from the fort, with stores of plaintains in their possession. They were thoroughly rousted out, and their camps were destroyed.

After a few days' experiences of life in the buildings we found we were to be annoyed by hosts of rats, fleas, and microscopically small mosquitoes. The rats destroyed our corn and bit our feet, sported wantonly over our faces, and played hide-and-seek under our bedclothes. It seems that by their wondrous craft they had discovered the natives were about to burn West Ibwiri, and had migrated in time out of harm's way into the deep bush and the corn fields, and they probably had a dim idea that such an eligible place would not remain long without tenants. When the commodious

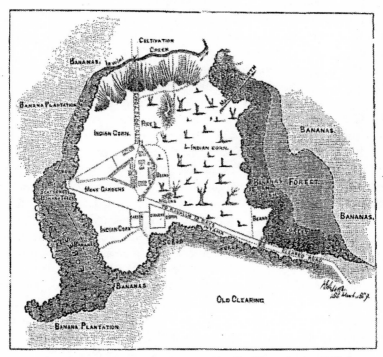

PLAN OF FORT BODO AND VICINITY. *By Lieut. Stairs, R.E.*

houses of the Europeans were erected, with spacious lofts, and corn-bins with an inexhaustible supply of grain, they had waited until everything was prepared; but in the meantime the strange white men had excavated a long and deep ditch half round the fort, the walls of which had been carved perpendicularly out of the clay, into which, in their scurry and hurry to take possession, several families of rats tumbled, and one morning "Randy," the fox-terrier, leaped in among them, and exterminated the unfortunates. Still, from the Zanzibari village some wise old rats had found safe entrance and multiplied so fast that, until we became accustomed to their playful though rude sport, we thought them to be an intolerable nuisance.

At the same time the warm dry clay floors began to breed fleas by myriads. Poor "Randy" was most miserable from these vexatious torments. We were in no better plight. While dressing they made our limbs black with their numbers. To suppress this pest we had recourse to keeping the floors constantly damp, and to sweeping the floors twice a day.

The ordinary mosquito netting was no protection against the mosquitoes of the clearing. They sailed through the open work as mice would creep through antelope nets, and the only remedy was to make mosquito curtains out of cotton muslin, which happily succeeded, but half suffocated the sleepers.

Our soap had long ago been exhausted, and as a substitute, though it was not agreeable to the smell, and was an altogether unsaleable article, we manufactured a soft soap out of castor-oil and lye, and, after a few experiments, succeeded in turning out a hard ball-like substance, which had all the desired effect.

Every night, from Yambuya to the plains, we had been troubled by harsh screams from the lemur. It began at a startling loud key, very deliberate, and as it proceeded the sounds became loader, quicker, and higher, in a quick succession of angry, grating, wailing cries. In the darkness and silence of the night, they sounded very weird. Soon, from a distance of perhaps 200 yards, commenced a response in the same strain, from another sexual mate. Sometimes two or three pairs of these would make sleep impossible, if any indisposition had temporarily disturbed the usual rest.

Armies of red ants would sometimes invade the fort from the clearing; their columns were not interrupted by the ditch. In long, thick, unbroken lines, guarded by soldiers on either flank, the innumerable insects would descend the ditch and ascend the opposite sides, over the parapets, through the interstices of the poles, over the banquette, and down into the plaza of the fort, some columns attacking the kitchen, others headquarters, the officers' mess-house, and woe betide any unlucky naked foot treading upon a myriad. Better a flogging with nettles, or cayenne over an excoriated body, or a caustic bath for a ravenous itch, than these biting and venomous thousands climbing up the limbs and body, burying themselves in the hair of the head, and plunging their shining, horny mandibles into the flesh, creating painful pustules with every bite. Every living thing seems disturbed at their coming. Men are screaming, bellowing with pain, dancing, and writhing. There is a general rustle, as of a host of migrant creatures among the crisp dry phrynia leaves overhead. The rats and mice, snakes, beetles, and crickets are moving. From a slung cot I have observed, by candle-light, the avengers advancing over the floor of my house, scaling the walls, searching the recesses of every layer of leaves, skirmish-ing among the nooks and crannies, mouse-holes, and cracks; heard moaning and crying of little blind mice, and terrified squealing of motherly and paternal rats, and hailed them as a blessing, encourag-ing them along on their career of destruction, until presently some perverse and undisciplined tribes would drop from the roof on my cot, and convert their well-wisher into a vindictive enemy, who, in his rage, would call aloud for hot glowing embers and roast them alive by thousands, until the air was heavy with the odour of friz-zling and frying ants. Bad luck to them!

While digging in the stiff yellow clay, to form the ditch, we have come across burnt wood in the hard compacted material, 5 feet below the surface of the humus. Yet there were stately trees, 100, 150, and 200 years old, above. The site was level, and appar-ently undisturbed.

One of our surprises has been the immunity we have enjoyed from snake-bites in tropical Africa. The continent swarms with rep-tiles of all kinds, from the silvery and blind typhlops to the huge python; but while travelling and navigating over 24,000 miles of land and water in Africa, only two men have been wounded, neither of which cases proved mortal. But the instant we begin clearing a forest, or hoeing a field or a roadway, we begin to realize the dan-gers we have escaped. During the work of clearing the prostrate logs, and rooting out the bushy undergrowth and preparing for cul-tivation, we came across many specimens, some remarkably beau-tiful. Coiled in the bushes, green as a tender young wheat-blade, were the slender whip-snakes, which dropped down among the men when the bill-hook was applied to destroy their perches. Various species of the Dendrophis, of brilliant colouring, also were revealed. Three bloated puff-adders, gorgeous in their complicated system of decorations, were killed; four horned snakes crept out of their holes to attack and be slain; one of the Lycodontidae, curious for its long fangs, was roasted out of its hiding-place, while several little, blind, blunt-headed, silvery snakes, not much larger than earthworms, were turned up by the hoes. Tortoises were very common, and the mephitis left frequent traces of his existence.

While kites, the most daring of their tribe, soared above every clearing in the forest, we never met a single vulture until we reached the grass-land. A few white-collared eagles now and then made their appearance, but there were parrots innumerable. From grey dawn to dusk these birds always and everywhere made their presence known. A few herons occasionally rested on trees in the clearing towards evening. They were probably fatigued with their flight from the Nyanza. The black ibis and wagtails were our constant companions in the wilds. Trees with weaver birds and their nests were a feature near every forest village. The neighbourhood, and finally our plantations, even within a dozen yards of the fort, were visited by troops of elephants. Buffalo and wild-hog tracks were common, but we were not naturalists. None of us had leisure, and probably but little taste, for collection of insects, butterflies, and birds. To us an animal or a bird was something to eat, but with all our efforts we seldom obtained anything. We only noted what happened to catch our eyes or cross our track. We had too many anxieties to be interested in anything save what was connected with them. If a native or a Zanzibari picked up a brilliant longicorn beetle or hawk-moth, or fine butterfly, or a huge mantis, or brought birds' eggs, or a rare flower, a lily or an orchid, a snake or a tortoise, my mind wandered to my own special business, even while gazing at and approving the find. My family was altogether too large to permit frivolity; not an hour passed but my fancies fled after Stairs at Ipoto; or my thoughts were filled with visions of Barttelot and Jameson struggling through the forest, overwhelmed with their gigantic task, or they dwelt upon the mystery surrounding the Pasha, or upon the vicious dwarfs and the murderous Balessé and their doings, or upon the necessities of providing, day after day, food and meat for the present, as well as for future months.

On the 7th of February the sounding line was stretched out to measure out the approaches to the gates of the fort, and most of the garrison were employed for several days in cutting broad, straight roads, east and west, for quick travel and easy defence. Mighty logs were cut through and rolled aside, the roads were cleaned, so that a mouse might be detected crossing them at 200 yards off, a bridge was built across the stream west of the fort, by which the scouts were enabled to proceed from each of the plantations in a short time, by night or by day. It may well be imagined what effect this flood of light had upon the crafty natives, who preferred burrowing in dark shades, and creep under the lee of monster logs, furtively spying out opportunities for attack. They felt that they could not cross the road at any point without becoming a target for a sentry's rifle, or their tracks would betray them to the patrols.

On the next morning we raised a flag-staff 50 feet high, and as the Egyptian flag was hoisted up, the Soudanese were permitted to salute it with twenty-one rounds.

We had scarcely finished the little ceremony when a shot was fired at the end of the western road, the sentry at the tower commanding it sang out, "Sail He," and we knew the caravan was coming in from Ipoto.

Surgeon Parke was the first to arrive, looking wonderfully well, but Nelson, who suffered from sore feet, and entered the fort an hour later, was prematurely old, with pinched and drawn features, with the bent back and feeble legs befitting an octogenarian.

The following account will speak for itself, and will prove that the stay of these officers at the Manyema village required greater strength of mind and a moral courage greater than was needed by us during our stormy advance across the grass-land. They were not inspired by energising motives to sustain or encourage them in their hour of suffering from physical prostration, sickness, and the wearying life they led among those fearful people, the Manyuema, whereas we had been borne up by the novelties of new scenes, the constant high pitch of excitement, the passion of travel and strife. They suffered from the want of the necessaries of life day after day, while we reveled in abundance, and the greatest difficulty of all was to bear all these sufferings inflicted upon them by Ismailia, Khamis, and Sangarameni, who were slaves of Kilonga-Longa, who was the slave of Abed bin Salim, of Zanzibar, sweetly and pleasantly.

Report of Surgeon T. H. Parke, Army Medical Department, in medical charge of E. P. R. Expedition.

Fort Bodo, 8 February, 1888.

Sir, – I have the honour to forward this report for your information. In compliance with your orders dated 24th October, 1887, I remained at the Manyuema Camp to take charge of invalids and impedimenta left there on your departure, 28th October, up to the time the relief party arrived, 25th January, 1888. Of those invalids whom you left at camp, seven were sufficiently recovered to send on with Captain Jephson, 7th November; those remaining were increased in number by the arrival of Captain Nelson, his two boys, and two men, 3rd November; also headman Umari and nine men, who were found in a starving condition in the bush by Kilonga-Longa, and brought to camp by him 9th January; this made a total of one sick officer and thirty-nine invalids remaining in camp; of this number Captain Nelson and sixteen men left with the relief party. Twelve men were away on a journey looking for food, therefore remain at Manyuema Camp, and eleven deaths occurred; this extremely high mortality will no doubt astonish you, especially as it was entirely due to starvation, except in two instances only. From the time you left the Manyuema Camp until our departure, 26th January, the chiefs gave little or no food to either officers or men; those men who were sufficiently strong to do a good day's work, sometimes got as many as ten heads of corn (Indian) per man, but as the working men were not constantly employed, their average ration of corn was about three per day; those invalids unable to work, of whom there were many, received no food from the chiefs, and were therefore obliged to exist on herbs. Remembering the wretched and debilitated condition of all these men, both from privation and disease, you will readily understand that the heartless treatment of the Manyuema chiefs was sufficient to cause even a much greater mortality.

The men were badly housed, and their scanty clothing consisted of about half a yard of native bark-cloth, as they sold their own clothes for food; they experienced not only the horrors of starvation, but were cruelly and brutally treated by the Manyuema, who drove them to commit theft by withholding food, and then scored their hacks with rods, and in one ease speared a man to death (Asmani bin Hassan) for stealing.

Captain Nelson arrived in a very weak condition, requiring good food and careful treatment. He visited the chiefs, and made them handsome presents of articles costing about £75, with a view to win their sympathy; however, they continued to give little or no food to officers or men: they said that no arrangement had been made for provisioning Captain Nelson, and any food they sent to me was entirely of their own generosity, as no arrangement had been made by you. I asked them to let me see the written agreement between you and them, which they did; also another document written in Arabic characters, which I could not read. In their agreement with you I saw that they had promised to provision the officers and men whom you would leave. I appealed to them, and remonstrated with them, nevertheless they supplied less and less food, until finally they refused to give any on the plea that they had none. The height of this generosity would be reached when they would send two or three cups of Indian meal to feed Captain Nelson, myself and the boys, until the next donation would turn up in six or seven days afterwards. During the last seven weeks we did not receive any food whatever from the chiefs. Owing to their refusal to give us food, we were obliged first to sell our own clothes, and eight rifles belonging to the Expedition to provide ourselves and boys with food. I repeatedly reminded Ismaili (chief) of the conversation he had with you in your tent the night before you left the camp, when he promised to look after and care for the officers and men whom you left in camp. Although the chiefs had no food to supply according to their agreement, yet they had always plenty to sell, their object being to com-

pel us to sell the arms and ammunition for food. I send you a complete list of effects left in my charge by Captain Jephson, 7th November, all of which were correct when the relief party arrived, with the following exceptions, viz.: – two boxes Remington ammunition, and one rifle, which were stolen by a Zanzibari (Saraboko), and, I believe, sold to the Nanyuema chiefs.

Several attempts were made to steal the arms, boxes, &c.; on the night of November 7th, the hut in which the baggage was stored was set on fire with a view to taking everything with a rush in the confusion caused by the fire: however, their dream was frustrated, as Captain Nelson, who was ever awake saw the blaze, and gave the alarm just in time for ourselves and our boys to put out the fire before it got to the baggage. I then had the tents pitched according to your directions, not being able to do so earlier, as I had no assistance. All the rifles, ammunition, boxes, &c., were packed in the tents, one of which was occupied by Captain Nelson, and the other by myself. Every effort was made to prevent things being stolen; nevertheless, even Captain Nelson's blankets were taken by a thief who got under the tent from behind. On another occasion I heard a noise at my tent-door, and, jumping out of bed quickly, I found a box of ammunition ten yards off, which had just been taken out of my tent. The thief escaped in the dark.

On the night of January 9th, I heard a noise outside my tent, and, suspecting a thief, I crept out noiselessly to the back, where I caught "Camaroni," a Zanzibari, in the act of stealing a rifle through a hole which he had cut in the tent for this offence. Life at the Manynema Camp was almost intolerable. Apart from starvation, the people, their manner and surroundings, were of the lowest order, and, owing to the mounds of fecal matter and decomposing vegetation which were allowed to collect on the paths and close to their dwellings, the place was a hotbed of disease. Captain Nelson was confined to his bed from sickness for over two months, and I got blood-poisoning, followed by erysipelas, which kept me in bed for five weeks. During our illness the chiefs paid us frequent visits, but always with a view to covet something which they saw in our teats. Their avarice was unbounded, and they made agreements one day only to be broken the next. After the arrival of Kilonga-Longa and his force of about 400, including women, children, and slaves, food became really scarce, therefore the Manyuema were obliged to send out large caravans to bring in food. Twelve Zanzibaris who are absent accompanied these caravans in search of food, and had not returned when I left the camp with the relief party. Starvation was so great just before we left that the native slaves seized one of their comrades, who had gone some distance from the camp to draw water, cut him in pieces, and ate him.

In conclusion, I may mention that Captain Nelson and myself did everything we could to preserve a good feeling with the Manyuema chiefs and people, and we parted on friendly terms.

T. H. Parke.
(Surgeon A. M. D.)
To H. M. STANLEY, Esq.,
Commanding E. P. R. Expedition.

The contrast between the sadly-worn men who reached us from that hot-bed of suffering at Ipoto and our beautifully sleek and glossy men who had reached the Albert was most marked. Their flesh was wasted, their muscles had become shriveled, their sinews were shrunk, and their distinctive and peculiar individualities seemed to have altogether vanished until it had become a difficult matter to recognise them.

On the 12th of February Lieutenant Stairs and his column appeared with every section of the boat in good order. He had been absent twenty-five days, and his mission had been performed with a sacred regard to his instructions and without a single flaw.

The evening of that date was remarkable for a discussion between the head-men and ourselves as to our future steps. I discovered that all the headmen were unanimous for proceeding to the Nyanza to launch the boat and search for news of Emin. My desire was equally great to obtain news of the Pasha; nevertheless, I think very little was required to induce me to abandon the search for the Pasha to obtain news of Major Barttelot, but officers and men were alike unanimous in their demand that we should resolve the fate of Emin Pasha. A compromise was finally effected. It was determined that couriers should be sent with our letters to Major Barttelot, with a map of our route and such remarks as would be of practical use to him. It was also decided that Lieutenant Stairs, after two days' rest, should escort these couriers as far as Ugarrowwa's, and see them safely across the river, and that on returning he should escort the convalescents, who, too feeble to march, had been housed in that settlement on the 18th September; that in order that Lieutenant Stairs should "participate in the honour of being present at the relief of Emin Pasha," we should wait for him until the 25th of March. Meantime we should continue the work of enlarging our domain for corn and bean planting, to prevent any scarcity of food while engaged in the forest.

The distance between Fort Bodo and Ipoto was seventy-nine miles,[11] or 158 miles the round journey, which had occupied Lieutenant Stairs twenty-five days, at the average of six and one-third miles per day, but he had reached Ipoto within seven days, and Jephson and Uledi had accomplished the distance in the same time, that is, at an average rate of travel of a little over eleven miles per day. Now, as Ugarrowwa was 104 miles beyond Ipoto, or 183 miles from Fort Bodo, it was estimated that the journey of 366 miles which Stairs was now about to undertake might be performed within thirty-four days, or at the rate of ten and three quarter miles per day. This would be magnificent travelling, especially in the forest, but as various circumstances might protract the period, it was agreed that if we moved towards the Nyanza on the 25th March, and as the carriage of the boat would necessitate short stages, we should travel slowly, that he might have the opportunity of overtaking us.

---

11. Seventy-nine miles one way, and eighty-four miles by another way.

On the morning of the 16th February, at muster, it was proclaimed that twenty first-class volunteers were required to convey our letters to Major Barttelot, at £10 reward for each man if they succeeded in reaching him, because, said I, "You have all combined to demand that we should find the Pasha first. It is well. But I feel as anxious about the Major as I do about the Pasha. We must find both. You who remember what we suffered must feel what the Major and his friends feel, in those horrible stretches of unpeopled woods, having no idea where they are going or what is waiting for them. You know how grateful we should have been, had we met anybody who could have warned us of the hunger and misery we should meet. Therefore every man who volunteers must be acknowledged as the fittest for this noble work by everyone here. Master Stairs, whom you all know as a man who is never tired, and never says 'enough' when there is something to be done, will show you the road as far as Ugarrowwa's, he will see that you are ferried over with food, and cartridges sufficient, and when you leave, you must race along our old road, which you cannot lose, like men running for a big prize. These letters must be put into the hands of the Major, that he and your brothers may be saved. Where are these fifty dollar men?"

Of course at such times the Zanzibaris are easily roused to enthusiasm, and every man considers himself a hero. Over fifty men came to the front challenging any one to say aught against their manliness or courage, but they had to undergo a searching criticism and bantering review from their fellows and officers, their courage, powers of endurance, activity, dispositions, strength, soundness of mind and body were questioned, but at last twenty men satisfactory to Commander and people received rations, and they were specially enrolled among the men of merit who for distinguished service were to be rewarded with varying sums of money, in addition to their pay, on reaching Zanzibar. Lieutenant Stairs left for Ipoto and Ugarrowwa's at 9 o'clock with fowls, goats, corn, and plantain flour rations for the long journey.

On the 18th my left arm, which had been very painful for four days previously, developed a large glandular swelling, which our surgeon said would prove to be an abscess.

The following is taken from my diary: –

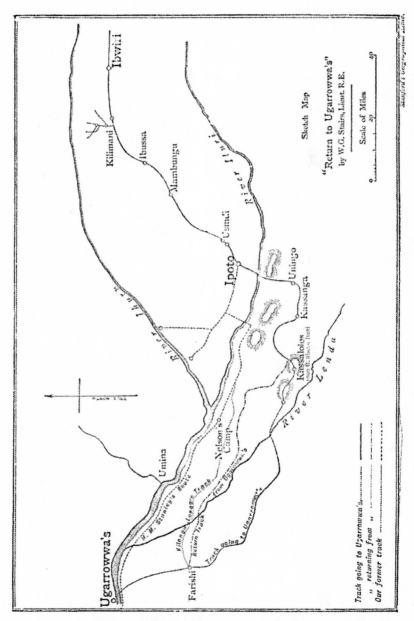

Sketch Map

"Return to Ugarrowwe's"
by W.G. Stairs, Lieut. R.E.

Scale of Miles

February 19th *to March* 13th. – On Sunday night, the 19th, I was attacked with inflammation of the stomach, which has been called by Dr. Parke sub-acute gastritis, of so severe a character that during the first week I had only a confused recollection of great pain in the arm and stomach, and general uselessness. Dr. Parke has been most assiduous in his application to my needs, and gentle as a woman in his ministrations. For once in my life every soul around me was at my service, and I found myself an object of universal solicitude night and day. My faithful friends, Parke and Jephson, waited, and watched, and served. Poor Nelson was himself a victim to ill-health, fevers, debility, eruptions and ulcers, the effects of his terrible agony at Starvation Camp, but he would come, sometimes tottering weakly, to express his sympathy. In the afternoons the Doctor would permit the headmen to visit me, to convey to the anxious Zanzibaris their personal opinions and views of my case. During most of these twenty-three days I have been under the influence of morphia, and the time has passed in unconsciousness. But I am now slowly recovering. Two days ago the abscess, which had become very large, was pierced, and I am relieved of that pain. Meanwhile my daily diet has consisted of a pint of milk – thanks to the Balegga cow – mixed with water. I am therefore so feeble as to be scarcely able to move.

During my illness I have to regret the loss of two good men, Sarmini and Kamwaiya, who have been killed with arrows, and one of the headmen has been severely wounded. This occurred during a patrolling tour as far as the Ihuru, fourteen geographical miles due north from here. Uledi and a party has discovered the haunts of the dwarfs and taller aborigines who rob our plantain groves to be at Alessé and Nderi, fourteen geographical miles east.

I find that Uledi has captured a Queen of the Pigmies, who is the wife of the Chief of Indekaru. She was brought in to be seen by me with three rings of polished iron around her neck, the ends of which were coiled like a watch spring. Three iron rings were suspended to each ear. She is of a light brown complexion, with broad round face, large eyes, and small but full lips. She had a quiet modest demeanour, though her dress was but a narrow fork clout of bark cloth.

Her height is about four feet four inches, and her age may be nineteen or twenty. I notice when her arms are held against the light, a whity-brown fell on them. Her skin has not that silky

THE QUEEN OF THE DWARFS

smoothness of touch common to the Zanzibaris, but altogether she is a very pleasing little creature.

March 13th *to April* 1st. – By the 25th I was well enough to be able to move about a few hundred yards at a time. My arm was still stiff and I was exceedingly feeble. Nelson has recovered somewhat from his successive fits of illness. During my convalescence I have been supported each afternoon to the centre of a lofty colonnade of trees, through which our road to the Nyanza leads, where in an easy chair I have passed hours of reading and drowsing.

It has been a daily delight while helped to my leafy arcade to observe the rapid change in the growth of the corn in the fields, and to see how we have been encroaching upon the forest. Our cultivable area, after being cleaned, hoed, and planted, was not long left with its bare brown face naked. On a certain day it became green with the young corn blades, it had sprouted by thousands as though at the word of command. Only yesterday, as it were, we smiled to see the tender white stalk arched for a spring under a slowly rising clod, and now the clods have been brushed aside, the arched stalks have sprung upright, and the virgin plants have unfolded their tender green crests. Day by day it has been a wonder how the corn has thriven and grown, with what vigour the stalks have thickened, enlarged in leaf, and deepened in green. Side by side in due rank and order they have risen, the blades have extended towards one another in loving embrace, until the whole has become a solid square field of corn, the murmur of which is like the distant wash of a languid sea over a pebbly beach.

This is the music to which I listen devoutly, while my medical friend sits not far off on the watch, and sentries stand still at each end of the avenue on guard. A gentle breeze blows over the forest and breathes upon the corn, causing a universal shiver and motion throughout, and I sit watching the corn tops sway and nod, and salute each other, with the beautiful grace and sweet undertones of many wavelets, until drowsiness overcomes me and seals my senses, and sleep bears me to the region of fantasy. As the sun appears low in the west, and lights the underwood horizontally with mellow light, my kind doctor assists me to my feet and props me, as I wend to the Fort, my corn with dancing motion and waving grace bidding me farewell.

In the warm teeming soil the corn has grown apace until it has reached a prodigious height, tall as the underwood of the forest. Only a few weeks ago I searched amid the clods for a sign of sprouting; a little later and I might still have seen a scampering mouse; a few days ago it was breast high; today I look up and I can scarcely touch the point of a rapier-like blade with a five-foot staff, and a troop of elephants might stand underneath undetected. It has already flowered; the ears, great and swelling, lying snug in their manifold sheaths, give promise of an abundant harvest, and I glow with pleasure at the thought that, while absent, there need be no anxiety about the future.

I am resolved to-morrow to make a move towards the Nyanza with the boat. This is the forty-sixth day of Stairs' absence. I had sent twenty couriers – one of whom returned later – to Major Barttelot. Stairs and his personal attendants numbered seven. I shall leave forty-nine in fort; inclusive of Nelson there will be 126 men left to escort the boat to the Nyanza. Total, 201 of advance column remaining out of 389, exclusive of such convalescents as may be obtained at Ugarrowwa's.

Tippu-Tib has evidently been faithless, and the Major is therefore working the double stages, some hundreds of miles behind; the nineteen couriers are speeding towards him, and are probably opposite the Nepoko at this date, and Stairs has found so many men yet crippled with ulcers that he is unable to travel fast. With 126 men I attempt the relief of Emin Pasha the second time. The garrison consists of all those who suffer from debility, anæmia – who were fellow-sufferers with Nelson at Starvation Camp – and leg sores, some of which are perfectly incurable.

The labour performed about the fort is extensive. Nelson has an impregnable place. The fields of corn and beans are thriving, and of the latter I have enjoyed a first dish to-day. The plantain groves appear to be inexhaustible.

Our broad roads extend about half a mile each way. Ten scouts patrol the plantations every morning, that the mischievous pigmies may not destroy the supplies of the garrison, and that no sudden onsets of natives may be made upon the field hands while at work.

Surgeon Parke accompanies us to the Nyanza tomorrow according to his own earnest request. Though his place is in the fort with the invalids, there are none who require greater attention than can be given by Captain Nelson through his boys, who have been instructed in the art of bathing the sores with lotions of carbolic acid and water.

Our men on the Sundays have amused themselves with performing military evolutions after the method taught by General Matthews at Zanzibar. They are such capital mimics that his very voice and gesture have been faithfully imitated.

Life at Fort Bodo, on the whole, has not been unpleasant except for Captain Nelson and myself. It is true we have fretted and never been free from anxiety respecting the whereabouts and fate of our friends. We have also been anxious to depart and be doing, some thing towards terminating our labours, but circumstances which we cannot control rise constantly to thwart our aims. We have therefore striven to employ every leisure hour towards providing unstinted supplies of food, in the hope that fortune will be good enough to veer round once in our favour, and bring Barttelot and our friends Jameson, Ward, Troup, and Bonny, with their little army of men, to Fort Bodo before our second return from the Nyanza.

Chapter 14

TO THE ALBERT NYANZA
A SECOND TIME

On the 2nd day of April, 1888, after a drizzly rain had ceased to fall, we filed out at noon with a view to attempt a second time to find the Pasha, or to penetrate the silence around him. We had now our steel boat in twelve sections, and the stem and stern being rather beamy we discovered very soon that a good deal of cutting with axes and bill-hooks was required to permit them to pass between the trees. The caravan in single file, laden with boxes, bales, and baggage, would find no difficulty; the narrower sections two feet wide passed through without trouble, but the plough-shaped stem and stern pieces soon became jammed between two colossal trees which compelled a retreat and a detour through the bush, and this could not be effected without clearing a passage. It was soon evident that our second trip to the Nyanza through the forest would consume some days.

The advance guard scanning the track, and fully lessoned in all the crooked ways and wiles of the pigmies and aborigines, picked up many a cleverly-hidden skewer from the path. At some points they were freely planted under an odd leaf or two of phrynium, or at the base of a log, over which, as over a stile, a wayfarer might stride and plant his foot deep into a barbed skewer well smeared with dark poison. But we were too learned now in the art of African forestcraft, and the natives were not so skilled in the invention of expedients as to produce new styles of molestation and annoyance.

The dwarfs' village at the crossing was our next resting-place, and Indé-mwani was reached on the 4th. The next day we moved to another dwarfs' village, and in the neighbouring plantain grove Saat Tato and a few friends, while collecting a few of the fruit, made a splendid capture of pigmies. We had four women and a boy, and in them I saw two distinct types. One evidently belonged to that same race described as the Akka, with small, cunning, monkey eyes, close, and deeply set. The four others possessed large, round eyes, full and prominent, broad round foreheads and round faces, small hands and feet, with slight prognathy of jaws, figures well formed, though diminutive, and of a bricky complexion. "Partial roast coffee," "chocolate," "cocoa," and *"café au lait,"* are terms that do not describe the colour correctly, but the common red clay brick when half baked would correspond best in colour to that of the complexion of these little people. Saat Tato reported that there were about twenty of them stealing plantains which belonged to the natives of Indepuya, who were probably deterred from defending their property by the rumour of our presence in the woods. The monkey-eyed woman had a remarkable pair of mischievous orbs, protruding lips overhanging her chin, a prominent abdomen, narrow, flat chest, sloping shoulders, long arms, feet turned greatly inwards and very short lower legs, as being fitly characteristic of the link long sought between the average modern humanity and its Darwinian progenitors, and certainly deserving of being classed as an extremely low, degraded, almost a bestial type of a human being. One of the others was a woman evidently a mother, though she could not have seen her seventeenth year. No fault could be found in the proportion of any one member; her complexion was bright and healthy; her eyes were brilliant, round, and large; her upper lip had the peculiar cut of that of the Wambutti noticeable in the woman at Ugarrowwas, and the chief's wife of Indekaru, which is the upper edge curving upward with a sharp angle and dropping perpendicularly, resembling greatly a clean up and down cut with a curl up of the skin as though it had contracted somewhat. I believe this to be as marked a feature of the Wambutti as the full nether lip is said to be characteristic of the Austrian. The colour of the lips was pinkish. The hands were small, fingers delicate and long, but skinny and puckered, the feet measured seven inches and her height was four feet four inches.

So perfect were the proportions of this girl-mother that she appeared at first to be but an undersized woman, her low stature being but the result of premature sexual intercourse or some other accidental circumstance, but when we placed some of our Zanzibar boys of fifteen and sixteen years old by her side, and finally placed a woman of the agricultural aborigines near her, it was clear to everyone that these small creatures were a distinct race.

Three hours beyond this great Mbutti village we reached Barya-Kunya amid a drizzly rain.

On the 8th we reached Indepessu, and two days later we travelled from the base of Pisgah, along an easterly path, a new track which led us through the little villages of Mandé to the Ituri river. The natives had all fled from Mandé and the slopes of Pisgah across the river with their movable property, and the men were awaiting events on the left bank, confident that they were beyond reach. As we emerged into view on the right bank I was quite struck with the light brown mass the warriors made against the blackish green of the vegetation behind them. Had they been of the colour of the Zanzibaris they would have formed an almost black mass, but they resembled in colour the ochreous clay banks of this river. They shot a few arrows amongst us across the 150 yards wide stream; some fell short and others hurtled harmlessly by us several yards. In our turn we replied and a general scamper occurred. Ninety minutes later the Expedition was across the Ituri by means of the boat. The vanguard picked up a ten-pound packet of clean native salt which had been dropped by the natives in their flight. Salt was a condiment greatly needed, and we were greatly rejoiced at the prize. We were now in the territory of the Bakuba, near the clearing of Kandekoré, which was one of the richest clearings in the forest of the Upper Congo basin. On the edge of the bank we were 3,000 feet above the sea.

Three-and-a-half hours' march from the Ituri, we issued out of the forest, and again the change from perpetual twilight to brilliant sunlight, and a blue sky was astonishing, and we all smiled to witness its effects on the nerves of our gentle friend and companion, the first son of Erin who had ever viewed the grass lands of these regions. This was the 289th day of Dr. Parke's forest life, and the effect of this sudden emergence out of the doleful shades in view of this enlarged view from the green earth to the shining and glowing concave of Heaven caused him to quiver with delight. Deep draughts of champagne could not have painted his cheeks with a deeper hue than did this exhilarating prospect which now met him.

On the road just before leaving the bush we passed a place where an elephant spear had fallen to the ground, and buried itself so deep that three men were unable to heave it up. Such a force, we argued, would have slain an elephant on the instant.

While sketching Pisgah Mountain in the afternoon from our first camp in the pasture land, I observed a cloud approaching it from the N.W., and all the forest beyond was shaded by its deep shadows, while the rolling plains still basked in hot sunshine. Presently another cloud from the S.E. appeared round the southern extremity of Mazamboni's range, and as it advanced, spread over the blue sky, and became merged with the cloud over the forest, and then rain fell.

At an altitude of 3,200 feet above the sea the village of Bessé is situated, seven hours' march from the Ituri. Though it was yet early forenoon we camped, the abundance of good ripe bananas, corn, fowls, sugar-cane, and banana wine being very tempting, and the distance to other villages east being unknown. Quite an active skirmish soon occurred while we were engaged making ready our quarters. Fetteh, the sole interpreter to the tribes of the plains, was grievously wounded over the stomach. The Babessé attempted various means to molest us as the long grass favoured them, but by posting sharpshooters in the native lookouts in the trees the knowledge that their tactics were supervised soon demoralised them.

We had some speech by means of a native of Uganda with one of these natives, who among his remarks said, "We are quite assured that you black men are creatures like ourselves, but what of those white chiefs of yours? Whence do they come?"

"Oh," our man replied, with wonderful facility for fraudful speech, "their faces change with the birth of each moon, when the moon is getting full their colour is dark like our own. They are different from us, as they came from above originally."

"Ah, true, it must be so," responded the astonished native, as he brought his hand up to his mouth from politeness, to cover the mouth that expanded with surprise.

The more we understand the language of these natives, the more we are struck with the identity of a common origin. How could such as these people have ever heard of such a thing as wit. I heard one native say to a Zanzibari who had met more than his match when he burst out so impatiently at one who had staggered against him,

"Such a fool as thou wast surely never seen elsewhere?"

To which the native replied, with a benevolent smile, "Ay, it is my lord, who is the sole possessor of wisdom."

"Ah, but you are wickedness itself" (personified). "I must not deny it, for all goodness is with thee." It is a common reply among a certain class of white folks when one is accused of being naughty, to reply to the accuser that he is a gentleman, but it must be admitted that the African reply is not inferior in politeness.

A little east of Bessé we lost the native track, and were obliged to strike across country, steering straight for Undussuma Peak which now began to lift itself into view, over the swells of grassland that spread in great waves towards its foot. The sun was fearfully hot, and as the march was mainly through tall grass, we were greatly fatigued. In the afternoon we reached a wooded hollow near a pellucid cool stream, which had its birthplace somewhere among the slopes of Undussuma Range now distant about five miles.

On the 14th, after a march of six hours, we were camped on the spur of Nzera Kum hill, and before us was the same scene which on the 10th and 11th of December witnessed our struggles for mastery with Mazamboni and his tribe. So far our experiences on this journey were very different. We saw no leaping exulting warriors, nor heard a single menace or war-cry; but, as we intended to halt here a day, it was necessary to know what to expect, and we despatched our Mganda interpreter to hail the natives, who were seated afar off on the hilltops looking down upon us. At 5 P.M. after several patient efforts, they were induced to descend and approach, and they finally entered our camp. The process of establishing a friendship then was easy. We could look into one another's faces, and read as in a book what each thought of the other. We mutually exchanged views, wherein they learned that we only needed a free passage to the Lake unmolested, that we had not appeared as enemies, but strangers seeking a halting-place for the night, to pursue our road the next day without disturbance. They pleaded, as an excuse for their former behaviour, that they were assured we were

Wara Sura (soldiers of Kabba Rega) who periodically visited their country, devastated their land, and carried off their cattle.

When we were both convinced that friendship was possible, that our former misunderstanding should not interfere with our future relations, they heard the mystery of our presence explained, that we were only travelling to discover a white chief, who years ago was reported to be somewhere near the sea of Unyoro. Had they ever heard of such a man?

They answered eagerly, "About two moons after you passed us – when you came from the Nyanza – a white man called *'Malleju,'* or the *Bearded One,* reached Katonza's in a big canoe, all of iron.

"Mother! however could she float; and in the middle of it there rose a tall black tree, and out of it came smoke and sparks of fire, and there were many many strange people aboard, and there were goats running about as in a village square, and fowls in boxes with bars, and we heard the cocks crow as merrily as they do among our millet. *Malleju* with a deep deep voice asked about you – his brother? What Katonza said to him we do not know, but *Malleju* went away in the big iron canoe, which sent as much smoke up into the air as though she was on fire. Have no doubt you will find him soon; Mazamboni shall send his runners to the Lake, and by to-morrow's sunset Katonza shall be told of the arrival of *Malleju's* brother."

This was the first news we had heard of Emin Pasha, and it was with the view of this news spreading abroad, and for preparing the natives for the irruption of strangers out of the unknown west, that I had sent couriers from Zanzibar in February, 1887. Had Emin, who expected us December 15th, but taken the trouble to have sent his steamers a nine-hours' steaming distance from his station of Mswa, we should have met with his people December 14th, been spared five days' fighting, a four months' loss of time, and on or about the 15th of March I should have been within the palisades of Yambuya in time to save Barttelot from his assassin, Jameson from his fatal fever attack, Troup from the necessity of being invalided home, Ward from his wholly useless mission to St. Paul de Loanda, and Mr. Bonny from days of distress at Banalya.

The next day was a severe one for me. All the talking was lev-eled at me, and I was imprisoned in my chair from dawn to dusk by crowds of Bavira agriculturists and Wahuma shepherds and herds-men, chiefs and slaves, princes and peasants, warriors and women. It was impolitic to stir from the close circle which the combined oligarchy and democracy of Undussuma had formed around me. What refreshments were taken were handed to me over the heads of nobles and serfs five deep. My chair was in the centre, three umbrella bearers relieved one another – the sun ran his course from east to west; it glowed at noon hours with the intense heat known in torrid deserts, from three to five it scorched my back, then it became cooler, but until the circles broke and were dissolved by the approaching cold accompanying the dusk, I was a martyr to the cause of human brotherhood.

At a very early hour Mazamboni appeared outside of the zeriba with an imposing retinue of followers. He was escorted to the mid-dle of the camp with every mark of respect, officers gracefully bowing their welcome, Zanzibaris and Soudanese, who had chased him and his legions over the hills in December, looking as innocent as though they had never tasted meat and smiling a summer greet-ing. Our best mats were spread under a sickly dwarf tree for the convenience of the august guest, ivory horns gave forth mellow blares, reminding me of the imperial court of the Ramessean auto-crat of Uganda, Usoga, and the island archipelagoes of the Victo-rian Sea. Nothing was omitted that experience with a thousand chiefs of dark Africa had taught me was necessary for lighting up a swarthy face with humour, pleasure, content, and perfect trust. Mazamboni accepted every attention as his by right Divine, but no smile or word greeted us. Was the man deaf and dumb? No; he spoke briefly and low to his sub-chiefs, and his satellites roared with bull voices, as though I needed an auricular trumpet to hear, and the sounds stunned me as though they were rung with a trip-hammer.

"My friends," said I, "my head will crack if you go on thus; besides, you know wisdom is precious. Why should the herd hear State policy?"

"Ah, truly!" said one sage with a beard as white as the father of the Commons ought to have. Nestor lowered his voice, and garru-lously rehearsed the history of the land, described the effect created upon it by the column's approach in December, the hasty councils that were held, and the rash resolution they had adopted, confessing that when they heard there were white men with the strangers they suspected they were wrong in continuing their hostile attitude, but the youthful warriors had been too impetuous and overruled the cautious counsels of the ancients of their tribe; that when they had seen us return from the Nyanza and depart in peace towards the forest, they then knew that the Wara Sura, as we were believed to be, would never have returned so soon from their own Lake, but would have crossed the Semliki to their own country, and then, when they had heard of *Malleju,* the white chief of the iron canoe, was seeking for us, they were convinced they had been all wrong." "But never mind," said we, "the strangers will return from the Kivira (forest), and we shall make it up with them. If they seek our friendship they shall have it, and Mazamboni's blood shall mingle with that of their chief; and we shall be one people, and lo! you have come, and the dreams of our wise men have become real facts. Mazamboni sits as a brother by the side of the white chief; let us see the blood mingle, and never a cloud shall come between you while you are in the land; the belongings of Mazamboni are yours, his warriors, wives, children, the land and all that stands on the face of it are yours. Have I said well, oh, warriors?"

"Well and truly you have spoken," murmured the circles.

"Shall Mazamboni be a son of 'Bula Matari?'"

"He shall."

"Shall there be true peace between us and the strangers?"

"Yea," came in an emotional shout from the mass. Then the mutual right hands of my son, Mr. Jephson, who volunteered to be sacrificed, were clasped crosswise over the crossed knees, the native Professor of Medicine made a slight incision in his arm until the red blood dyed it. My Professor of Secret Ritualism caused the dark red blood of Mazamboni to well out of the vein, and as the liquid of life flowed and dropped over the knees, the incantations were commenced by the sage with the white beard, and as he shook the pebbles in the magic gourd at the range of the peak opposite, and at the horse-shoe range yonder in the plains, and to eastward and westward of the valley, he delivered his terrible curses from the summit of Nzera-Kum, and all men listened unto him with open lips: –

"Cursed is he who breaks his plighted vow.

"Cursed is he who nourisheth secret hate.

"Cursed is he who turneth his back against his friend.

"Cursed is he who in the day of war denieth his brother.

"Cursed is he who deviseth evil to his friend whose blood has become one with his own.

"May the itch make him loathsome, and the hair of his head be lost by the mange; may the adder wait for him by the path, and the lion meet him on his way; may the leopard in the darkness besiege his house, and his wife when she draweth water from the stream, be seized; may the barbed arrow pin his entrails, and the sharp spear be dyed in his vitals; may sickness waste his strength, and his days be narrowed with disease; may his limbs fail him in the day of battle, and his arms stiffen with cramps," and so on, invoking every evil and disease most dreaded, and the Zanzibari Professor of Secret Ritualism, somewhat dumbfounded at first at the series of curses delivered so volubly by Nestor, seized his magic gourd, and shook it at the hills and the valley, at the head of Mazamboni with awful solemnity; at Nestor himself, and the awe-struck following around, and outdid Nestor, from perverted ambition, by frenzy, voice, and gesture, in harmony with it; his eyes rolled wildly, foam came from his lips; he summoned every blight to fall upon the land and its productions, every damnable agency in his folk-lore to hound Mazamboni for ever; every dark and potent spirit out of the limbo of evil imagination to torture him in his waking and sleeping hours, until his actions were so fantastic, his

ONE OF MAZAMBONI'S WARRIORS.

denunciation so outrageous, his looks so like one possessed with a demon, that everyone, native and Zanzibari, broke out into uncontrollable laughter, which caused Murabo, our "medicine man," to sober instantly, and to say in Swahili to us, with a conceited shake of the head,

"Ay! master, how do you like that style for high acting?" which reminded me of nothing so much as Hamlet out-ranting Laertes.

Mazamboni, though undoubtedly paramount chief of Undussuma, seems to be governed by an unwritten constitution. His ministers also are his principal kinsmen, who conduct foreign and home policy even in his presence, so that in affairs of government his voice is seldom heard. Most of the time he sat silent and reserved – one might almost say indifferent. Thus this unsophisticated African chief has discovered that – whether from intuition or traditional custom it is hard to say – it is best to divide government. If the principle has been derived from custom, it proves that from the Albert Nyanza down to the Atlantic the thousand tribes of the Congo basin spring from one parent tribe, nation, or family. The similarity in other customs, physiognomy, and roots of languages, lend additional proofs to substantiate this.

We discovered that the chiefs, as well as the lesser folk, were arrant beggars, and too sordid in mind to recognise a generous act. Though a peace was strenuously sought by all, yet the granting of it seemed to them to be only a means of being enriched with gifts from the strangers. Mazamboni, even after a long day's work, could only be induced to give more than a calf and five goats as a return for a ten-guinea rug, a bundle of brass wire, and ivory horns from the forest. The chief of Urumangwa and Bwessa, that flourishing settlement which in December had so astonished us with its prosperity, likewise thought that he was exceedingly liberal by endowing us with a kid and two fowls.

Among our visitors today were Gavira, the chief of the Eastern Bavira, who proclaimed from a hill that the land lay at our feet when we were returning from the Lake; and also a Mhuma chief, who wore unblushingly the fine scarlet cloth of which we had been mulcted in December to buy peace. He never offered a return gift so long deferred. We discovered that there were two different and distinctly differing races living in this region in harmony with each other, one being clearly of Indo-African origin, possessing exceedingly fine features, aquiline noses, slender necks, small heads, with a grand and proud carriage; an old, old race, possessing splendid traditions, and ruled by inflexible custom which would admit of no deviation. Though the majority have a nutty-brown complexion, some even of a rich dark brown, the purest of their kind resemble old ivory in colour, and their skins have a beautifully soft feel, as of finest satin. These confine themselves solely to the breeding of cattle, and are imbued with a supercilious contempt for the hoemen, the Bavira, who are strictly agricultural. No proud dukeling in England could regard a pauper with more pronounced contempt than the Wahuma profess for the Bavira. They will live in the country of the Bavira, but not in their villages; they will exchange their dairy produce for the grain and vegetables of the hoemen, but they will never give their daughters in marriage but to a Mhuma born. Their sons may possess children by Bavira women, but that is the utmost concession. Now in this I discover the true secret of the varying physiognomies, and the explanations in the variation of facial types.

We have the true negroidal cast of features in the far-away regions of West Africa, with which this proud high-caste race could not possibly come in contact during many centuries; we have the primitive races of the forest, the Akkas, Wambutti, Watwa, and Bushmen, of which the Wambutti are by far the handsomest; have the Zulus, the Mafitte, Watuta, Wahha, Warundi, Wanya-Ruanda, semi-Ethiopic; we have the Ethiopic, slightly degraded, except in the aristocratic families, as in the Wahuma, or, as they are variously called, Waima, Wachwezi, Wawitu, and the Wataturu, who reprosent two human streams, one coming from Ethiopia by way of South-East Galla into Unyoro and the high pastoral lake regions, and the other flowing direct south. The Victoria Lake lies between these sections of superior African humanity.

A Bavira chief complained to me of the haughty contempt with which the Bavira were regarded by the Wahuma, in just such words as these: "They call us hoemen, and laugh to scorn the sober regularity with which we, tilling the dark soil, live through our lives in honest labour. They sweep round on foraging excursions, and know no loved and fixed home; they settle down wherever they are tempted (by pasture), and when there (is trouble) they build a house in another spot."

But to my narrative, as I may deal with the subject further in a special chapter. On the 16th, furnished by Mazamboni with twelve guides, escorted by Gavira and fifty warriors, accompanied by a long line of new friends behind the rear guard, assisted by more than a hundred carriers, we marched to the territory of Gavira, to the village where we had rested in the naked hill-village, after a terrible day of excitement, on the 12th of December. We were now a peaceful procession, with somewhat of a triumphal character. For at every village we appeared the warriors came out and hailed us with friendly greetings, and at Makukuru, the name of the village which we already knew, the women lu-lu-lued. From this settlement in Uzanza we enjoyed an extensive view, embracing all eastward to the brow of the high land overlooking the gulf of the Albert Lake westward as far as Pisgah, six marches distant northward to the cones of Bemberri, southward the hills of the Balegga rose, a mile off.

The Chief of the Bavira is known as Gavira – an hereditary title, though his name is Mpinga. He was a pleasant little man, but stingy; and when not engaged in State councils, talkative. He and his tribe begged for friendship similar to that which was established with Mazamboni; we were only too willing to accede – the conditions being that he should be hospitable to the Expedition on its journeys through his country. Having halted one day at Mazamboni's, it was necessary that we should do equal honour to Gavira; and as this place was only two short marches, or one long march, to the Nyanza, we agreed.

In the evening, two natives arrived from Mbiassi, of the tribe Babiassi, chief of the district of Kavalli, which extended, in a broad strip, down to the Nyanza, who informed me that their chief possessed a small packet, covered with dark cloth, for me, which had been given him by Mpigwa, of Nyamsassi, who had received it from a white man known to them as *Malleju*.

We were surrounded on the next day by hundreds of friendly people who seemed unable to gaze sufficiently at us. They therefore placidly squatted on their haunches, quietly contemplating our movements; the younger members were deputed by the old to gather fuel and sweet potatoes, and to bring millet grain to camp. For trifling gifts, the Zanzibaris obtained their most devoted service for building their huts, and carrying water and attending to their fires, grinding their millet grain into flour; while our men contentedly sat down, encouraging them to hard labour with a friendly nod and bland smile, some bit of iron-work, a pinch of beads, a cowrie or two, or a wristlet of brass wire. Every man picked up a warm-hearted, and ingenious brother; and, excepting in cooking, the natives were admitted into the privilege of fast friendship.

The chief Gavira was robed, in the afternoon, in bright scarlet cloth of first-class quality, and escorted around the camp, with all honour, by our headmen, who introduced him to the various messes with high tribute to his good disposition. He was afterwards shown a mirror, at which he and his elders expressed extraordinary astonishment and fright. They took the reflection of their own faces to be a hostile tribe advancing from the earth towards them, and started to run to a safer distance; but instinctively they halted, as they saw that we did not stir. They then returned on tip-toe, as if to ask what that sudden vision of black faces could possibly have been; for the mirror had been dropped on its face into the ease. In answer to their mute appeal, it was opened again, and they gazed at it fixedly. They whispered to one another – "Why, the faces resemble our own!" They were told that what they saw was a reflection of their own remarkably prepossessing features; and Mpinga, with pride, blushed darkly at the compliment. Perceiving that he could be trusted with it without shock to his nerves, it was put into his hand; and it was amusing to see how quickly personal vanity increased; his elders crowded around him, and all grouped around and were pleased to note how truthfully the mirror reflected each facial characteristic. "See that scar – it is just and exact; but lo! look at your broad nose, Mpinga; why, it is perfect! Ay, and look at that big feather; it actually waves! It is too – too wonderful! What can it be made of? It is like water; but it is not soft by any means; and on the back it is black. Ah, but we have seen a thing to-day that our fathers never saw, eh?"

Uzanza exposed, and open to every blast from each quarter of heaven, will be remembered for a long time. As the sun set, the cold winds blew from lakeward, and smote us sorely; we were so accustomed to the equable temperature of the forest, and so poor in clothing. One officer armed himself with his waterproof; another put on his ulster, and still the wind penetrated to the marrow; and there was no warmth but in the snug beehive huts of the Bavira – whither we retired.

Instead of pursuing along our first course to the Lake, we struck north-east to the village of Kavalli, where the mysterious packet was said to be. The grass was short cropped by numerous herds of cattle, and covered every inch and made it resemble a lawn, save where the land dipped down into the miniature cañons, which had been scooped out by centuries of rain.

As we traversed the smiling land, hailed, and greeted, and welcomed, by the kindly Bavira, we could not forbear thinking how different all this was from the days when we drove through noisy battalions of Bavira, Babiassi, and Balegga, each urging his neighbours, and whooping and hallooing every one to our extermination, with the quick play of light on crowds of flashing spears, and yard-long arrows sailing through the air to meet us; and now we had 157 Bavira actually in front of the advance guard, as many behind the rear guard, while our 90 loads had been distributed among voluntary carriers who thought it an honour to be porters to the same men whom they had hounded so mercilessly a few months previous.

Soon after the arrival of the now numerous column before the thorny zeriba of Kavalli, the chief, a handsome young Mhuma, with regular features, tall, slender, and wonderfully composed in manner, appeared, to show us where we might camp. To such as chose to avail themselves of shelter in his village he accorded free permission; and on being asked for the packet of *Malleju,* he produced it; and, as he handed it to me, said that only his two young men, of all the country, knew that he possessed it; and anxiously asked if he had not done an excellent thing in keeping the secret safe.

Untying the cover, which was of American oil-cloth, I found the following letter: –

Dear Sir, –

Rumours having been afloat of white men having made their apparition somewhere south of this Lake, I have come here in quest of news. A start to the furthest end of the Lake, which I could reach by steamer, has been without success, the people being greatly afraid of Kabba Rega people, and their chiefs being under instructions to conceal whatever they know.

To-day, however, has arrived a man from Chief Mpigwa, of Nyamsassi country, who tells me that a wife of the said chief has seen you at Undussuma, her birthplace, and that his chief volunteers to send a letter of mine to you. I send, therefore, one of our allies, Chief Mogo, with the messenger to Chief Mpigwa's, requesting him to send Mogo and this letter, as well as an Arabic one, to you, or to retain Mogo and send the letter ahead.

Be pleased, if this reaches you, to rest where you are, and to inform me by letter, or one of your people, of your wishes. I could easily come to Chief Mpigwa, and my steamer and boats would bring you here. At the arrival of your letter or man, I shall at once start for Nyamsassi, and from there we could concert our further designs.

Beware of Kabba Rega's men! He has expelled Captain Casati.

Believe me, dear Sir, to be

Yours very faithfully,

(Signed) Dr. Emin.
Tunguru (Lake Albert).[12]
25/3/88. 8 P.M.

The letter was translated to our men, upon hearing which, they became mad with enthusiasm; nor were the natives of Kavalli less affected, though not with such boisterous joy, for they perceived that the packet they had guarded with such jealous care was the cause of this happiness.

Food poured in gratuitously from many chiefs, and I directed Mbiassi to inform the districts around that a contribution from each tribe or section would be gladly received.

On the 20th, I despatched Mr. Jephson and Surgeon Parke, with 50 rifles and two native guides of Kavalli, to convey the steel boat, *Advance,* down to Lake Albert. I am informed by the guides that Mswa station was distant two days only, by boat sailing along the western shore. Mr. Jephson was entrusted with the following letter to Emin Pasha: –

April 18th, 1888.

Dear Sir, –

Your letter was put into my hands by Chief Mbiassi, of Kavalli (on the plateau), the day before yesterday, and it gave us all great pleasure.

I sent a long letter to you from Zanzibar by carriers to Uganda, informing you of my mission and of my purpose. Lest you may not have received it, I will recapitulate in brief its principal contents. It informed you first that, in compliance with instructions from the Relief Committee of London, I was leading an Expedition for your relief. Half of the fund necessary was subscribed by the Egyptian Government, the other half by a few English friends of yours.

It also informed you that the instructions of the Egyptian Government were to guide you out of Africa, if you were willing to leave Africa; if not, then I was to leave such

---

12. When, after reaching Zanzibar, I read Emin Pasha's letter to the Editor of Petermann's 'Mitteilungen' (see No. 4 of the 'Gotha Geog. Journal'), dated 25th March, 1888 (the same date that the above letter was written), which concluded with the significant words: "If Stanley does not come soon, we are lost," most curious thoughts came into my mind which the intelligent reader will find no difficulty in guessing Happily, however, the Pasha kept his own secret until I was far away from Bagamoyo, and I was unable to inquire from him personally what were his motives for not coming to Kavalli, December 14th, 1887, the date he expected us; for remaining silent two months and a half in his own stations after that date, and then writing two such letters as the one above and that to Petermann's Magazine on the same date.

ammunition as we had brought with us for you, and you and your people were then to consider yourselves as out of the service of Egypt, and your pay was to cease upon such notification being given by you. If you were willing to leave Africa, then the pay of yourself, officers and men, was to continue until you had landed in Egypt.

It further informed you that you yourself was promoted from Bey to Pasha.

It also informed you that I proposed, on account of the hostility of Uganda, and political reasons, to approach you by way of the Congo, and make Kavalli my objective point.

I presume you have not received that letter, from the total ignorance of the natives at Kavalli about you, as they only knew of Mason's visit, which took place ten years ago.

We first arrived here after some desperate fighting on the 14th December last. We stayed two days on the shore of the Lake near Kavalli, inquiring of every native that we could approach if they knew of you, and were always answered in the negative. As we had left our boat a month's march behind, we could get no canoe by fair purchase or force, we resolved to return, obtain our boat, and carry it to the Nyanza. This we have done, and in the meantime we constructed a little fort fifteen days' march from here, and stored such goods as we could not carry, and marched here with our boat for a second trial to relieve you. This time the most violent natives have received us with open arms, and escorted us by hundreds on the way. The country is now open for a peaceful march from Nyamsassi to our fort.

Now I await your decision at Nyamsassi. As it is difficult to supply rations to our people on the Nyanza plain, I hope we shall not have to wait long for it. On the plateau above there is abundance of food and cattle, but on the lower plain, bordering the Nyanza, the people are mainly fishermen.

If this letter reaches you before you leave your place, I should advise you to bring in your steamer and boats, rations sufficient to subsist us while we await your removal, say about 12,000 or 15,000 lbs. of grain, millet, or Indian corn, &c., which, if your steamer is of any capacity, you can easily bring.

If you are already resolved on leaving Africa, I would suggest that you should bring with you all your cattle, and every native willing to follow you. Nubar Pasha hoped you would bring all your Makkaraka, and leave not one behind if you could help it, as he would retain them all in the service.

The letters from the Ministry of War, and from Nubar Pasha, which I bring, will inform you fully of the intention of the Egyptian Government, and perhaps you had better wait to see them before taking any action. I simply let you know briefly about the intentions of the Government, that you may turn the matter over in your mind, and be enabled to come to a decision.

I hear you have abundance of cattle with you; three or four milk cows would be very grateful to us if you can bring them in your steamer and boats.

I have a number of letters, some books and maps for you, and a packet for Captain Casati. I fear to send them by my boat, lest you should start from your place upon some native rumour of our having arrived here, and you should miss her. Besides, I am not quite sure that the boat will reach you; I therefore keep them until I am assured they can be placed in your hands safely.

We shall have to forage far and near for food while we await your attendance at Nyamsassi, but you may depend upon it we shall endeavour to stay here until we see you.

All with me join in sending you our best wishes, and are thankful that you are safe and well.

Believe me, dear Pasha,

Your most obedient servant,

Henry M. Stanley.
Commanding Relief Expedition
His Excellency Emin Pasha,
Governor of Equatorial Provinces, &c., &c., &c.

During our halt at Kavalli several hundred natives from the districts round about paid us friendly visits, and the chiefs and elders tendered their submission to me. They said the country was mine, and whatever my commands might be, would be promptly done. By the ready way food was brought in, there was no reason to doubt their sincerity, though as yet there was no necessity to take it too literally. So long as we were not starving, nothing could happen to disturb the peaceful relations commenced with Mazamboni.

According to my means each chief received a present of cloth, beads, cowries, and wire. Mbiassi furnished me with a quart of milk daily in a wooden bowl of this pattern.

MILK VESSEL OF THE WAHUMA.

Chapter 15

THE MEETING WITH EMIN PASHA

On the 25th we departed from Kavalli and camped at Bundi, at an altitude of 4,900 feet above the sea. The village proper was situated 400 feet higher, on the crest of one of those ranges of hills which form the dividing-line between the Congo basin and that of the Nile. From its folds westerly escaped the first infant streams which flowed into East Ituri. On the other side of the narrow rocky spine issued streams which dropped into the gulf of the Albert. Our camp was situated on the very brow of the plateau, in full view of a large portion of the south end of the Albert.

Mbiassi, the handsome chief of Kavalli, accompanied us to do the honours of his tribe to his guests. He commanded the people of Bundi to hurry forward an ample contribution to the camp, and also despatched messengers to the redoubtable Komubi, chief of the Eastern Balegga, who seemed to be considered by these stubborn foes of Kabba Rega as their "Only General," with a message not to lag behind in supplying with food a man, who might be induced to lend his aid in punishing Kabba Rega some day. Mbiassi, commonly called Kavalli by his people, after his district, was a diplomat.

On the 26th we descended the plateau slope once more in 2 hours 45 minutes – and at the foot of it we were quartered in the Balegga village of Badzwa, 2,300 feet below Bundi camp. The Balegga had decamped, but as it was Kavalli's property, he assumed charge, and distributed corn from its granaries, according to the needs of our united followers, sufficient for five days' rations.

Messengers from Katonza, the chief who had declined our friendship on December 14th, who had refused our proffered gifts, who had sent his men to throw arrows into our bivouac of the 16th, and murdered our two sick men, came to say that he was "dying" to see me. He had now heard that Mazamboni, Gavira, Kavalli, and many others were hand-and-glove with the strangers who had humbly begged a drink of water from his people, and he had hastened to make reparation, like Shimei the Benjamite. Before I could frame an answer, stalwart Komubi, the "only general," had descended from the Balegga Hills with a white cow, several goats, and bundles of sweet potatoes, besides many jars of potent beer. It was Komubi and his stubborn fellows who had clung to the rear guard on the 13th December with such persistency, and had attempted a night attack. He now frankly came to express contrition and sorrow that he had mistaken us for Kabba Rega's bandits, and to surrender his country wholly into my hands, and his life, if I so wished it. With this bold chieftain we made friends quickly enough, and after a lengthy interview parted. To Katonza we replied that we would think of his message.

I now turn to the diary form.

August 27th. – Halt at Badzwa. The kites are very bold in this neighbourhood. Seeing their daring, we amused ourselves with putting pieces of meat on the roof of a hut within arm's length of a man standing by, and each time the kite succeeded in escaping with the meat, as the bird, sailing and wheeling round the spot, seemed to know when the attention was relaxed, and that moment dropped plump upon the meat, and sailed away with it fast gripped before the outstretched hand could seize him.

Our hunter, "Three o'clock," went out, and returned with the meat of a fine kudu he had shot.

April 28th. – Halt. Wadi Mabruki, another hunter, went out this morning to compete at game-hunting with "Three o'clock," and in the afternoon he and his followers brought three young roan antelope.

April 29th. – At 8 A.M., as we were about to break camp to march to the Lake, a native guide appeared with a note from Jephson, dated April 23rd, which stated that he had safely reached Mswa, a station of Emin Pasha's, and that messengers had been despatched by the Commandant, Shukri Agha, to apprise Emin

Pasha of our appearance on the lake. A basket of onions – a gift from Shukri Agha – accompanied the note.

At 9 A.M. we set out for the Lake. Two hours later we were camped about a quarter of a mile from the shore, not far from the bivouac ground occupied by us on the 16th December, and on the site of old Kavalli, as the chief showed us. We had five days' rations of grain with us, and meat could be procured from the plain behind us, as it swarmed with large game of various kinds.

From my tent-door, at 4.30 P.M., I saw a dark object loom up on the north-east horizon of the lake. I thought it might be a native canoe, or perhaps the steel boat *Advance* returning, but a binocular revealed the dimensions of a vessel much larger than a boat or canoe could possibly be, and presently a dark puff of smoke issuing from it declared her to be a steamer. An hour later we could distinguish a couple of boats in tow, and at 6.30 P.M. the steamer dropped anchor in the baylet of Nyamsassi, in shore of the island of that name. Scores of our people were on the beach in front of our camp firing guns, and waving signals, but though we were only two miles from the island, no one appeared to observe us.

Ardent messengers were therefore sent. along the shore to inform the party on board of our presence, and these were, unhappily, so exuberant, that as they fired their rifles to give notice, they were fired at in return by the Soudanese, who naturally enough took the wild figures for Kabba Rega's people. However, no harm was done; the boat's crew distinguished their comrades' cries, the word was passed that the people on shore were friends, and the boat was made ready to convey our visitors to the beach near the camp. At eight o'clock, amid great rejoicing, and after repeated salutes from rifles, Emin Pasha himself walked into camp accompanied by Captain Casati and Mr. Jephson, and one of the Pasha's officers. I shook hands with all, and asked which was Emin Pasha? Then one rather small, slight figure, wearing glasses, arrested my attention by saying in excellent English, "I owe you a thousand thanks, Mr. Stanley; I really do not know how to express my thanks to you."

"Ah, you are Emin Pasha. Do not mention thanks, but come in and sit down. It is so dark out here we cannot see one another."

At the door of the tent we sat, and a wax candle threw light upon the scene. I expected to see a tall thin military-looking figure, in faded Egyptian uniform, but instead of it I saw a small spare figure in a well-kept fez and a clean suit of snowy cotton drilling, well-ironed and of perfect fit. A dark grizzled beard bordered a face of a Magyar cast, though a pair of spectacles lent it somewhat an Italian or Spanish appearance. There was not a trace on it of ill-health or anxiety; it rather indicated good condition of body and peace of mind. Captain Casati, on the other hand, though younger in years, looked gaunt, care-worn, anxious, and aged. He likewise was dressed in clean cottons, with an Egyptian fez for a head-covering.

Brief summaries of our incidents of travel, events in Europe, occurrences in the Equatorial Provinces, and matters personal, occupied the best part of two hours, after which, to terminate the happy meeting, five half-pint bottles of champagne – a present from my friend Greshoff, of Stanley Pool – were uncorked and duly drank to the continued good healths of Emin Pasha and Captain Casati.[13]

The party were conducted to the boat, which conveyed them to the steamer.

April 30th. – Marched Expedition to Nsabé, a fine dry grassy spot, fifty yards from Lake and about three miles from Nyamsassi Island. As we passed the anchorage of the steamer *Khedive,* we found a detachment of the Pasha's Soudanese drawn up on the Lake shore on parade to salute us with music. The Pasha was dressed in his uniform coat, and appeared more of a military man than last night.

Our Zanzibaris, by the side of these upright figures, seemed altogether a beggarly troop, and more naked than ever. But I was not ashamed of them. It was by their aid, mean as they appeared, that we had triumphed over countless difficulties, and though they did not understand drill, nor could assume a martial pose, the best of these Soudanese soldiers were but children to them for the needs of a Relief Expedition. After this little ceremony was over I delivered to the Pasha thirty-one eases of Remington ammunition, and I

---

13. The following entries must be read while bearing in mind that thirty-five days previously the Pasha had written to the Editor of Petermann's 'Mitteilungen' a letter, which he concluded with the significant words, *"If Stanley does not come soon, we are lost."*

went aboard the steamer, where I breakfasted on millet cake fried in syrup, and a glass of new milk.

The steamer proved to be the *Khedive,* built by Samuda Brothers in 1869, and is about ninety feet long by seventeen or eighteen feet wide; draught five feet. Though nearly twenty years old, she is still serviceable, though slow. The upper works look well enough, but she is much patched below water, I am told.

On board, besides the Pasha, were Casati, Vita Hassan, a Tunisian apothecary, some Egyptian clerks, an Egyptian lieutenant, and some forty Soudanese soldiers, besides a fine crew. Sometimes, from the familiar sounds heard during moments of abstraction, I fancied myself at Alexandria or on the Lower Congo; but, looking up, and taking a sweeping view around, I became assured that I was on board of a steamer afloat on Lake Albert. As we move slowly about a mile and a half from the shore northward, the lofty mass of the plateau of Unyoro is to our right, and to our left is an equally formidable plateau wall, the ascents and descents of which we know so well. By a glance at the mass of Unyoro, which is darkly blue, I see the reason Baker gave the name of Blue Mountains to our plateau wall, for were we steaming along the Unyoro shore the warm vapour would tint our plateau wall of similar colour. When we have left Nyamsassi Island astern, a damp sheet of rock, wetted by the stream we crossed yesterday in our descent, glistens in the sun like a mirror, and makes it resemble a clear falling sheet of water. Hence Baker gave it the name of a Cascade, as seen by him from the eastern side.

Dr. Junker and Dr. Felkin, especially in the *Graphic* numbers of January, 1887, made us expect a nervous, wiry, tall man of six feet, or thereabouts, but in reality Emin Pasha does not exceed 5 feet 7 inches in height. I remember that the former was anxious that the trousers ordered in Cairo for his friend should be long enough in the extremities. About six inches were cut off the legs before they fitted. He tells me he is forty-eight years old. In appearance he does not indicate such an age; his beard is dark almost to blackness, while his activity would befit a man of thirty or thirty-five.

The Pasha tells me that he has visited Monbuttu, but, like the travellers Schweinfurth, Casati, Piaggia, and Junker, he has not made any astronomical observations, but confined himself solely to the compass survey. The meteorology of this climate, however, has received greater attention, as might be expected from his methodical habitude of mind.

About noon we anchored off Nsabé, and I went ashore to bestir the men to make a respectable camp suitable for a protracted halt in a country that we might well call dangerous owing to the proximity of Kabba Rega. That king, having thrown down the gage of battle to Emin Pasha, might fancy himself strong enough, with his 1,500 rifles, to test our strength; or the Waganda, during their raids, might hear of our vicinity and be tempted by expected booty to make a visit to us.

This evening Emin Pasha came ashore, and we had a lengthy conversation, but after all I am unable to gather in the least what his intentions may be. I have delivered to him his mails, the Khedive's "High Order," and Nubar Pasha's letter.

I had an idea that I might have to wait about two weeks, when we would all march to the plateau and occupy a suitable spot in Undusuma, where, after seeing everything done for complete security and comfort, I could leave him to return to the assistance of the rear column. On being re-united we could resume our march within a few days for Zanzibar; but the Pasha's manner is ominous. When I propose a return to the sea to him, he has the habit of tapping his knee, and smiling in a kind of "We shall see" manner. It is evident he finds it difficult to renounce his position in a country where he has performed viceregal functions.

After laying before him at some length the reasons of the abandonment of the Equatorial Provinces by Egypt he replied, "I see clearly the difficulty Egypt is in as regards retention of these provinces, but I do not see so clearly my way of returning. The Khedive has written to me that the pay of myself, officers and men will be settled by the Paymaster General if we return to Egypt, but if we stay here we do so at our own risk and on our own responsibility, and that we cannot expect further aid from Egypt. Nubar Pasha has written to me a longer letter, but to the same effect. Now, I do not call these instructions. They do not tell me that I must quit, but they leave me a free agent."

"Well, I will supplement these letters with my own positive knowledge, if you will permit me, as the Khedive and Nubar Pasha are not here to answer for themselves. Dr. Junker arrived in Egypt telling the world that you were in great distress for want of ammunition, but that you had a sufficient quantity to defend your position for a year or perhaps eighteen months, providing no determined attack was made on you, and you were not called upon to make a prolonged resistance; that you had defended the Equatorial Provinces so far successfully; that you would continue to do so to the utmost of your ability, until you should receive orders from your Government to do otherwise; that you loved the country and people greatly; that the country was in a prosperous state – quiet and contented – possessed of almost everything required to maintain it in this happy condition; that you would not like to see all your work thrown away, but that you would much prefer that Egypt should retain these provinces, or failing Egypt, some European Power able and willing to continue your work. Did Dr. Junker report you correctly, Pasha?"

"Yes, he did."

"Well, then, the first idea that occurred to the minds of the Egyptian officials upon hearing Dr. Junker's report was, that no matter what instructions you received, you would be disinclined to leave your provinces, therefore the Khedive says that if you remain here, you do so upon your own responsibility, and at your own risk, and you are not to expect further aid from Egypt.

"Our instructions are to carry a certain quantity of ammunition to you, and say to you, upon your obtaining it, 'Now we are ready to guide and assist you out of Africa, if you are willing to accompany us, and we shall be delighted to have the pleasure of your company; but if you decline going, our mission is ended.'

"Let us suppose the latter, that you prefer remaining in Africa. Well, you are still young, only forty-eight; your constitution is still good. Let us say you will feel the same vigour for five, ten, even fifteen years longer; but the infirmities of age will creep on you, and your strength will fade away. Then you will begin to look doubtingly upon the future prospect, and mayhap suddenly resolve to retire before it is too late. Some route will be chosen – the Monbuttu route, for instance – to the sea. Say that you reach the Congo, and are nearing civilization; how will you maintain your people, for food must then be bought for money or goods? And supposing you reach the sea, what will you do then? Who will assist you to convey your people to their homes? You rejected Egypt's help when it was offered to you, and, to quote the words of the Khedive, 'You are not to expect further aid from Egypt.'

"If you stay here during life, what becomes of the provinces afterwards? Your men will fight among themselves for supremacy, and involve all in one common ruin. These are grave questions, not to be hastily answered. If your provinces were situated within reasonable reach of the sea, whence you could be furnished with means to maintain your position, I should be one of the last to advise you to accept the Khedive's offer, and should be most active in assisting you with suggestions as to the means of maintenance; but here, surrounded as this lake is by powerful kings and warlike peoples on all sides, by such a vast forest on the west, and by the fanatic followers of the Mahdi on the north, were I in your place, I would not hesitate one moment what to do."

"What you say is quite true," replied the Pasha, "but we have such a large number of women and children, probably 10,000 people altogether! How can they all be brought out of here? We shall want a great many carriers.

"Carriers for what?"

"For the women and children. You surely would not leave them, and they cannot travel."

"The women must walk; for such children as cannot walk, they will be carried on donkeys, of which you say you have many. Your people cannot travel far during the first month, but little by little they will get accustomed to it. Our women on my second expedition crossed Africa; your women, after a little while, will do quite as well."

"They will require a vast amount of provisions for the road."

"Well, you have a large number of cattle, some hundreds, I believe. Those will furnish beef. The countries through which we pass must furnish grain and vegetable food. And when we come to countries that will accept pay for food, we have means to pay for it, and at Msalala we have another stock of goods ready for the journey to the coast."

"Well, well. We will defer further talk of it till to-morrow."

May 1st. – Halt at Nsabé.

About 11 A.M. Emin Pasha came ashore, and upon being seated we resumed in a short time our conversation of last evening.

"What you told me last night," began the Pasha, "has led me to think that it is best we should retire from Africa. The Egyptians are very willing to go I know. There are about fifty men of them besides women and children. Of those there is no doubt, and even if I stayed here I should be glad to be rid of them, because they undermine my authority, and nullify all my endeavours for retreat. When I informed them that Khartoum had fallen and Gordon Pasha was slain they always told the Nubians that the story was concocted by me, and that some day we should see the steamers ascend the river for their relief. But of the Regulars, who compose two battalions I am extremely doubtful. They have led such a free and happy life here, that they would demur at leaving a country where they enjoy luxuries such as they cannot hope for in Egypt. They are married, and besides, each soldier has his harem; most of the Irregulars would doubtless retire and follow me. Now supposing the Regulars refused to leave, you can imagine my position would be a difficult one. Would I be right in leaving them to their fate? Would it not be consigning them all to ruin? I should have to leave them their arms and ammunition, and on my retiring all recognized authority and discipline would be at an end. There would presently rise disputes and factions would be formed. The more ambitious would aspire to be chiefs by force, and from rivalries would spring hate and mutual slaughter, involving all in one common fate."

"It is a terrible picture you have drawn, Pasha," I said. "Nevertheless, bred as I have been to obey orders, no matter what may happen to others, the line of your duty, as a faithful officer to the Khedive, seems to me to be clear.

"All you have to do, according to my idea, is to read the Khedive's letter to your troops, and ask those willing to depart with you to stand on one side, and those preferring to remain to stand on the other, and prepare the first for immediate departure, while to the latter you can leave what ammunition and guns you can spare. If those who remain number three-fourths or four-fifths of your force, it does not at all matter to any one what becomes of them, for it is their own choice, nor does it absolve you personally from the line of conduct duty to the Khedive directs."

"That is very true," replied the Pasha; "but supposing the men surround me and detain me by force?"

"That is unlikely, I should think, from the state of discipline I see among your men; but of course you know your own men best."

"Well, I shall send the steamer down to-morrow with the Khedive's letter, and you would oblige me greatly if you would allow one of your officers to go and show himself to the troops at Dufflé. Let him speak to the men himself, and say that he has come from the representative of the Government, who has been specially sent by the Khedive to bring them out, and perhaps when they have seen him, and talked with your Soudanese, they will be willing to depart with us. If the people go, I go; if they stay, I stay."

"Now supposing you resolve to stay, what of the Egyptians?"

"Oh, those I shall have to ask you to take charge of."

"Now will you be good enough to ask Captain Casati if we are to have the pleasure of his company to the coast, for we have been instructed to lend him every assistance in our power?"

Captain Casati answered through Emin Pasha.

"If the Governor Emin goes, I go; if he stays, I stay."

"Well, I see, Pasha, that in the event of your staying your responsibilities will be great, for you involve Captain Casati in your own fate."

(A laugh), and the sentence was translated to Casati, and the gallant Captain at once replied.

"Oh, I absolve Emin Pasha from all responsibility connected with me, for I am governed by my own choice entirely."

"May I suggest then, Pasha, if you elect to remain here, that you make your will?"

"Will! What for?"

"To dispose of your pay of course, which must by this time be considerable. Eight years I believe you said? Or perhaps you meditate leaving it to Nubar Pasha?"

"I give Nubar Pasha my love. Pho! There can be only about two thousand and odd pounds due. What is such a sum to a man about to be shelved? I am now forty-eight and one of my eyes is utterly gone. When I get to Egypt they will give me some fine words and bow me out. And all I have to do is to seek out some corner of Cairo or Stamboul for a final resting-place. A fine prospect truly!"

In the afternoon Emin Pasha came again to my tent, and during our conversation he said that he had resolved to leave Africa – "if his people were willing; if not, he would stay with them."

I learned also that the Egyptians were only too willing to leave for their mother-land, and that there were about sixty-five of them. That the first battalion of Regulars numbered a little over 650, and that the second battalion amounted to nearly 800. That he had about 750 Remington rifles, and that the rest were armed with percussion muskets.

May 2nd. – The *Khedive* steamer left this morning for the northward, first to Mswa Station, thence to Tunguru, fourteen and a half hours' steaming from hence; two days later she will sail for Wadelai, the third day for Dufflé. She carries letters from the Pasha to bring up sixty or seventy soldiers, a Major, and as many carriers as can be mustered. She will probably be fourteen days absent. In the meantime we await here her return.

I omitted to state before that the Pasha brought with him, according to my letter, a few bullocks and milk cows, about forty sheep and goats, and as many fowls, besides several thousand pounds of grain, as rations to subsist the Expedition pending the time we should remain on the Nyanza, as the shore in the neighbourhood of Nsabé is entirely destitute of food except what may be obtained by hunting. With care we have quite three weeks' provisions on hand.

Meanwhile the Pasha remains here with Captain Casati and about twenty soldiers, and is camped about 300 yards south of us. He and his people are comfortably hutted. There is every prospect of a perfect rest free from anxiety for some two weeks, while myself and officers will have the society of a most amiable and accomplished man in the Pasha. Casati does not understand English, and his French is worse than my own, so I am excluded from conversing with him. I learn from the Pasha, however, that Casati has had a difficult time of it in Unyoro. Until December last, things progressed tolerably well with him. Residing in Unyoro as Emin Pasha's Agent, he was the means of forwarding the Pasha's letter to Uganda, and transmitting such packets of letters, books, medicines, etc., that Mr. Mackay, Church Missionary Agent, could spare.

Then from Uganda there came suddenly news to Kabba Rega of our Expedition, whose force rumour had augmented to thousands of well-appointed soldiers, who intended to unite with the Pasha's force, and sweep through Unyoro and Uganda devastating every land; and presently a packet of letters for myself and officers was put in Kabba Rega's hands, confirming in a measure the truth of this report. An officer was sent to Casati's house, and the Wanyoro pillaged him of every article, and bound him and his servants to a tree, besides treating him personally with every mark of indignity. Mohammed Biri, an Arab, who had been mainly the medium of communication between Casati and Mr. Mackay, was, I am told, treated in a worse fashion – probably executed as a spy and traitor. Captain Casati and his personal servants, after a while were led out from Unyoro, by Kabba Rega's officials, and when beyond the frontier were tied to trees again in a nude state. By some means, however, they managed to untie themselves and escape to the neighbourhood of the Lake, where one of the servants discovered a canoe and set out for the western shore across the Lake to Tunguru to obtain help from Emin Pasha. One of the Pasha's steamers came across the daring fellow, and the captain on hearing the news, after supplying his vessel with fuel, steamed away to acquaint the Pasha. In a few hours the *Khedive* steamer was under way, commanded by the Governor in person, who had a detachment of soldiers with him. After searching for some time the eastern shore, as directed by Casati's servant, the steamer was hailed from shore by Casati, who in a few moments found himself safe in the arms of his friend. Some soldiers were sent on shore, and Kibero was burnt in retaliation for the injuries done to his agent. Of course, Casati, having been turned out naked into the wilderness, lost all his personal property, journals and memoirs, and with these our letters.

The Captain placed a way-bill in my hand, wherein I learn that postal carriers left Zanzibar on the 27th July, just one month after we had left Yambuya, so that our letters were duly received at Msalala on the 11th September, and arrived at the Church Missionary Station in Uganda, November 1st; and that Captain Casati received six packets of letters on the 1st December, just twelve days before we arrived on the western shore of the Nyanza. As he was expelled on the 13th February, 1888, according to his account our mails seem to have long lain on his hands, probably no means having been presented of sending them to the Pasha.

This morning 3 o'clock (Saat Taro) the hunter set out to shoot game for the camp, accompanied by a few young fellows anxious to participate in the sport. Two buffalo fell victims to the hunter's unerring aim, but a third one, wounded only in the leg, according to the cunning instinct of the beast, rushed away, and making a circle hid himself in some branchy acacias to await his opponent. Mabruki, the son of Kassin, thought he knew the art of buffalo hunting, and set out on the tracks of the wounded animal. The buffalo on the alert no sooner discovered his enemy, than uttering a hoarse bellows charged and tossed him, one of his horns entering the thigh of the unhappy man. While thus prostrate, he was pounded with the head, gored in the side, arms, and ripped in the body, until Saat Taro, hearing the screams, rushed to the rescue when almost too late, and planting a shot in the buffalo's head, rolled him over, dead. A young man hurried to camp to acquaint us with the sad accident. "Three O'clock" set out again, and shot four fine buck roan antelope. While Mabruki was being borne, shockingly mangled, in a cot to our camp, a strong detachment of men were bearing the remains of three buffaloes, and four roan antelopes to serve as provisions for a people already gorged with beef and grain, but, strange to say, there was as much eager clamour and loud demand for their due share as if the men were famished.

On the night of April 30th a strong gale blew nearly all night, and the Pasha signaled to the *Khedive* to drop two anchors. As there was good holding ground the steamer rode the gale safely. Since then we have had several strong squalls accompanied with rain day and night.

May 3rd. – Nsabé Camp.

Kavalli's people, like good subjects to their absent prince, came to visit him to-day, bringing with them ten baskets of potatoes, which were kindly distributed between us and Emin Pasha.

During a long conversation this afternoon Emin Pasha stated, "I feel convinced that my people will never go to Egypt. But Mr.

Jephson and the Soudanese whom you are kind enough to leave with me will have an opportunity to see and hear for themselves. And I would wish you would write out a proclamation or message which may be read to the soldiers, in which you will state what your instructions are, and say that you await their declaration. From what I know of them I feel sure they will never go to Egypt. The Egyptians, of course, will go, but they are few in number, and certainly of no use to me or to any one else."

This has been the most definite answer I have received yet. I have been awaiting a positive declaration of this kind before venturing upon any further proposition to him. Now, to fulfil my promise to various parties, though they appear somewhat conflicting, I have two other propositions to make. My first duty is to the Khedive, of course; and I should be glad to find the Pasha conformable, as an obedient officer who kept his post so gallantly until ordered to withdraw. By this course he would realise the ideal Governor his letters created in my mind. Nevertheless, he has but to speak positively to induce me to assist him in any way to the best of my power.

"Very well," I said; "and now pray listen, Pasha, to two other propositions I have the honour of making to you from parties who would be glad to avail themselves of your services. Added to that which comes from His Highness the Khedive, these two will make three, and I would suggest that, as there appears to be abundant time before you, that you examine each on its merits and elect for yourself.

"Let me repeat them. The first proposition is that you still continue to be an obedient soldier and accompany me to Egypt. On arrival, yourself, your officers and men, will receive your pay up to date. Whether you will be employed by the Government in active service I do not know; I should think you would. Officers of your kind are rare, and Egypt has a frontier where such services as you could render would be valuable. In answer to this proposition you, however, say that you feel convinced your men will not depart from here, and that in the event of a declaration to that effect being given by them that you will remain with them.

"Now, my second proposition to you comes from Leopold, King of the Belgians. He has requested me to inform you that in order to prevent the lapse of the Equatorial Provinces to barbarism, and provided they can yield a reasonable revenue, the Congo State might undertake the government of them if it could be done by an expenditure of about £10,000 or £12,000 per annum; and further, that his Majesty King Leopold was willing to pay a sufficient salary to you – £1,500 as Governor, with the rank of General – in the belief that such employment agrees with your own inclination. Your duty would be to keep open the communications between the Nile and Congo, and to maintain law and order in the Equatorial Provinces.

"My third proposition is: If you are convinced that your people will positively decline the Khedive's offer to return to Egypt, that you accompany me with such soldiers as are loyal to you to the north-east corner of Victoria Nyanza, and permit me to establish you there in the name of the East African Association. We will assist you to build your fort in a locality suitable to the aims of such an association, leave our boat and such things as would be necessary for your purpose with you, and then hasten home across the Masai Land, lay the matter before the East African Association, and obtain its sanction for the act, as well as its assistance to establish you permanently in Africa. I must explain to you that I have no authority to make this last proposition, that it issues from my own goodwill to you, and with an earnest desire to save you and your men from the consequences of your determination to remain here. But I feel assured that I can obtain its hearty approval and co-operation, and that the Association will readily appreciate the value of a trained battalion or two in their new acquisition, and the services of such an administrator as yourself.

"Pray, grant me a patient hearing for a moment or two while I explain definitely to you your position here. The whole system of Egyptian extension up to the Albert Nyanza was wrong. In theory it was beautiful, and it was natural, What more natural than that the Government established at the mouth of a river should desire to extend its authority up along the banks to its source, and such a source as the Nile has. Unhappily, however, it was an Egyptian Government, which, however honest in its intentions, could only depend upon officials of the lowest moral quality and mental calibre. It is true the chief official in these regions has been a Baker, or a Gordon, or an Emin, but all the subordinates were Egyptians or Turks. As you multiplied your stations and increased your posts, you lessened your own influence. While in the centre of your orbit there might be a semblance of government; the outer circles remained under the influences of Turkish and Egyptian officers of some Cairene Pasha, or Bey, or Effendi, whose conduct was licentious and capricious. By military force the country was taken and occupied, and by force the occupation has been maintained ever since. A recognized Government, even if it be that of Egypt, has a legal and moral right to extend its authority and enlarge its domain. If it executes its will effectively, so much the better. Civilization will be benefited, and all peoples are better under a constituted Government, than under none. But was there an effective Government? As far as Lado and Gondokoro, near the White Nile Cataracts, it was tolerable I admit. Steamers could steam from Berber as far as Lado, and the chief official could superintend such sub-Governments as were established, but when, before making roads or preparing and ensuring the means of communication, the Egyptian Government approved the acts of expansion undertaken over the immense, trackless, inaccessible area of the extreme Soudan, it invited the catastrophe that happened. When Mohammed Achmet fired the combustible material that the extortionate subordinates had gathered, the means for extinguishing the flames were scattered over an area of about 500,000 square miles. The Governor-General was slain, his capital taken; one province after another fell; and their governors and soldiery, isolated and far apart, capitulated; and you, the last of these, only saved yourself and men by retreating from Lado. Expanded on the same system, and governed only by the presence of the military, these former Egyptian acquisitions, if retaken, would invite a similar fate. If the military occupation were effective, and each sub-Government cohered to the other, the collapse of the Government need not be feared; but it can never be effective under Egypt. Neither her revenues nor her population can afford it. In the absence of this, only self-interest of the peoples governed can link these distant territories to the Government of Egypt; and this is an element which seems never to have been considered by those responsible for this sudden overgrowth of Cairene empire. When has this self-interest of the people been cultivated or fostered? The captains marched their soldiery to a native territory, raised a flag-staff, and hoisted the red banner with the crescent, and then with a salute of musketry declared the described district around formally annexed to Egypt. Proclamations were issued to all concerned, that henceforth the ivory trade was a monopoly of the Government; and in consequence, such traders as were in the land were deprived of their livelihood. When, to compensate themselves for the loss of profit incurred by these measures, the traders turned their attention to slaves, another proclamation crushed their enterprise in that traffic also. A large number of the aborigines derived profit from the sale of ivory to the traders, others had large interests in the capture and sale of slaves, while the traders themselves, having invested their capital in these enterprises, discovered themselves absolutely ruined, both money and occupation gone. Remember, I am only considering the policy. Thus there were left in the Soudan hundreds of armed caravans, and each caravan numbered from a score to hundreds of rifles. When Mohamed Achmet raised the standard of revolt he had some advantages to offer to the leaders of these caravans made desperate by their losses. What had the Government officials to offer? Nothing. Consequently all vestiges of the Government that had been so harsh, so arbitrary, and unwise, were swept away like chaff. It was to the interest of traders to oppose themselves to the Government, and to endeavour to restore a state of things which, though highly immoral as considered by us, to them meant profit, and, what is more, relief from oppression.

"Now consider the Congo State, which has extended itself much more rapidly than Egyptian authority was extended in the Soudan. Not a shot has been fired, no violence has been offered to either native or trader, not a tax has been levied except at the seaport where the trader embarks his exports. Native chiefs voluntarily offered their territories, and united under the blue flag with the golden star. Why? Because there were many advantages to be derived from the strangers living among them. First, they were protected against their stronger neighbours, every eatable they could raise and sell brought its full value to them of such clothing and other necessaries they needed. Whatever trade they had – ivory, rubber, palm-oil, or kernels – was free and untaxed, and their native customs, or domestic matters, were not interfered with. It was founded without violence, and subsists without violence; when, however, the Congo State initiates another policy, taxes their trade, lays hands upon the ivory as a Government monopoly, meddles with their domestic institutions, absorbs tyrannically all the profits of the European trader, before it is firmly established on the soil, and gathered about its stations sufficient physical force to enable it to do so with impunity, the Congo State will collapse just as disastrously and as suddenly as was the case with Egyptian authority in the Soudan. The disaster that occurred at Stanley Falls station is an indication of what may be expected.

"Now every man who reflects at all will see that these Provinces of yours can never be re-occupied by Egypt while Egypt is governed by Egyptian officials. Egypt cannot afford the sums necessary to maintain an effective occupation over a territory so remote. They are too distant from Wadi Halfa, the present true limit of her territory. When she connects Wadi Halfa with Berber, or Khartoum or Suakim with Berber by railway, Lado may be considered the extreme southern limit of her territory. When a railway connects Lado with Dufflé the true limit of Egyptian authority will be the southern end of this Lake, provided always that the military force will be sufficient to maintain this mode of communication uninterrupted. When do you think all this will happen? During your lifetime?

"Who else, then, will be so quixotic as to cast a covetous eye on these Provinces? The King of the Belgians? Well, there is a stipulation connected with this proposal, and that is, if the Provinces can 'give a reasonable revenue.' You are the best judge of this matter, and whether £10,000 or £12,000 subsidy will suffice for the support of the Government of these Provinces. The revenue, whatever it may be with this additional sum, must be sufficient to maintain about twenty stations between here and Yambuya, a distance of 650 miles or thereabouts; that is, to pay about 1,200 soldiers, about fifty or sixty officers, and a supreme Governor, furnish their equipments, the means of defence, and such transport force as may be necessary to unite the most distant part with the Congo.

"Failing the King of the Belgians, who else will undertake your support and maintenance, befitting your station and necessity?

There are enough kindhearted people in this world possessed of sufficient superfluous means to equip an Expedition once, say, every three years. But this is only a temporary expedient for mere subsistence, and it scarcely responds to your wishes. What then? I await your answer, Pasha, again begging to be excused for being so talkative."

"I thank you very much, Mr. Stanley, I do assure you, from my heart. If I fail to express my gratitude, it is because language is insufficient. But I feel your kindness deeply, I assure you, and will answer you frankly.

"Now, to the first proposition you have made me, I have already given my answer.

"To the second I would say that, first of all, my duty is to Egypt. While I am here, the Provinces belong to Egypt, and remain her property until I retire. When I depart they become 'no man's land.' I cannot strike my flag in such a manner, and change the red for the blue. I have served the first for thirty years; the latter I never saw. Besides, may I ask you if, with your recent experience, you think it likely that communication could be kept open at reasonable cost?"

"Undoubtedly not at first. Our experiences have been too terrible to forget them soon; but we shall return to Yambuya for the rear column, I anticipate, with much less suffering. The pioneer suffers most. Those who follow us will profit by what we have learned."

"That may be, but we shall be at least two years before any news can reach us. No, I do not think that proposition, with all due gratitude to His Majesty King Leopold, can be entertained, and therefore let us turn to the last proposition.

"I do not think that my people would object to accompanying me to the Victoria Nyanza, as their objection, so far as I know, only applies to going to Egypt. Assuming that the people are willing, I admire the project very much. It is the best solution of the difficulty, and by far the most reasonable. For consider that three-fourths of the 8,000 people are women, children, and young slaves. What would the Government do with such a mass of people? Would it feed them? Then think of the difficulty of travel with such an army of helpless people. I cannot take upon myself the responsibility of leading such a host of tender-footed people to die on the road. The journey to the Victoria is possible. It is comparatively short. Yes, by far the last proposition is the most feasible."

"There is no hurry, since you are to await the arrival of the rear column. Turn the matter over in your mind while I go to bring the Major up. You have certainly some weeks before you to consider the question the-roughly."

I then showed him the printed Foreign Office despatches furnished to me by order of Lord Iddesleigh. Among these was a copy of his letter to Sir John Kirk, wherein he offered the Province in 1886 to England, and stated that he would be most happy to surrender the Province to the British Government, or, in fact, any Power that would undertake to maintain the Province.

"Ah," said the Pasha, "they should never have published this letter. It was private. What will the Egyptian Government think of my conduct in venturing to treat of such a matter?"

"I cannot see the harm," I replied; "the Egyptian Government declares its inability to keep the Province, the British Government will have nothing to do with it, and I do not know of any company or body of men who would undertake the maintenance of what I regard, under all the circumstances, as a useless possession. In my opinion it is just 500 miles too far inland to be of any value, unless Uganda and Unyoro have been first brought under law; that is, if you persist in declining King Leopold's offer. If you absolutely decline to serve the King of the Belgians, and you are resolved to stay in Africa, you must trust in my promise to get a British Company to employ you and your troops, which probably has by this time been chartered with the purpose of constituting a British possession in East.

Chapter 16

WITH THE PASHA (CONTINUED)

May 4th. – Mswa, I am told, is 9 hours' distance from Nsabé camp by steamer, thence to Tunguru is 5 hours, and to Wadelai 18 hours. The other fortified stations are named Fabbo, east of Nile; Dufflé end of navigation; Horiyu, Laboré, Muggi, Kirri, Bedden, Rejaf, and three or four small stations inland, west of the Nile.

He has spoken in a more hopeful tone to-day of the prospects of returning, from the shores of the Albert, the Victoria Lake region appearing even more attractive than at first. But there is something about it all that I cannot fathom.

May 6th. – Halt at Nsabé.

Another storm broke out to-day, commencing, at 8 A.M., blowing from the north-east. The previous gales were south-easters, veering to east. Looking toward the steep slope of the plateau walls east and west of us, we saw it shrouded in mist and vapour, and rain-clouds ominous of tempests. The whole face of the Nyanza was foam, spray, and white rollers, which, as they approached the shore, we saw were separated by great troughs, very dangerous to any small craft that might be overtaken by the storm. *May* 7th. – Halt at Nsabé

While at dinner with me this evening, the Pasha informed me that Casati had expressed himself very strongly against the route proposed to be taken, *viâ* Usongora, south, and advised the Pasha to take the Monbuttu route to the Congo. From which I conclude that the Pasha has been speaking to Casati about going home. Has he then altered his mind about the Victoria?

May 8th. – Halt at Nsabé.

Each day has its storm of wind and rain, loud thunder-claps, preceded by a play of lightning flashes, most beautiful, but terrible.

Discovered a nest of young crocodiles, thirty-seven in number, having just issued from their egg-homes. By-the-bye, to those unacquainted with the fact, a crocodile has five claws on the fore feet, and only four claws on the hinder. It has been stated that a crocodile raises the upper jaw to devour, whereas the fact is it depresses the lower jaw like other animals.

May 9th, 10th. – Halt at Nsabé.

May 11th. – Food supply is getting low. Five men have wandered off in search of something, and have not returned since yesterday. I hope we are not going to be demoralized again.

Mr. Jephson is suffering from a bilious attack.

Lake Ibrahim, or Gita Nzige according to the Pasha, is only an expansion of the Victoria Nile, similar to that below Wadelai and Lake Albert, the Upper Congo, and Stanley Pool. Consequently it has numerous channels, separated by lines of islets and sand-bars. Both Gordon and Emin Pasha have travelled by land along its right bank.

At 9 P.M. I received dismal intelligence. Four men, whom I observed playing on the sandy shore of the lake at 4 o'clock, suddenly took it into their heads to make a raid on some Balegga villages at the foot of the plateau N.N.W. from here. They were surrounded by the natives, and two of them seemed to have been killed, while the other two, who escaped, show severe wounds.

May 12th. – Halt at Nsabé.

This morning sent Doctor Parke with forty-five rifles to hunt up the two missing men. One of them came in at 9 A.M. after a night spent in the wilderness. He has a deep gash in the back from a spear that had been hurled at him. Fortunately it did not penetrate the vital parts. He tells me he was exchanging meat for flour when he heard rifle shots ahead, and at once there was general alarm. The natives fled one way and he fled another, but presently found himself pursued, and received a spear wound in the back. He managed to outrun the pursuer, until in the deep grass of watercourse he managed to hide while a number of natives were searching for him. He lay there all night, and when the sun was up, lifted his head to take a look round, and seeing no one, made his way to the camp.

I am never quite satisfied as to the manner of these accidents, whether the natives or the Zanzibaris are the aggressors. The latter relate with exceeding plausibility their version of the matter, but they are such adepts in the art of lying that I am frequently bewildered. The extraction of the truth in this instance seems to be so hopeless that I tell them I judge of the matter thus:

"You Zanzibaris, so long as you receive five or six pounds of flour and as many pounds of meat daily, become so lazy, you would not go to the steamer for more to provide rations while she would be absent. She has been gone now several days, your rations are nearly exhausted, of course, for who can supply you with as much meat as you can waste, and you left camp without permission, to steal from the Balegga. There was quite a party of you, I hear, and most of you, on seeing the village fairly crowded with natives, were more prudent than others, and traded a little meat for flour, but your bolder companions passed on, and began to loot fowls. The natives resented this, shot their arrows at the thieves, who fired in return, and there was a general flight. One of your number has been killed. I have lost a rifle, and three more of you have been wounded, and will be unfit for work for a long time. That is the truth of the matter, and therefore I shall give you no medicines. Cure your own wounds if you can, and you three fellows, if you recover, shall pay me for my rifle.

May 13th. – Halt at Nsabé.

The doctor returned from his quest of the missing without further incident than burning two small villages and firing a few shots at distant parties. He was unable to recover the body of the Zanzibari, or his Winchester rifle. Where he fell was marked with a good deal of blood, and it is probable that he wounded some of his foes.

A real tornado blew last night. Inky clouds gathering to the S.E.E. and N.E. prepared us somewhat for a wet night, but not for the fearful volume of wind which pressed on us with such solid force as to wreck camp and lay low the tents. The sound, as it approached, resembled that which we might expect from the rupture of a dam or the rush from a collapsed reservoir. The rain, swept by such a powerful force, pierced everywhere. No precaution that we had been taught by past experience of this Nyanza weather availed us against the searching, penetrative power of the rain and its fine spray. From under the huts and tents, and along the ridge poles, through close shut windows, ventilators, and doors, the tornado drove the rain in until we were deluged. To contend against such power of wind and water in a pitchy darkness in the midst of a deafening uproar was so hopeless a task that our only refuge was to bear it in silence and with closed lips. Daylight revealed a placid lake, a ragged sky, plateau tops buried in masses of vapour, a wrecked camp, prostrate tents, and soaking furniture. So terrible was the roar of the surf that we should have wished to have viewed the careering rollers and tempestuous face of the lake by daylight. It is to be hoped that the old *Khedive* was safely harboured, otherwise she must have foundered.

May 14th. – Halt at Nsabé.

The steamer *Khedive* arrived this afternoon, bringing in a supply of millet grain and a few milch cows. The Pasha came up smiling with welcome gifts for each of us. To me he gave a pair of stout walking shoes in exchange for a smaller pair of boots to be given him on my return with the rear column. Mr. Jephson was made happy with a shirt, a singlet, and a pair of drawers; while Dr. Parke, whose grand kit had been stolen by an absconding Zanzibari, received a blue jersey, a singlet, and a pair of drawers. Each of us also received a pot of honey, some bananas, oranges, and water melons, onions, and salt. I also received a pound of "Honeydew Tobacco" and a bottle of pickles.

These gifts, such as clothes, that our officers have received from Emin Pasha, reveal that he was not in the extreme distress we had imagined, and that there was no necessity for the advance to have pressed forward so hurriedly.[14] We left all our comforts and reserves of clothing behind at Yambuya, that we might press on to the rescue of one whom we imagined was distressed not only for want of means of defence from enemies, but in want of clothing. Besides the double trip we have made to Lake Albert, I fear I shall have to travel far to go to the rescue of Major Barttelot and the rear column. God only knows where he is. He may not have left Yambuya yet, and if so we shall have 1300 miles extra marching to perform. It is a terribly long march through a forbidding country, and I

---

14.   Yet, Emin Pasha wrote a letter on the 25th March, 1888, to the Editor of Petermann's Magazine, fifty days previously, which he concluded with the words, "If Stanley does not come soon, we are lost."

fear I shall lose many and many a good soul before it is ended. However, God's will be done.

He introduced to me to-day Selim Bey and Major Awash Effendi, and other officers. I had suggested to him two or three days ago that he could assist me greatly if he constructed a small station on Nyamsassi Island, where we would be sure to have easy communication with his people, on which he also could store a reserve of corn ready for the arrival of the united Expedition, and he readily promised me. But I confess to experiencing some wonder to-day when he turned to Awash Effendi, the Major, and said, rather pleadingly I thought, "Now promise me before Mr. Stanley that you will give me forty men to build this station, which Mr. Stanley so much desires." There is something about this that I do not understand. It is certainly not like my ideal Governor, Vice-King, and leader of men, to talk in that strain to subordinates.

Had another conversation with Emin Pasha to-day, from which I feel convinced that we shall not only have to march to the Albert, Nyanza again, but that we shall have to wait afterwards at least two months before he can get his people together. Instead of setting to work during our absence to collect his people and prepare for the journey, it is proposed to wait until my return with the rear column, when it is expected I shall go as far as Dufflé to persuade the people to follow me. He still feels assured his people will not go to Egypt, but may be induced to march as far as the Victoria Nyanza.

I asked him if the report was true that he had captured 13,000 head of cattle during an incursion to the western cattle-lands.

"Oh, no; it is an exaggeration. A certain Bakhit Bey succeeded in taking 8000 head during a raid he made in Makraka, during Raouf Pasha's Governor-Generalship; but he was severely censured for the act, as such wholesale raiding only tended to depopulate a country. That has been the greatest number of cattle obtained at one time. I have had occasion to order forays to be made to obtain food, but 1600 head has been the greatest number we have ever succeeded in obtaining at one time. Other forays have resulted in bringing us 500, 800, and 1200 head."

Both yesterday and to-day have been very pleasant.

May 16th. – Nsabé Camp.

The steamer *Khedive* departed this morning for Mswa Station and Tunguru, and probably for Wadelai, to hurry up a certain number of porters to replace our men lost by starvation in the, wilderness. Captain Casati and Mons. Vita Hassan, the Tunisian apothecary, have sailed with her. In order to keep my men occupied, I have begun cutting a straight road through the plain towards Badzwa Village. When we take our departure hence we shall find our advantage in the shorter cut than by taking the roundabout path by Nyamsassi Island and the site of old Kavalli. Fetteh, our interpreter, wounded in the stomach at the skirmish of Bessé, is now quite recovered, and is fast regaining his old weight. Mabruki, the son of Kassim, so mangled by the buffalo the other day, is slowly improving. The man wounded by a spear in the back during his foray into the villages of Lando, shows also signs of rapid recovery. We live in hay-cock huts now, and may consider ourselves householders (according to Emin Pasha) of the Albert Nyanza Province.

May 17th. – Nsabé Camp. Our road is now 2,360 paces long towards Badzwa Village.

May 18th. – Nsabé Camp. Our hunters, when receiving cartridges, insist on their being laid on the ground. Ill luck would follow if the cartridges were delivered to them from the hand.

I have been instructing the Pasha in the use of the sextant the last two days preparatory to taking lessons in navigation. His only surveying instrument hitherto has been a prismatic compass, and as he has never been taught to discover its variation, it is probable that his surveys have been from magnetic bearings.

The son of Kassim, the victim to the fury of an angry buffalo, called me this morning to his bedside, that I might register his last wishes respecting the wages due to him. His friend Maruf and adopted brother Sungoro are to be the legatees. Poor Mabruki desired to remember another friend, but the legatees *begged him not to fill the Master's book with names.* He was so dejected that I told him that the doctor had great faith that he would recover. "You are in no danger. Your wounds are very bad, but they are not mortal, and as the Pasha will take care of you in my absence, I shall find you a strong man when I return. Why do you grieve to-day?"

"Ah, it is because something tells me I shall never see the road again. See, is not my body a ruin?" Indeed he was a pitiable sight, right eye almost obscured, two ribs broken, right thigh and fork lacerated in the most dreadful manner.

The Chief Mbiassi of Kavalli departed homeward two days ago. Mpigwa, Chief of Nyamsassi, and his retinue left yesterday. Kyya-nkondo or Katonza, for he has two names, also went his way (which, by the way, is in the wilderness owing to a late visit of Kabba Rega's brigands), while Mazamboni's people after entertaining the Pasha and his officers with a farewell dance last night, took their leave this morning.

Three buffalo and a water buck were shot yesterday by two of our hunters.

The last four days and nights have given us better thoughts of this African land and lake shore than we previously entertained. The weather has been somewhat warm, but the lake breeze blowing light and soft, just strong enough to swing pendulous foliage, has been cooling and grateful. The nights have been more refreshing. In a sky of radiant brightness the moon has stood high above the plateau's crown, turning the lake into a quivering silver plain, the lake surf so blustering and restless, rolls in a slow and languid cadence on a gray shore of sand before the light breath of an eastern wind. As if to celebrate and honour this peaceful and restful life, the Zanzibaris and natives, who, last December were such furious foes, rival one another with song and chorus and strenuous dance to a late hour each night.

May 19th. – *Nsabé* Camp.

Our road towards Badzwa is now three and a third miles long. We have but to hoe up the grass along a line, and we have a beautiful path, with the almost imperceptible rise of 1 foot in 200.

May 20th. – Nsabé Camp.

Captured two small brown snakes of a slight coppery tint in my tent this morning.

May 21st. – Nsabé Camp.

The Pasha is now able to read the sextant very well. He has also made an advance towards finding index error; though he labours under the infirmity of short sight, he is quick and devoted to his intention of acquiring the art of observing by the instrument. At noon we took meridian altitude for practice. He observed altitude was 70° 54' 40" at one-and-half miles distant, height of eye five feet. Index error to add 3' 15".

May 22nd. – Nsabé Camp.

The steamers *Khedive* and *Nyanza,* the latter towing a lighter, appeared to-day about 9 A.M., bringing 80 soldiers, with the Major and Adjutant of the 2nd Battalion, and 130 carriers of the Madi tribe. We received gifts of raki (ten-gallon demijohn, a kind of Russian vodka, from the Pasha's distillery, pomegranates, oranges, water-melons, and more onions, besides six sheep, four goats, and a couple of strong donkeys, one for myself and one for Doctor Parke). The *Nyanza* steamer is about 60 feet by 12. I propose leaving the Albert Lake for my journey in search of the rear column of the Expedition the day after tomorrow.

I leave with the Pasha, Mr. Mounteney Jephson, three Soudanese soldiers, and Binza, Doctor Junker's boy, besides the unhappy Mabruki. Of the baggage we carried here, exclusive of thirty-one cases Remingtons already delivered, I leave two boxes Winchesters, one box of brass rods, lamp, and sounding iron; also my steel boat, *Advance,* with her equipments.

In accordance with the request of the Pasha, I have drawn up a message, which Mr. Jephson will read to the troops. It is as follows: –

Soldiers, – After many months of hard travel, I have at last reached the Nyanza. I have come expressly at the command of the Khedive Tewfik, to lead you out of here and show you the way home. For you must know that the River el Abiad is closed, that Khartoum is in the hands of the followers of Mohamed Achmet, that the Pasha Gordon and all his people were killed, and that all the steamers and boats between Berber and the Bahr Ghazal have been taken, and that the nearest Egyptian station to you is Wady Halfa, below Dongola. Four times the Khedive and your friends have made attempts to save you. First, Gordon Pasha was sent to Khartoum to bring you all home. After ten months of hard fighting Khartoum was taken, and Gordon Pasha was killed, he and his soldiers. Next came the English soldiers under Lord Wolseley to try and help Gordon Pasha out of his troubles. They were four days too late, for they found Gordon was dead and Khartoum was lost. Then a Doctor Lenz, a great traveller, was sent by way of the Congo to find out how you could be assisted. But Lenz could not find men enough to go with him, and so he was obliged to go home. Also a Doctor Fischer was sent by Doctor Junker's brother, but there were too many enemies in the path, and he also returned home. I tell you these things to prove to you that you have no right to think that you have been forgotten in Egypt. No, the Khedive and his Wazir, Nubar Pasha, have all along kept you in mind. They have heard by way of Uganda how bravely you have held to your post, and how stanch you have been to your duties as soldiers. Therefore they sent me to tell you this; to tell you that you are well remembered, and that your reward is waiting for you, but that you must follow me to Egypt to get your pay and your reward. At the same time the Khedive says to you, through me, that if you think the road too long, and are afraid of the journey, that you may stay here, but in that case you are no longer his soldiers; that your pay stops at once; and in any trouble that may hereafter befall you, you are not to blame him, but yourselves. Should you decide to go to Egypt, I am to show you the way to Zanzibar, put you on board a steamer and take you to Suez, and thence to Cairo, and that you will get your pay until you arrive there, and that all promotions given you will be secured, and all rewards promised you here will be paid in full.

I send you one of my officers, Mr. Jephson, and give him my sword, to read this message to you from me. I go back to collect my people and goods, and bring them on to the Nyanza, and after a few months I shall come back here to hear what you have to say. If you say, Let us go to Egypt, I will then show you a safe road. If you say, We shall not leave this country, then I will bid you farewell and return to Egypt with my own people.

May God have you in His keeping.

Your good friend,

(Signed) Stanley.

May 23rd. – Halt.

The Zanzibaris entertained the Pasha and his officers to-night with a farewell dance. Though they are quite well aware of the dangers and fatigue of the journey before them, which will commence to-morrow, there are no symptoms of misgiving in any of them. But it is certain that some of them will take their last look of the Pasha to-morrow.

May 24th. – March to Badzwa village, 10 miles; performed it in 4 hours.

Emin Pasha marched a company along our new road at dawn this morning, and halted it about two miles from the Lake. Having arranged the Madi carriers in their place in the column, the advance guard issued out from camp and took the road towards the west at 6.15 A.M. In half-an-hour we found the Pasha's Soudanese drawn up in line on one side of the road. They saluted us as we passed on, and the Pasha fervently thanked us and bade us good-bye. At the end of the new road twenty-one of the Madis broke from the line of the column and disappeared towards the north rapidly. Fourteen men were sent back to inform the Pasha, while we held on our way to Badzwa. About a mile from the village there was another stampede, and eighty-nine Madis deserted in a body, but not without sending a shower of arrows among the rear guard. The doctor, believing that this was preliminary to an attack on his small detachment, fired his rifle, and dropped a Madi dead, which precipitated the flight of the deserters. The remaining nineteen out of the 130 were secured.

A second message was therefore sent to the Pasha acquainting him with the events of the march.

When about five miles from Nsabé Camp, while looking to the south-east, and meditating upon the events of the last month, my eyes were directed by a boy to a mountain said to be covered with salt, and I saw a peculiar shaped cloud of a most beautiful silver colour, which assumed the proportions and appearance of a vast mountain covered with snow. Following its form downward, I became struck with the deep blue-black colour of its base, and wondered if it portended another tornado; then as the sight descended to the gap between the eastern and western plateaus, I became for the first time conscious that what I gazed upon was not the image or semblance of a vast mountain, but the solid substance of a real one, with its summit covered with snow. I ordered a halt and examined it carefully with a field-glass, then took a compass bearing of the centre of it, and found it bear 215° magnetic. It now dawned upon me that this must be the Ruwenzori, which was said to be covered with a white metal or substance believed to be rock, as reported by Kavalli's two slaves.

This great mountain continued to be in sight most distinctly for two hours, but as we drew nearer to Badzwa at the foot of the plateau, the lofty wall of the plateau hid it from view.

This discovery was announced to the Pasha in the second message I sent. When I come to reflect upon it, it strikes me as singular that neither Baker, Gessi, Mason, or Emin Pasha discovered it long ago.

Gessi Pasha first circumnavigated the Albert Lake, steaming along the western shore towards the south, rounding the southern end of the lake and continuing his voyage along, the eastern shore.

Mason Bey, in 1877, is the next visitor, and he follows the track of Gessi with a view of fixing positions by astronomical observations, which his predecessor was unable to do.

Emin Pasha, eleven years later, comes steaming south in quest of news of the white men reported to be at the south end of the Lake.

If a fair view of this snowy mountain can be obtained from the plain of the Nyanza, a much better view ought to be obtained from the Lake, and the wonder is that none of these gentlemen saw it. Whereas Baker, casting his eyes in its direction, on a "beautifully clear day," views only an illimitable Lake.

Messrs. Jephson and Parke, while carrying the boat from Kavalli's to the Lake, report that they saw snow on a mountain, and the latter officer, pointing to the little range of Unya-Kavalli, inquired of me on his return if it was possible that snow would be found on suck hills. As their highest peak cannot be 5,500 feet above the sea, I replied in the negative, but the doctor said that he was equally certain that he had seen snow. I explained to him then that a certain altitude of about 15,000 feet in the Equatorial regions is required before rain can be congealed into permanent snow; that there might be a hail-storm or a fall of snow, caused by a cold current, even on low altitudes in a tropic region, but such cold would only be temporary, and the heat of tropic waters or tropic soil would in a few moments cause the hail and snow to disappear. Standing as we were in camp at Bundi, on the crest of the plateau, in plain view of Unya Kavalli and other hills, there was no height visible anywhere above 6000 feet of an altitude above the sea.

Considering the above facts, it will be evident that it requires a peculiar condition of the atmosphere to enable one to see the mountain from a distance of 70 miles, which I estimate it at. Near objects, or those 10, 15, or 20 miles, an ordinarily clear atmosphere may enable us to distinguish; but in such a humid region as this is, on a bright day such a quantity of vapour is exhaled from the heated earth, that at 30 miles it would be intensified into a haze which no eyesight could penetrate. But at certain times wind-currents clear the haze, and expose to the view objects which we wonder we have not seen before. As, for instance, in December last, returning from Nyanza to Fort Bodo, I took compass bearings of a lofty twin-peak mountain from a table hill near the East Ituri River. I noted it down that the twin-peak mass was already seen, and I pointed it out to Mr. Jephson. Strange to say, I have never seen it since, though I have been twice over the ground.

Kavalli passed our camp this afternoon with 400 men to assist Emin Pasha in a demonstration he proposes to make against Kabba Rega. Katonza and Mpigwa of Nyamsassi will also, perhaps, lend an equal number to his assistance.

I received the following letters to-day from the Pasha. When he talks of pride and joy at being in our company, I think we are all unanimous in believing that he has given us as much pleasure as we have given him.

Nsabé Camp,
25th May, 1888, 5 A.M.

Dear Sir,

I should not need to tell you how distressed I have been when I heard of the misfortune happened by the desertion of our Madi people. I at once sent out different searching parties, but I am sorry to state that up to noon their efforts were of no avail, although Shukri Agha and his party, who went yesterday to Kahanama, have not returned.

By a mere chance it happened that when Dr. Parke came a boat from Mswa station had arrived, bringing me intelligence of the arrival there of 120 porters from Dufflé. I therefore started immediately the Khedive steamer to bring them here, and expect her back this very night, when, at her arrival, I shall start the whole gang, accompanied by a detachment of my people.

Allow me to he the first to congratulate you on your most splendid discovery of a snow-clad mountain. We will take it as a good omen for further directions on our road to Victoria.[15] I propose to go out on your track to-day or to-morrow, just to have a look at this giant.

In expectance of two words of you this morning I venture to offer you my best wishes for the future. I always shall remember with pride and joy the few days I was permitted to consort with you.

Believe me, dear Sir,
Yours very sincerely,

(Signed) Dr. M. Emin.

Nsabé Camp,
26th May, 1888, 2.30 A.M.

---

15. It is clear that he was smitten with the Victoria Lake proposition.

Dear Sir,

Your very welcome and most interesting note of yesterday has reached me at the hands of your men. The steamer has come in this very instant, but she brought only eighty-two carriers, the rest having run away on the road between Tunguru and Mswa. I send, therefore, these few men, accompanied by twenty-five soldiers and an officer, hoping they may be of some use to you. Their arms having been collected I handed them to the officer, from whom you will kindly receive them. We heard yesterday evening that your runaways had worked their way to Muganga, telling the people they were sent by me.

The ten men you kindly sent here accompanying the carriers as well as Kavalli and his men. Having caught yesterday a spy of Ravidongo[16] in Katonza's Camp, I told this latter he would better retire, and he acted on this advice. I have acquainted Kavalli with my reasons for not interfering just now with Ravidongo, and have asked him to return to you. He readily assented; he had some presents, and starts now with the courier. He entreats me, further, to beg you to send some of your men to take hold of his brother Kadongo, who stays, says he, with the Wawitu somewhere near to his residence.

I shall try hard to get a glimpse of the new snow mountain, as well from here as from some other points I propose to visit. It is wonderful to think how, wherever you go, you distance your predecessors by your discoveries.

And now as this, for some time at least, is probably the last word I will be able to address you, let me another time thank you for the generous exertions you have made, and you are to make for us. Let me another time thank you for the kindness and forbearance you have shown me in our mutual relations. If I cannot find adequate words to express what moves

---

16. Ravidongo, one of the principal generals of Kabba Rega.

me in this instant you will forgive me. I lived too long in Africa for not becoming somewhat negrofied.

God speed you on your course and bless your work!

Yours very faithfully,

(Signed) Dr. Emin.

May 25th and 26th. – Halt at Badzwa.

The Pasha has abandoned his idea of making a demonstration against Unyoro, and his allies, who have much to avenge, have been quickly dismissed homeward.

In the afternoon Balegga descended from Bundi Hill Village, and secretly informed us that Kadongo and Musiri – the latter a warlike and powerful chief – have banded their forces together and intend to attack us on the road between Gavira's and Mazamboni's. We have given neither of them any cause for this quarrel, unless our friendship with their rivals may be deemed sufficient and legitimate. I have only 111 rifles and ten rounds of ammunition for each rifle, to reach Fort Bodo, 125 miles distant. If any determined attack is made on us in the open country, a few moments' firing will make us helpless. Therefore I shall have to resort to other measures. It was held by Thomas Carlyle that it was the highest wisdom to know and believe that the stern thing which necessity ordered to be done was the wisest, the best, and the only thing wanted there. I will attack Kadongo first, and then march straight upon Musiri, and we will spend our last shots well, if necessary. It may be this bold movement will upset the combination.

The Pasha has acted quickly. Eighty-two fresh carriers arrived at noon, under a strong guard, and three soldiers specially detailed to accompany me. On their delivery to us, each Zanzibari received a Madi to guard.

At half-past three in the afternoon we commenced the steed ascent up the terrible slope of the plateau, with a burning sun in our front, and reached the crest at Bundi camp at 6.30P.M., a half-hour after sunset.

After placing strong guards round the camp, I selected a band of forty rifles of the choicest men under two Zanzibari chiefs, and prepared them for a surprise party to attack Kadongo's camp by night. A few of our native allies volunteered to show the hill village he was occupying.

At 1 A.M. the party was despatched.

May 27th. – At 8 A.M. the party detailed against Kadongo returned, having effected their mission most successfully, but Kadongo himself escaped by crying out that he was a friend of "Bula Matari." No cattle or goats were taken, because the place was only occupied by Kadongo's band for temporary purposes.

We then lifted our burdens and began our march towards Gavira's. We had barely started when we discovered a large band of men advancing towards us, preceded by a man bearing a crimson flag, which at a distance might be taken for that of Zanzibar or Egypt. We halted, wondering what party this might be, but in a few moments we recognised Katto, Mazamboni's brother, who had been sent by his chief to greet us and learn our movements. We admired the aptness of these people in so soon learning to follow the direction given to them, for had not the flag held us in suspense, we might have injured our friends by taking them for the van of Musiri's war-party.

Retaining a few of them to follow us, I ordered Katto to return quickly to Mazamboni, his brother, and secretly inform him that as Musiri intended to attack us on the road, I intended to attack him at dawn the day after to-morrow, and that I expected from Mazamboni, as my ally, that he would bring as many men as he could sometime that next day. Katto declared the thing possible, though it was a short notice for the distance to be travelled. We were at the time six miles from Gavira's, thence to Mazamboni's village was thirteen miles, and back again to Gavira's would be another thirteen miles, and in the meantime some delay would be necessary to secretly muster a sufficient body of warriors becoming Mazamboni's rank, and prepare rations for a few days.

We arrived at Gavira's about noon. Here I proposed to Gavira to join me in the attack, which the chief as readily promised.

May 28th. – Halt. We have received abundant contributions of food for our force, which numbers now 111 Zanzibaris, 3 whites, 6 cooks and boys, 101 Madis, and 3 soldiers belonging to the Pasha – total 224, exclusive of a few dozen natives who voluntarily follow us.

An hour after sunset Mazamboni arrived in person with about 1000 warriors armed with bows and spears. His force was camped in the potato fields between Gavira's and Musiri's district.

May 29th. – At three o'clock A.M. we set out for Usiri on a N.W. road, a bright moon lighting the way. About 100 of the boldest of Mazamboni's corps preceded our force. The others fell in line behind, and Gavira's tribe, represented by about 500 men, brought up the rear. A deep silence, befitting our purpose, prevailed.

At 6 A.M. we reached the outskirts of Usiri, and in a few moments, each chief having received his instructions, Dr. Parke, in charge of sixty rifles to keep the centre, Katto, in charge of his brother's warriors to form the left wing, and Mpinga and Gavira with his men to form the right, the attacking force moved on swiftly.

The results were ludicrous in the extreme. Mpinga's Wahuma herdsmen had given notice to Musiri's Wahuma herdsmen, and Mazamboni's Wahuma had been just as communicative to their fellow-countrymen with the enemy. Consequently the herdsmen had driven all the herds from Usiri by other roads; a half of them arrived at Gavira's, and the other half at Mazamboni's, just at the same morning when the attacking force poured over the land of Usiri, and Musiri, the chief, after hearing of the disaster to Kadongo, and of the mighty army to be brought against him, took tender care that not one soul under his sway should be injured. The land was quite empty of people, herds, flocks, and fowls, but the granaries were heaped full of grain, the fields exhibited abundant crops of potatoes, beans, young Indian corn, vegetables, and tobacco. I am secretly glad of the bloodless termination of the affair. My object has been gained. We have saved our extremely scanty supply of ammunition, and the road is clear from further trouble. Mazamboni and Gavira, I believe, were also delighted, though they expressed themselves mortified.

In one of the huts was discovered the barrel of a carbine and percussion lock. The latter bore the brand of "John Clive III., 530."

This is a relic of Kabba Rega's visit, whose men were sadly defeated by Musiri about a year ago.

In the afternoon Mazamboni's warriors, 1000 strong, joined to celebrate the bloodless victory over Musiri in a phalanx dance. Dancing in Africa mainly consists of rude buffoonery, extravagant gestures, leaping and contortions of the body, while one or many. drums keep time. There is always abundance of noise and loud laughter, and it serves the purpose of furnishing amuse-merit to the barbarians, as the dervish-like whirling and pirouetting give to civilised people. Often two men step out of a semicircle of their fellow villagers, and chant a duet to the sound of a drum or a horn amid universal clapping of hands, or one performs a solo while dressed most fantastically in cocks' feathers, strings of rattling gourds, small globular bells, and heaps of human, monkey, and crocodile teeth, which are the African jewels; but there must always be a chorus, the grander the better, and when the men, women, and children lift their voices high above the drums, and the chatter and murmur of the crowd, I must confess to having enjoyed it immensely, especially when the Wanyamwezi are the performers, who are by far the best singers on the African continent. The Zanzibaris, Zulus, Waiau, Wasegara, Waseguhha, and Wangindo are in the main very much alike in method and execution, though they have each minor dances and songs, which vary considerably, but they are either dreadfully melancholiac or stupidly barbarous. The Wasoga, Waganda, Wakerewé, Wazongora, around Lake Victoria, are more subdued, a crude bardic, with something of the whine of the Orient – Mustapha, or Hussein, or Hassan, moaning below lattices to the obdurate Fatima or stony-eared Roxana. Except the Wanyamwezi, I have not heard any music or seen any dance which would have pleased an English audience accustomed to the plantation dances represented in a certain hall in Piccadilly until this day, when the Bandussuma, under Katto, the brother of Mazamboni, led the chief warriors to the phalanx dance. Half a score of drums, large and small, had been beaten by half a score of accomplished performers, keeping admirable time, and emitting a perfect volume of sound which must have been heard far away for miles, and in the meantime Katto, and his cousin Kalengé, adorned with glorious tufts of white cocks' feathers, were arranging thirty-three lines of thirty-three men each as nearly as possible in the form of a perfect and solid and close square. Most of these men had but one spear each, others possessed two besides their shields and quivers, which were suspended from the neck down the back.

The phalanx stood still with spears grounded until, at a signal from the drums, Katto's deep voice was heard breaking out into a wild triumphant song or chant, and at a particular uplift of note raised his spear, and at once rose a forest of spears high above their heads, and a mighty chorus of voices responded, and the phalanx was seen to move forward, and the earth around my chair, which was at a distance of fifty yards from the foremost line, shook as though there was an earthquake. I looked at the feet of the men and discovered that each man was forcefully stamping the ground, and taking forward steps not more than six inches long, and it was in this manner that the phalanx moved slowly but irresistibly. The voices rose and fell in sweeping waves of vocal sound, the forest of spears rose and subsided, with countless flashes of polished iron blades as they were tossed aloft and lowered again to the hoarse and exciting thunder of the drums. There was accuracy of cadence of voice and roar of drum, there was uniform uplift and subsidence of the constantly twirling spear blades, there was a simultaneous action of the bodies, and as they brought the tremendous weight of seventy tons of flesh with one regular stamp of the feet on the ground, the firm and hard earth echoed the sound round about tremulously. With all these the thousand heads rose and drooped together, rising when venting the glorious volume of energy, drooping with the undertone of wailing murmur of the multitude. As they shouted with faces turned upward and heads bent back to give the fullest effect to the ascending tempest of voices, suggestive of quenchless fury, wrath and exterminating war, it appeared to inflate every soul with the passion of deadly battle and every eye of the onlookers glowed luridly, and their right arms with clenched fists were shaken on high as though their spirits were thrilled with the martial strains; but as the heads were turned and bowed to the earth we seemed to feel war's agony, and grief, and woe, to think of tears, and widows' wails, and fatherless orphans' cries, of ruined hearths and a desolated land. But again as the mass, still steadily drawing nearer, tossed their heads backward, and the bristling blades flashed and clashed, and the feathers streamed and gaily rustled, there was a loud snort of defiance and such an exulting and energising storm of sound that man saw only the glorious colours of victory and felt only the proud pulses of triumph.

Right up to my chair the great solid mass of wildly chanting natives advanced, and the front line lowered their spears in an even line of bright iron; thrice they dropped their salute and thrice they rose, and then the lines, one after another, broke into a run, spears clenched in the act of throwing, staffs quivering, war-whoops ringing shrilly. The excitement was intensified until the square had been transformed into wheeling circles three deep, and after three circlings round the open plaza, Prince Katto took his position, and round him the racing men coiled themselves until soon they were in a solid circle. When this was completed the square was formed, it was divided into halves, one half returning to one end, the other half to the other end. Still continuing the wild chant, they trotted towards one another and passed through without confusion, exchanging sides, and then once more in a rapid circling of the village common with dreadful gestures until the eye was bewildered with the wheeling forms, and then every man to his hut to laugh and jest, little heeding what aspects they had conjured by their evolutions and chants within me, or any one else. It was certainly one of the best and most exciting exhibitions I had seen in Africa.

May 30th. – March to Nzera-Kum Hill in Ndusuma, three hours.

We marched to Mazamboni's country to our old camp at Chongo, which name the Zanzibaris have given to the hill of Nzera-Kum, and we had abundant evidence that Mazamboni was deeply implicated in the acts of the Wahuma herdsmen, for the track was fresh and large of many a fine herd of cattle. Presently we came in sight of the fine herds, who, all unconscious of trouble, were browsing on the fine pasture, and the Zanzibaris clamoured loudly for permission to capture them. For an instant only there was a deep silence, but Mazamboni, on being asked the reason for the presence of Musiri's herds on his territory, answered so straightforwardly that they belonged to the Wahuma who had fled from his territory last December when he was in trouble with us, and now to avoid the same trouble in Usiri had returned to their former place, and he had not the heart to prevent them, that the order was given to move on.

May 31st – Halt. Mazamboni gave us a present of three beeves and supplied our people with two days full rations of flour, besides a large quantity of potatoes and bananas. A large number of small chiefs from the surrounding districts paid visits to us, each bringing into camp a contribution of goats, fowls, and millet flour. Urumangwa, Bwessa, and Gunda have also made pacts of friendship with us. These villages form the very prosperous and extensively cultivated district which so astonished us by its abundance one December morning last year.

Towards evening I received a communication from Musiri, saying that as all the land had made peace with me, he wished to be reckoned as my friend, and that the next time I should return to the country he would be prepared with suitable gifts for us.

As to-morrow I propose to resume the journey towards Fort Bodo and Yambuya, let me set down what I have gleaned from the Pasha respecting himself.

Chapter 17

PERSONAL TO THE PASHA

It is not my purpose to make a biographical sketch of Emin Pasha, but to furnish such items of information as he delivered them to me, day by day, concerning the life he has led in the Soudan, and his acquaintance with his illustrious chief – the ever-lamented Gordon.

By birth he is a German, but whether Austrian or Prussian I know not, and I have no curiosity to know the name of the obscure village or town where that event happened. He declares he is forty-eight years old, and must therefore have been born in the year 1840. I fancy that he must have been young when he arrived in Constantinople, that some great man assisted him in his medical studies, that through the same influence probably he entered the Turkish service, and became medical attendant on Ismail Hakki Pasha. If for thirty years he has served under the crescent flag as he himself reported, he must have begun his service in Turkey in the year 1858. He became attracted to the "Young Turk" party, or to the reform party, in Stamboul. It had an organ, which, by its bold advocacy of reform, was three times suppressed by the authorities. On the last suppression he was expelled from the country.

He admits that he was in Constantinople when the assassination of the Sultan Abdul Aziz occurred, though he was absent during the trial of those suspected to be concerned in it. Coming to Egypt in December, 1875, he entered the Egyptian service, and was despatched to Khartoum.

..."Gordon first appointed me as surgeon at £25 a month. He then raised me to £30, and after my mission to Uganda he surprised me with increasing my pay to £40, but when I became Governor of this Province my pay like other Provincial Governors' became £50 monthly. What the pay of a General is I do not know, but then I am only a 'Miraman,' a kind of civilian Pasha, who receives pay while employed, but immediately his services are not required he becomes unpaid. I expected to be made a military Pasha – a General of Division."

..."Now Gordon appointed the German Vice-Consul at Khartoum as my agent, to receive my pay, without any advice from me about it. For several months I believe it was paid to him regularly. But finally Gordon appointed the same Vice-Consul Governor of Darfour, when he shortly after died. When his effects were collected and his small debts paid, there were found sufficient funds to present his wife with £500 and send her to Cairo, and to transfer £50 to my account as his principal creditor. A few months afterwards Khartoum fell, and what money had been deposited there after the Vice-Consul's death was lost of course. So that for eight years I have received no pay at all."

..."My last interview with Gordon Pasha was in 1877. There had been an Expedition sent to Darfour, under Colonel Prout, and another under Colonel Purdy, for survey work. When Gordon became Governor-General, he requested Stone Pasha, at Cairo, to despatch to him one of these officers, for survey work in the Equatorial Province. Gessi Pasha had already circumnavigated the Albert, but his survey was by compass only. Both Prout Bey and Mason Bey were capital observers. Prout Bey was the first to arrive. He travelled from Lado to Fatiko, thence to Mruli, on the Victoria Nile, and from there he proceeded to Magungo, on the Albert Nyanza, and by a series of observations he fixed the position of that point for all time. Illness compelled him to retire to my station at Lado. Just then Mason Bey arrived in a steamer, to survey the Albert Lake, and by that steamer I received an order to descend to Khartoum, to be made Governor of Massowah, on the Red Sea. The French Consul of that place had a misunderstanding with the civil Governor there, and he had begged that if another Governor was appointed, he should be some person who could understand French. I suppose Gordon, knowing me to be familiar with the language, had elected me. On reaching Khartoum I was very cordially received by Gordon, and he insisted on my taking my meals with him, which was a great favour, as he seldom invited anybody to eat with him. However, I declined living in the palace, and breakfasted at home, but lunch and dinner Gordon insisted I should take with him. He had abundance of work for me – letters to the Egyptian Pashas and Beys of the various provinces; letters to the Catholic Mission of Gondokoro; letters to the Pope, to the Khedive, &c., in Italian, German, and Arabic. This went on for some time, when one day he sent me on a mission to Unyoro. A little later I ascended the river, and I have never seen Gordon since."

..."In June, 1882, Abdul Kader Pasha wrote me that in a couple of months he would despatch a steamer to me with provisions and ammunition. After waiting nine months I obtained fifteen cases only of ammunition, in March, 1883. That is really the last supply of anything received from the outside world until your recent arrival in April, 1888. Five years exactly!"

..."During five years I have remained isolated in this region; not idle, I hope. I have been kept busy in the affairs of my Province, and have managed to find pleasure in many things. Still, the isolation from the civilized world has made life rather burthensome. I could enjoy life here to the end, could I but obtain regular news, and was certain of communication with the outer world, receive books, periodicals, every month, two months, or even three months. I envy those missionaries in Uganda who receive their monthly packet of letters, newspapers and books. Mr. Mackay has quite a library in Uganda. That packet of "honeydew" tobacco I gave you the other day I obtained from him. I received also a couple of bottles of liquor, have had clothes, writing paper, and such news as I know I discovered in the *Spectators* and *Times* now and then sent me by him. But there are certain books upon subjects which I am interested in that I could never obtain through him without giving him and his friends far too great a trouble. Therefore I should wish a postal service of my own, then my life would be relieved of its discontent. Ah, those eight years of silence! I cannot put my feelings in words. I could not endure them again."

...I have already described his person and age, and certain qualities of his character may be discerned in the conversation reported above; still, the man would be scarcely understood in the full compass of his nature if I stopped here. His abilities, and capacity, and fitness for the singular position in which he has been placed will be seen in the manner in which he has managed to clothe many of his troops. Among the gifts he pressed upon us were pieces of cotton cloth woven by his own men, coarse but strong, and slippers and shoes from his own bootmakers. The condition of his steamers and boats after such long service, the manufacture of oil suitable for the engines (a mixture of sesamum oil and tallow), the excellent sanitary arrangements and cleanliness and order of the stations under his charge, the regular and ungrudging payment of corn tribute twice a year by his negro subjects, all serve to demonstrate a unique character, and to show that he possesses talents rarely seen in those who select Africa for their field of labour. In endeavouring to estimate him, I pass in mental review hundreds of officers who have served on the Nile and the Congo, and I know of but few who would be equal to him in any one of his valuable qualities. Besides his linguistic attainments, he is a naturalist, something of a botanist, and, as a surgeon, I can well believe that thirty years of an adventurous life such as his has been would furnish him with rare opportunities to make him wise and skilful in his profession. The language he has used, as may be seen above, is something higher than colloquial, and marks his attainments in English. With his full sonorous voice and measured tones, it sounded very pleasantly, despite the foreign accent. Upon any policy treated of in newspapers and reviews I found him exceedingly well informed, no matter what country was broached. His manner is highly courteous and considerate, somewhat, perhaps, too ceremonious for Central Africa, but highly becoming a Governor, and such as one might expect from an official of that rank, conscious of serious responsibilities.

Industry seems to be a vital necessity of life with him. He is a model of painstaking patient effort. No sooner has he camped than he begins to effect arrangements orderly and after method. His table and chair have their place, his journals on the table, the aneroids on a convenient stand, dry and wet bulb thermometers duly exposed in the shade, with ample air-flow about them. The journals are marvels of neatness – blotless, and the writing microscopically minute, as though he aimed at obtaining a prize for accuracy, economy, neatness and fidelity. Indeed, most Germans of my acquaintance are remarkable for the bulk of their observations and superfine calligraphy, while English-speaking travellers whom I have known possess note-books which, useful as they may be to themselves, would appear ill-kept, blotchy and scrawly in comparison to them, and furnish infinite trouble to their executors to edit.

...The following will illustrate something of his troubles during the five years he has been cut off from headquarters at Khartoum.

Shukri Agha, Commandant of Mswa station, who paid me a visit on the evening of the 19th May, relates that about a year ago 190 rifles of the First Battalion set out from Rejaf Station for Kirri, where the Pasha resided, with the intent to capture and hold him captive among themselves. A letter had been received from Dr. Junker from Cairo, stating that an expedition was to be sent to their relief, had created a confused impression in the minds of the soldiers of the First Battalion that their Governor intended to fly in that direction, leaving them to their fate. Convinced that their safety lay in the presence of their Civil Governor among them, they conceived the idea of arresting him and taking him with them to Rejaf, which, with the more northern stations, was garrisoned by this battalion. "For," said they, "we know only of one road, and that leads down the Nile by Khartoum."[17] The Pasha was suddenly informed of their intention by the officers of the Second Battalion, and cried out, "Well, if they kill me, I am not afraid of death; let them come – I will await them." This the officers of the Second Battalion at Kirri would not permit, and implored him to make his escape before the malcontents appeared, and argued that "the violent capture and detention of the Governor would put an end to all government, and be the total ruin of all discipline." For some time he refused to move, but finally, yielding to their solicitations, escaped to Mswa. Soon after his departure the detachment of the First Battalion appeared, and, after surrounding the station, cried out a peremptory demand that the' Governor should come out and deliver himself to them. They were answered that the Governor had already departed south to Muggi and Wadelai, upon which the mutineers advanced to the station, and seized the Commandant and his subordinate officials, and soundly flogged them with the kurbash, and afterwards

---

17. The correspondence these people maintained with Khartoum compel me to doubt whether this is the correct reason. Read Omar Sale's letter to the Khalifa at Khartoum, farther on.

took most of them prisoners and carried them to Rejaf, whither they returned.

Shukri Agha continued thus: – "You must know that all the First Battalion guard the northern stations, and every soldier of that battalion is opposed to making any retreat, and any suggestion of leaving their watch post at Rejaf, the northernmost station, only makes them indignant. They have been all along waiting to hear of the arrival of a steamer at Lado, and are still firm in the belief that some day the Pasha at Khartoum will send for them. Whatever the Pasha says to the contrary receives utter disbelief. But now that you have arrived by an opposite road, and some of us who were with Linant Bey in 1875 saw you in Uganda, and many more of us have known you by name, it is most likely all of them will be convinced that the Nile is not the only road to Egypt, and that you, having found them, can take them out of the country. They will see your officers, they will see your Soudanese, they will listen respectfully to your message, and gladly obey. That is my own opinion, though God only knows what the sentiments of the First Battalion are by this time, as sufficient time has not elapsed to enable us to hear from them."

...On telling Emin Pasha the next day the story of Shukri Agha, he said: –

"Shukri Agha is a very intelligent and brave officer, promoted to his present rank for distinguished service against Karamalla, one of the Mahdi's generals, when he came here with some thousands to demand our surrender to the authority of Mohamed Achmet."

"His story is quite true, except that he has omitted to mention that with the 190 rifles of the First Battalion there were 900 armed negroes. Subsequently I learned that it had been their intention to have taken me to Gondokoro, and detain me there until the garrisons of the southern stations, Wadelai, Tunguru, and Mswa, were collected, and then to have marched along the right bank towards Khartoum. On reaching the neighbourhood of Khartoum, and there learning that the city had really fallen, they were then to disperse, each to his own house, leaving the Cairenes and myself to shift as we might for ourselves."[18]

...The following are some natural history facts he related to me: –

"The forest of Msongwa (see map) is infested with a large tribe of chimpanzees. In summer time, at night, they frequently visit the plantations of Mswa station to steal the fruit. But what is remarkable about this is the fact that they use torches to light the way! Had I not witnessed this extraordinary spectacle personally I should never have credited that any of the Simians understood the art of making fire."

"One time these same chimpanzees stole a native drum from the station, and went away pounding merrily on it. They evidently delight in that drum, for I have frequently heard them rattling away at it in the silence of the night."

He observed that parrots are never seen along the shores of Lake Albert. Up to lat. 2° N. they are seen in Unyoro, but the Lake people do not seem to understand what is referred to when parrots are mentioned.

Our people captured a pair of very young mongoose, which were taken to the Pasha. They were accepted, and ordered to be nursed on milk. He declared that the mongoose, though he becomes very tame and is exceedingly droll, is a nuisance. Instruments are broken, ink scattered, papers and books are smeared and soiled by this inquisitive little beast. To eggs it is especially destructive. If it finds an egg of more than ordinary hard shell, it lifts it with its forefeet and lets it drop until it is broken.

The Pasha has much to say respecting the Dinkas. Proprietors of cattle among the Dinka tribe own from 300 to 1500 head. They rarely kill, their cattle being kept solely for their milk and blood. The latter they mix with sesamum oil, and then eat as a delicacy. At the death of a herd-owner his nearest kinsman invites his friends, and one or two beeves may be slaughtered for the funeral feast; otherwise one scarcely ever hears of a Dinka killing his cattle for meat. Should one of the herd die a natural death, the love of meat demands that it be eaten, which is a proof that conscience does not prohibit satisfying the stomach with meat, but rather excessive penuriousness, cattle being the Dinka's wealth.

---

18. Knowing this, the Pasha seems to me to have been very imprudent in adventuring into the presence of these rebels without satisfying himself as to the effect his presence would have on them.

These Dinkas also pay great reverence to pythons and all kinds of snakes. One of the Soudanese officers killed a snake, and was compelled to pay a fine of four goats. They even domesticate them, keeping them in their houses, but they are allowed every liberty, and to crawl out for prey, after which they return for rest and sleep. They wash the pythons with milk and anoint them with butter. In almost every hut the smaller snakes may be heard rustling in the roofs as they crawl, exploring for rats, mice, etc.

On the east side of the Nile he found a tribe exceedingly partial to lions; in fact, one of them would prefer to be killed than be guilty of the death of a lion. These people dug a pit at one time for buffaloes and such game to fall into, but it unfortunately happened that a lion was the first victim. The Soudanese who discovered it were about to kill it, when the chief vetoed the act and implored that the lion should be given to him. The Soudanese were willing enough, and curiously watched what he would do with it. The chief cut a long stout pole and laid it slantwise to the bottom of the pit, up which the lion immediately climbed and bounded away to the jungle to enjoy his liberty. It should be added that the noble beast did not attempt to injure any person near the pit – probably he was too frightened; though as pretty a story might be made out of it as that of Androcles and the lion, did we not live in such a veracious and prosaic age.

"Bird studies," the gray-haired lieutenant from Cairo declared, were the Pasha's delight. Indeed, he seems to find as great pleasure in anything relating to birds or animals as in his military and civil duties, though I have not observed any neglect of the last, and the respectful soldierly bearing of his people in his presence marks a discipline well impressed on them.

...From the above gleanings of such conversation as I have noted it will be clear to any one that the Pasha has had a varied life, one that would furnish to quiet home-keeping people much valuable and enchanting reading matter. It may be hoped he will see fit some day to exhibit to them in book form some of his startling life incidents in Asia and Africa, and rehearse in his own pleasing manner some of the most interesting observations he has made during a long residence amid a new and wild nature.

Chapter 18

START FOR THE RELIEF OF THE REAR COLUMN

On the 1st of June, escorted by a score of Mazamboni's people, we marched westward from Undussuma. In an hour and a half we reached Urumangwa. This district furnished an escort of about a hundred, the Mazambonis withdrawing to their homes. At Unyabongo, after a two hours' march, the people of Urumangwa likewise withdrew, yielding their honourable duties to the people of the new district, and these escorted us for an hour and a half, and saw us safely housed and abundantly fed at Mukangi. For a short time before the latter place we were drawn up in battle array, and a fight was imminent, but the courage and good sense of its chief enabled both parties to avoid a useless rupture.

A good example has its imitators as well as bad examples. The chiefs of Wombola and Kametté heard how quickly we had embraced the friendly offers of Mukangi, and when we marched through their districts the next day not one war-cry was heard or a hostile figure appeared. Those of Kametté. called out to us to keep on our way, it is true, but it was just, as we had no business in Kametté, and the day was yet young; but on our arrival at the next village, Ukuba, we were tired, and disposed to rest after a five hours' march. But Ukuba, of Bessé district, had already experienced our weapons on the 12th April last, and we were permitted to camp quietly. At sunset we were gratified at seeing several of the natives walking unarmed to camp, and in the morning they came again with presents of a milch goat, some fowls, and enough plantains for all.

On the 3rd we pressed on rapidly, and captured the canoes to ferry our party across the Ruri, which, though there had been but little rain of late, we found to be as full as in rainy April.

On the next day we captured a woman of Mandé after crossing the river, and released her to tell her people that we were harmless enough if the road was undisturbed. It may extend the area over which peace between us and the natives is established.

On the 5th we camped at Baburu, and on the next day at W. Indenduru. On the 7th a seven hours' march brought us to a stream called Miwalé River, from the great number of raphia palms; and the next day we entered Fort Bode, bringing with us six head of cattle, a flock of sheep and goats, a few loads of native tobacco, four gallons of the Pasha's whisky, and some other little luxuries, to joy the hearts of the garrison.

Such an utter silence prevails in the forest that we were mutually ignorant of each other's fate during our sixty-seven days' separation. Until we approached within 400 yards of Fort Bode we could not divine what had become of Lieutenant Stairs, who, it will be remembered, had been despatched on the 16th February to Ugarrowwa's to conduct such convalescents as could be found there to us to share in such fortune as might happen to us in the open country, whose very view had proved so medicinable to our men. Nor could the garrison guess what luck had happened to us. But when our rifles woke up the sleeping echoes of the forest with their volleys, the sounds had scarcely died away before the rifles of the garrison responded, and as we knew that Fort Bode still existed, those immured within the limits of the clearing became aware that we had returned from the Nyanza.

Lieutenant Stairs was first to show himself and hail us, and close after him Captain Nelson, both in excellent condition, but of rather pasty complexion. Their men then came trooping up, exuberant joy sparkling in their eyes and glowing in their faces, for these children of Nature know not the art of concealing their moods or disguising their emotions.

But, alas! for my estimates. Since I have entered the forest region they have always been on the erring side. After computing carefully, as I thought, every mile of the course to be travelled and every obstacle likely to be met by him and his lightly-laden escort,

I was certain Lieutenant Stairs would be with us after an absence of thirty-nine days. We stayed forty-seven days, as we were assured it would please him to be present at the successful termination or crowning triumph of our efforts. He arrived after seventy-one days' absence, and by that date we had already communicated with Emin Pasha.

I had estimated also that out of the fifty-six invalids left in the care of Ugarrowwa, and boarded at our expense, at least forty convalescents would be ready, fit for marching, but Mr. Stairs found most of them in worse condition than when they parted from us. All the Somalis were dead except one, and the survivor but lived to reach Ipoto. Out of the fifty-six there were but thirty-four remaining. One of these was Juma, with foot amputated; three were absent foraging. Out of the thirty sorry band of living skeletons delivered to him fourteen died on the road, one was left at Ipoto, the remaining fifteen survived to exhibit their nude bodies disfigured by the loathliest colours and effects of chronic disease. The following is the letter describing Mr. Stairs' remarkable journey, which amply accounts for his detention: –

Fort Bodo, Ibwiri, Central Africa,
June 6th, 1888.

Sir, –

I have the honour to report that in accordance with your orders of the 15th February, 1888, I left this place on the 16th of that month with an escort of twenty couriers and other details, to proceed to Ugarrowwa's station on the Ituri, forward the couriers on their journey to Major Barttelot's column, relieve the invalids left in charge of Ugarrowwa, and bring them on to this station.

Leaving this place, then, on the 16th, we reached Kilimani Hill village on the 17th. Next day I decided to follow a large native track, well worn, about two miles west of Kilimani on our through track to Ipoto; accordingly we started off this up till 11 a.m. After we had gone this length, the track struck too much to the north and east; I therefore looked for other tracks, hoping by following one to at last get on to a large road, and thus work through to the Ihuru. Finding one, we followed it up some two miles or so, and then found that it ended abruptly, and no further trace could be found of it. Returning to our former road we moved on, and that day made four more endeavours to get north-west or somewhere in that direction; late at night we camped, just before dark, having found a blazed track. On the next day, 19th, we followed this track north-west at a fast rate, and about 10 a.m. came on to an old village. The blazes here ended; no further signs of a track could we find leading out of the village, though we hunted thoroughly in every direction. Returning again, and following a large track northeast, we made still another try, but here again the track ended.

After some consideration I returned to our camp of yesterday, and decided on following a road leading towards Mabungu, and then take a side road, said by the natives to lead to the Ihuru, but on following this we found it lead merely up to some Wambutti huts, and here ran out.

After taking my head men's opinion, I then decided on returning and following our old road to Ipoto, there to procure two guides and follow on the track to Uledi's village, and there cross the Ihuru and follow down on north side, &c. My reasons for doing these were: If I should go on like this, looking for tracks, I should lose probably four or five days, and this with my limited time would not be admissible; and, secondly, that to attempt to split our way on a bearing through the bush to the river would take perhaps five days, which would quite counterbalance any advantage a north road might possess, Reaching Kilonga Longa's on the 22nd, we arranged for a party to take us by a road south of Ituri, and on the 24th left. On the 1st of March crossed the Lenda, courses now N.W. and N.N.W. On the 9th reached Farishi, the upper station of Ugarrowwa. On the 14th we reached Ugarrowwa's, on the Ituri, early in the morning. For many days we had been having rains, and owing to these I suffered very much from fevers, and on getting to Ugarrowwa's had to remain in bed for two days.

At U.'s some eight or ten were away foraging, and to get these required three and a half days.

Fifty-six (56) men were left with Ugarrowwa, viz., five Somalis, five Nubians, and forty-six Zanzibaris, on the 18th of September, 1887. Of this total twenty-six had died, including all the Somalis except Dualla. There were still two men out when I left. Baraka W. Moussa I detailed as a courier in place of another (who had been left at Ipoto with bad ulcer), and Juma B. Zaid remained with Ugarrowwa.

The majority of the men were in a weak state when I arrived, and on leaving I refused to take seven of these. Ugarrowwa, however, point blank refused to keep them, so thus I was obliged to bring on men with the certainty of their dying on the march.

Early on the 16th, Abdullah and his couriers were despatched down river. On the 17th took our forty-four rifles from Ugarrowwa, and out of these made him a present of two and forty-two rounds Remington ammunition.

On the 18th closed with U. for $870, being $30 for twenty-nine men; also handed him his bills of exchange and your letter.

On same day left for Ibwiri with following.

From the 19th to 23rd, when I reached Farishi, the rain was constant, making the track heavy and the creeks difficult in crossing. From here on to Ipoto I had bad fevers day after day, and having no one to carry me, had to make marches of five to seven miles per day. The constant wettings and bad roads had made all the men very low-spirited, some doubt-

*ing even that there was help ahead. Reached Ipoto April
11th, left 13th; and after more trouble from fever reached
here on 26th April. All glad to see the Fort. Dualla, the
Somali, I was obliged to leave at Ipoto. Tam, a former don-
key-boy, deserted on the road. Of the draft of invalids
(twenty-six) ten had died. Kibwana also died from chest disease in camp near Mambungu. Out of fifty-six invalids
brought fourteen alive to the Fort.*

*On reaching Fort Bodo I found you had been so long gone
that I could not follow up with safety with the few rifles I
could command, and so remained at this station and
reported myself to Captain Nelson, who was left in charge of
the Fort by you.*

*Floods, rains, fevers, and other illnesses had been the cause
of our long delay, and those of us who were in fit condition
at all, felt bitterly the disappointment at not being able to
reach you.*

I have the honour to be, &c.,

> *W. G. Stares, Lieut. R.E.*
> *To M. H. Stanley, Esq.*

Of the condition of the garrison at Fort Bodo there was but little to complain; the ulcerous persons, though nothing improved,
were not worse; the anæmic victims of the tortures of Manyuema at
Ipoto had gained possibly a few ounces in weight; the chronically
indolent and malingerers still existed to remind us by their aspects
of misery that they were not suitable for the long and desperate
journey yet before us. We expected all this. The long journey to
Yambuya and back, 1,070 miles, could never be performed by
unwilling men. It would be volunteers, fired by interest, stimulated
by the knowledge that, this one task ended, forest miseries, famine,
damp, rain, mud, gloom, vegetable diet, poisoned arrows, would be
things and griefs of the past; and then the joys of the grass land,
divine light, brightness and warmth of full day, careering of grass

before the refreshing gales, the consolation of knowing that heaven is above, and the earth, yet full of glad life, glowing with beneficence and blandness, ever before them. Oh, gracious God! hasten the day. But can black men, the "brutes," "niggers," "black devils," feel so? We shall see.

One crop of Indian corn had been harvested, and was stored snugly in granaries, the fields were being prepared anew for replanting, the banana plantations still furnished unlimited supplies of food, the sweet potatoes grew wild in various places, and there was a fair stock of beans.

The malicious dwarfs (the Wambutti) had paid nocturnal visits, and ravaged somewhat the corn fields, and Lieut. Stairs, with a few choice spirits of the garrison, had given chase to the marauders and had routed them, losing one man in the action, but scaring the undersized thieves effectually.

The Fort now contained 119 Zanzibaris of the Advance, four of Emin Pasha's soldiers, ninety-eight Madi carriers, and three whites from the Albert Nyanza, besides fifty-seven Zanzibaris and Soudanese, and two officers who formed the garrison – total, 283 souls. It was out of this number we were to form a column of Zanzibari volunteers and Madi carriers to hasten to the relief of Major Barttelot and the Rear Column.

After a two days' rest a general muster was made. The necessities of our condition were explained aloud to them; our white brothers were labouring under God alone knew what difficulties – difficulties that appeared greater to them than they did to us, inasmuch as we had gone through them and survived, and could afford to make light of them. For knowledge would teach us to be more prudent of our rations, where to refresh our jaded bodies, and when to hasten through the intervening wildernesses, husbanding our resources. Our meeting would rejoice our poor friends, distressed by our long absence, and our good news would reanimate the most feeble and encourage the despairing. They all knew what treasures of cloth and beads were in charge of the Rear Column. We could not carry all, as indeed there was no need for so much. How could it better be bestowed than on the tireless faithful fellows who had taken their master twice to the Nyanza and back to his long-lost friends! "I pray you, then, come to my side ye that are willing, and ye that prefer to stay in the Fort remain in the ranks."

Exulting in their lusty strength, perfect health, and in their acknowledged worth, 107 men cried aloud, "To the Major!" "To the Major!" and sprang to my side, leaving only six, who were really indisposed by illness and growing ulcers, in their places.

Those who understand men will recognize some human merits exhibited on this occasion, though others may be as blind in perceiving the finer traits in human nature, as there are many utterly unable to perceive in a picture the touches which betray the masterful hand of a great painter, or in a poem the grace and smoothness, combined with vigour and truth, of the true poet.

After selecting out a few of the garrison to replace those unable to undertake the long march before us, there remained only to distribute twenty-five days' rations of Indian corn to each member of the Relief Force, and to advise that in addition each man and boy should prepare as much plantain flour as he could carry.

Until the evening of the 15th of June all hands were engaged in reducing the hard corn with pestle and mortar and sieve into flour, or corn rice, called "grits," in peeling the plantains, slicing, drying them on wood grating over a slow fire, and pounding them into fine flour. I, on my part, besides arranging the most needful necessaries required for general uses, had many personal details to attend to, such as repairs of pantaloons, shoes, chair, umbrella, rain-coat, etc.

My intention was to conduct the Relief Force in person, unattended by any officers, for many reasons, but mainly because every European implied increase of baggage, which was now required to be of the very smallest limit consistent, with the general safety. Besides, Lieut. Stairs, in my opinion, deserved rest after his trip to Ipoto to bring the steel boat to Fort Bodo, and his journey to Ugarrowwa's was to conduct the convalescents. Captain Nelson, ever since the latter part of September, 1887, had been subject to ever-varying complaints – first ulcers, then a general debility which almost threatened his life, then skin eruptions, lumbago, tender feet, and fits of obstinate ague. To a person in such a vitiated condition of blood a journey of the kind about to be undertaken would doubtless prove fatal. Dr. Parke, the only other officer availing, was needed for the sick at the Fort, as in truth the entire garrison consisted mainly of people requiring medical Attendance and treatment.

With great difficulty we were able to select fourteen men of the garrison to accompany Captain Nelson as far as Ipoto, to convey the dozen loads of baggage still remaining there; but as we were about to start, the Captain was prostrated with another attack of intermittent fever, and a strange swelling of the hand, which made it necessary for Dr. Parke to replace him for this short journey.

The faithful little fox-terrier "Randy," which had borne the fatigues of the double march to the Albert Nyanza so well, and had been such a good friend to us in an hour of great need, and had become the pet of every one, though "Randy" would not permit a Zanzibari to approach me unannounced, was committed to the care of Lieutenant Stairs, in the hope of saving him the thousand-mile journey now before us. But the poor dog misjudged my purpose, and resolutely refused his food from the moment I left him, and on the third day after my departure he died of a broken heart.

Upon carefully considering the state of the Fort, and the condition of its garrison, and the capacity of its Commandant, Lieut. Stairs, who would be assisted by Captain Nelson and Dr. Parke, I felt the utmost assurance that, with sixty rifles and abundant stores of ammunition, they were invulnerable from any attack of forest natives, however strong their forces might be. A wide and deep ditch ran round two-thirds of it. At each of its angles a commanding platform, closely fenced, had been erected, with approaches and flanks duly under rifle range, and each angle was connected by a continuous stockade, well banked with earth without and supported within by a firm banquette. The main roads leading to the Fort were also fenced, to serve as obstructions. The village inhabited by the garrison lay on the side unprotected by the ditch, and was arranged in V shape, to mask the entrance into the Fort. During daylight no hostile party could approach within 150 yards of the Fort unperceived. At night ten sentries would be sufficient precaution against surprise and fire.

This protection was not so much designed against natives alone as against a possible – and by no means unlikely – combination of Manyuema with natives. As much might be urged for the likelihood of such a combination as against it; but it is a totally wrong policy to be idle before an uncertain issue, and of the hundreds of camps or stations established by me in Africa, not one has been selected without considering every near or remote contingency.

I was about to leave Fort Bodo without the least anxiety respecting the natives and Manyuema, as also without fear of incompatibility between the officers and Zanzibaris. The officers were now acquainted with the language of their people, as well as with their various habits, tempers, and moods, and the men could equally distinguish those of their officers. Both parties also believed that their stay at Fort Bodo was not likely to be protracted, as the Pasha had promised to visit them within two months, and from a visit of one of his considerate and thoughtful character they might surely infer they would derive pleasure as well as profit. On his return to the Nyanza they could accompany him, abandoning the Fort to its fate.

Of the fidelity of the Zanzibaris there was also no room for doubt. However tyrannical or unjust the officers might be – an extreme conjecture – the Zanzibaris could only choose between them on the one hand, and the cannibalism of the Wambutti and the incarnate cruelty of the Manyuema on the other.

Would that I could have felt the same confidence and content-ment of mind regarding the Rear Column. With the lapse of months had been the increase of my anxiety. As week after week had flown by, my faith in its safety had become weakened and my mind fatigued – with the continual conflict of its hopes and doubts, with the creation of ingenious and fine theories, and their no less subtle demolition, was, perforce, constrained for its own repose and health to forbear thought and take refuge in the firm belief that the Major was still at Yambuya, but abandoned. Our duty was, therefore, to proceed to Yambuya, select the most necessary material equal to our carrying force, and march back to the Nyanza again with what speed we might.

On this supposition I framed an estimate of the time to be occu-pied by the journey, and handed it, with a letter of instructions, to the Commandant of the Fort for his use: –

Whereas the distance between Fort Bodo to the Nyanza is

*125 miles, and has been performed in 288 hours' marching,
or 74 days, inclusive of halts.*

*Whereas we travelled the distance from Yambuya to Ugar-
rowwa's in 289 hours =74 days.*

*Whereas Lieutenant Stair's marched from Ugarrowwa's to
Fort Bodo in26 days*

100 days

*Therefore our journey to Yambuya will probably occupy 100
days, and the same period back. From June 16th, 1888, to
January 2nd, 1889, is 200 days. We may reasonably be
expected on January 2nd at Fort Bodo, and on the 22nd of
the same month at Lake Albert.*

Or thus: Starting June 16th, 1888: −

The last evening of my stay at Fort Bodo, while re-citing over
the several charges, general and personal, entrusted to him, Lieut.
Stairs suggested that perhaps the non-arrival of the steamer Stanley
at Yambuya accounted for the utter silence respecting the Rear Column. I then replied in the following terms: −

"That is rather a cruel suggestion, my dear sir; that is the least I
fear, for as well as I was able I provided against that accident. You
must know that when the *Stanley* departed from the Yambuya on
the 28th of June, I delivered several letters to the captain of the
steamer. One was to my good friend Lieut. Liebrichts, Governor of
Stanley Pool district, charging him, for old friendship's sake, to
despatch the steamer back as soon as possible with our goods and
reserve ammunition.

"Another was to Mr. Swinburne, my former secretary, who was
the soul of fidelity, to the effect that in case the *Stanley* met with
such an accident as to prevent her return to Yambuya, he would be
pleased to substitute the steamer *Florida* for her, as the owners
were business men, and full compensation in cash, which I guaran-

teed, would find as ready an acceptance with them as profits from the ivory trade.

"A third letter was to Mr. Antoine Greshoff, the agent at Stanley Pool for the Dutch house at Banana, to the effect that, failing both steamers *Stanley* and *Florida,* he would find a large ready money profit if he would undertake the transport of the stores of the Expedition from Stanley Pool, and 128 men from Bolobo, to Yambuya. Whatever reasonable freight and fare he would charge, immediate payment was guaranteed by me.

"A fourth letter was to our officer in charge at Stanley Pool, Mr. John Rose Troup, to the effect that, failing the steamers *Stanley, Florida,* and Mr. Greshoff's, he was to use his utmost powers and means to collect boats and canoes, at whatever cost, ready at hand, and communicate with Messrs. Ward and Bonny at Bolobo. Mr. Ward at Bolobo was also enjoined to do the like in Uyanzi, and man these vessels with the Zanzibaris and natives, and transport by stages the various stores to the intrenched camp at Yambuya. This last would scarcely be needed, as it is extremely improbable that from June 28th, 1887, to June 16th, 1888 – nearly twelve months – neither the *Stanley,* the *Florida,* nor Mr. Greshoff's steamer would be available for our service.

"Besides, you must remember that both captain and engineer of the *Stanley* were each promised a reward of £50 sterling if they would arrive within reasonable time. Such amounts to poor men are not trifles, and I feel assured that if they have not been prevented by their superiors from fulfilling their promise, all goods and men arrived safely at Yambuya."

"You still think, then, that in some way Major Barttelot is the cause of this delay?"

"Yes, he and Tippu-Tib. The latter of course has broken his contract. There is no doubt of that. For if he had joined his 600 carriers, or half that number, with our Zanzibaris, we should have heard of them long ago, either at Ipoto, when you returned there for the boat, or later, when you reached Ugarrowwa's, March 16th this year. The letter of September 18th, 1887, when only eighty-one days absent from Yambuya, and which the Arab promised without delay, would certainly have produced an answer by this if the Major had departed from Yambuya. Those carriers, all choice men, well armed, acquainted with the road, despatched with you to Ugar-rowwa's on February 16th, and seen by you safely across the river opposite his station on the 16th of the following month, would surely by this have returned if the Rear Column was only a few weeks' march from Yambuya; therefore I am positive in my mind that Major Barttelot is in some way or other the cause of the delay."

"Well, I am sure, however you may think the Major is disloyal, I –"

"Disloyal! Why, whoever put you in mind of that word? Such a word has no connection with any man on this Expedition, I hope. Disloyal! Why should any one be disloyal? And disloyal to whom?"

"Well, not disloyal, but negligent, or backward in pressing on; I feel sure he has done his best."

"No doubt he has done his level best, but as I wrote to him on September 18th, in my letter to be given to him by Ugarrowwa's carriers, it is his 'rashness and inexperience I dread,' not his disloy-alty or negligence. I fear the effect of indiscriminate punishments on his people has been such that the vicinity of Stanley Falls and the Arabs has proved an irresistible temptation to desert. If our let-ters miscarry in any way, our long absence – twelve months nearly to this day, and by the time we reach Yambuya fourteen months at least! – will be a theme for all kinds of reports. When the Zanzi-baris from Bolobo reached him he ought to have had over 200 car-riers. In twelve months – assuming that the goods and men arrived in due date, and that, finding Tippu-Tib had broken faith, he began the move as he promised – he would be at Panga Falls; but if the severe work has demoralized him, and he has demoralized his carri-ers, well, then, he is stranded far below Panga Falls – probably at Wasp Rapids, probably at Mupé or at Banalya, or at Gwengweré Rapids – with but 100 despairing carriers and his Soudanese, and he is perforce compelled by the magnitude of his task to halt and wait. I have tried every possible solution, and this is the one on which my opinion becomes fixed."

"Do you allow only 100 left? Surely that is very low."

"Why? I estimate his loss at what we have lost – about 50 per cent. We have lost slightly less; for from our original force of 389 souls there are 203 still alive: – 4 at Nyanza, 60 in the Fort, 119 going with me, and 20 couriers."

"Yes, but the Rear Column has not endured a famine such as we have had."

"Nor have they enjoyed the abundance that we have fed upon for the last seven months, therefore we are perhaps equal. But it is useless to speculate further upon these points.

"The success which was expected from my plans has eluded me. The Pasha never visited the south end of the Lake, as I suggested to him in my letter from Zanzibar. This has cost us four months, and of Barttelot there is not a word. Our men have fallen by scores, and wherever I turn there is no comfort to be derived from the prospect. Evil hangs over this forest as a pall over the dead; it is like a region accursed for crimes; whoever enters within its circle becomes subject to Divine wrath. All we can say to extenuate any error that we have fallen into is, that our motives are pure, and that our purposes are neither mercenary nor selfish. Our atonement shall be a sweet offering, the performance of our duties. Let us bear all that may be put upon us like men bound to the sacrifice, without one thought of the results. Each day has its weight of troubles. Why should we think of the distresses of to-morrow? Let me depart from you with the conviction that in my absence you will not swerve from your duty here, and I need not be anxious for you. If the Pasha and Jephson arrive with carriers, it is better for you, for them, and for me that you go; if they do not come, stay here until my return. Give me a reasonable time, over and above the date – the 22nd of December; then if I return not, consult with your friends, and afterwards with your men, and do what is best and wisest. As for us, we shall march back to the place where Barttelot may be found, even as far as Yambuya, but to no place beyond, though he may have taken everything away with him down the Congo. If he has left Yambuya and wandered far away south-east instead of east, I will follow him up and overtake him, and will cut through the forest in the most direct way to Fort Bodoe. You must imagine all this to have taken place if I do not arrive in December, and consider that many other things may have occurred to detain us before you yield to the belief that, we have parted for ever."

The following is the letter of instructions to Lieut. Stairs: –

Fort Bodo, Central Africa,
June 13th, 1888.

Sir, –

During my absence with the advance party of the Expedition, now about to return to the assistance of Major Barttelot and Rear Column, I appoint you Commandant of Fort Bodo. I leave with you a garrison, inclusive of sick, numbering nearly sixty rifles. The men mainly are not of the calibre requisite for a garrison in a dangerous country. Still they can all shoot off their rifles, are in good condition, and you have abundance of ammunition. My principal reliance is on the Commandant himself. If the chief is active and wary, our fort is safe, and no combination of natives can oust the garrison from its shelter. I need not tell you that I leave you with confidence.

Respecting the improvements to be made in the Fort, which I have verbally explained to you, I would suggest that as the Fort when completed will be more extensive than at present, you elect about twenty or thirty of the more decent and cleanly of the men to occupy the buildings in the Fort, until such time as they are wanted for other persons, because –

1st. You are in no danger, then, of being cut off by a daring foe from your garrison.

2nd One-third of your men will be then within the gates ready at your most sudden call.

3rd. The buildings within the Fort will be kept dry and in a habitable condition by being occupied.

Corn. Begin planting corn about July 15th. 1st July you should begin hoeing up, clearing the ground.

Bananas. I am exceedingly anxious about the bananas. Twice a week there should be sent a strong patrol round the plantations to scare the natives, and also elephants. For the latter half-a-dozen fires at as many points might suffice.

An officer should be sent out with the patrol, to have a reliable report of what transpires; should he report the bananas as getting scanty, then you should begin rationing your people, always obtaining your supplies by detachments from the most distant points of the plantations. Let the bananas nearest the Fort reach maturity, just as you would your corn. Along the main roads it would also be well to leave plantations alone until they mature.

I leave Captain Nelson as second in command, to take charge when you are incapacitated by illness or accident.

Dr. T. H. Parke, A.M.D., remains here as surgeon to take charge of the sick.

It is, of course, impossible to say when we shall return, as we have not the least idea whereabouts the Rear Column is, but we shall do our best. If the Major is still at Yambuya, you may expect us in December sometime.

I expect Emin Pasha and Mr. Jephson in here about two months hence- say about the middle of August.

Should Mr. Jephson appear with a sufficient force of carriers, then I should recommend the evacuation of the Fort and take the garrison, and accompany Mr. Jephson to the Nyanza, and put yourself and force at the disposition of Emin Pasha until my return. As I come eastward I propose following a northerly and easterly track from the Nepoko and make for the Ituri ferry.

In order that on reaching the Ituri ferry I may know whether you have evacuated the Fort or not, please remember that on the right bank of the river, near the ferry, there are a number of very tall trees, on which you could carve a number of broad arrows, which would indicate that you had passed. You could also carve date of crossing the Ituri on a conspicuous place near the ferry. This would save me a great deal of time and anxiety respecting you.

As our twenty couriers left here 16th February, it will be four months, June 16th, since they left. If Jephson appears in about two months, say, the time will then be about six months since the couriers left Fort Bodo – quite sufficient time to dispel all doubt about them.

I wish you and your associates good health and safe arrival at the Nyanza. On our part we will do our work with what celerity circumstances will permit.

Yours faithfully,

(Signed) Henry M. Stanley,
Commanding E. P. R. Expedition.
To Lieut. W. G. Stairs,
Commandant Fort Bodo.

Chapter 19

ARRIVAL AT BANALYA:
BARTTELOT DEAD

On the 16th of June, in the early morning we set out Fort Bode towards Yambuya in excellent spirits, loudly cheered by the garrison and with the best wishes of the officers. We numbered 113 Zanzibaris, ninety-five Madi carriers, four of Emin Pasha's soldiers, two whites besides Dr. Parke and his little band of fourteen men, whose company we were to have as far as Ipoto. Indekaru was reached on the evening of the 17th, amid a heavy storm of rain. The next day was a halt to collect more plantains. On the 19th we camped at Ndugubisha, the day following at Nzalli's. We had by this time been introduced to the difficulties of forest marching. The cries of the column leaders recalled most painfully what an absence of seven months had caused us almost to forget.

"Red ants afoot! Look out for a stump, ho! Skewers! A pitfall to right! a burrow to left! Thorns, thorns, 'ware thorns! Those ants; lo! a tripping creeper, Nettles, 'ware nettles! A hole! Slippery beneath, beneath! look out for mud! A root! Red ants! red ants amarch! Look sharp for ants! A log! Skewers below!" And so on from camp to camp.

Most of the villages along this route still stood, but all awry and decaying; reeling from rotten uprights, the cave corners on the ground, green mould covering the floors within, hollows filled with slime, and fungi flourishing along the sides, and nitrous excrescences abounding; roofs covered with creepers, nettles, and prolific gourd vines – veritable nests of ague, into which, however, necessity compelled us and our men to seek shelter by reason of excessive fatigue, or imminence of a rainstorm.

Mambungu's was reached on the 21st, and on the edge of the Busindi clearing we camped on the following day. After forty-seven hours marching from Fort Bodo we entered the Arab settlement of Ipoto, where it will be remembered our people, maddened by distress of hunger, caused me such serious losses of arms and ammunition. But the change in their condition was so great, and their eyes flashed such lively glances of scorn at their tormentors, that in the afternoon Kilonga-Longa, with his head-men, dreading reprisal, began with many apologies for the behaviour of his Manyuema during his absence to extenuate the heinousness of their crimes, and to offer to atone for them as well as he was able. Nineteen Remingtons were laid before me, out of thirty I knew to be in their possession. Six of these had been left as pledges of payment by myself, two were given by Mr. Stairs acting in my name, one was sold by Captain Nelson, and ten were sold by Zanzibaris, besides eleven not yet recovered; but out of 3000 cartridges and two entire cases these receivers of stolen goods purchased from the starving Zanzibaris, only fifty were returned. Whatever fears the Manyuema may have felt, the fit time for reprisal and retaliation had not arrived, though fifty rifles could have captured the settlement easily, the majority of Kilonga-Longa's people being absent raiding eastward. We had far more important business afoot than the destruction of Ipoto, nor must it be forgotten that our little garrison at Fort Bode was not so secure but that a few hundreds of men made desperate by their losses might not avenge themselves fully by a siege or midnight assault.

We therefore, bending under the necessities of the occasion, accepted the rifles and gifts of goat and rice, and the Zanzibaris were permitted to sell such ivory as they had packed up for 100 pecks of rice, which to them was most welcome provender.

The next day the chief returned two more rifles, but all my men being sufficiently armed, he was requested to retain them as pledges, in addition to the six remaining in his hands, for payment of ninety doti of cloth promised to him and his people for the grudging and scant sustenance given to Captain Nelson and Dr. Parke while they were compulsory guests of this ill-natured community.

In the afternoon Dr. Parke and his little band of fourteen men commenced their return journey to Fort Bode, conveying thirteen loads, and bearing the very last instructions I could give.

On the 25th June we set out from Ipoto accompanied by a guide and our escort of fifteen Manyuema, who were ostentatiously detailed for this duty as far as the next Arab settlement, one of Ugarrowwa's outlying stations. We arrived at the Ituri River, and a canoe capable of carrying nine men was delivered over to us at 3 P.M. to serve as the means of ferriage. As one trip to the left bank and back occupied on an average twenty-three minutes, night fell before a half of our force was across.

The work of ferrying was resumed early next morning, and continued until two o'clock, when every soul had crossed excepting the Manyuema escort whose fears that sudden vengeance would be inflicted on them, caused them to decline the venture they had been ordered to undertake.

We were now fairly in the wide uninhabited wilderness through which last October the Expedition struggled, gaunt victims of a merciless famine. No consideration would have tempted us to a revisit of these dreadful shades, but that we fostered a lively hope that we should soon meet our returning couriers, who we expected would gratify us with news from the Major's column. Imbued with the fond belief that as they had not arrived at Ipoto we should meet them on this road – none other being known to them – we marched briskly from the landing-place, and in two and three-quarter hours reached the camp whence we had crossed over to the north bank on the 14th of October last. Indications of our stay here were yet fresh – the charcoal broad arrows drawn on the barked tree stems, the lead pencil writing to Khamis Parry still plainly legible.

At 1.15 P.M. of the 28th we arrived at Nelson's camp, opposite the confluence of the Ihuru with the Ituri, a place which last October witnessed such death and agony, where poor Nelson sat so many hours, so many wretched days with ulcered feet, waiting anxiously the arrival of news from us, and where he was found by his friend Mounteney Jephson, haggard, and reduced by his feelings of forlornness and despair into a state of abject helplessness, in the midst of his dying and dead companions. We had performed the march in twenty hours, or in four days inclusive of our detention while ferrying with one small craft. Last October, despite our strenuous endeavours, the same distance had occupied us thirty-nine hours' marching, or thirteen days inclusive of the halt! The condition of the stomach made all this great difference.

We found our *cache* untouched, though we had strong doubts, and unearthed our buried stores which Jephson's relief party was unable to carry away. The ammunition, made by Kynoch of Birmingham, after eight months' burial in the sand, subject to tropic damp and an eternal rain, was not so much injured as we expected, a full eighty per cent. of it being still sound, and the well-waxed brass cases and copper caps yet exhibited their native brightness and gloss. Distributing 1,000 rounds to the men for the refilling of their pouches, selecting such other articles as were useful, we made up eight loads, and after burying the rest as superfluous, we hurried away from the hateful spot, camping far inland.

Arriving at camp, we discovered four Madi carriers to have deserted with the kits of their Zanzibari mates. Had they known, what we could never forget, of the evil repute of this wilderness, they probably would have chosen the brawling river for their graves than the slow torture of famine in the ruthless forest.

At sunset we were surprised to see the Manyuema escort reach our camp. They had fled to Kilonga Longa's, and that gentleman had sternly ordered them to follow us again, and not to return without a note reporting they had performed the duty on which they had been sent.

On the 29th we left the river route and steered a south-westerly course through the pathless forest, in order to strike the road taken by Mr. Stairs' party on their return from Ugarrowwa's. As the head-man Rashid bin Omar was of our party, we presumed – as he asserted his faith in himself – that he would recognize the path if it were shown to him, after which of course there would be no difficulty. The whole of the 29th and 30th were occupied in this south-westerly course undeviating. We meanwhile crossed several native paths, but as Rashid failed to recognize any of them, we continued on our way. On the 1st July, early in the morning's march, we entered the basin of the Lenda River, and then, as Rashid expressed himself of the opinion that we must have passed the path, we took a direct westerly course, steering straight on through the forest by compass. At noon of the 2nd we struck the Lenda River which generally flowed, as we observed during the afternoon march of the 2nd and until noon of the 3rd, N.N.W. Discovering a narrow chasm thirty yards wide through which the Lenda rushed furiously, we conceived it would be to our advantage to throw a bridge across this river, and trust to fortune showing us the path to Ugarrowwa's station on the other bank, rather than continue along the Lenda River on the right bank, lest we might be forced to wander for days without finding the means of crossing. Accordingly we selected three of the tallest trees, 115, 110, and 108 feet respectively, which we managed to launch across the chasm, and these resting on stout forked uprights, with railings to steady the laden men, made a commodious and safe bridge. Early on the morning of the 5th the bridge was completed, and by ten o'clock every man was safe across.

The Madi carriers having purposely scattered their corn provision along the road to lighten their loads, began now to pay the penalty of their wastefulness. Though the camp-crier cried out daily the number of days yet remaining for which the provisions must last, the ignorant savages were, however, too dense-headed to profit by the warning; consequently we had a dozen feeble wretches already faltering in their gait. We were already short of seven – four of whom had deserted.

We continued on the left bank our westerly course, and meantime crossed several native paths inclining S.E. and N.W., but we found none that can be made available for our necessity.

On the 6th we stumbled across a clearing garnished with a small but thriving plantation of plantains. The famished Madis rushed on this supply like hungry wolves on their prey, and soon devoured the whole, but three of them trod on cunningly-hidden sharp-pointed skewers set in the ground.

Through a pelting rain we travelled on the 7th, and, wet and miserable, camped in the bosom of untraversed woods. One hour's march next day brought us to the small village of Balia, and five hours later halted for the night at Bandeya.

This day had been replete with miseries and singular accidents. A shower of cold rain fell on us after leaving Balia, and three of the naked Madis fell dead within a few paces of each other. At the first indications of this shower I had ordered a halt, and spread out about

150 square feet of tenting, inviting everyone to huddle under it. The shower over, we rolled up the canvas and resumed the march, but we were still subject to the heavy cold dripping of the foliage. The Zanzibaris, more accustomed to it and in better condition of body, were not much inconvenienced; but three Madis, depressed in mind, depleted in body, fell dead as suddenly as though shot. A Lado soldier of Emin Pasha's and a Zanzibari were skewered in the feet, and so crippled by these painful wounds that we were obliged to carry them. Near Bandeya another Madi native succumbed to illness caused by insufficient food, and a Zanzibari was shot by a bold and crafty dwarf with an arrow which penetrated between the ribs, but not to a fatal depth. Arriving at the village, my cook Hassan, in an unfortunate moment, while drawing his Winchester rifle towards him, caused it to explode, tearing a large portion of the muscles of the left arm; and near midnight a youth named Amari, while blowing up to a brighter flame a watch-fire, was suddenly wounded in the head by a bullet from a Remington cartridge that some one had carelessly dropped near the embers.

The next day, guided by some women who said they knew the way to Ugarrowwa's, there was a most tedious march through an immense clearing lately abandoned by the natives. None that I can remember was so full of vexations. It was a strained position at every stride we took – now treading on a slippery trunk which bridged a chasm bristling with dangers from a number of dead branches, their sharp points erected upwards threatening impalement to the unfortunate man who fell from such a height on them; then balancing oneself on a log thrown across a rushing stream; anon plunged into a brake suffocatingly close from the dense masses of myriads of creepers growing above and around; soon stumbling through a deep green slough, its depth hidden by floating vegetable parasites, then over a fearful array of logs, the relics of the old forest, and every step the difficulties repeated until near noon we had traversed with streaming bodies the vast clearing of Ujangwa. On the confines of the virgin forest we formed camp, despatched the people to gather plantains and to prepare them as provisions for the few days yet remaining of the wilderness.

By solar observations I discovered we were in N. lat. 1° 0' 16".

On the 10th I suspected we were taking a course which, if continued, would lead us not far from our camp of the 8th, but the Zanzibaris were so wedded to the belief that the natives knew their own country best, that in a fit of spleen I permitted them to rest in that opinion. About ten o'clock of the 11th we came upon the clearing and a little village we had left on the morning of the 8th. Thus we had made a complete circle, and in revenge for this the people demanded that the women should be slaughtered. Poor things, they had only acted according to their nature! It is we who were in error in supposing that the natives would show us a way leading them further and further from their own country. Were the faith continued in them they would have persisted in guiding us round about their clearings until they had dropped dead on their native earth. The women were therefore sent away home, and with compass in hand we steered a west by north course to strike the main road. We continued this course the whole of the 11th, and early next day succeeded in finding he path, which ran north by east.

At nine o'clock of the 13th July we reached our old camp on the Ituri River, opposite Ugarrowwa's station, but the place, as we looked across the river, we found to be abandoned. Therefore no news could be obtained of our long absent carriers, or of the Major and his people. We resumed our march, our course being along the Ituri River, every mile, every creek, every crossing-place and every camp, well known to us.

The next day, rations all exhausted, Madis perishing by twos and threes daily, we reached Amiri Falls. No sooner was camp pitched than there was a rush for food. It was not to be obtained in the immediate vicinity, for Ugarrowwa's multitude of 600 people had preceded us and devoured every edible, and that the supply had been insufficient for them was evident by the number of skeletons in his old camp. Distance would not deter our fellows from the Nyanza; they hastened onward, pursuing a track leading southward, until finally after some hours they reached a hill the base of which was one continuous thriving plantation of plantains. At a late hour in the night they brought the good news to camp, gratified our famished eyes with a view of the prodigious fruit, which caused us all to dream ecstatically on fruity banquets of which the mellow and flavoury plantain was the most conspicuous.

Of course a halt at such a critical period within reach of such abundance was imperative, and at an early hour the camp was emptied of nearly every able hand, excepting sentries, to procure food. In the afternoon the well-furnished foragers returned, often in couples, with an immense bunch between them, like to the old engraving of Caleb and. Joshua bearing the grapes of Eshcol. The more provident, however, bore larger quantities of the fruit, peeled and sliced, ready for drying, thus avoiding the superfluous stalk and plantain skin. During the absence of the foragers the weaker of the messes had erected the wooden grates and collected the fuel for the drying overnight. The fruit when thus dry could be converted into cakes, or palatable plantain porridge, or a morning's, draught of plantain gruel. Many of the finest specimens were reserved to ripen to make a sweet pudding, or a sweet brew, or for sauce for the porridge.

On the 16th July we resumed our march along the river, following our old road as closely as possible, and in seven hours reached the Little Rapids above Navabi Falls. On the next day passed Navabi Falls, and took a look at the place where we submerged our canoes, to discover that they had been taken away. Within four hours we arrived at our old camp at Avamburi landing-place. The path was now considerably improved, for nearly a thousand pairs of feet had trodden it since our two score of bill-hooks had first carved a passage through the bush. Many a skeleton lay along the road, and our moribund Madis were destined to add a few more to the number, for day by day they dropped down never to rise again. Nothing that we could say would prevail to induce them to provide provision for the morrow. Ten plantains they thought an inexhaustible stock, but the evening would find them hungering for more. The only other means left to save their lives was to halt as often as possible, to enable them to eat their fill. Accordingly we halted two days at Avamburi landing-place, to rest and comfort the drooping and dying Madis.

On the 20th we marched for seven and a half hours, and camped a few miles above Bafaido Cataract, losing one Zanzibari and four Madis *en route.* One of the latter was a chief among them, who suffered from a skewer wound in the foot. As we were starting he stated his intention to die on the spot, called his countrymen together, distributed his bracelets, anklets, shiny iron collars and ear-rings among them, and then lay down with a placid countenance, wherein not the slightest emotion was discernible. All this was very admirable, but it would have been still more admirable to have bravely struggled, than to have so doggedly died. Three hours later we discovered a canoe into which we were enabled to place a few weaklings. Before reaching camp we had found three canoes, into which we embarked nearly all the ailing ones. It would have been cruel to have halted and sent back people for the Madi chief; besides there were many chances against our finding him alive, for as soon as the rearguard left the camp it was generally visited by hosts of natives, who would feel no remorse for ending the feeble life of the sick man lagging behind the column.

The next day was a short march of two hours. Ugarrowwa had also halted at Bafaido Cataract, and for several days, judging from the elaborate arrangements of his large camp, which from a distance appeared like a large town, occupying the extremity of the river-head terminated by the cataract. Before arriving at Hippo Broads we were in possession of four canoes. On the next day, lunching at the cataract camp, where we buried our shovels and some articles which our weakening force could not carry, we examined the caché, and discovered that the deserters had unearthed the ten tusks of ivory, and the natives had possessed themselves of all the remaining articles. Late in the afternoon we camped at Basopo Cataract. Between the two cataracts the Zanzibaris discovered several canoes hidden away in the creeks emptying into the Ituri, and joyfully, but most recklessly, embarked in them, and notwithstanding their knowledge of the dangerous channels of the Basopo Cataract, continued on their course down the furious stream, which caused us the loss of a Zanzibari and a boy belonging to the soldiers of Emin Pasha. In the capsized canoe were also two of the Pasha's soldiers, both of whom lost their rifles and their kit, and barely escaped with their lives.

Two Zanzibaris, called Juma and Nassib, wandered away from the column and were missing this day, and we were therefore obliged to halt on the 24th to send out a party to hunt for them. In the afternoon the party returned unsuccessful, but an hour later we were startled to hear a bullet hissing over our heads. A search was

made, and the culprit was found to be Nassib, who, accompanied
by his friend Juma, was returning to camp, and who informed us
that he had seen one of our people in the bush just outside the
camp, and had fired at him, supposing him to be a prowling native.
He still more astonished us when he related that the cause of his
parting from the column was that he and Juma had seen some fine
plantains in a plantation, and had sat down to peel and dry a supply
for the road. This had consumed some eighteen hours at least, and
they say that when they sought the road they could not find the
track of 200 men. It is difficult to decide which compelled most
admiration, the folly of these two third-rate men sitting calmly
down in the midst of a plantation belonging to ferocious cannibals,
who generally closed the rear of the columns to avenge themselves
on the stragglers, or the alarm which in this solitary instance possessed the natives.

On the 25th we camped above the Little Rapids of Bavikai, and
on the next day entered the populous district of Avé-jeli, opposite
the mouth of the Nepoko affluent, taking our quarters in the village
where Dr. Parke so successfully amputated the foot of an unfortunate Zanzibari thirteen months before.

I was never so sensible of the evils of forest marching as on this
day. My own condition of body was so reduced, owing to the mean
and miserable diet of vegetables on which I was forced to subsist,
that I was more than usually sympathetic. At this time there were
about thirty naked Madis in the last stages of life; their former ebon
black was changed to an ashy grey hue, and all their bones stood
out so fearfully prominent as to create a feeling of wonder how
such skeletons were animated with the power of locomotion.
Almost every individual among them was the victim of some hideous disease, and tumours, scorched backs, foetid ulcers, were
common; while others were afflicted with chronic dysentery and a
wretched debility caused by insufficient food. A mere glance at
them, with the mal-odour generated by ailments, caused me to gasp
from a spasm of stomach sickness. With all this, the ground was
rank with vegetable corruption, the atmosphere heated, stifling,
dark and pregnant with the seeds of decay of myriads of insects,
leaves, plants, twigs and branches. At every pace my head, neck,
arms, or clothes was caught by a tough creeper, calamus thorn,

coarse briar, or a giant thistle-like plant, scratching and rending whatever portion they hooked on. Insects also of numberless species lent their aid to increase my misery, especially the polished black ant, which affects the trumpet tree. As we marched under the leaves these ants contrived to drop on the person, and their bite was more vexatious than a wasp's or red ant's; the part bitten soon swelled largely, and became white and blistery. I need not name the other species, black, yellow and red, which crossed the path in armies or clung to almost every plant and fed on every tree. These offensive sights and odours we met day after day, and each step taken was fraught with its own particular evil and annoyance, but with my present fading strength and drooping spirits, they had become almost unbearable. My mind suffered under a constant strain of anxiety respecting the fate of my twenty choice men which were despatched as couriers to the rear column under Major Barttelot, as well as of the rear column itself. I had had no meat of any kind, of bird or beast, for nearly a month, subsisting entirely on bananas or plantains, which, however varied in their treatment by the cook, failed to satisfy the jaded stomach. My muscles had become thin and flabby, and were mere cords and sinews, every limb was in a tremor while travelling, and the vitals seemed to groan in anguish for a small morsel of meat.

At camp I overheard a conversation carried on between my tent-boy Sali and another Zanzibari. The boy was saying that he believed the "Master" would not last long, how he had observed that his powers were declining fast. "Please God," said the other, "we shall find goats or fowls in a few days. It is meat he needs, and he shall get it if Ugarrowwa has not cleared out the country."

"Ah," said Sali, "if the Zanzibaris were men instead of being brutes, they would surely share with the master what meat they get while foraging. Do they not use his guns and cartridges, and are they not paid wages for using them. I can't understand why they should not share what they obtain with the master's own rifles."

"There are few here so wicked as not to do it – if they get anything worth sharing," replied the other.

"But I know better," said Sali. "Some of the Zanzibaris find a fowl or a goat almost every day, but I do not see any of them bringing anything to the master."

At this juncture I called out to Sali, and enjoined him to tell me all he knew. By dint of questioning, the fact was elicited that there was some truth in what he had stated. Two of the Zanzibari chiefs, Murabo, of Bumbiré fame, and Wadi Mabruki, had discovered a goat and three fowls on the 25th, and had secretly eaten them. This was one of the first instances of signal ingratitude discovered in these two men. From this day the effect of the disclosure resulted in obtaining a share in the spoils. Three fowls were delivered to me before evening, and a few days later I had regained normal strength. This happy result in my own case proved what the needs of the poor naked Madis were.

A heavy stock of provisions of dried plantains was prepared at Avé-jeli, and our increasing flotilla of canoes enabled us to embark all our Madis, baggage, and half of the Zanzibari force.

We formed our next day's camp near Avugadu Rapids, and on the 27th passed the canoes over the rapids, and halted for the night a few miles below.

We lunched at our old camp, where I remained so many days while waiting and searching for the lost Expedition in August, '87, on the 30th July, and took up our night's quarters at Mabengu village.

At this village we observed about sunset an immense number of large bats, called "pope" in Swahili, sailing over our heads to their night roosts across the river. A thin riband of sky was alone visible above where I stood, and I counted 680 of the number that flew within view. As the army of bats must have spread over several miles of the forest, a rough approximation of the many thousands that were flying may be made.

On the last day of July we reached Avisibba, famous for its resistance to our advance column last year, and for the fatal effects of the poisoned arrows employed in the conflict. In one of the huts we found the top of one of our tent-poles, wrapped carefully in leaves, with a small piece of cartridge paper, a bit of green velvet from our surgical instrument case, and the brass case of a Remington cartridge. The curious package was hung up to one of the rafters, and probably consecrated to some fetish.

In another hut we discovered a collar of iron rings, and ten unfired cartridge cases. These last must have belonged to one of our unfortunate deserters, whose flesh must have simmered in a pot over a fire and formed a family repast. An old jacket was also picked up later, which deepened the probability.

Shortly after landing at the village a little naked girl about eight years old walked composedly into view and surprised us all by addressing us in the Zanzibari language.

She cried out, "It is true, then? I heard a gunshot, and I said to myself while in my hiding-place, these must be my own people, and I will go and see them, for the Pagans have no guns."

She gave her name as "Hatuna-mgini" (we have no other), and related that she and five full-grown women were abandoned by Ugarrowwa at that place because they were very sick, and that soon after Ugarrowwa had departed with his large flotilla of canoes the natives rushed in and killed the five women, but that she had run away and hidden herself, where she had remained ever since, living on raw wild fruit, but in the night she had succeeded in gathering bananas, which, when ripe, she could eat uncooked, since no fire was possible. Ugarrowwa had had a skirmish with the Avisibbas, in which he had killed a great number. He had stayed here five days preparing food, and had departed many days – "more than ten days."

A march of four and a half hours to Engwedde, and another of seven and a half hours, took us to a camp opposite an island occupied by the Bapaiya fishermen, a few miles above the Nejambi Rapids. Rifles, accoutrements, were disembarked, and the canoemen were ordered to pass their canoes down the left branch. While the land party was engaged in the portage, the majority of the canoemen preferred to take the right branch, in which act of disobedience the Zanzibari chief and five Madis lost their lives, one canoe was lost, and two others capsized, but afterwards recovered. A Zanzibari named Salim was so bruised and battered by the flood sweeping him against the rocks that he was unable to walk for nearly a month afterwards.

About 3 P.M. we resumed our journey, and arrived about 5 P.M. at Panga Falls. Leaving a detachment of them to guard the canoes, we formed camp below the Falls. The land party succeeded in finding a small, supply of Indian corn, which, converted into meal, made me a porridge supper.

A downpour of rain, commencing at midnight and continuing until 1 P.M. of the 5th of August, much impeded our work, but by night we had our flotilla of nineteen canoes safe below the Falls, in front of our camp.

The natives of Panga had betaken themselves into an island near the right bank, with all their goats, fowls, and other property, but they had left several nets and wires within reach in the various branches on our side, whence we obtained some fine large fish. The natives were practically safe, inasmuch as no body of men with other business in view would incur the trouble of molesting them. They, however, manifested most plausibly a desire to make terms of amity with us by pouring water on their heads and sprinkling their bodies with it, and some of our men good-naturedly approached their island and responded reciprocally. The daring natives pushed across the cataract, and one of them contrived to draw himself unperceived' near one of our men, and stabbed him in the back.

A halt was ordered the next day, and a band of forty men proceeded inland to forage, returning towards night, each with a load of eatables; but one of their number, a Madi, received a severe wound in the back with an arrow.

Our old camp opposite the confluence of the Ngula River and the Ituri was reached on the 7th in two and a half hours by the canoes, but the land party occupied eight hours in marching the distance, which I estimated at eleven miles.

At Mambanga's on the north bank, which we reached the next day, we found a good supply of food, but a Zanzibari named Jaliffi was seriously wounded with a wooden arrow in the chest. A portion an inch and a half long was imbedded in the wounded part, which incapacitated him from duty for over two months. On the point of the arrow being ejected, the wound soon closed.

At Mugwye's – or My-yui – the next place, a great change had occurred. All the villages were obliterated by fire, and the fine plantain plantations cut down, and at Mugwye's own village there stood an immense camp. Believing that Ugarrowwa was present, we fired a signal shot, but no answer being returned, we proceeded to our old camp on the left, bank, where on one of the trees Lieutenant Stairs had carved the date "July 31st" (1887) for the benefit of the Major.

Arriving at our old camp, we were surprised to see the body of a woman belonging to Ugarrowwa's, freshly killed and washed, laid out on the bank close to the river, and near by three bunches of plantains, two cooking-pots, and a canoe capable of carrying five people. It was evident to us that a party of natives hearing the signal shot, had decamped, and had been obliged to abandon their intended feast.

A party of men was sent across the river to reconnoitre, and in a short time they came back reporting that Ugarrowwa must have departed that same morning down the river. This was very regrettable to me, as I burned to ascertain what he had heard of the news from down river, and I also wished to beg of him not to ravage the country for the benefit of succeeding caravans, which would suffer serious loss from the wholesale havoc and devastation attending his journey.

On the 10th of August I delivered over to the care of the senior Zanzibar chief, Rashid, thirty-five of the ablest of our men, with a charge to pursue our old track along the river as I intended to descend the river with our canoe flotilla without a halt as far as Wasp Rapids, where no doubt we should overtake Ugarrowwa, and where we should stay together until he should reach us.

At 6.40 A.M. we set out, and, paddling vigorously, were in the neighbourhood of Wasp Rapids at 11 A.M. Long before we heard the roar of the rushing river over the rocky reefs which obstruct its course there, we descried an immense camp on the right bank, and in a short time the forms of men in white dresses moving about the bush. When we had approached within rifle range we fired some signal shots and hoisted our flag, which was no sooner seen than the deep boom of heavily-loaded muskets announced that we were recognized. Soon several large canoes pushed from the right bank towards us, as we were descending along the left bank, and hailed us in the Swahili language. After the usual exchange of compliments we then asked the news, and to our great joy, not unmixed with grief, we learned that our couriers, who had now been absent from us nearly six months, were in Ugarrowwa's camp. The couriers had left Lieutenant Stairs at Ugarrowwa's station on the 16th of

March, and had reached Wasp Rapids in seventeen days, or on the 1st of April, where they had been driven back with a loss of four of their number. Perceiving that they were unable to pierce through the hostile crowds, they had travelled back to Ugarrowwa's station, which they reached on the 26th of April, and where they placed themselves in Ugarrowwa's hands. A month later, Ugarrowwa, having collected his people from the outlying stations, commenced his descent of the Ituri River, our couriers accompanying him, reaching Wasp Rapids on the 9th of August, having been seventy-six days *en route*. That same period we had occupied in travelling from the Albert Nyanza, the 10th of August being the twenty-ninth day since we had left Ugarrowwa's old station.

After forming our camp on the left bank in the deserted village of Bandeyah, opposite the camp of Ugarrowwa's, in the deserted village of Bandekiya, the surviving couriers, accompanied by Ugarrowwa and his head men, visited us. Amid a deep silence the head man related his tragic story:

"Master, when you called for volunteers to bear your letter to the Major, there was not a man of us but intended to do his very best, knowing that we were all to receive a high reward and great honour if we succeeded. We have done our best, and we have failed. We have, therefore, lost both reward and honour. It is the men who have gone with you to the Nyanza and found the Pasha, and can boast of having seen him face to face, who deserve best at your hands. But if we have not succeeded in finding the Major and gladdening his heart with the good news we had to tell, God he knows it has not been through any fault of our own, but rather because it is His will that we should not do so. We have lost four of our number, and I am the only one who cannot show a wound received during the journey. We have two, who though alive, seem to be incurable from the poison in their blood. Some of our men have as many as five arrow wounds to show you. As far as Avisi-bba we came down the river smoothly enough, but then the sharp work soon commenced. At Engwedde two were wounded. At Panga Falls three men were most seriously hurt by arrows. Between Panga Falls and here was a continued fight day after day, night after night; the natives seemed to know long before we reached them our full strength, and set on us either in full daylight or in the darkness, as though resolved to exterminate us. Why they should show so much courage with us when they had shown themselves so cowardly when we went up with you, I cannot say, unless our deserters, coming down river by half-dozens, have enabled the Pagans to taste the flavour of Zanzibari blood, and they having succeeded so well with them, imagined they could succeed with us. However, when we reached this village wherein you are now encamped, there were only eleven of us fit for anything; all the rest were sore from their wounds and one was helpless; and soon after our coming the fight began in real earnest. Those from that great village opposite us joined with the natives of Bandeya; the river seemed to swarm with canoes, and the bush around this village was alive with natives. After an hour's trial, during which time many of them must have been killed, for they were so crowded, especially on the river, we were left in peace. We availed ourselves in fortifying, as well as we could, the few huts we had selected for our quarters during the night.

"When night fell we placed sentries as usual, as you and Lieut. Stairs and Ugarrowwa, all of you, enjoined on us; but, wearied with work and harassed by care, our sentries must have slept, for the first thing we knew was that the natives had pulled down our zeriba and entered into the camp, and a wild cry from a man who received a fatal thrust with a spear woke us up to find them amongst us. We each grasped our rifles and fired at the nearest man, and six of them fell dead at our feet. This for a moment paralysed them; but we heard a chief's voice say, 'These men have run away from Bula Matari. Not one of them must live.' Then from the river and the bush they came on in dense crowds, which the flashes of our rifles' fire lit up, and their great numbers seemed for a short time to frighten the best of us. Lakkin, however, who is never so funny as when in trouble, shouted out, 'These fellows have come for meat — give it them, but let it be of their own people,' and wounded men and all took their rifles and took aim as though at a target. How many of them fell I cannot say; but when our cartridges were beginning to run low they ran away, and we were left to count the dead around us. Two of our men never answered to their names, a third called Jumah, the son of Nassib, called out to me, and when I went to him I found him bleeding to death. He had just strength enough to charge me to give the journey up. 'Go back,' said he. 'I give you my last words. Go back. You cannot reach the Major; therefore whatever you do, go back to Ugarrowwa's.' Having said this, he gave up his last breath, and rolled over, dead.

"In the morning we buried our own people, and around our zeriba there were nine natives dead, while within there were six. We beheaded the bodies, and after collecting their heads in a heap, held council together as to the best course to follow. There were seventeen of us alive, but there were now only four of us untouched by a wound. Jumah's last words rung in our ears like a warning also, and we decided to return to Ugarrowwa's. It was easier said than done. I will not weary you with details – we met trouble after trouble. Those who were wounded before were again wounded with arrows; those who were unwounded did not escape – not one excepting myself, who am by God's mercy still whole. A canoe was capsized and we lost five rifles. Ismailia was shot dead at Panga Falls. But why need we say over again what I have already said? We reached Ugarrowwa's after an absence of forty-three days. There were only sixteen of us alive, and fifteen of us were wounded. Let the sears of those wounds tell the rest of the story. We are all in God's hands and in yours. Do with us as you see fit. I have ended my words."

Among those who heard this dreadful story of trials for the first time there was scarcely a dry eye. Down many faces the tears ran copiously, and deep sighs and ejaculations of pity gushed from the sympathetic hearts. When the speaker had finished, before my verdict was given, there was a rush towards him, and hands stretched out to grasp his own, while they cried out with weeping eyes, "Thank God! thank God! You have done bravely: yes, you have shown real worth, and the mettle of men."

It was thus we welcomed our long-lost couriers, whose fate had been ever in our minds since our departure from Fort Bodo. They had been singularly unsuccessful in the object of their mission, but somehow they could not have been more honoured by us had they returned with letters from the Major. The story of their efforts and their sufferings was well told, and was rendered more effective and thrilling by the sight of the many wounds each member of the gallant band had received. Through the kindness of Ugarrowwa, whose sympathies had been won by the same sad but brave story, their wounds had soon healed, with the exception of two, who though now only greatly scarred were constantly ailing and weak. I may state here that one finally recovered in the course of two months his usual strength, the other in the same time faded away and died.

In Ugarrowwa's camp were also discovered three famous deserters, and two of our convalescents who were absent foraging during Lieut. Stairs' visit. One of these deserters had marched away with a box of ammunition, another had stolen a box containing some of Emin Pasha's boots and a few pairs of my own. They had ventured into a small canoe which naturally was capsized, and they had experienced some remarkable hair-breadth escapes before they arrived at Ugarrowwa's. They had been delivered as prisoners to Lieut. Stairs, but a few days later, they again escaped to Ugarrowwa's, who was again induced to deliver them up to me. These two afterwards behaved exceedingly well, but the third, while a victim to small-pox, some few weeks later, escaped from the care of his friends and leaped into the Nejambi Rapids, where he was drowned.

Ugarrowwa, being out of powder, was more than usually kind. A notable present of four goats, four sacks of rice, and three large canoes was made to me. The goats and rice, as may be imagined, were very welcome to us, nor were the canoes a despicable gift, as I could now treble the rate of our descent down the river; for in addition to our own canoes the entire Expedition of 130 fighting men, boys, followers, and Madi, carriers, besides the baggage could be embarked.

No news had been obtained of our Rear Column by either the couriers or Ugarrowwa. The letter to the Major, which I had delivered to Ugarrowwa for despatch by his couriers last September, was now returned to me with the letters from my own couriers. He had sent forty-five men down the river, but at Manginni, about half-way between Wasp Rapids and My-yui, they had been obliged to return. Thus both effects to communicate with Major Barttelot had been unsuccessful, and could not but deepen the impression that something exceedingly awry had occurred with the Rear Column. Among the letters delivered to me by Ugarrowwa was one open. It is descriptive and amusing, and characteristic of our Doctor: –

Fort Bode,
15th February, 1888.

My Dear Old Barttelot,

I hope you are 'going strong,' and Jameson 'pulling double.'
None of us here have any idea where you are. Some of us
officers and men say you are on the way up river, others say
you are still at Yambuya, unable to move with a large num-
ber of loads, and amongst the men there is an idea that your
Zanzibaris may have gone over to Tippu Tib. Stanley
reached the Lake 14th December, 1887, but could not com-
municate with Emin Pasha. As he had not got his boat, he
then came back from the Lake into the bush, and made this
fort to store his baggage, while he again goes on to the Lake
with Jephson and boat. Stairs goes to Ugarrowwa's to-mor-
row with twenty men, who are to go on to you and who bring
this letter. Stairs returns here with about forty or fifty men
who were left at Ugarrowwa's, and then goes on after Stan-
ley, as the place is only 80 or 100 miles from the Lake. I am
to stay at this fort with forty or fifty men. Nelson, who has
been ailing for months, therefore also remains here. We had
an awful time coming here. I often said I was starved at
school, but it was stuffing compared with what we have gone
through. I am glad to say all the white men are very fit, but
the mortality amongst the men was enormous, something like
50 per cent. Up to Ugarrowwa's there is plenty of food, but
little or none along the river this side of Ugarrowwa's. Stan-
ley, I know, is writing you all about the starvation and the
road. To-day, Stanley fell in all the men, and asked them all
if they wanted to go to the Lake or go back for you. Most of
the men at first wanted to go back, but afterwards the major-
ity were for the Lake; both Stairs, Jephson, and myself were
for the Lake, so as to decide if Emin Pasha was alive or not,
so as not to bring your column up all this way and then go
back to Muta Nzigé. All the men are as fat as butter, some of

them, However, who stayed with me at an Arab camp for three months, where I was left to look after Nelson, and sick men, and boxes, etc., are reduced to skin and bone. Out of thirty-eight, eleven died of starvation. Stairs was the only officer wounded, but many of the men died from their wounds.

"We are all in a bad way for boots; none of us have a good pair. I have made two pairs, but they did not last long, and all my clothes have been stolen by 'Rehani,' a Zanzibari. Stanley has had me working hard all day, and I have only time to write these few lines as the sun is going down. Our party have lost and sold a great quantity of ammunition.

Give my best wishes to old Jameson, also the other fellows whom I know; and hoping to see you up here before long,

Believe me, yours very sincerely,

J. H. P.

We are all awfully sick of this 'bush'; it continues to within a few miles of the Lake.

The next day was a halt. The senior Chief Rashid and his land party did not arrive before 2 P.M. of the 11th. The current had carried our flotilla in five hours, a journey which occupied him fifteen hours' march. But on the 12th of August, having safely passed the canoes below the rapids, we embarked at noon and proceeded down river. Opposite Elephant-playground camp we met one of Ugarrowwa's scouting canoes ascending, the men of which related wonderful stories of the strength, fierceness, and boldness of the Batundu natives. Two hours later the Batundu drums announced our advent on the river; but when their canoes advanced to reckon the number of our vessels, they quietly retired, and we occupied their chief village in peace, and slept undisturbed during the night.

At S. Mupé we arrived on the 13th, and halted one day to prepare food for our further journey down river, but on the next day, the 15th, we passed the flotilla safely down the various rapids, and camped below the lowest Mariri Rapids.

Resuming the journey on the 16th, we floated and paddled past three of our land march camps, and on a large island possessing huts sufficient to accommodate 2,000 people we halted for the night. Both banks of the river were unpeopled and abandoned, but no one could impart any reason for this wholesale devastation. Our first thought was that our visit had perhaps caused their abandonment, but as the natives had occupied their respective villages in view of the rear guard, we concluded that probably some internecine war was the cause.

This day was the eighty-third since we had departed from the shores of the Albert Nyanza, and the sixtieth since we had left Fort Bodo. Our progress had been singularly successful. Of the naked Madi carriers we had lost a great many, nearly half of the number that we had departed from the Nyanza with; but of the hardened and acclimatised Zanzibaris we had lost but three, two of whom were by drowning, and one was missing through a fit of spleen. Five hundred and sixty miles of the journey had been accomplished, there were only ninety miles remaining between Bungangeta Island and Yambuya, yet not a rumour of any kind had been heard respecting the fate of our friends and followers of the rear column. This constant and unsatisfied longing, pressing on my mind with a weight as of lead, with the miserable unnourishing diet of dry plantains, was fast reducing me into an aged and decrepit state of mind and body. That old buoyant confident feeling which had upheld me so long had nearly deserted me quite. I sat near sunset by the waterside alone, watching the sun subside lower and lower before the horizon of black foliage that bounded Makubana, the limits of my view. I watched the ashen grey clouds preceding the dark calm of night, and I thought it represented but too faithfully the melancholy which I could not shake off. This day was nearly twelve months from the date the rear column should have set out from Yambuya – 365 days. Within this period 100 carriers only might have been able to have advanced as far as Bungangeta, even if they had to make seven round trips backwards and forwards?

What could possibly have happened except wholesale desertion caused by some misunderstanding between the officers and men? In the darkness I turned into my tent, but in my nervous and highly-strung state could find no comfort there; and at last I yielded and implored the all-seeing and gracious Providence to restore to me my followers and companions, and allay the heartache that was killing me.

At the usual hour on the 17th, we embarked in our canoes and resumed our journey down the river, paddling languidly as we floated. It was a sombre morning; a heavy greyness of sky painted the eternal forest tops of a sombrous mourning colour. As we glided past Bungangeta district we observed that the desolation had not been confined to it, but that Makubana also had shared the same fate; and soon after coming in view of the mighty curve of Banalya, which south or left bank had been so populous, we observed that the district of the Banalya had also been included. But about half past nine we saw one village, a great way down through the light mist of the morning, still standing, which we supposed was the limit of the devastation. But as we drew near we discovered that it had a stockade. In July 1887, when we passed up, Banalya was deemed too powerful to need a stockade. Presently white dresses were seen, and quickly taking up my field glass, I discovered a red flag hoisted. A suspicion of the truth crept into my mind. A light puff of wind unrolled the flag for an instant, and the white crescent and star was revealed. I sprang to my feet and cried out, "The Major, boys. Pull away bravely." A vociferous shouting and hurrahing followed, and every canoe shot forward at racing speed.

About 200 yards from the village we stopped paddling, and as I saw a great number of strangers on the shore, I asked, "Whose men are you?" "We are Stanley's men," was the answer delivered in mainland Swahili.

But assured by this, and still more so as we recognised a European near the gate, we paddled ashore. The European on a nearer view turned out to be Mr. William Bonny, who had been engaged as doctor's assistant to the Expedition.

Pressing his hand, I said, "Well, Bonny, how are you? Where is the Major? Sick, I suppose?"

"The Major is dead, sir."

"Dead? Good God! How dead? Fever?"

"No, sir, he was shot."

"By whom?"

"By the Manyuema – Tippu-Tib's people."

"Good heavens! Well, where is Jameson?"

"At Stanley Falls."

"What is he doing there, in the name of goodness?"

"He went to obtain more carriers."

"Well then, where is Mr. Ward, or Mr. Troup?"

"Mr. Ward is at Bangala."

"Bangala! Bangala! what can he be doing there?"

"Yes, sir, he is at Bangala, and Mr. Troup has been invalided home some months ago."

These queries, rapidly put and answered as we stood by the gate at the water side, prepared me to hear as deplorable a story as could be rendered of one of the most remarkable series of derangements that an organized body of men could possibly be plunged into.

Despite Mr. Bonny's well written report of the events which had occurred, it was many days before I could find time to study and understand the details. The strangers I had observed belonged to Tippu-Tib, and they now pressed congratulations upon our arrival, and our people hurrying in through the narrow gate with the baggage from the canoes, bawling out recognition of their friends, leaping with joy, or homing with grief, made Banalya Camp indescribably tumultuous.

Let us imagine the baggage stored orderly, the canoes lashed to stakes firmly driven in the bank, the congratulations of the strangers over, the Zanzibaris of the advance column departed from our immediate vicinity to seek their long-lost friends and to hear the news, the Soudanese and Zanzibari survivors of the rear column having uttered their fervid thanks that we had at lash – at last, thank God – come, and such letters as had arrived hastily read, despatches hastily written, sent by couriers to Stanley Falls, one for Tippu-Tib himself, and one for the Committee of the Relief Fund, and we shall be at liberty to proceed with the story of the rear column, as gathered from Mr. Bonny's reports oral and written, and from the surviving Soudanese soldiers and Zanzibaris, and we shall then see how the facts differed or agreed with our anticipations.

Chapter 20

THE SAD STORY OF THE REAR COLUMN

The principal characters of the following narrative are: –

First. Tippu-Tib, *alias* Sheikh Hamed bin Mohammed, a man who is a native of the East Coast of Africa, of Arab descent. He has thousands of men under his command. He is a renowned slave trader, with a passion for extending his conquests and traffic in ivory and slaves, who, while meditating war against an infant State lately created in Africa, is persuaded to agree to a peace pact, to confine his destructive raids within certain limits, and, finally, to lend the services of 600 carriers to our Expedition, which is destined for the rescue of a worthy Governor beleaguered by many enemies at the north end of the Albert Nyanza.

While exhibiting the utmost goodwill, ungrudging hospitality, and exercising numerous small kindnesses to the officers of the Expedition, he contrives to delay performing the terms of his solemn contract, and months are wasted before he moves to take the necessary steps for accomplishing his duties. Finally, as the officers provoke him by constant and persistent entreaties, he makes a journey of over 700 miles, collects the carriers, and after eleven months' systematic delay, surrenders them to his white friends. But a few weeks later a catastrophe occurs: one of the head-men of these carriers, named Sanga, points his musket at the principal European officer in charge, and shoots him dead.

Second, is Major Edmund Musgrave Barttelot, a generous, frank, and chivalrous young English officer, distinguished in Afghanistan and on the Soudanese Nile for pluck and performance of duty. His rank and past experience in the command of men entitle him to the appointment of commander of the rear column. He is instructed to remain at Yambuya until the arrival of a certain contingent of carriers from Bolobo, in the charge of three subordinate officers, Messrs. Ward, Troup, and Bonny. If Tippu-Tib has arrived previous to or by that date, he is to lose no time in following the track of the advance column, which has preceded him by about seven weeks. If Tippu-Tib has not arrived by the time the Bolobo contingent has reached Yambuya, he is to make a forward move by slow stages with his own force of about 210 carriers, making repeated trips backwards and forwards until all the essentials are removed from camp to camp; he is allowed discretion what to dispense with in order to be enabled to march; the articles arc mentioned which may be thrown away. He declares the instructions to be clear and intelligible. He vows that he will not wait longer at Yambuya than the arrival of the Bolobo people, and satisfies us all that in him we have a man of energy, resolution, and action, and that there is no need of anxiety respecting the conduct of the rear column. In every letter and report he appears animated by the utmost loyalty and willing spirit.

Third, is a young civilian named James Sligo Jameson, a gentleman of wealth, with a passion for natural history studies, who, professing a fraternal attachment for his friend the Major, is appointed second in command of the rear column. It is reported of him, that "his alacrity, capacity, and willingness to work are unbounded"; whatsoever his friend the Major proposes receives the ready sanction of Mr. Jameson; and he has a claim to having much experience and judgment for former adventurous travels in Mashona Land and Matabele. Barely four weeks after the assassination of his friend he dies, utterly worn out by fever and trouble.

Three young Englishmen come last, who are attached to the Major's staff, two of whom, Mr. Herbert Ward and Mr. Troup, are to be associated with the commander and his second in the discussion of every vital step, and no important decision can be taken unless a council of the four has been convened to consider it as to its bearing upon the enterprise for which they have assembled on the verge of the unknown region of woods. They are therefore implicated in the consequences of any resolution and every sequent act. They are not boys new from school, and fresh from the parental care. They are mature and travelled men. Mr. Herbert Ward has seen service in Borneo, New Zealand, and Congo land; is bright, intelligent and capable. Mr. John Rose Troup has also served under command in the-Congo State, and has been mentioned in my record of the founding of that State as an industrious and zealous officer. Mr. William Bonny has seen service in the Zulu and Nile campaigns, has lived years in South America, and appears to be a staid and observing man.

Now here is the inexplicable mystery. We have parted from them while warmly and even affectionately attached to each other. We have plighted our words one to the other. "Fear not," say they; "we shall be doing and striving, cheerfully and loyally." We believe them, and hand in hand we pledge ourselves.

We return from our quest of Emin Pasha, and according to Major Barttelot's own Report (see Appendix) we learn the following striking facts: –

1st. "Rumour is always rife, and is seldom correct, concerning Mr. Stanley. He is not dead to the best of my belief. I have been obliged to open Mr. Stanley's boxes, as I cannot carry all his stuff."

He sends to Bangala all my clothing, maps, and charts, reserved medicines for the Expedition, photo chemicals and reserve negatives, extra springs for Winchesters, Remingtons, essentials for tents, and my entire canteen. He reduces me to absolute nakedness. I am so poor as to be compelled to beg a pair of pants from Mr. Bonny, cut another pair from an old white blanket in the possession of a deserter, and another from a curtain in my tent. But Messrs. Jameson, Troup, and Bonny are present, concurring and assisting, and the two last-named receive salaries, and both present their accounts and are paid, not a penny deducted, and a liberal *largesse* besides in first-class passages home is granted to them.

2nd. "There are four other Soudanese and twenty-nine Zanzibaris who are unable to proceed with us."

"Two cases of Madeira were also sent him (Mr. Stanley). One case I am sending back" – that is, down the Congo. He also collects a choice assortment of jams, sardines, herrings, wheaten flour, sago, tapioca, arrowroot, &c., and ships them on board the steamer which takes Mr. Troup homeward. And there are thirty-three dying men in camp. We may presume that the other gentlemen concurred in this deed also.

3rd. "I shall go on to Wadelai, and ascertain from Emin Pasha, if he be there still, if he has any news of Mr. Stanley; also of his own intentions as regards staying or leaving, I need not tell you that all our endeavours will be most strenuous to make the quest in which we are going a success. It may be he only needs ammunition to get away by himself, in which case I would in all probability be able to supply him."

On the 14th of August Mr. John Rose Troup has delivered over to Major Barttelot 129 cases Remington rifle cartridges, in addition to the twenty-nine left by me at Yambuya. These 158 cases contain 80,000 rounds. By June 9th (see Barttelot's Report) this supply has dwindled down to 35,580 rounds. There has been no marching, no fighting. They have decreased during a camp life of eleven months in the most unaccountable manner. There are left with the rear column only sufficient to give fifty rounds to each rifle in the possession of Emin Pasha's troops. Half of the gunpowder, and more than two-thirds of the bales of cloth, have disappeared. Though Yambuya. originally contained a store of 300,000 percussion-caps, it has been found necessary to purchase £48 worth from Tippu-Tib.

4th. "The loads we do not take are to be sent to Bangala. They will be loaded (on the steamers) on June 8th (1888), a receipt being given for them by Mr. Yan Kerkhoven, which is forwarded to you; also a letter of instructions to him and to Mr. Ward. Perhaps you would kindly give the requisite order concerning the loads and two canoes purchased for Mr. Ward's transport, as it is nearly certain I shall not return that way, and shall have, therefore, no further need of them or him." (See Appendix – Barttelot's Report).

Mr. Ward has been despatched down river to telegraph to the Committee for instructions; he was supposed to bring those instructions back from the sea with him. Here we are told the Major has no further need of him. He has also written to Captain Van Kerkhoven, of Bangala, not to allow him to ascend above Bangala. In the last paragraph of Mr. Jameson's letter to Mr. Bonny I note a reference to this change.

5th. The rear column consisted of 271 souls rank and file when we parted from Yambuya, June 28th, 1887.

In October, 1887, this force, according to a letter from the Major, had decreased to 246 men.

On June 4th, 1888, while the rear column lies still in the same camp (see the Major's Report) it has diminished to 135 men rank and file.

On August 17th, 1888, I demand from Mr. William Bonny, who is in sole charge at that date, an official report as to the number of men left of the rear column, and he presents me with the following: –

"List of Zanzibaris left by Mr. Stanley at Bolobo and Yambuya, inclusive of eleven men, deserters, picked up from advance column: –

    78 dead.
    26 deserted.
    10 with Mr. Jameson (Bangala).
    29 left sick at Yambuya.
    5 left sick on road.
    75 present at Banalya, August 17th, 1888.

Return of Soudanese and Somalis and Syrians left at Yambuya:

    21 died.
    1 killed by natives.
    1 executed by order of Major Barttelot.
    3 sent down Congo to Egypt.
    4 left sick at Yambuya.
    1 sick handed over to care of Congo State.
    22 present at Banalya, August 17th, 1888.

Return of British officers left by Mr. Stanley at Bolobo and Yambuya: –

    1 John Rose Troup, invalided home.
    1 Herbert Ward, sent down river by Major Barttelot
    1 James S. Jameson, proceeded down Congo.
    1 Edmund M. Barttelot, Major (murdered).
    1 William Bonny, present at Banalya, August 17th, 1888.
    11 deserters from advance column
    1 error.

Dead and lost.

> 78 Zanzibaris dead.
> 29 left sick at Yambuya.
> 4 left sick at Yambuya.
> 5 left sick on road.
> 21 Soudanese dead.
> 1 killed by natives.
> 1 executed.

6th. The steamer *Stanley* arrived at Yambuya on the 14th of August, within a few days of the date mentioned in the Letter of Instructions. On the 17th she departs to her port at Leopoldville, and has severed all connection with the Expedition. The officers of the Congo State have behaved loyally according to their Sovereign's promise. It only remains now for the rear column to pack up and depart slowly but steadily along our track, because Tippu-Tib has not arrived, and according to the issue anticipated will not come.

I turn to Mr. Bonny, and ask, "Were you not all anxious to be at work?"

"Yes, sir."

"Were you not burning to be off from Yambuya?"

"Yes, sir."

"Were you all equally desirous to be on the road?"

"I believe so. Yes, sir."

"Well, Mr. Bonny, tell me – if it be true that you were all burning, eager, and anxious to be off – why you did not devise some plan better than travelling backwards and forwards between Yambuya and Stanley Falls?"

"I am sure I don't know, sir. I was not the chief, and if you will observe, in the Letter of Instructions you did not even mention my name."

"That is very true; I ask your pardon; but you surely did not remain silent because I omitted to mention your name, did you – you a salaried official of the Expedition?"

"No, sir. I did speak often."

"Did the others?"

"I don't know, sir."

I have never obtained further light from Mr. Bonny, though at every leisure hour it was a constant theme.

A year after this we were at Usambiro, south of the Victoria Nyanza, and I received a clipping of a newspaper wherein there was a copy of Major Barttelot's letter of October, 1887. There was a portion which said, "We shall be obliged to stay here until November." I know that they thought they were obliged to remain until June 11, 1888. I turn to Major Barttelot's letter of June 4th, 1888 (see Appendix), wherein he says, "I feel it my bounden duty to proceed on this business, in which I am fully upheld by both Mr. Jameson and Mr. Bonny; to wait longer would be both useless and culpable, as Tippu-Tib has not the remotest intention of helping us any more, and to withdraw would be pusillanimous, and, I am certain, entirely contrary to your wishes and those of the Committee."

I turned to my Letter of Instructions, and I find in Paragraph 10:

"It may happen that though Tippu-Tib has sent some men, he has not sent enough to carry the goods with your own force. In that case you will of course use your discretion as to what goods you can dispense with, to enable you to march."

Paragraph 11. "If you still cannot march, then it would be better to make marches of six miles twice over, if you prefer marching to staying for our arrival, than throw too many things away." (See Letter of Instructions in a preceding chapter.)

At Usambiro also I received the answer which the Committee sent in reply to Mr. Ward's cablegram from St. Paul de Loanda, asking them to "wire advice and opinion."

To Major Barttelot, Care Ward, Congo.

Committee refer you to Stanley's orders of the 24th June. If you still cannot march in accordance with these orders, then stay where you are, awaiting his arrival, or until you receive fresh instructions from Stanley.

A committee 6000 miles away penetrate into the spirit of the instructions instantly, but a committee of five officers at Yambuya do not appear to understand them, though they have been drawn up on the clear understanding that each officer would prefer active movement and occupation to an inactive life and idle waiting at Yambuya.

7th. Mr. William Bonny, whose capacity to undertake serious responsibilities is unknown to me, is not mentioned in the Letter of Instructions.

On my return to Banalya, Mr. Bonny hands me the following order written by Major Barttelot.

Yambuya Camp,
April 22nd, 1888.

Sir, – In event of my death, detention of Arabs, absence from any cause from Yambuya camp, you will assume charge of the Soudanese company, the Zanzibar company, and take charge of the stores, sleeping in the house where they are placed. All orders to Zanzibaris, Somalis, and Soudanese will be issued by you and to them only. All issues of cloth, matako (brass rods), etc., will be at your discretion, but expenditure of all kinds must as much as possible be kept under. Relief to Mr. Stanley, care of the loads and men, good understanding between yourself and the Arabs must be your earnest care; anything or anybody attempting to interfere between you and these matters must be instantly removed.

I have the honour to be, Sir, &c.,

Edmund M. Barttelot,
Major.

What remains for the faithful Jameson, "whose alacrity, capacity, and willingness to work are unbounded," to do? Where is the promising, intelligent, and capable Ward? What position remains for the methodical, business-like, and zealous Mr. John Rose Troup? Mr. Bonny has been suddenly elevated to the command of the rear column in the event of any unhappy accident to Major Barttelot.

My first fear was that I had become insane. When I alone of all men attempt to reconcile these inexplicable contrarinesses with what I know animated each and every officer of the rear column, I find that all the wise editors of London differ from me. In the wonderful log-book entries I read noble zeal, indefatigable labour, marches and countermarches, and a limitless patience. In the Major's official report, in Mr. Jameson's last sad letter (see Appendix), I discern a singleness of purpose, inflexible resolve and the true fibre of loyalty, tireless energy, and faith, and a devotion which disdains all calculation of cost. When H came to compare these things one with another, my conclusion was that the officers at Yambuya had manifestly been indifferent to the letter of instructions, and had forgotten their promises. When Mr. Bonny told me that one of them had risen at a mess meeting to propose that my instructions should be cancelled, and that the ideas of Major Barttelot should be carried out in future – it did appear to me that the most charitable construction that could be placed upon such conduct was that they were indifferent to any suggestions which had been drawn out purposely to satisfy their own oft-repeated desire of "moving on."

But how I wish that I had been there for just one hour only on that August 17th, 1887, when the five officers were assembled – adrift and away, finally from all touch with civilization – to discuss what they should do, to tell them that

Joy's soul lies in the doing,
And the rapture of pursuing
Is the prize.

To remind them that

The path of duty is the way to glory.

What! count your hundreds of loads! What are they? Look, it is simply this: 200 carriers are here to-day. There are 500 loads. Hence to the next village is ten miles. In six days your 200 men have carried the 500 loads ten miles. In four months you are inland about 150 miles. In eight months you are 300 miles nearer to the Nyanza, and long before that time you have lightened your labours by conveying most of your burdens in canoes; you will have heard all about that advance column as early as October, the second month of work; for powder and guns, you may get Ugarrowwa's flotilla to help you, and by the time the advance column starts from Fort Bodo to hunt you up, you will be safe in Ugarrowwa's settlement, and long before that you will have met the couriers with charts of the route with exact information of what lies before you, where food is to be obtained, and every one of you will be healthier and happier, and you will have the satisfaction of having performed even a greater task than the advance column, and obtained the "kudos" which you desired. The bigger the work the greater the joy in doing it. That whole-hearted striving and wrestling with Difficulty; the laying hold with firm grip and level head and calm resolution of the monster, and tugging, and toiling, and wrestling at it, today, to-morrow, and the next until it is done; it is the soldier's creed of forward, ever forward – it is the man's faith that for this task was he born. Don't think of the morrow's task, but what you have to do to-day, and go at it. When it is over, rest tranquilly, and sleep well.

But I was unable to be present; I could only rely on their promise that they would limit their faith in Tippu-Tib until the concentration of all officers and men attached to the rear column, and insist that the blazing on the trees, the broad arrow-heads pointing the way, should be well made for their clear guidance through the almost endless woods, from one side of the forest to its farthest edge. Yet curiously hungering to know why Barttelot, who was "spoiling for work," and Jameson, who was so earnest, and had paid a thousand pounds for the privilege of being with us, and Ward, who I thought was to be the future Clive of Africa, and Troup, so noted for his industry, and Bonny, so steady and so obedient, so unconsciously acted as to utterly prevent them from doing what I believe from my soul they wished to do as much as I or any other of us did, a conviction flashes upon my mind that there has been a supernatural malignant influence or agency at work to thwart every honest intention.

A few instances will tend to strengthen this conviction. I freely and heartily admit that the five officers burned to leave Yambuya, and. to assist in prosecuting unto successful issue the unique enterprise they had sacrificed so much comfort to join. But they are utterly unable to move, try how they may. They believe I am alive, and they vow to make a strenuous quest for me, but they reduce me to nakedness. They are determined to start in quest and relief of Emin Pasha, because "to withdraw would be pusillanimous, and to stay longer would be culpable," and yet they part with the necessary ammunition that they wish to carry to him. They confess that there are thirty-three sick men unable to move at Yambuya, and yet the very stores, medicaments, and wine that might have saved them they box up and send to Bangala, after first obtaining a receipt for them. They have all signed agreements wherein each officer shall have a fair share of all European preserved provisions, perfect delicacies, and yet they decline to eat them, or allow the sick men to eat them, but despatch them out of the hungry woods to the station of Bangala. Mr. Bonny, as I understand, expressed no regret or audible dissent at their departure. From pure habit of discipline he refrained from demanding his fair share, and like a good Englishman, but mighty poor democrat, he parted with his inalienable right without a murmur. They searched for Manyuema slaves, cannibals of the Bakusu and Basongora tribes to replace their dead Zanzibaris and Soudanese, Somalis and Syrians, and it came to pass a few weeks after they had obtained these cannibals that one of their head men assassinates the English commander. Also on a fatal date, fatal because that resolution to wait sealed their fate, an officer of the advance column was straying through an impenetrable bush with 300 despairing men behind him, and on this fatal date the next year, Mr. Bonny, the sole survivor of the English band, pours into my ears a terrible tale of death and disaster, while at the same hour poor Jameson breathes his last, tired and worn out with his futile struggles to "move on" at Bangala, 500 miles west of me; and 600 miles east of me, the next day, Emin Pasha and Mr. Jephson walk into the arms of the rebel soldiery of Equatoria.

This is all very uncanny if you think of it. There is a supernatural *diablerie* operating which surpasses the conception and attainment of a mortal man.

In addition to all these mischiefs a vast crop of lying is germinated in these darksome shades in the vicinity of Stanley Falls, or along the course of the Upper Congo, showing a measureless cunning, and an insatiable love of horror. My own murder appears to be a favourite theme, quantities of human bones are said to be discovered by some reconnoitering party, human limbs are said to be found in cooking-pots, sketches by an amateur artist are reported to have been made of whole families indulging in cannibal repasts; it is more than hinted that Englishmen are implicated in raids, murder, and cannibalism, that they have been making targets of native fugitives while swimming in the Aruwimi, all for the mere sake of infusing terror, alarm, and grief among quiet English people, and to plague our friends at home.

The instruments this dark power elects for the dissemination of these calumnious fables are as various in their professions as in their nationality. It is a deserter one day, and the next it is an engineer of a steamer; it is now a slave-trader, or a slave; it is a guileless missionary in search of work, or a dismissed Syrian; it is a young artist with morbid tastes, or it is an officer of the Congo Free State. Each in his turn becomes possessed with an insane desire to say or write something which overwhelms common sense, and exceeds ordinary belief.

From the official written narrative of Mr. William Bonny I glean the following, and array the facts in clear order.

The *Stanley* steamer has departed from Yambuya early in the morning of August 17th, 1887. The goods she has brought up are stored within the magazine, and as near as I can gather there are 266 men within the entrenched camp. As they are said to have met to deliberate upon their future steps we may assume that the letter of instructions was read, and that they did not understand them. They think the wisest plan would be to await Tippu-Tib, who, it will be remembered, had promised to Major Barttelot that he would be after him within nine days.

On this day the officers heard firing across the river almost opposite to Yambuya. Through their binoculars they see the aborigines chased into the river by men dressed in white clothes, who are shooting at them from the north or right bank. Conceiving that the marauders must be some of Tippu-Tib's men, they resolve upon electing an officer and a few men to interview them, and to cease from molesting the natives who have long ago become friendly and are under their protection. The officer goes across, finds their camp, and invites Abdallah, their chief, to visit the English commander of Yambuya. The Major thus learns that these marauders really belong to Tippu-Tib, and that Stanley Falls is but six days' march overland from Yambuya. Probably believing that, after all, Tippu-Tib may be persuaded to assist the Expedition, he inquires for and obtains guides to conduct some of his party to Stanley Falls, to speak and treat in his behalf with that chieftain whom we have conveyed from Zanzibar to Stanley Falls, with free rations in consideration of the help he had solemnly contracted to furnish.

On August 29, Mr. Ward returns from the Falls with a reply from Tippu-Tib, wherein he promises that he will collect the carriers needed and send them within ten days. The first promise in June was "in nine days"; the promise is in August "in ten days." A few days later Mr. Jameson returns from Stanley Falls in company of Salim bin Mohammed, a nephew of Tippu-Tib, and a large party of Manyuema. This party is reported to be the vanguard of the carrier contingent, which Tippu-Tib will shortly bring in person.

In the interval of waiting for him, however, trouble breaks out on the Lumami, and Tippu-Tib is obliged to hurry to the scene to settle it. The Yambuya garrison, however, are daily expecting his presence.

Unable to bear the suspense, the second visit to Stanley Falls is undertaken, this time by Major Barttelot in person. It is the 1st of October. Salim bin Mohammed accompanied him, and also Mr. Troup. On the way thither they met Tippu-Tib advancing towards Yambuya, having six deserters from the advance column, each bearing a weighty tusk. The Major graciously remits the six ivory tusks to the Arab chief, and, as they must have a palaver, they go together to Stanley Fails.

After one month the Major returns to his camp, on the Aruwimi, and states that Tippu-Tib, unable to muster 600 carriers in the Stanley Falls region, is obliged to proceed to Kasongo, about 350 miles above Stanley Falls, and that this journey of about 700 miles (to Kasongo and back) will occupy forty-two days.

Meantime, twenty of the Major's own people have been buried outside the camp.

The English commander learns that during his absence, Majato, a head man of the Manyuema, has been behaving "badly," that he has been, in fact, intimidating the natives who marketed with the garrison, with the view of starving the soldiers and Zanzibaris, or reaping some gain by acting as the middleman or factor in the exchange of goods for produce. Hearing these things, the Major naturally becomes indignant, and forthwith despatches Mr. Ward, who makes the third visit to the Falls to complain of the arbitrary conduct of Majato. The complaint is effective, and Majato is immediately withdrawn.

In the beginning of 1888, Salim bin Mohammed arrives at Yambuya for the second time, and presently becomes so active in enforcing certain measures against the natives that the food supply of the camp is wholly cut off and never renewed. He also commences the construction of a permanent camp of substantial mud-built huts, at half a bow-shot's distance from the palisades of Yambuya, and completely invests the fort on the land side, as though he were preparing for a siege of the place.

After a futile effort to bribe Salim with the offer of a thousand pounds to lead a Manyuema contingent to follow the track of the advance column, Major Barttelot and Mr. Jameson, about the middle of February, undertake the fourth visit to Stanley Falls. Salim, fearing unfavourable accounts of his behaviour, accompanies them *en route*; the party meet 250 Manyuema, but as they have no written instructions with them, they are permitted to scatter over the country in search of ivory.

In March Salim returns to Yambuya, and intimates to the officers that no doubt the carriers would be ultimately forthcoming, not however for the purpose of following Mr. Stanley's track, but to proceed *viâ* Ujiji and Unyoro; a mere haziness of geography!

On the 25th of March, Major Barttelot returns to the camp with information that Mr. Jameson, the indefatigable Jameson, has proceeded up river in the track of Tippu-Tib with the intention of reaching Kasongo. He also announces his intention of forming a flying column, and leaving the larger part of his goods at Stanley Falls in charge of an officer! He also prepares a telegram to the committee in London which is as follows: –

> St. Paul de Loanda,
> 1st May, 1888.

"No news of Stanley since writing last October. Tippu-Tib went to Kasongo, Nov. 16th, but up to March has only got us 250 men. More are coming, but uncertain in number, and as precaution, presuming Stanley in trouble (it would) be absurd in me to start with less number than he did, while carrying more loads – minus Maxim gun. Therefore I have sent Jameson to Kasongo to hasten Tippu-Tib in regard to originally proposed number of 600 men, and to obtain as many fighting men as possible up to 400, also to make as advantageous terms as he can regarding service, and payment of men, he and I guarantee the money in name of Expedition. Jameson will return about the 14th, but earliest day to start will be June 1st, when I propose leaving an officer with all loads not absolutely wanted at Stanley Falls. Ward carries this message; please obtain wire from the King of the Belgians to the Administrator of the Free State to place carriers at his disposal, and have steamers in readiness to convey him to Yambuya. If men come before his arrival I shall start without him. He should return about July 1st. Wire advice and opinion. Officers all well. Ward awaits reply.

> *Barttelot.*

Mr. Ward proceeded down the Congo, and in an unprecedentedly short time reached the sea-board, cabled his despatch, received the following reply, and started up the Congo again for the Yambuya camp.

Major Barttelot, care Ward, Congo.

Committee refer you to Stanley's orders of the 24th June, 1887. If you still cannot march in accordance with these orders, then stay where you are, awaiting his arrival or until you receive fresh instructions from Stanley. Committee do not authorise the engagement of fighting men. News has been received from Emin Pasha viâ Zanzibar, dated Wadelai, November 2nd. Stanley was not then heard of: Emin Pasha is well and in no immediate want of supplies, and goes to south-west of lake to watch for Stanley. Letters have been posted regularly viâ East Coas.

Chairman of Committee.

Mr. Ward on arriving at Bangala is detained there by order.

The Committee have made a slight mistake in calling my letter of instructions "orders." The instructions are not exactly "orders." They are suggestions or advices tendered by the Commander of the Expedition to the Commanding Officer of the rear column, which he may follow or reject at his own discretion. Major Barttelot has expressed an impatient desire to be of active service to the Expedition. He declares that it is his dearest wish to leave Yambuya to follow on our track. The Commander of the Expedition, strongly sympathising with the impetuous young officer, writes out a series of suggestions by which his desire may be realised, and gives him further a pencilled estimate (see Appendix) by what manner the forward advance after us may be done. The Major earnestly promises to conform to these suggestions, and the parting between him and myself is on this understanding. But they are not positive "orders," as a man's epitaph can best be written after his death, so the measure of "kudos" to be given a man is best known after the value of his services has been ascertained.

At the end of March the Major is on bad terms with Salim bin Mohammed, which compels him to make a fifth visit to Stanley Falls to obtain his removal.

About the middle of April Major Barttelot returns to his camp, and Salim has orders to quit Yambuya. Instead, however, of proceeding to Stanley Falls, he proposes a raid upon a large village below Yambuya, but in a few days he reappears, stating that he has heard a rumour that the advance column is descending the upper waters of the Aruwimi.

On the 9th of May, 1888, the Major proceeds to make a sixth visit to Stanley Falls, and on the 22nd of the month makes his reappearance with the indefatigable Jameson and a large party of Manyuema. Three days later the procrastinating Tippu-Tib, who, on the 18th of June, 1887, said that he would be at Yambuya within nine days, and in August within ten days, arrives by steamer *A. I. A.* The *Stanley* also steams up to deliver letters for the expedition.

As Tippu-Tib suggested that the loads 60 lbs. weight were too heavy for his people, the officers were obliged to reduce them to 40, 30, and 20 lb. weights, to suit his views. This was no light task, but it had to be performed. As an advance payment, Mr. Bonny relates that forty-seven bales of cloth, a vast store of powder and fixed ammunition are delivered, and £128 worth of stores are given to Muini Sumai, the head man of the Manyuema battalion. The European provisions are then overhauled, and such articles as Madeira wine, jams, sago, tapioca, arrowroot, sardines, herrings, and wheat flour are boxed up, and with eight boxes of my baggage are shipped on board the steamer for Bangala as unnecessary and superfluous, in the same vessel on which Mr. Troup is an invalid passenger bound home.

Finally, on the 11th of June, 1888, after weeding out twenty-nine Zanzibaris and four Soudanese who are too feeble to work, Messrs. Barttelot, Jameson, and Bonny leave the camp they should have left not later than the 25th of August, 1887, with a following of Zanzibaris, Soudanese, Somalis, and Manyuema, aggregating nearly 900 men, women, and children, with the intention of making that "strenuous quest" for the lost Commander and to relieve Emin Pasha.

These six visits to Stanley Falls which the Major and his friends have made amount in the aggregate to 1200 English miles of marching. The untiring Major has personally travelled 800 miles, while Jameson has performed 1200 miles. If only these 1200 miles had been travelled between Yambuya and the Albert, the rear column would have reached Pangs Falls. Even by travelling sixty miles, to gain a direct advance of ten miles, they would have been cheered and encouraged by our letters and charts to press on to Avejeli to recuperate among the abundant plantains of that rich and populous settlement.

But while the Major and his officers were endeavouring to stimulate an unwilling man to perform his contract with forty-five guinea rifles, Remington rifles, ivory-handled revolvers and ammunition, with many a fair bale of cloth, their own faithful men were dying at a frightful rate. Out of the original roll of 271, there are only 132 left of rank and file, and out of these 132 by the time they have arrived at Banalya there are only 101 remaining, and nearly a half of these are so wasted by famine and disease that there is no hope of life in them.

Thirteen days after the departure of the horde of Manyuema and the anæmic Zanzibaris from the fatal camp of Yambuya, the Major undertakes a seventh visit to Stanley Falls, and leaves the column to struggle on its way to Banalya without him. On the forty-third day of the march of ninety miles the van of the rear column enters the palisaded village of Banalaya, which has become in my absence a station of Tippu-Tib's in charge of an Arab called Abdallah Karoni, and on the same day the restless and enterprising Major enters it on his return from Stanley Falls. On the next day some misunderstanding takes place between him and the chief Abdallah Karoni. The Major storms at him, and threatens to start to Stanley Falls for the eighth visit on the 20th of July to complain of his conduct to Tippu-Tib; but at dawn on the 19th of July the unfortunate commander is shot through the heart by the assassin Sanga.

I will permit Mr. William Bonny's official report to detail what occurred in a revised form.

18th July, 1888. – The Major continued to threaten Abdalla that if he did not get the carriers promised by Tippu-Tib he would return to Stanley Falls on the 20th, and he ordered the Arab to accompany him. The Major informed me he would be back on the 9th of August, but before concluding his remarks, he asked me, 'Don't you think I am doing the correct thing by going to Stanley Falls?' I answered, 'No, I don't see why you want sixty more men; you have men enough and to spare! You had better issue the rifles and ammunition to the men, and that will reduce the number of our burdens by fifteen, and trust the men. Mr. Stanley is obliged to trust the men. If they run away from you, they run away from him, but if you leave them in my hands I don't think they will run.' The Major said, 'I intend that you shall have command of the Zanzibaris and Soudanese from here, and you shall precede the Manyuema a day's march. Mr. Jameson and I will march with the Manyuema and get them into some order, and see they do not mix up with your people. I don't want to go to the Falls, but I want you to try to get some few men. If you only get me twenty I shall be satisfied. I asked Abdallah if he could let me have a few carriers. I obtained seven.

19th July. – Early this morning a Manyuema woman commenced beating a drum and singing. It is their daily custom. The Major sent his boy Soudi, who was only about thirteen years old, to stop them, but at once loud and angry voices were heard, followed by two shots by way of defiance. The Major ordered some Soudanese to go and find the men who were firing, at the same time getting up from bed himself and taking his revolvers from the case. He said, 'I will shoot the first man I catch firing.' I told him not to interfere with the people's daily custom, to remain inside, and not go out, inasmuch as they would soon be quiet. He went out revolver in hand to where the Soudanese were. They told him that they could not find the men who were firing. The Major then pushed aside some Manyuema and passed through them towards the woman who was beating the drum and singing, and ordered her to desist. Just then a shot was fired through a loophole, in an opposite hut from within, by Sanga, the woman's husband. The charge penetrated just below the region of the heart and passed out behind, lodging finally in a part of the verandah under which the Major fell dead.

The Soudanese ran away, and refused to follow me to get the Major's body; but I went, and was followed by one Somali, and one Soudanese, who with myself carried the body to my house. From the screaming I thought a general massacre had commenced, for I had not seen a single Zanzibari. They were either hiding within their houses or joining in the gen-

eral stampede that followed. I now turned and saw one of the headmen of the Manyuema, who with rifle and revolver in hand was leading a body of sixty of his people to attack me. I had no arms. I walked up to him and asked him if he was leading his men to fight me. He replied 'No' I said, 'Then take your men quietly to their houses and bring all the headmen to me, for I wish to speak to them.' Some headmen shortly afterwards made their appearance, and I said to them, 'The trouble is not mine, but Tippu-Tib's. I want you to bring me all the loads, and tell all your fellows to do the same. Tippu-Tib knows what each of you has in charge and is responsible for them, This is Tippu-Tib's trouble. Tippu-Tib will have to pay up if the goods are lost, and will punish the headman who causes him a loss. I shall write to him, and he will come here, and he shall know the name of him who refuses to do what I now wish.' This resulted in my getting back to the storeroom about 150 loads. I now sent my men to collect what goods they could, and before long I recovered 299 porter loads. They had been scattered all over the place, some in the forest, in the rice field, and in the village huts hidden away within and without, in fact everywhere. Some of the bead sacks and ammunition boxes had already been ripped or broken open, and the whole of their contents, or in part, gone. After counting up I found I was forty-eight loads short. The inhabitants of the village numbered about 200 or 300 people. I had arrived with about 100 men; Muni Sumai, the chief headman of the Manyuema, with 430 carriers and about 200 followers, making a total of about 1000 people, of whom 900 were cannibals, all confined within an area 160 yards by 25 yards. You can therefore better judge than I can describe the scene when the general stampede commenced, the screaming, firing, shouting, looting our stores, &c., &c. I regret to say that the Soudanese and Zanzibaris without exception joined in the looting, but in my turn I raided their houses and haunts and captured a quantity of cloth, beads, rice, &c. I had to punish severely before I succeeded in stopping it. I now wrote to Mr. Jameson, who was about four days off bringing up the remaining loads. I also wrote to

Mons. Baert, a Congo State officer, and secretary to Tippu-Tib at Stanley Falls, explaining what had taken place, how I was situated, and asking him to use all his tact with Tippu-Tib to get him to come here or send some chief to replace Muini Sumai, who had been one of the first to abscond. I told Mons. Baert to tell Tippu-Tib that all Europe would blame him if he did not assist us. I then buried the Major, after sewing the body up in a blanket. I dug a grave just within the forest, placing leaves as a cushion at the bottom of the grave, and covered the body with the same. I then read the church service from our Prayer-Book over the body, and this brought the terrible day to a close.

The Major wrote and handed me the official order appointing me in command of the Zanzibari and Soudanese when the camp at Yambuya was in great danger, and his own life especially. I therefore take command of this Second Column of the Emin Pasha Relief Expedition until I see Mr. Stanley or return to the coast.

It shall be my constant care under God's help to make it more successful than heretofore. Mr. Jameson will occupy the same position as shown in Mr. Stanley's instructions to Major Barttelot on his going to Stanley Falls to settle with Tippu-Tib for another headman of the Manyuema He has free hands, believing himself to be in command. I did not undeceive him. On his return here I will show him the document a copy of which I have given above.

I have the honour to be, Sir,

&c., &c.,
William Bonny.
To H. M. Stanley, Esq.,
Commander E.P.R.E.

Three days after the tragedy Mr. Jameson appears at Banalya with the rear guard of the rear column, and assumes command; but on the 25th of July, after leaving words of encouragement to Mr. Bonny, he undertakes the eighth visit to Stanley Falls in the hope that by making liberal offers of gold to satisfy the avaricious Tippu-Tib he may induce him either to head the Rear Column himself, or send one of his fiery nephews in his place – Salim bin Mohammed, or Rashid, who assaulted and captured Stanley Falls from Captain Deane.

On August 12th he writes his last letter (see Appendix) to Mr. Bonny, and begins it, "The Expedition is at a very low ebb at present, as I think you will acknowledge." This is a sad fact very patent to everybody.

After seeing the act of justice performed on the wretched assassin Sanga, and witnessing the shooting of him and the body tossed into the Congo, he departs from Stanley Falls for Bangala. For Mr. Jameson and Major Barttelot were both concerned in the detention of Ward for some reason at Bangala, and therefore the answer of the Committee to their cablegram of the 1st of May was in his possession. Mr. Jameson is anxious to know what its tenor is before a final movement, and he departs in a canoe with ten Zanzibaris. Night and day they float, and when opposite the Lumami he is attacked with fever. His constitution is open to its virulence, filled as his mind is with despondency, for the fortunes of the Expedition are – despite every strenuous endeavour on his part, his whole-hearted devotion, his marches and countermarches, his tramp of 1400 miles (1200 miles before leaving Yambuya, thence to Bana-lya, and then to Stanley Falls), his sacrifice of money, physical comforts, and the pouring out of his soul to effect what he thinks ought to be done – but alas! "at their lowest ebb." And the fever mounts to his brain. By day and night the canoe-men press on to the goal of Bangala Station, and arrive in time to put him in the arms of Mr. Ward, where he breathes his last, as the advance column, returning after its rushing and swinging pace through forest and by river from the Albert Nyanza, enter Banalya to demand "Where is Jameson?"

Twenty-eight days after the tragic death of Major Barttelot, and twenty-three days after the departure of Jameson, the advance column returning from the Albert Nyanza, much reduced in numbers, and so tattered in their clothing that they were taken for pagans picked up by the way and their old comrades failed to recognise them, appeared at Banalya to learn for the first time the distressful story of the rear column.

The life of misery which was related was increased by the misery which we saw. Pen cannot picture nor tongue relate the full horrors witnessed within that dreadful pest-hold. The nameless scourge of barbarians was visible in the faces and bodies of many a hideous-looking human being, who, disfigured, bloated, marred and scarred, came, impelled by curiosity, to hear and see us who had come from the forest land east, and who were reckless of the terror they inspired by the death embodied in them. There were six dead bodies lying unburied, and the smitten living with their festers lounged in front of us by the dozen. Others worn to thin skin and staring bone from dysentery and fell anæmia, and ulcers as large as saucers, crawled about and hollowly sounded their dismal welcome – a welcome to this charnel yard! Weak, wearied, and jaded in body and mind, I scarcely know how I endured the first few hours, the ceaseless story of calamity vexed my ears, a deadly stench of disease hung in the air, and the most repellent sights moved and surged before my dazed eyes. I heard of murder and death, of sickness and sorrow, anguish and grief, and wherever I looked the hollow eyes of dying men met my own with such trusting, pleading regard, such far-away yearning looks, that it seemed to me if but one sob was uttered my heart would break. I sat stupefied under a suffocating sense of despondency, yet the harrowing story moved on in a dismal cadence that had nought else in it but death and disaster, disaster and death. A hundred graves at Yambuya – thirty-three men perishing abandoned in the camp, ten dead on the road, about forty in the village about to yield their feeble hold of life, desertions over twenty, rescued a passable sixty! And of the gallant band of Englishmen? "Barttelot's grave is but a few yards off, Troup went home a skeleton, Ward is somewhere a wanderer, Jameson has gone to the Falls, I don't know why." "And you – you are the only one left?" "The only one, sir."

If I were to record all that I saw at Banalya in its deep intensity of unqualified misery, it would be like stripping the bandages off a vast sloughing ulcer, striated with bleeding arteries, to the public gaze, with no earthly purpose than to shock and disgust.

Implicitly believing as we did in the *élan* of Barttelot, in the fidelity of Jameson, in the vigorous youth and manly promise of Ward, in the prudence and trustworthiness of Troup, and the self-command and steadiness of Bonny, all these revelations came to me with a severe shock. The column was so complete with every requisite for prolonged and useful work, but the "flood-tide of opportunity" flowed before them unseen and unnoted, therefore their marches became mere "marking time."

What, Barttelot! that tireless man with the ever-rushing pace, that cheery young soldier, with his dauntless bearing, whose soul was ever yearning for glory. A man so lavishly equipped with Nature's advantages to bow the knee thus to the grey craftiness at Stanley Falls! It was all an unsolved riddle to me. I would have wagered he would have seized that flowing grey beard of Tippu-Tib and pounded the face to pulp, even in the midst of his power, rather than allow himself to be thus cajoled time and time again. The fervid vehemence of his promise not to wait a day after the fixed date yet rings in my ears; I feel the strong grip, and see the resolute face, and I remember my glowing confidence in him.

It is said that "Still waters run deep." Now Jameson was such a still, and patient, and withal determined man that we all conceded a certain greatness to him. He had paid £1000 sterling, and had promised diligence and zealous service, for the privilege of being enrolled as a member of the Expedition. He had a passion for natural history to gratify, with a marked partiality for ornithology and entomology. According to Barttelot, "his alacrity, capacity, and willingness to work were unbounded," which I unqualifiedly endorse. What else he was may be best learned in his letter of August 12, and his entries in the log book. Zeal and activity grow into promise and relief as we read, he seals his devotion by offering out of his purse £10,000, and by that unhappy canoe voyage by day and by night, until he was lifted to his bed to die at Bangala.

Granted that Tippu-Tib was kind to these young gentlemen during their frequent visits to Stanley Falls, and welcomed and feasted them on the best, and that he sent them back to Yambuya with loads of rice and flocks of goats, which is admitted. But his natural love of power, his ignorance of geography, his barbarous conceit, his growing indolence, and his quickened avarice proved insuperable obstacles to the realizing of Barttelot and Jameson's wishes, and were as fatally opposite to their interests and dearest desires as open war would have been. The wonder to me is that the officers never seem to be conscious that their visits and rich gifts to him are utterly profitless, and that the object they have at heart, their inherited qualities, their education, habits, and natures forbid any further repetition of them. For some mysterious reason they pin their faith with the utmost tenacity to Tippu-Tib, and to his promises of "nine days," then "ten days," then "forty-two days," &c., &c., all of which are made only to be broken.

But the most icy heart may well be melted with compassion for these young men so prematurely cut off – and so near rescue after all. They bravely attempt to free their clouded minds and to judge clearly in which course lies their duty. At their mess-table they sit discussing what ought to be done. Mind gravitates to mind, and ignites a spark of the right sort; it is uttered, but some one or something quenches the spark as soon as it flashes, and the goodly purpose goes astray. They propose a number of schemes wide apart from the simple suggestions that I have furnished them with, and each project as soon as it is born is frustrated by some untoward event soon after. Though they all are undoubtedly animated by the purest motives, and remain to the end unquestionably loyal – throughout every act they are doing themselves irreparable injury, and unconsciously weighing their friends of the advance column down to the verge of despair with anxieties.

The following is Mr. Herbert Ward's report, which in justice I feel bound to publish: –

Windsor Hotel,
New York City,
Feb. 13th, 1890.

On August 14th, 1887, Troup, Bonny, and myself, with the men and loads, arrived at Yambuya from Bolobo. We found that since your departure on June 28th, 1887, nothing had teen heard of Tippu-Tib, and that the Major and Jameson had occupied their time in obtaining firewood for the steamer. On the following afternoon after our arrival, a band of Manyuema attacked the temporary village that the Chief Ngunga had built on the opposite side of the river, just below the rapids. Bonny and I crossed in a canoe to discover who they were, but apparently as soon as they saw the steamer lying alongside our camp, they cleared off into the forest, and returned to their own camp, which the natives told us was but a few hours' journey up the river. The next day the head man of the Manyuemas, named Abdallah, came to us with a few followers, and gave an account of how Tippu-Tib, true to his word, had sent about 500 men to us in canoes under Salim bin Mohammed, but that they had encountered much hostility from the natives, and after paddling against the stream for several days, and finding no indication of our camp they disbanded, and Salim sent small bands of Manyuemas in different directions to try and discover our whereabouts, and Abdallah represented himself as being the head-man of one of the parties sent in search of our camp. Another version of the story to account for the 500 men disbanding when on their way up the Aruwimi, was that their ammunition had given out, and the natives proved too strong for them. Abdallah stated that Tippu-Tib was quite willing to supply the men, and that as Stanley Falls was only a few days' journey, we could easily go ourselves and see Tippu-Tib, and that he himself would be ready the next day to accompany us and act as guide.

The Major instructed Jameson and myself to proceed to the Falls. We were there told the same story again, of how Tippu-Tib had sent a large number of men to us, but that they had disbanded on the Aruwimi River on account of their being unable to pass some populous village, where the natives had attacked and driven them back, as they were short of gunpowder. Tippu Tib professed his willingness to supply the men, but said that it would require some time to collect them together again.

As there were upwards of 600 valuable loads stored in Yambuya Camp, and only a sufficient number of able-bodied men to carry 175, we all considered it better to guard the loads in the camp where there was abundance of food for the men, until the arrival of Tippu-Tib's promised aid than to discard a portion of the loads and to make triple marches; for we were all convinced from evidence we had of men even deserting from the camp, that after the first few days' marching most of our men would desert and join the Arab band of Waswabili and Manyuema raiders, who, we found, were traversing the country in all directions, and whose free, unrestrained manner of living rendered our men dissatisfied with their lot, and tempted them to desert us and accompany their compatriots. The Major, our chief, personally disliked the Zanzibaris, and lucked the proper influence over them.

Tippu-Tib continued to procrastinate, and in the meantime a large number of our Zanzibaris, many of whom, however, from the first were organically diseased and poorly, sickened and died. They were always employed, and the cause of their death cannot be attributed to inaction. Being fatalists, they resigned themselves without an effort, for the Bwana Makubwa, with their comrades, had gone into the dark forests, and they all verily believed had perished. They themselves, when they found that upon no consideration would there ever be a chance of returning to their own country except by the deadly forest route, looked upon the situation as hopeless, gave way, and died.

We expected you to return to Yambuya about the end of November; but time passed away and we received no news from you. We were unable to make triple marches owing to the sad condition of our people. Every means was tried to urge Tippu-Tib to produce the men, but without avail.

In February, 1888, the Major and Jameson went again to the Falls, and on the 24th March the Major returned to Yambuya. He stated that he had guaranteed the payment of a large sum of money to Tippu-Tib if he would produce the men, that Jameson had gone to Kasongo to hurry them up, and that he considered that the Committee should be informed of the state of affairs; firstly, that no news whatever had been received from you since your departure, nine months before; secondly, that Tippu-Tib's aid was not forthcoming, that we were still in Yambuya unable to march. No steamers had visited the camp since the arrival of the last contingent.

It appeared to us that evidently circumstances had prevented you from communicating with us after your departure, and that news about your movements might have reached the east coast.

As it appeared possible to reach Loanda and communicate by cable with the Committee and return to Yambuya by the time Jameson was expected from Kasongo, the Major instructed me to convey and despatch a cablegram which be himself worded and signed. I accomplished the journey in thirty days, and immediately upon receiving their reply (the clause "we refer you to Mr. Stanley's instructions of June 24th," was precisely what both Troup and I expected before my departure), I hastened back as far as Bangala, where I was instructed to remain by the Major until I received further news from the Committee, to whom he had written, that he had no further use for my services or the loads he had sent down in Le Stanley.

Five weeks after my arrival at Bangala, news came down by the En Evant that the Major had been assassinated. Jameson, who was at the Falls seeing to the punishment of the murderer and reorganisation of the Manyuema contingent, wrote and urged me to stay at Bangala. Having descended from the Falls in canoes, he was in the last stage of bilious fever. Despite every care and attention, he died the following day. He came down to Bangala to learn the Committee's reply to the Major's cable, and to take back the Bangala loads and myself in the steamer that the State officer at the Falls had assured him would be at Bangala on its way up to

*the Falls just about the time he would arrive. This informa-
tion about the steamer was false, and on the first day of his
journey down in the canoes he caught a fatal chill, which
resulted in his death from bilious fever. There being no possible chance of my joining Bonny, as no steamer was to
again visit the Falls for some months, I went to the coast to
acquaint the Committee with the fact of Jameson's death,
and the position of affairs as I learnt them from Jameson
before his death. They cabled an order for me to return to
the Falls, and hand over the remaining stores to the State
Station there, and to bring down Bonny and the men for
shipment. Upon reaching Stanley Pool I found that news had
just been received of your arrival at Banalya and return to
Emin Pasha. I continued my journey, however, to the Falls,
and took up with me all the loads that the Major had sent
down to Bangala. I remained one month at the Falls anxiously hoping for further news of you.*

*After collecting all that remained of the sick men whom the
Major handed over to Tippu-Tib, I descended the Congo
again in canoes and returned to Europe according to the
cabled instructions of the Committee.*

*The above is a simple and truthful statement of facts relating
to the failure of the rear guard.*

*No one can feel more bitterly disappointed at the unfortunate
condition of affairs than myself. I regret most sincerely that
my services were so profitless.*

I remain,

Always yours faithfully,

(Signed) Herbert Ward.
Henry M. Stanley, Esq.

Mr. Ward informed me that he had discovered my eight boxes of reserve clothing and Expedition necessaries at Bangala; that he took them with him to Stanley Falls – 500 miles above Bangala – and then brought them down to Banana Point on the sea-coast, where he left them. No person knows – though diligent enquiry has been made – what has become of them.

APPENDIX

Major Barttelot's Last Report of events at Yambuya: –

Yambuya Camp
June 4, 1888.

Sir, – I have the honour to report to you that we are about to make a move, though with far less numbers than I originally intended. Tippu-Tib has at last, but with great reluctance, given us 400 men. I have also obtained from another Arab called Muini Somai thirty more carriers; we shall move not earlier than the 9th of June, and our forces will be as follows: – Soudanese 22, rifles 22; Zanzibaris 110, rifles 110, loads 90; Manyuema 430, muskets 300, loads 380. The officers who are going are Major Barttelot, in command; Mr. J. S. Jameson, second in command; Mr. W. Bonny; Sheik Muini Somai in command of Manyuema force.

Sheik Muini Somai is an Arab of Kibongé, who volunteered to accompany the Expedition as commander under me of the native contingent.

On May 8, the Belgian steamer *A.I.A.*, with M. van Kerkhoven, the chief of Bangala, arrived here, having on board Mr. Ward's escort of thirty Zanzibaris and four Soudanese, one Soudanese dying at Bangala.

May 11th. – They left us to go to Stanley Falls.

May 14th. – I left for Stanley Falls, going overland and catching the steamer at Yallasula, on the Congo. I proceeded with the Belgians to the Falls on May 22.

Mr. Jameson and Tippu-Tib, with 400 men, returned from Kasongo.

Mr. Jameson wrote to you while at Kasongo of his proceedings there. He told me on arrival that Tippu-Tib had promised him 800 men, but would make no written agreement with him.

May 23rd. – I had my palaver with Tippu-Tib; he then told me he could only let me have 400 men, 300 of whom were to carry 40-lb. loads, and 100 20-1b. loads. He said the men were present, and ready to start as soon as I had my loads ready. I told him of what he had promised Mr. Jameson at Kasongo, but he said never had any mention of 800 men been made, only of the 400. That it was quite impossible he could give us more men, as he was short of men at Kasongo and Nyangwé, as he was at present engaged in so many wars that he had completely drained the country. I was forced to submit, but hoped that he might be able to collect another 100 or so at and around Yambuya.

Tippu then asked me if I wanted a headman, stating that in the former agreement Mr. Stanley had said that if a headman was taken he should be paid. I replied, 'Certainly I want a headman.' He then presented me to the Arab, Muini Somai. This man agreed to come, and I send you the terms I settled with him.

I got back to Camp Yambuya May 30.

June 4th. – The *Stanley* steamer arrived, and the *A. I. A.*, the former bringing Belgian officers for the Falls Station, the latter Tippu-Tib himself.

June 5th. – I had another palaver with Tippu-Tib, asking him where were the 250 men already sent; he explained to me that they had been dispersed, and on trying to collect them they refused to come, owing to the bad reports brought in by the deserters, and that as they were subjects and not slaves he could not force them. That was the reason why he had brought 400 entirely fresh men from Kasongo for us.

However, Tippu said he could let me have thirty more men of Muini Somai. This, as I was so terribly short of men, I agreed to.

Muini Somai himself appears a willing man, and very anxious to do his best. He volunteered for the business. I trust you will not think his payment excessive, but the anxiety it takes away as regards his men and the safety of the loads is enormous, for he is responsible for the Manyuema and the loads they carry, and thus saves the white officers an amount of work and responsibility which they can now devote to other purposes.

The loads we do not take are to be sent to Bangala. They will be loaded up in the *A. I. A.*, or *Stanley,* on June 8, a receipt being given for them by Mr. Van Kerk-hoven, which is marked B and forwarded to you, also a letter of instruction to him and to Mr. Ward. Perhaps you would kindly give the requisite order concerning the loads and the two canoes purchased in March for Mr. Ward's transport, also for those stores purchased by Mr. Ward on behalf of the Expedition, as it is nearly certain I shall not return this way, and shall therefore have no further need of them or him. Mr. Troup, who is in a terrible condition of debility and internal disarrangement, is proceeding home at his own request. Mr. Bonny's certificate of his unfitness is attached, and his application marked E, also letters concerning passage, &c., to M. Fontaine, marked F. I have given him a passage home at the expense of the Expedition, as I am sure it would be your and their wish.

The interpreter, Assad Farran, I am also sending home. He has been, and is, utterly useless to me, and is in failing health; and if I took him with me I would only, after a few marches, have either to carry or leave him, and I am terribly short of carriers. So I have ventured to send him home with a steerage passage to Cairo, and have sent a letter to the Consul-General, Cairo, concerning him; also copy of agreement made by Assad Farran with me on his proceeding home; also papers of interpreter, Alexander Hadad, who died June 24, 1887, both marked G. These two interpreters made no sort of agreement concerning pay, terms of service, &c., when they agreed to come on this Expedition in February, 1887, so perhaps you would kindly inform the proper authorities on that subject. With British troops in Egypt, as interpreters, they would have received not more than £6 a month and their rations, for as interpreters they were both very inferior.

A Soudanese soldier with a diseased leg is also proceeding down country. Besides these there are four other Soudanese and twenty-nine Zanzibaris who are unable to proceed with us. Tippu-Tib has kindly consented to get these to Zanzibar as best he can. A complete list of them, their payments, &c., will be forwarded to the Consul at Zanzibar, and I have requested him to forward on the Soudanese to Egypt.

My intentions on leaving this camp are to make the best of my way along the same route taken by Mr. Stanley; should I get no tidings of him along the road, to proceed as far as Kavalli, and then if

I hear nothing there to proceed to Kibero. If I can ascertain either at Kavalli or Kibero his whereabouts, no matter how far it may be, I will endeavour to reach him. Should he be in a fix I will do my utmost to relieve him. If neither at Kavalli nor Kibero I can obtain tidings of him, I shall go on to Wadelai and ascertain from Emin Pasha, if he be there still, if he has any news of Mr. Stanley, also of his own intentions as regards staying or leaving. I will persuade him, if possible, to come out with me, and, if necessary, aid me in my search for Mr. Stanley. Should it for sundry reasons be unnecessary to look further for Mr. Stanley, I will place myself and force at his disposal to act as his escort, proceeding by whichever route is most feasible, so long as it is not through Uganda, as in that event the Manyuemas would leave me, as I have promised Tippu-Tib they shall not go there, and that I will bring them back or send a white officer with them back to their own country by the shortest and quickest route on completion of my object. This is always supposing Emin Pasha to be there and willing to come away. It may be he only needs ammunition to get away by himself, in which case I would in all probability be able to supply him, and would send three-fourths of my Zanzibar force and my two officers with him, and would myself, with the other Zanzibaris, accompany the Manyuemas back to the Tippu-Tib's country, and so to the coast, by the shortest route – viz., by the Muta-Nzigé, Tanganika and Ujiji. This is also the route I should take should we be unable to find Stanley, or, from the reasons either that he is not there or does not wish to come, relieve Emin Pasha.

I need not tell you that all our endeavours will be most strenuous to make the quest in which we are going a success, and I hope that my actions may meet with the approval of the committee, and that they will suspend all judgment concerning those actions, either in the present, past, or future, till I or Mr. Jameson return home.

Rumour is always rife, and is seldom correct, concerning Mr. Stanley. I can hear no news whatever, though my labours in that direction have been most strenuous. He is not dead, to the best of my belief, nor of the Arabs here or at Kasongo. I have been obliged to open Mr. Stanley's boxes, as I cannot carry all his stuff, and I had no other means of ascertaining what was in them. Two cases of Madeira were also sent him. One case I am sending back, the other has been half given to Mr. Troup, the other half we take as medical comforts. Concerning Tippu-Tib I have nothing to say beyond that he has broken faith with us, and can only conjecture from surrounding events and circumstances the cause of his unreasonable delay in supplying men, and the paucity of that supply.

I deem it my bounden duty to proceed on this business, in which I am fully upheld by both Mr. Jameson and Mr. Bonny; to wait longer would be both useless and culpable, as Tippu-Tib has not the remotest intention of helping us any more, and to withdraw would be pusillanimous, and, I am certain, entirely contrary to your wishes and those of the committee.

I calculate it will take me from three to four months to reach the lakes, and from seven to nine more to reach the coast.

Should you think and the committee agree that the sum is excessive to give Muini Somai and are not prepared to meet it, or may be, are prepared to place only a portion of that at my disposal for that purpose, both Mr. Jameson and I are fully prepared to meet it or the remaining portion of it, as it is entirely for our benefit he is coming: though of course it must be remembered that our object is to reach our destination with as many of our loads as possible, and that our individual hold over the Manyuema without outside aid would be *nil*. Should you agree to place the sum at my disposal, please arrange accordingly; if only a portion, that portion, for he has received an advance in powder, cloth, beads, and cowries to the value of £128. In case of not meeting it or only a portion of it, please inform Sir Walter Barttelot, Carlton Club. I insert this as it is most necessary the money should be there when wanted, as Arabs and Orientals are most punctilious on pecuniary transactions.

I have much pleasure in stating that from all the officers of the State with whom I have come in contact or from whom I have solicited aid, I have met with a most willing and ready response, which is highly gratifying. I would particularly mention Captain Van Kerk-hoven, Chief of Bangala, and Lieutenant Liebrechts, Chief of Stanley Pool, and I trust that they may meet with the reward and merit they deserve.

June 6th. – This morning Tippu-Tib sent for me and asked me if I thought he would got his money for the men. I told him I could give no assurance of that. He then said he must have a guarantee, which I and Mr. Jameson have given; terms of agreement and guarantee are attached. All receipts, agreements, &c., made between Arabs and myself and signed by them I have sent to Mr. Holmwood, and the copies to you.

June 8th. – This morning I had the loads for Tippu-Tib's and Muini Somai's men stacked, and Tippu-Tib himself came down to see them prior to issuing. However, he took exception to the loads, said they were too heavy (the heaviest was 45 lbs.), and his men could not carry them. Two days before he had expressed his approbation of the weight of the very same loads he refused to-day. I pointed out to him that he as well as I knew the difficulty of getting any load other than a bale, to scale the exact weight, and that the loads his men carried were far above the prescribed weight of 60 lbs. We were to have started to-morrow, so we shall not now start till the 11th or 12th of June, as I am going to make all his loads weigh exactly 40 lbs. It is partly our fault, as we should have been more particular to get the exact weight. The average weight over due was about 2 lbs., some loads being 2 lbs. under. But it is not the weight of the loads he takes exception to – in reality it is having to perform the business at all. He has been almost forced to it by letters received from Mr. Holmwood against his own and more than against the wish of his fellow Arabs, and, filled with aspirations and ambitions of a very large nature, the whole business has become thoroughly distasteful to him, which his professed friendship for Stanley cannot even overcome. His treatment of us this morning showed that most thoroughly. But should he not act up to his contract I hope it will be taken most serious notice of when it comes to the day of settling up. He has got us tight fixed at present, but it should not always be so.

On our road lie many Arab settlements to within a month of Lake Albert Nyanza, though the distance between some of them is bad, and the inhabitants of that distance warlike. I shall, whenever opportunity offers, hire carriers, if not for the whole time at any rate from station to station, for of course death, sickness, and desertions must be looked for, and I must get my loads in as intact as possible to my destination.

This is when Muini Somai will be so useful. We seem to have paid a big price for his services, but then he is a big Arab, and in proportion to his bigness is his influence over the Manyuema to keep them together, to stop desertions, thefts, &c. A lesser Arab would have been cheaper, hut his influence would have been less, and in consequence our loads gradually less, and loads mean health and life and success, and therefore cannot be estimated at too high a value. We are carrying light loads, and intend to do at first very easy marches, and when I get into the open country by Uganda to push on.

We weighed all our loads before one of Tippu-Tib's headmen, and he passed loads which had been condemned shortly before in the morning, which fully shows that for some reason or other he wishes to delay us here, but for what purpose I cannot say.

June 9th. – We shall easily be able to start by the 11th, but I am sorry to say our loss of ammunition by the lightening of the loads – for it was the ammunition they particularly took notice of – is something enormous.

Both the *A. I. A.* and the *Stanley* left this morning for Stanley Falls, but Tippu-Tib and his Belgian secretary remain behind; also four ships' carpenters, whom Captain Vangele and M. van Kerkhoven left with us to help us. The Belgians have behaved with very great kindness to us, and helped us on our way enormously.

Before I close I would wish to add that the services of Mr. J. S. Jameson have been, are, and will be invaluable to me. Never during his period of service with me have I had one word of complaint from him. His alacrity, capacity, and willingness to work are unbounded, while his cheeriness and kindly disposition have endeared him to all. I have given Ward orders about any telegram you may send, and Tippu-Tib has promised he will send a messenger after me should it be necessary, provided I have not started more than a month. Tippu-Tib waits here to see me off.

I am sending a telegram to you to announce our departure, and I will endeavour through the State to send you news whenever I can; but it would not surprise me if the Congo route was not blocked later on.

I have not sent you a copy of Mr. Holmwood's letter, as it was not official, but of all others I have. I think I told you of everything of which I can write. There are many things I would wish to speak of, and no doubt I will do so should I be permitted to return home.

Our ammunition, Remington, is as follows: – Rifles, 128; reserve rounds, per rifle, 279; rounds with rifle, 20 = 35,580.

June 10th. – The loads have been weighed and handed over; powder and caps issued to the Manyuema force, and we are all ready to start, which we shall do to-morrow morning. I have told you of all now I can think of, but I would bring finally to your notice that Tippu-Tib has broken his faith and contract with us. The man Muini Somai I think means business, and therefore I trust all will be well.

I have, &c.,

Edmund M. Barttelot, *Major.*

To Mr. William Mackinnon,

President of the Emin Pasha Relief Committee.

Copy of Log of Rear Column.

Note. – This "Log" may not appear to be very lively reading at first, but it presently deepens in interest, and will repay perusal to the reader who has shared in our anxieties respecting the fate of the rear column.

H.M.S.

June 11th, 1888. – Left Yambuya at 7 A.M. Slight excitement prevailed at first, firing off guns, &c., but this was soon checked. The Zanzibar Company went ahead, Mr. Jameson in advance, Mr. Bonny in the centre, Major Barttelot in rear. The Manyuema contingent under Muini Somai started later, but soon caught up the Zanzibar Company; the rear reached camp at the Batuka village called Sudi at noon. One sick man was left behind on the road, but he found his way to camp later on. All loads correct.

The rear column left Yambuya with strength as follows: –

Major Edmund M. Barttelot, *Commanding.*

Mr. James S. Jameson, *Second in Command.*

Mr. William Bonny, *Command of Zanzibar Co.*

Zanzibar Company, 108 men.

Zanzibar Company Boys, 7

Soudanese soldiers, 22

Somali, 1

Manyuema carriers, 430

Total, 568

Distance travelled about five miles.

Road fair, through jungle and plantations, the best roadways being the streams.

General direction S.E.

(Signed) E. M. B.

June 23rd. Halted in camp to await arrival of search party, who returned at 3 P.M., having done nothing. Major Barttelot went to explore road, following it for five miles to the N.E. Major Barttelot's boy Soudi deserted with his revolver, belt and 85 rounds of ammunition, owing to Major Barttelot's thrashing him, though doubtless he was put up to it. In consequence all rifles taken from Zanzibaris. Major Barttelot will proceed to-morrow to Stanley Falls to see Tippu-Tib concerning deserters, and if possible to obtain fresh men from him to get back loads and rifles. He will send a note to Mr. Jameson to come here and bring as many Manyuema as he can to take ammunition and rifles and escort Zanzibari to Abdulla Karoni's (Banalya), where they will await Major Barttelot's arrival. Major Barttelot and Mr. Bonny both thinking this the most feasible plan, as if the desertions last much longer, there will not be a load left. Kindness has been shown in every way to the Zanzibaris throughout, and the marches have been uniformly short.

Weather fine, shower in the evening.

E. M. B.

June 24th. – Major Barttelot, with fourteen Zanzibaris and three Soudanese and boys, left here this morning for Stanley Falls. Kuchu, a Zanzibari, who, when ordered to accompany the Major, ran away, came in at 8 A.M. He was tied up and kept in the guard-room.

Copy of orders to Mr. Bonny, June 23rd, 1888.

I. Take over charge of the camp, remaining till Mr. Jameson's arrival.

II. To have special care of all Zanzibari rifles and ammunition.

III. When move is made, to see that all loads, such as ammunition, are under Soudanese escort.

IV. Any attempt at mutiny to be punished with death.

V. To try to obtain information of whereabouts.

VI. To hand over command to Mr. Jameson when he arrives, and not to proceed further than Abdulla Kihamira's (Banalya).

Edmund M. Barttelot.

You will retain command of the Zanzibaris as before.

A case of small-pox I ordered to be removed some distance off from the camp.

Weather fine.

Wm. Bonny, *Commanding (pro tem.).*

Note .from Mr. Jameson.

"My Dear Bonny, – I have just arrived here. I suppose it is Nassur bin Saifi, and have met Kuchu and soldiers with slaves. They told me that the Major is gone to Stanley Falls four days ago. I don't knew how he could have missed us. Have captured sixteen guns and two men, but only part of two loads. No medicine. I will come to your camp to-morrow as early as I can.

"Yours &c.

"J.S. Jameson"

Wm. Bonny, *Commg.*

July 2nd. – Got away at 7 A.M., and marched till noon. Camping in a village named Mkwagodi, tribe Baburu, general direction N.E., distance about eight miles. Road bad, running through many swamps and old plantations. No desertions on road, or in camp last night. Found some of Tippu-Tib's people here, who say they will carry a letter to Stanley Falls. They knew a road to the Congo which can be traversed in four days' march. The Aruwimi R. distant from this camp about three hours. Tippu-Tib's men state that Abdallah Kihamira's station (Banalya) is but three days' march from here, and that the blazing of trees on his road beyond that place is still visible.

Weather fine.

J. S. J.

6 P.M. – Mr. Bonny reports non-arrival of two Zanzibaris. Each possessed a rifle, and one was loaded with loose ammunition.

July 3rd. – Returned to Ujeli Camp for extra loads, and arrived at 1 P.M. Muini Sumai reported arrivals of letters, stating that the whole force was to return to Stanley Falls. Received two letters from Major Barttelot, dated June 25th, to the effect that we were to proceed with all despatch to Banalya. Muini Sumai told me he had received the news in a letter from Sala Sala, conveyed by some messenger, and that on receipt of it he had sent to stop the men and loads *en route* here from Nassur bin Saifi village. I replied that the Major's orders were still to proceed to Banalya. He sent messengers at once to tell the people behind to come on. He reports many cases of smallpox and other diseases, about sixty men unfit for work, that seven of his men have deserted. Met the two men reported missing last night. Both were sick and had slept at a village close by.

Weather fine.

J. S. J.

July 4th. – Told Muini Sumai that my last orders to him were to get the whole of his force together at once, and come on to my camp with all speed. He promised to leave following day. Rain came down in torrents shortly after leaving, but pushed on and reached Mpungu about noon, when it cleared up for a fine day. Heavy rain until noon. Double loads borne remarkably well.

J. S. J.

July 5th. – Reached Mkwagodi, Mr. Bonny's camp, about noon. Swamps very bad after rain. He reports all quiet during my absence. One Zanzibari had died. My letters to Stanley Falls left about 9 A.M. of the 3rd. Tippu-Tib's people had brought a few fowls for sale. Weather fine.

J. S. J.

July 6th. – Sent Mr. Bonny on to next village, which I hear is a large one, and quite an easy march from here, with orders to send back Soudanese escort and carriers to carry extra loads tomorrow. This is a very small village with not sufficient accommodation for our force, so determined to await his arrival at the next. Men returned from Mr. Bonny about 2 P.M.

J. S. J.

July 7th. Moved up with all extra loads to Sipula, about fifteen miles. Road a bad one, much fallen timber, and manioc very thick. Bonny reported Zanzibari bearer of our chop-box as lagging behind yesterday, and breaking open his box. Was caught red-handed in the act. One tin of corn-beef and one tin of milk were missing, also a broached tin of cocoa still in box. Man volunteered to show where these were. Sent him back with Soudanese, who returned with both tins opened. Dr. Parke's box, whilst being carried here yesterday, fell and burst open; damaged beyond repair. The clothing I packed in Messrs. Stairs' and Nelson's bags, which were underweight; the shot and cartridge cases were discarded, being short of carriers. Collected all the cartridges carried by the Zanzibari, and will have them carried as loads, as I mean to send Mr. Bonny on to Banalya. The road is a perfectly safe one, and food all the way. The small-pox is rife amongst the Manyuema, and I wish to prevent it from spreading among our people. Banalya is four easy marches from here, and Mr. Bonny will have guides to show the road. Have sent to Muini Sumai to join me to-morrow here. Weather fine.

J.S.J.

July 8th. – Mr. Bonny left here for Banalya. Muini Sumai with nearly all the Manyuema arrived here. Muini Sumai tells me that he has received a second letter from Sala saying that the whole force is to return to Stanley Falls. Upon further inquiry I find that the way Sala got the news was the following. Men of Salim Mohamed's returning from Stanley Falls after the steamer had arrived at Yambuya spread this report among the people, who communicated the same to Sala's people.

J. S. J.

July 9th. – Last night, as if at a given signal, nearly every man in the camp began to fire off his gun; several of the shots were fired beside my tent. I jumped out of bed, sent for Muini Sumai, got my rifle, and told him before every one that I would shoot the very next man that fired close to my tent. There were no more shots.

About noon to-day several of Bonny's men came into camp telling me he had lost the road. Started out to Bonny's camp. Met messenger with a note from him on road. He tells me the guides yesterday took him all wrong and then ran away. He afterwards got too far N., sighting the Aruwimi. He is camped at a village about half-an-hour from here. Went with him along road, and found a well blazed one going to the eastward which he had missed. Got back to his camp at dusk.

Weather fair. Mr. Bonny reports a goat missing.

J. S. J.

July 10th. – Started shortly after daylight and joined Mr. Bonny. Went ahead on road, general direction S.E. which I found he had followed the day before. Had just determined to go to where he had camped when Arabs from Banalya arrived. The head-man told me that he had brought the percussion-caps from Stanley Falls to Banalya, and also four letters. He handed over to me three deserters from Mr. Stanley's force, Musa Wadi Kombo, Rehani Wadi Mabruki and Jumah Wadi Chandi. (Note from Mr. Stanley: these three men deserted from the advance on or about Aug. 98th., just half way between Yambuya and Albert Nyanza.) They all declare that they did not desert from him, but were left sick on the road. They say they belong to Captain Stairs' Company. I got them to guide us to the right road, and they took us to the very village where Mr. Bonny and his men slept the day before yesterday, close to the. Aruwimi, and from which point he had turned back. He camped there again to-day and goes on to-morrow morning. Abdulla Kihamira handed me the 40,000 percussion-caps for which Tippu-Tib is to be paid £48.

Weather fine.

J. S. J.

July 11th. Muini Sumai informed me to-day that he could not leave for Banalya until the day after to-morrow. I warned him that every day lost on the road would be a day less at Banalya, as Major Barttelot would expect us to be ready to start on his arrival. He has not the slightest power over the other head-men.

Heavy and continuous rain in afternoon.

J. S. J.

July 12th. – Muini Sumai requested percussion-caps to be distributed among his men. Told him to address himself to "Major Barttelot on the latter's arrival. He made another excuse for not starting to-morrow, as he did not like leaving the white man behind. I told him that was my business not theirs, and that every man and load must leave this place to-morrow.

Weather cloudy, but fine.

J. S. J.

July 13th. – Muini Sumai and Manyuema left to-day for Banalya. One sick chief going on slowly with men. Several dying of smallpox left in village. Stench around village frightful, but all villages near here are in a similar condition.

Weather fine.

J. S. J.

July 14th. – Sent for Tippu-Tib's men from Mampuya, and told them we would remain here some days. They have no news of Major Barttelot's being on the road. Heavy rain all afternoon.

J.S.J.

July 15th. – Still at Sipula awaiting return of men from Banalya. J. S. J.

July 16th. – Tippu-Tib's people came from Mampuya with plantains for sale. Purchased some for the sick. Cannot understand the non-arrival of men from Banalya.

J. S. J.

July 17th. – Nyombi, Tippu-Tib's head man at Mampuya, came into camp to-day. Reports return of the men who took letters to Stanley Falls. Had seen Major Barttelot, who has gone by a short road to Banalya. Said he would be there to-day. Still no signs of the men from Banalya to carry the extra loads. They are now a full two days over date. Weather fine.

J.S.J.

July 18th. – Between 3 and 4 P.M. the men from Banalya arrived. Told them to collect plantains and manioc at once, as we should march to-morrow. Much grumbling.

The following received from Mr. Bonny:

Abdullah's Camp (Banalya),

July 15th, 1888.

"My Dear Jameson, – I arrived here about 10 A.M. this day. The Zanzibaris did not know the road well, and I had to keep to the front nearly the whole distance. When you arrive at my first camp on the river bank you had better get three days' manioc – you will not find any for three days. The Soudanese in charge of the Zanzibari prisoner let him escape on my second day's march. You may see this escaped prisoner. (Here follows list.) Twenty-three men have deserted. The Manyuema who came with us left us on the wrong road early on second day; they had blocked the right road in several places. I did not see any native on the road, although I am certain they look after people left behind. On my four-days' march

Feraji Wadi Zaid ran away, leaving his load on the road. I hear Selangi, who was sick, is also absent; loads correct.

"Yours, etc.,

"William Bonny."

Weather fine.

J. S. J.

July 19th. – Started about 7 A.M. and marched to Mr. Bonny's first camp. Aruwimi R. distance between five and six miles, general direction north-east. Passed through five villages and over two streams. Road generally good, through old manioc plantations broken up with patches of forest. Halted to let men collect manioc. Threatening thunder, but fine.

J. S. J.

July 20th. – Left camp a little before 7 A.M. and reached Mr. Bonny's camp on the bank of the Aruwimi R. 11 o'clock. Distance between five and six miles. General direction E. Road a bad one, lying along the bank of the river and crossing all the deep cuttings with muddy inlets to them. Latter part of march through old sites of very large villages. The natives were all living on opposite bank. Very large plantations of manioc and plantain.

Weather fine.

J. S. J.

July 21st. – When nearly ready to start this morning a heavy shower of rain fell, and I kept the tent standing; it cleared, however, shortly, and we made a start, when it began to pour again and rained steadily until we reached Mr. Bonny's first camp in forest, when we halted. When about a mile from the camp we were met by messengers from Mr. Bonny, who handed me a letter, and whilst opening it overheard some of the men saying that Major Barttelot was dead. This was only too true, for my letter contained the sad news that he was shot dead early on the morning of the 19th at Banalya, and further that Muini Sumai and all the Manyuema had left.

J. S. J.

Mr. Bonny's letter follows: –

"19th *July,* 1888.

"My Dear Jameson, – Major Barttelot shot dead early this morning; Manyuema, Muini Sumai and Abdullah Kihamira all gone. I have written to Tippu-Tib through Mons. Baert.

"Push on.

"Yours,

"Bonny."

July 22nd. – After seeing all loads ready to start, got away about an hour after daybreak and reached Banalya an hour before sunset – a long march over one of the worst roads in this country. On arrival found all quiet, and that Mr. Bonny had done all that could be done under the circumstances. He had recovered about 300 of the loads carried by the Manyuema, and had succeeded in quieting these who had remained near camp. Muini Sumai halted on the morning of the 19th instant without a word to any one, and has gone to Stanley Falls. The other head men under him, with the exception of two or three who are camped outside this village, are camped in the bush some distance away. Major Barttelot was buried on the 19th. A full account of the circumstances of his death is given by Mr. Bonny later on.

J. S. J.

July 23rd. – Made an inventory of the effects of Major Barttelot, and packed all things considered necessary to send home, a full account of everything being sent to Sir Walter Barttelot. Offered a reward for the arrest of the man who shot Major Barttelot.

J. S. J.

July 24th. – Made a complete list of all leads recovered; the majority of the Manyuema head men came into camp, and from them gathered the following information: –

There are 193 Manyuema carriers still camped in this vicinity; Muini Sumai, six head men, and Sanga, the man who shot Major Barttelot, are all at Stanley Falls. On my march to Stanley Falls I will meet more of the head men, who will give information about their loads and men. I then told them I was going to Stanley Falls to-morrow, to see Tippu-Tib, and try to make such arrangements with him as would admit of our still continuing the Expedition; would not remain away long, and when returned would let them know whether it would be an advance or otherwise. Told them I wished them to remain quietly in whatever camp they chose in the neighbour-hood, but not in this village, so that there would be no chance of further trouble until my return. They said they were perfectly willing to do this. We have recovered 298½ loads, and are now 47½ loads short.

Letters handed by me to Major Barttelot before our departure from Yambuya. Two loads of the Expedition found missing. Believed them to have been lost on the way, which one of his men (Hamed bin Daoud) ran away with on his return from Stanley Falls.

J. S. J.

Mr. Bonny's Log.

July 11th. – I struck camp early, and started along the bank of Aruwimi. I soon found out why I had not taken this road. Every village has been burnt down, and everything destroyed. Elephants are very numerous here. New roads have been made, the old ones destroyed; but after an hour's march I came on Mr. Stanley's road.

Wm Bonny,
Commanding Advance Party.

July 12th. – Made a long march, taking throe days' manioc to enable me to pass through the forest. The Arabs who joined with the Zanzibaris deserted after leading us an hour on the wrong road, and, blocking up the right ones in several places, ran away. I found right road, and continued my march until mid-day. Camped in forest.

Wm. Bonny,
Commanding Advance Party.

July 15th. – I arrived at Banalya at about 10 A.M., after a march of four days and four hours from where I last saw Mr. Jameson. Nothing worth noting occurred on the 13th and 14th instant. Abdullah, the head man of this village, treating me very kindly, giving me a large house, rice, fish, and bananas. Camp quiet.

Wm. Bonny, *Commanding Advance Party.*

July 16th. — Some of Muini Sumai's Manyuema came in today.

Wm. Bonny,
Commanding Advance Party.

The dates 17th, 18th, and 19th have been already published in Chapter XX. – "The Sad Story of the Rear Column."

H. M. S.

July 20th. – Sent out to headmen to try and get more loads. I find I am short of the following loads, viz., 8 bags beads, 3 3/4 brass wire, 10 sacks of hkfs., 9 bales Zanzibar cloth, 5 loads of powder, 10 sacks rice, 1 sack cowries; total 47 loads, I discovered that the man who shot the Major is named Sanga and is a bead man charged with the care of ten loads. He has fled Stanley Falls with Muini Sumai.

William Bonny, *Commanding.*

July 22nd. – It has been raining now thirty-six hours. Jameson arrived to-day. Camp quiet.

William Bonny, *Commanding.*

July 25th. – Mr. Jameson left here for Stanley Falls, taking with him the late Major's effects.

William Bonny, *Commanding.*

July 27th. – The Soudanese paraded to-day, without being asked, and said they wished to speak to me. They said "We wish to fight the Manyuema; we are waiting for orders, and are ready to fight."... I think they are now ashamed of their conduct on the 19th instant in not following me when called upon.

William Bonny, *Commanding.*

Following from Mr. Jameson: –

"July 26th, 1888.

"My Dear Bonny, –

"We have been doing good work, marching eight hours yesterday, and nine and a haft hours to-day...

"Met Muini Sumai. He was on his way back to Banalya, having been persuaded to return by other Arabs coming from Stanley Falls.

"Muini Sumai told me that one of Sanga's women was beating the drum when the Major came up, and the Major went to the house saying 'Who is that?' Sanga says he thought that the Major was going to beat the woman as he had beaten the man the day before, and so fired at him. He is at Stanley Falls.

"Yours,

"J. S. Jameson"

August 1st. – I raided the Zanzibari houses to-day, which resulted in my getting ten pieces of cloth.

William, Bonny, *Commanding.*

August 2nd. – Empty Remington box found in forest. A Zanzibari was found in possession of forty-eight hkfs., being part of stores lost on 19th.

William Bonny, *Commanding*.

August 6th. – The natives came last night and stole a canoe from our gate, and not two yards from a Soudanese sentry. I fined the three Soudanese sentries each £1 for neglect of duty.

William Bonny, *Commanding*.

August 8th. About 10 P.M., hearing an unusual noise, I got up, and discovered that it proceeded from about 100 to 150 canoes knocking together. The natives were in force across the river, and I soon posted my men. The natives observing our movements returned up river. No shot was fired. I want to make friends with them.

William Bonny, *Commanding*.

August 12th. – The Manyuema, through Chief Sadi, brought me a present of 15 lbs. of wild pig meat. I have had no meat since 25th July.

William Bonny, *Commanding*.

August 14th. – I received a letter from Mr. Jameson, now at Stanley Falls, in which he states that my letter of the 19th July, 1888, was lost. It was addressed to Mons. Baert, Stanley Falls, announcing the death of Major Barttelot to Tippu-Tib, and enclosed one to Sir Walter Barttelot, Bart., M.P. Tippu-Tib has tried Muini Sumai, and finding him guilty, has torn up his contract. Muini Sumai has to return all rifles, &c. Mr. Ward is at Bangala with letters from the committee, which Jameson has ordered to be sent up. Tippu-Tib has agreed to hand over Sanga, the murderer of the Major, to Jameson for justice. The state officers claim that power, and will try him, as Banalya is within their territory.

William Bonny, *Commanding*.

August 17th. – Mr. Stanley arrived here about 11 A.M. this morning in good health, but thin. He came by water with about thirty canoes, accompanied by about 200 followers. Some of whom are natives belonging to Emin Pasha.

I briefly told Mr. Stanley the news, handed to him eleven letters addressed to himself, and four addressed to Emin Pasha.

Rain.

W. Bonny.

August 18th. – A Manyuema admits to Mr. Stanley that he had two bales of Zanzibar cloth, and knew a man who had a bag of beads, taken from me on the 19th July. Mr. Stanley advised the head-man to return the goods to me. Kimanga brought two half bales of Zanzibar cloth, being part of the stores looted on the 19th July. A receipt was given to him. I received a letter dated August 12th, Stanley Falls, from Mr. Jameson. Muini Sumai came in and saw Mr. Stanley.

William Bonny.

August 19th. – Muini Sumai has now returned all rifles, revolvers, and ammunition, besides top of tent.

William Bonny.

August 20th. – Soudanese and Zanzibaris paraded to-day of their own accord before Mr. Stanley, and complained to him that they had been badly treated.

The following is from Mr. Jameson: –

"Stanley Falls,

"*August* 12, 1888.

"My Dear Bonny, – The Expedition is at a very low ebb at present, as I think you will acknowledge. No head-man will go in charge of Manyuema although I have done all in my power to get one. Tippu-Tib said he would go for £20,000 paid unconditionally, and said further that if he met with any really superior force, or saw his men threatened with any serious loss, he would return. It is not likely that the Committee would agree to this proposal. Secondly, he proposed for the same sum to take the loads *viâ* Nyangwe and Tanganika to Kibero in Unyoro, guaranteeing first to pay for all loss of loads. Secondly, to deliver all loads at Kibero in Unyoro within six months of date of starting. Thirdly, after delivering leads at Kibero will look for Stanley. But if war between Unyoro and Uganda, could not guarantee delivery of loads at Kibero. I had a final interview with him last night. I told him that Mr. Stanley's very last orders were to follow the same road he had taken. Major Barttelot's intentions were, at the time of his death, to continue on that road. Major Barttelot wrote to Mr. Mackinnon to say he had started on that road. The reply of the Committee could not have been to go by another, or we would have received it. Emin Pasha's last statement was to the effect that if he were not soon relieved he would put himself at the head of his men and try and get out *viâ* the Congo. That Emin Pasha had received the messages which Mr. Stanley sent from Zanzibar telling him his route would be by the Congo. That did he start, the Congo would without doubt be the route he would choose to come out. And that finally, in the face of all this, I could not go by a new route unless ordered to do so. Tippu-Tib then said, 'You are right.' I then told him that as regards our old route, he could not get me a head-man over the Manyuema, no matter what I did to induce them. He said he would command them himself for £20,000, yet told me that if any serious less was threatened to his men he would turn back. I replied, 'You will accept no less a sum than £20,000, and that unconditionally.' Many of the Manyuema openly avow their intention should I go without a headman from you, they will proceed a certain distance, and when they come to a good village, throw down our loads and begin ivory hunting. (This Tippu-Tib acknowledged.) Therefore, if I start from here without a head-man it might be fatal to the whole expedition.

"The only thing left for me to do now was to get a canoe, and go to Bangala at once. Read the Committee's reply, and if it was to the effect, go on at all hazards. Then I would take thirty or forty loads to be carried by the men Tippu-Tib is going to give me to replace those of Muini Sumai, bring Mr. Ward with me, as in case the Manyuemas chucked their loads, there would be one of us who might get back with the news, and bring no headman. I shall have plenty to do with the Manyuema. Return here at once in the *Stanley* Steamer, which will be at Bangala immediately after I arrive there, and start at night away again. If the reply of the Committee would justify my stopping, knowing all I do, I would send Ward with a telegram at once to Banana by same canoes I go down in, return in the *Stanley*, go up to you, and all men and loads would be sent to Yarukombé on the Congo. Tippu-Tib guarantees that he will dismiss his men, and keep them close to the Aruwimi, and should the reply from the Committee be to still go on, on either route, he will have them all collected in a few days. There is no one to go down but me. Were I to wait the answer of the Committee here, then if we started at once I would have no loads to replace those lost at Banalya, and Ward could not come with us, and if I thought right to stop and send a telegram, a very serious delay would accrue in Ward's starting with it.

"What I wish you to do now is to stop at Banalya until you hear from me, which ought to be in three weeks or a month.

"If we have to come down to Yarukombé, the thing will be to make Zanzibaris believe that we are going to Zanzibar, then there will not be many desertions. Tippu-Tib has found out the refuge of the deserters. It is at Yatuka, Said bin Habib's place. He has sent men to catch all who are there. Daoud was captured at Yambuya with the Major's sack of cloth with him. Pieces of our cloth are being brought here to Tippu-Tib from villages all over the country.

"Yesterday Sanga (the murderer) was tried before Tippu-Tib and the Belgian Resident. He was found guilty, and shot immediately afterwards.

"My hopes sometimes have been raised to the highest pitch, and then thrown to the ground the next moment. When Tippu Tib said he would go for £20,000, I told him I did not think the Committee would give it, but if he would give me certain guarantees I would pay half the sum myself as a subscription to the Expedition. But after what he had said no one would take him.

"You remember that in camp I had serious thought for reasons you know of not bringing Ward; but if we do start this time without any head-man, it is most necessary that there should be three of us. I assure you that his coming will not in the least interfere with your command of the Zanzibaris. And now, old man, good-bye, and God bless you,

"Very sincerely yours,

"James S. Jameson."

Copy of pencilled remarks and calculations made in presence of Major Barttelot, June 24th, 1887, when he demanded further light upon his duties, and regarding Tippu-Tib. Fourteen months after it had been handed to Major Barttelot it was restored to me by Mr. William Bonny. It was copied, and the document was returned to him.

"Str. *Stanley*, let us assume, arrives here in August, Mr. Stanley hopes to be at Nyanza same date. He stops two weeks with Emin Pasha, say to 1st September. September and October to come back.

"So you have got seventy-four days with 550 loads; you have 155 carriers, besides two garrisons of fifty men each, to occupy ends of your days' march.

Going 6 miles per day.155 loads} 4 trips to make

6155 loads} 6 miles forward, 8 trips

6155 loads} to make 1 day's journey

6155 loads} for a caravan.

"Therefore in seventy-four days you will have made nine marches forward nearer to us.

"If Tippu-Tib sends 400 men with your 208 carriers you can march with all goods towards Muta Nzigé. Then I shall meet you thirteen days from Muta Nzigé."

List of Stores landed at Yambuya Camp, August 14th, 1887, per s.s. *Stanley* from Leopoldville: –

100 cases gunpowder.

129 cases Remington rifle cartridges.

10 cases percussion caps.

7 cases biscuits (ship).

2 cases Madeira wine.

2 cases Savelist.

114 bales cloth (assorted).

33 sacks beads.

13 sacks cowries.

20 sacks rice.

8 sacks salt.

1 sack empty sacks.

26 loads of brass rods.

27 loads brass and iron wire.

1 case tinware.

List Of Stores left at Yambuya in charge of Major Barttelot June 28th. 1887: –

2 boxes general and private baggage – Mr. Stanley.

20 boxes Remington rifle cartridges.

88 boxes Winchester rifle cartridges

24 boxes Maxim rifle cartridges

24 boxes European provisions.

10 loads officers' baggage.

15 loads brass rods.

1 loads tobacco.
1 loads cowries.
12 loads rice.
7 loads biscuits.
1 loads salt.
 3 loads tents.
167 loads

THE NARRATIVE PRESS
FIRST PERSON ACCOUNTS OF ADVENTURE & EXPLORATION

The Narrative Press prints only true, first-person accounts of adventures — explorations, circumnavigations, shipwrecks, jungle treks, safaris, mountain climbing, spelunking, treasure hunts, espionage, polar expeditions, and a lot more.

Some of the authors are famous (Ernest Shackleton, Kit Carson, Sir Richard Burton, Francis Chichester, Henry Stanley, T. E. Lawrence, Buffalo Bill). Some of the adventures are scientifically or historically important. Every one of these stories is fascinating.

All of our books are available as high-quality, lifetime softcover paper books. Each is also available as an electronic ebook, ready for viewing on your desktop, laptop, or handheld computer.

Visit our on-line catalog today, or call or write to us for a free copy of our printed catalogue.

THE NARRATIVE PRESS
P.O.Box 2487, Santa Barbara, California 93120 U.S.A.
(800) 315-9005
www.narrativepress.com

Printed in the United States
30325LVS00002B/157-162

9 781589 760448